Kandinsky
The path to abstraction

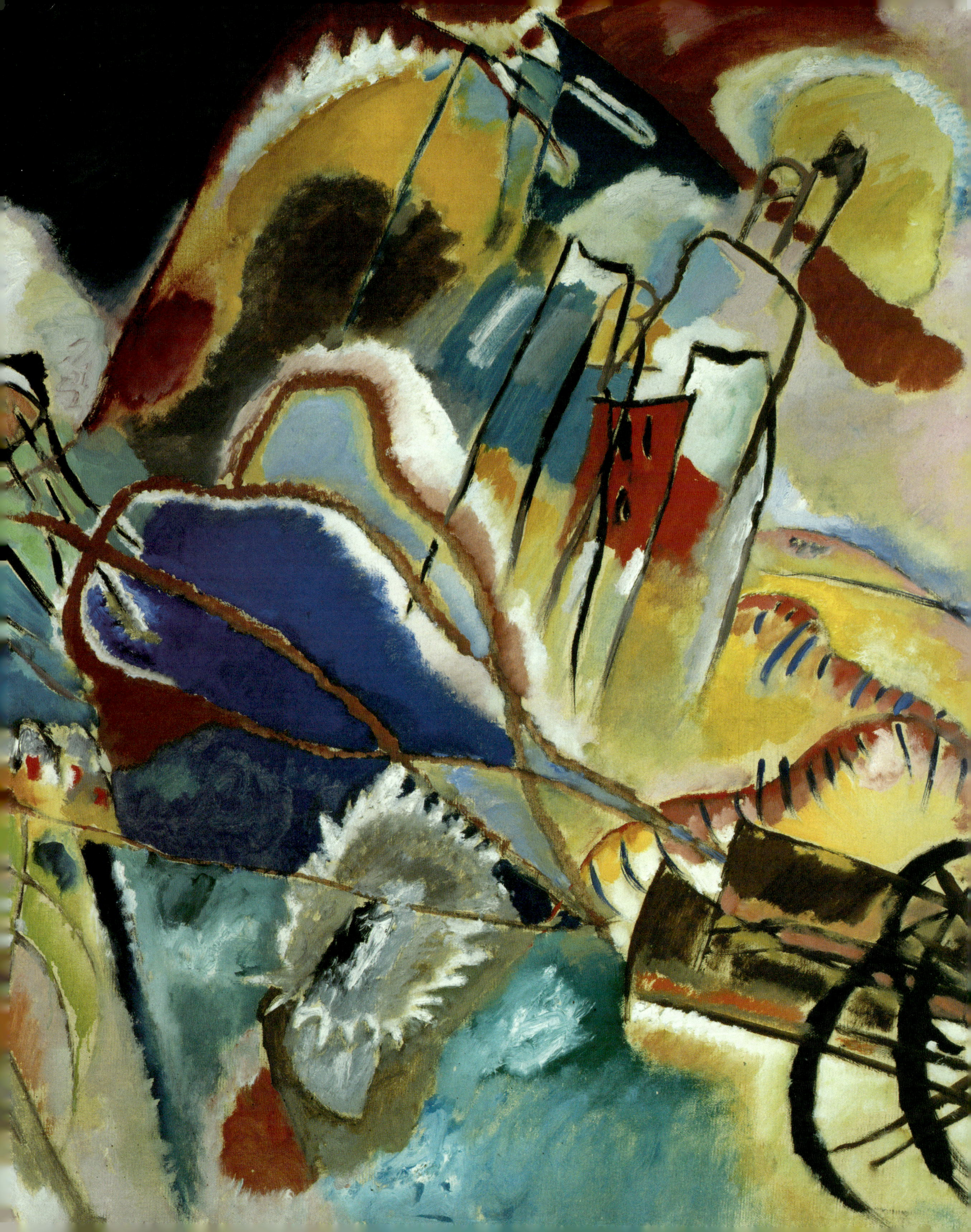

Kandinsky
The path to abstraction

Edited by Hartwig Fischer and Sean Rainbird
With essays by Shulamith Behr, Bruno Haas,
Noemi Smolik and Reinhard Zimmermann

TATE PUBLISHING

Supported by
TATE MEMBERS

Additional support from

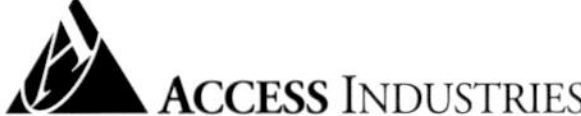
ACCESS INDUSTRIES

First published 2006
by order of the Tate Trustees
by Tate Publishing, a division of
Tate Enterprises Ltd,
Millbank, London SW1P 4RG
www.tate.org.uk/publishing

on the occasion of the exhibition
Kandinsky
The path to abstraction
Tate Modern, London
22 June – 1 October 2006

Kandinsky
Malerei 1908 – 1921
Kunstmuseum Basel
21 October 2006 – 4 February 2007

British Library Cataloguing in Publication Data
A catalogue record for this book is available from
the British Library

ISBN-13 978-185437-677-0 (hbk)
ISBN-13 978-185437-624-4 (pbk)
ISBN-10 1-85437-677-2 (hbk)
ISBN-10 1-85437-624-1 (pbk)

Distributed in the United States and Canada by
Harry N. Abrams, Inc., New York

Library of Congress Cataloging in Publication Data
Library of Congress Control Number: 2006926363

Designed and typeset in Monotype Bembo by Tilley&Tilley
www.tilleyandtilley.com

Pre-press and printing by GZD, Germany

Measurements are given in centimetres, height before width.

FRONT COVER
Cossacks
1910-11
(NO.31, DETAIL)

BACK COVER
Murnau – Kohlgruberstrasse
1908
(NO.5, DETAIL)

FRONTISPIECE
Improvisation 30 (Cannons)
1913
(NO.51, DETAIL)

Contents

Sponsor's Foreword   6

Foreword   7

Acknowledgements   9

Introduction   12
HARTWIG FISCHER AND SEAN RAINBIRD

Early Imprints and Influences   16
REINHARD ZIMMERMANN

Plates 1905 – 1910   43

Kandinsky, Münter and the Creative Partnership   76
SHULAMITH BEHR

Plates 1910 – 1914   101

Kandinsky – Resurrection and Cultural Renewal   138
NOEMI SMOLIK

Plates 1916 – 1921   159

Syntax   184
BRUNO HAAS

Chronology   208
BETTINA KAUFMANN

Notes   213
Select Bibliography   216
List of Exhibited Works   218
Lenders and Credits   220
Index   221

Tate Members are delighted to support the first major exhibition in the UK to focus on the paintings of Wassily Kandinsky (1866-1944), one of the most important figures in the evolution of abstraction. The exhibition examines the first half of Kandinsky's career, during which he moved beyond the observed world, towards images generated by an inner vision.

The charity Tate Members was founded in 1958 specifically to support the work of Tate; it has proved to be one of the most successful schemes of its kind. The Members' contribution is vital in helping Tate build and care for the Collection and extend exhibition, educational and outreach programmes. In the last financial year Members gave nearly £3 million in direct funding to Tate. This included £250,000 to the Collections campaign, the second instalment of an overall commitment of £1 million to this permanent fund to develop the Collection of British and International Modern Art.

This is the sixth exhibition that Tate Members have supported at Tate Modern, the first being *Eva Hesse* in 2002, followed by *Donald Judd* and *Luc Tuymans* in 2004, *August Strindberg* and *Jeff Wall* in 2005. Members are proud to be associated with this exhibition of works by such a key figure in twentieth-century art.

Tate Members are central to the success of all four galleries and play an important role in helping Tate fulfil its duty to increase public knowledge, understanding and enjoyment of art. We hope that many of you who view the exhibition and read this catalogue will join us and support Tate's vision.

Francine Stock
Chair, Tate Members

Foreword

Kandinsky remains one of the most important artists of the twentieth century. He is celebrated as a leading modern artist and as an originator in the field of abstraction, one of the pioneering practitioners of a form of art that emerged only at the beginning of the twentieth century. His early works, landscapes and scenes from folk art gave few clues that he would make paintings with no, or at most vestigial, connections with observed reality. This move away from the material world opened for Kandinsky a connection with a more profound spiritual reality. He sought access to it by analogy with innately more abstract art forms, principally music. After 1920 his work coalesced from informal flowing shapes rendered with vibrant colours, to a more measured style based upon more muted colours and more settled geometric forms. In this his art anticipated the spectrum explored by many other abstract artists as the century progressed. This extended from the divining of a purely spiritual reality beyond experiences at one extreme, to a rigorous geometricism based upon mathematical logic at the other.

This exhibition shines the spotlight on the period in Kandinsky's career during which he evolved the abstract style so characteristic of his painting. It begins with the first of many breakthroughs, in 1908, when his observation of the landscape in Murnau, near Munich, began to take on a more autonomous pictorial reality which moved his paintings away from the intense observation of landscape that had characterised his art up to that point. This complex process proceeded by trial and error, during which one is usually able to discern a residual sense of landscape or figure in otherwise quite abstract works. A highpoint in this development is a group of paintings from before the First World War, inspired by apocalyptic imagery and dramatic landscapes, in which a full-blown abstraction triumphed. After the outbreak of war in 1914 Kandinsky was obliged to return to Russia, where he experienced, and contributed to, the invigorating but ultimately ideologically directed innovations, after 1917, of post-revolutionary artistic and cultural policy in the new republic. The exhibition concludes in 1921 with his return to Germany, to Weimar by way of Berlin, to teach at the Bauhaus, a move which marks a watershed in his style and approach.

The present exhibition is a collaboration between Tate Modern, London, and Kunstmuseum Basel. It has been selected by Hartwig Fischer, lately of Kunstmuseum Basel and newly installed as Director of the Folkwang Museum, Essen, and Sean Rainbird, Tate Collection and Director-designate of the Staatsgalerie, Stuttgart. Through all the twists and turns they have been ably supported by Bettina Kaufmann in Basel and Ann Coxon in London. We are grateful for the commitment they have shown in supporting the realisation of this project.

We have relied on the goodwill and generosity of many lenders to realise this ambitious project. To the curators' thanks to our many institutional and private lenders, given in detail below, we add our own profound gratitude.

Vicente Todolí
Director, Tate Modern, London

Bernhard Mendes Bürgi
Director, Kunstmuseum Basel

Acknowledgements

Both institutions are indebted to the many museums and private collectors who have supported this project with vitally important loans. With a principal responsibility towards the works in their care, collectors, museum curators, directors, and trustees acknowledge the special role of temporary exhibitions by making available pictures for loan. With Kandinsky, this means responding to continual requests for a myriad of exhibitions where his art is a vital presence. In many cases it means removing centrally important paintings from their own displays to be shown elsewhere. We give them heartfelt thanks that they have entrusted their treasured possessions to this exhibition.

What makes this exhibition particularly special is the level of cooperation we have enjoyed from our partners in Russian museums, with substantial groups of works coming from The State Tretyakov Gallery, Moscow and The State Russian Museum, St Petersburg, and truly significant works from elsewhere, especially The State Hermitage Museum, St Petersburg and The State Pushkin Museum of Fine Arts, Moscow. Our colleagues at the Tretyakov Gallery gave further invaluable assistance in securing loans from regional Russian museums (The State Museum of Fine Arts of Tatarstan, Kazan; Tula Museum of Fine Arts; The Ekaterinburg Museum of Fine Arts; The State Art Museum, Nizhny Novgorod). No Kandinsky exhibition can take place without the support of the three institutions which hold the bulk of his paintings, works on paper and documents. This present exhibition was planned in the knowledge that those three collections, the Solomon R. Guggenheim Museum, New York, the MNAM Centre Georges Pompidou, Paris, and the Städtische Galerie im Lenbachhaus, Munich, were in the initial stages of preparing a major exhibition based around their combined, extensive holdings. We are particularly indebted to their generosity in supporting our project with many significant loans.

We wish to thank Shulamith Behr, Bruno Haas, Noemi Smolik, and Reinhard Zimmermann for their contributions to this catalogue, and Bettina Kaufmann, with assistance from Jacob Dabrowski, for compiling the chronology. We also wish to thank the translators, Fiona Elliott, Ishbel Flett, and Catherine Schelbert, for their excellent, highly professional collaboration in translating some of the contributions. We thank Martin Tilley of Tilley & Tilley, who designed the catalogue: he deserves our grateful recognition for his enormous commitment.

At Tate Publishing we would like to thank Nicola Bion for her diligence in seeing through this complex project, ably supported by Alessandra Serri, picture research, and Emma Woodiwiss in production, as well as Jenny Knight, copyeditor, and Karen George, Russian language consultant.

Much valued support has been given by senior staff at both institutions, especially Bernhard Mendes Bürgi, Director Kunstmuseum Basel; Vicente Todolí, Director, Tate Modern; Sheena Wagstaff, Head of Exhibitions and Displays, Tate Modern; and Nicholas Serota, Director of Tate. Particular thanks are due to Ann Coxon and Bettina Kaufmann for their precise and committed curatorial assistance at Tate Modern and Kunstmuseum Basel.

Such an exhibition project cannot come to fruition without the assistance of many colleagues and we would like to thank the following people in London and Basel.

At Tate Modern: Registrar Stephen Dunn and Exhibitions Co-ordinator Stephen Mellor; interns Jacob Dabrowski, Renata Smialek and Claire Mander for their dedication to the project; Press Officer Ruth Findlay; Caroline Priest, Louise Ramsay and Rosie Blackmore in Marketing, Communications and Merchandise; Phil Monk and the Art Handling team; Conservators Patricia Smithen (paintings) Rosie Freemantle (paper); Stuart Comer for organising the related film programme; Craig Burnett, Simon Bolitho, Marko Daniel and Sophie Howarth, Education and Interpretation; Fernando Gutierrez at Pentagram for design work in the exhibition.

At Kunstmuseum Basel: Registrar Charlotte Gutzwiller; Press Officer Christian Selz; Restoration and Conservation Peter Berkes, Amélie Jensen and Sara de Bernardis.

Many other people have given us valuable assistance in the form of advice, encouragement, important indications about condition, quality and the location of works which we have sought to include. Among these many friends of this project we would like to thank in particular: William Acquavella, Galina Andreeva, Irina A. Antonova, Boris Asvarišč, James Attlee, Elise Bauduin, Agnès de la Beaumelle, Christoph Becker, Richard Bernas, Christiane Berndes, Ernst Beyeler, Bettina Blohm, Mrs and Mr Werner Blohm, Gottfried Boehm, Katie Boot, Christopher Brown, Mieke Chill, Celia Clear, Melanie Clore, James Cuno, Stephanie D'Alessandro, Susan Davidson, Lisa Dennison, Christian Derouet, David Elliott, Roger Emery, Charles Esche, Sjarel Ex,

Helmut Friedel, Matthew Gale, Adrian Glew, Geraldine Glynn, Grigori Goldovsky, Vladimir Gusev, Tatiana Goubanova, Anita Haldemann, Martin Hentschel, Margareta Helleberg, Jacqueline Hill, Annegret Hoberg, Olga Illmenkova, Doris Im Obersteg, Fumiko Ito, Howard Karshan, Katharina Katz, Christian Klemm, Ulf Küster, Serge Lemoine, Tomás Llorens, Oxana Lopatina, Rona McKenzie, Olga Mahkroff, Natalia Markova, Vladimir Matveev, Henriette Mentha, Werner and Gabrielle Merzbacher, Magdalena Moeller, Christian Müller, Ulrich Mosch, Helly Nahmad, Lars Nittve, Alfred Pacquement, Evgenia Petrova, Michail Piotrovsky, Sabine Röder, Valentin Rodionov, Ludmilla Sala, Barbara Schellewald, Irina Serebryakova, Dieter Schwarz, Guillermo Solana, Natalia Sukhowa, Alain Tarica, Roger Thorp, Jean Torrent, Elena Tyun, Wim van Krimpen, Gijs van Tuyl, Christoph Vitali, Mario-Andreas von Lüttichau, Ortrud Westheider, Timothy Wilson, Nina Zimmer, Armin Zweite.

In London the exhibition has been generously supported by Tate Members. Their commitment to such an important exhibition in Tate Modern's programme of groundbreaking shows is deeply appreciated. We are also delighted to welcome Access Industries as a supporter of Tate and are extremely grateful for their most generous support of the exhibition.

Without the very generous financial contribution made by the Stiftung Patronatskomitee Basler Kunstmuseen the exhibition in Basel could not have been realised. Kunstmuseum Basel would therefore like to extend express thanks to the Board of Trustees, and especially to the committee's president, Professor Dr Peter Böckli.

Hartwig Fischer   **Sean Rainbird**

Introduction

HARTWIG FISCHER AND SEAN RAINBIRD

Kandinsky holds a special place as one of the prime movers in the evolution of modern art in the early twentieth century. He was one of the first artists to move beyond figuration, from a direct connection based on observation of the world as expressed in western art since the Renaissance until the dissolution of form by the Impressionists. Kandinsky strived to articulate a pure, non-objective painting which found its subject and content within the emotions of the artist and translated them through the materials of the painting to trigger an empathic response in the viewer. What once had been the subject of a painting, a motif drawn from nature or, after Impressionism the pictorial effects of how objects might be optically perceived, became an essence that endowed a painting in the absence of the material object or its representation, with, primarily, a spiritual reality. This new reality, which Kandinsky termed 'pure painting', was art made by someone he conceived of as a spiritual, intuitive creator.

In order to achieve these aims, towards which he inched by a mixture of practical experimentation, observation, instinct and frequent recourse to writing about art in general as well as his own, Kandinsky investigated the tools at his disposal. He made line, traditionally descriptive of form by way of delineating outlines or combined in parallel hatching to give the impression of volume, into a measure of energy. Lines of varying width, length and texture gave direction and thrust, and created fundamental elements of structure in a picture. Within and around the linear elements Kandinsky employed colour. Colour was not codified to trigger specific associations, but was invested with the intention of releasing subconscious feelings through the relationship between different colours as juxtaposed on the canvas. Indeed, on reading Kandinsky's own writings and reminiscences, it becomes clear that colour, his responses to it and how optical effects can be handled to shape an emotional impact, forms the bedrock of his art. Both in descriptions and in diagrammatic form Kandinsky theorised about the optical effects of colour and how these translated into psychological responses that took the form of sympathetic vibrations within the viewer. He wrote that some colours seem to recede while others appeared to project forward; how some had the effect of turning inward while others spread laterally from the area they occupy;

how some areas of colour appeared still while others possessed an inherent mobility.

Looking back in 1914 over the passage towards greater abstraction in his pictures of the past half decade, Kandinsky claimed not to want a revolutionary break with the motif. Only that he had approached a breaking point where the physiology of the subject had become so distorted in order for him to achieve what he wished for in a picture – which he differentiated from a painting illustrative of the natural world – that the natural elements became first residual, then largely disappeared. This watershed was passed in 1908 in the many landscapes he painted in Murnau, south of Munich. His observation of the landscape around Murnau, where one can encounter deep greens and purples at certain times in the day, reached a point in their translation into paintings where colour values became independent of the motif. Kandinsky found he was building pictures around particular experiences of colour he observed, or around the intensity in his experience of certain light conditions. Such experiences forced the importance of the landscape motif to recede in favour of purely pictorial questions of colour and composition. The pictures he painted after December 1913 mark the moment when Kandinsky himself asserted a fully fledged purity of abstraction as expressed by the absence of any residual motifs. However, this progress was not irreversible and did not exclude a return to figuration, as demonstrated by the bagatelle watercolours and *Moscow, Red Square*, both from 1916. It was not until Kandinsky left Russia in 1921 to take up a post at the Bauhaus the following year, the end point of the present exhibition, that the more rigorous geometricism of his pictures excluded any further residual figuration.

To advance towards what became a prolonged break within the representational traditions of western art, Kandinsky drew painting into proximity with other creative art forms which applied different senses to their realisation and existed in temporal dimensions unknown to painting. Thus music, which is both transitory and plays to the aural rather than the visual sense, supplied analogies by which Kandinsky extracted painting from its dependence on descriptive line and naturalistic colour. Through reference to the resonance and vibration caused by the juxtaposition of colours, music also provided Kandinsky with the analogy of the bodily effect he argued a work of art can have on the viewer. Even those paintings, his, 'impressions' based on observed events, move far beyond the illustrational, to present more of a vibrant after-image commemorating the intensity of the actual event witnessed by the artist. It is, however, Kandinsky's 'improvisations' and the more highly structured and replete 'compositions' (the former analogous with concertos, the latter with symphonies, if a parallel in symphonic music of the period might be sought), that the achievements of Kandinsky's incremental shift towards a non-objective, or pure, art find their fullest and most complex expression.

While in the period covered by this exhibition it is almost always possible to find the residue of an observed motif within a painting, certain aspects characteristic of this new form of expression become apparent. First, Kandinsky unsettled the relations between work as something essentially static not only in the fact of it hanging on the wall but also in the scene it depicted. He achieved this predominantly by creating mobility within the picture, removing motifs that might give an indication of relative scale and enabling areas of colour and swirling lines to move forwards and backwards in the space within the picture. Moreover by frequently omitting visual stepping stones that guided the viewer into the foreground of the picture, he extended this dynamic to an ambiguous and unstable relationship between the spectator and the internal space of the picture. This applied also to shifts in scale in elements of line and form which might be identified with familiar motifs (from nature or from his own earlier works), and the presence of areas of colours merging and shifting within dynamically conceived linear constructions. Sometimes thin, at others thicker, both linear and colour elements push and pull, laterally as much as into and out of the pictorial space of the painting.

The early parts of Kandinsky's career covered in this exhibition were spent in Germany then, after 1914, mainly in Russia. In each country Kandinsky both responded to and contributed to the cultural life of the cities of Munich and Moscow where he spent much of his time. His willingness to create opportunities to exhibit art, his own and others, to publish in support of the dissemination of his ideas and those of like-minded artists and creative individuals expanded still further in Moscow to embrace his leadership of institutions. These activities included the formation of the first museums of contemporary art into which he and others channelled the newest Russian art which reflected the radical changes brought about by the October Revolution in 1917. His Russian roots and the period of great activity there during and immediately after the First World War were critically important in his life, even though he spent most of it abroad, first in Germany, latterly in Paris.

At the turn of the new century Munich and its surroundings played a vital role in the origination and transmission of Jugendstil, the German variant of art nouveau. Through the secession exhibitions and commercial gallery network, the city was equally pivotal in the dissemination of advanced art made in other parts of Europe, particularly from Paris but also elsewhere in France, the Low Countries, Scandinavia and Germany.

When the outbreak of war in 1914 forced Kandinsky to leave Germany, he returned to find Russia in a revolutionary fervour, where the power of avant garde visual ideas was encouraged, before being appropriated by a cultural and political elite, after the Revolution in 1917, to help forge a new world. Kandinsky's independence of artistic expression and credo of intuition and subjectivity as creative forces alongside logic and reason made him unwilling to subordinate his creativity to the rationalist precepts of the Constructivists. When he left Russia in 1921, never to return to his homeland, his art was at a pivotal moment. The rational, geometrical forms – circles, triangles, rectangles – employed by Constructivists such as Kasimir Malevich and El Lissitzky became a feature of the few paintings Kandinsky completed before leaving Moscow in late 1921, and became the basis of his art after that. Well aware of the emphasis on the two-dimensional flatness of the picture surface that the single dominant form imposed on a white ground in Malevich's *Black Square* 1913 implied, implicit too in the presence of newspaper glued directly onto the surface of Cubist collages, Kandinsky continued to create space within the picture. This autonomous space constituted a new, wholly subjective universe removed from the objects and elements of the world outside. By implanting more stable forms in the more rationally organised spaces within his pictures and by leaving behind the cosmic swirl and atmospherics of his 1912-19 paintings Kandinsky achieved greater equilibrium and clarity of expression. The abstraction thus created was, however, in a very different key – formally more stable, chromatically more muted – from his art after 1908. In that year, evolving from his many small landscapes painted principally in Murnau, Kandinsky's work was poised to transcend the observation of landscape and to acquire its own specific values and referents as a wholly new form of – abstract – art.

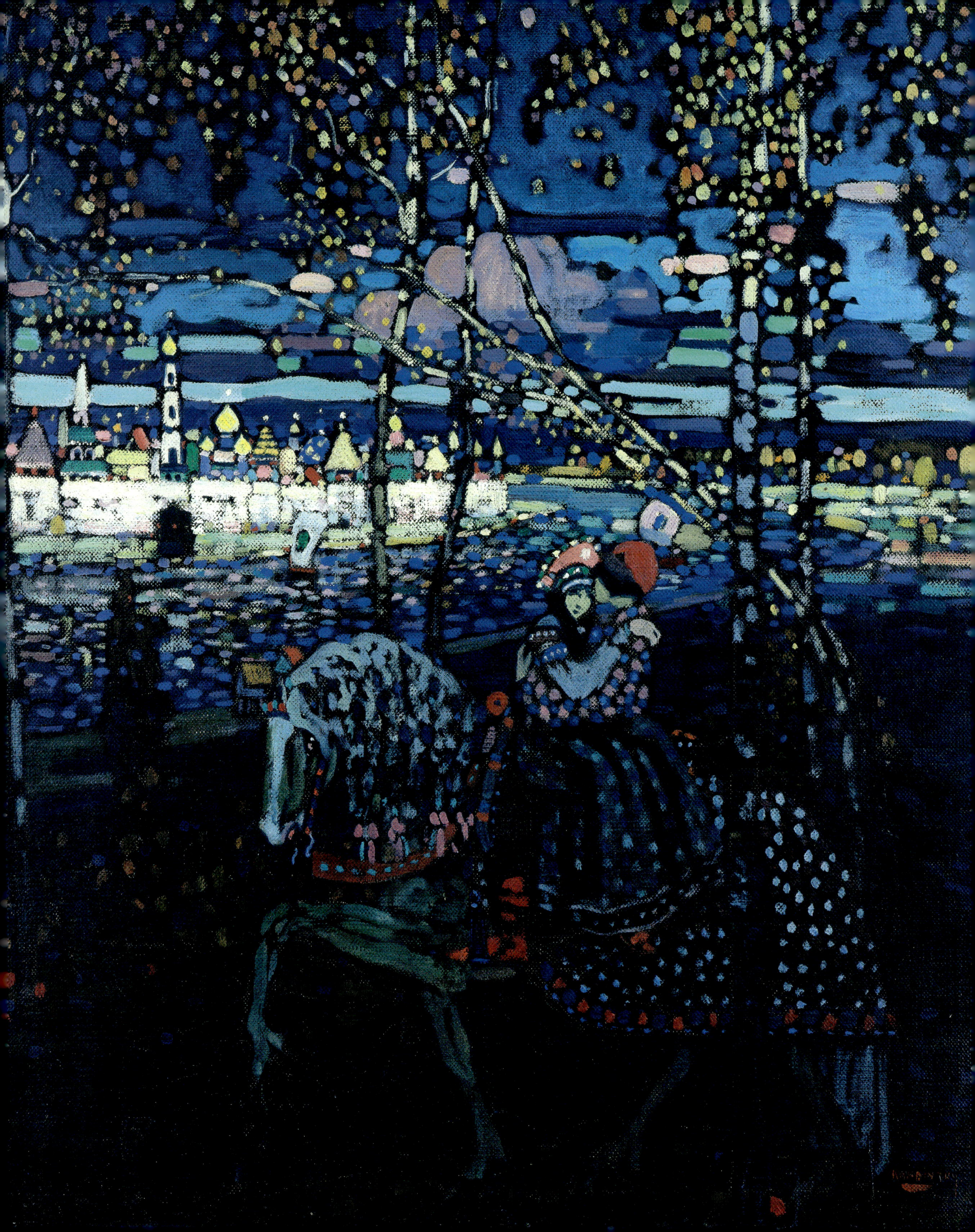

Early Imprints and Influences

REINHARD ZIMMERMANN

'And I noticed with surprise and confusion that the picture not only gripped me, but impressed itself ineradicably on my memory, always hovering quite unexpectedly before my eyes, down to the last detail … Painting took on a fairy-tale power and splendor.'

Riding Couple
1907
(FIG. 7, DETAIL)

ALL HIS LIFE KANDINSKY WAS ON THE MOVE BETWEEN DIFFERENT WORLDS. Thirty-seven of his seventy-eight years were spent in Russia; however, if we look only at the years he actively devoted to art, Germany comes top of the list with twenty-six, followed by France with twelve and Russia with seven, which leaves three years spent travelling. The transnational nature of his existence is fundamental to his artistic being, too – and it is significant that Kandinsky made his home in Munich, choosing not to exchange Moscow for Paris, but to settle instead at the midway point between the two. Although he was indebted to modern French art for the inspiration he found in it (which he always freely recognised), nevertheless – as some hardly flattering remarks from his time in Munich show – he had certain serious reservations about French culture which, even in his last years in Paris, lingered on in his frequently reiterated critique of Surrealism.

In 1913 – at the point when he had just achieved his great goal, his breakthrough to abstraction – he looked back in his 'Reminiscences'[1] at the three poles of his artistic identity, which he saw in his original artistic ideal and the two events that encouraged, even prompted him, to pursue his career as an artist. His original artistic ideal accounts for the Russian factor in his art, and it took the form of what he himself called 'fairy-tale Moscow', the overwhelming sight of the city of Moscow bathed in the intoxicating colours of the setting sun. In his 'Reminiscences' Kandinsky memorably eulogised this Moscow (which he later also described as the original inspiration for his art).[2]

The German factor is embodied in the music of Richard Wagner: Kandinsky cites a performance of *Lohengrin* at the Court Theatre in St Petersburg as one of the key moments in his decision to dedicate his life to art.[3] For Kandinsky there was an associative connection here with painting: the colours in a painting should have the same power as the sounds that make up a piece of music, and painting should be as 'abstract' as music. And for Kandinsky, the sounds he heard in that Wagner orchestra evoked his own vision of a fairy-tale Moscow.

In terms of Kandinsky's actual artistic development during the first phase of his artistic career, the third pole, and undoubtedly the most important, was the French factor. He came face to face with it in the work of Claude Monet, specifically in a painting from his *Haystacks* series, shown in an exhibition of Impressionist paintings in Moscow in 1896. Kandinsky described this moment:

Previously, I had known only realistic art, in fact only the Russians, and had often remained standing for a long time before the hand of Franz Liszt in the portrait by Repin, etc. And suddenly, for the first time, I saw a *picture*. That it was a haystack, the catalogue informed me. I didn't recognize it … I had a dull feeling that the object was lacking in this picture. And I noticed with surprise and confusion that the picture not only gripped me, but impressed itself ineradicably on my memory, always hovering quite unexpectedly before my eyes, down to the last detail … Painting took on a fairy-tale power and splendor. And, albeit unconsciously, objects were discredited as an essential element within the picture.[4]

So it was French Impressionism that first gave Kandinsky at least an approximate notion of what abstract art might look like. The 'lack of clarity' in the representation of objects which resulted from the freely painted lineature and the greater luminescence of the colours, compared to those in realistic paintings, embodied – in Kandinsky's eyes – a new artistic ideal that was concerned with the painting as a painting and was no longer reliant on references to objects.

Colour and the Inner Sound

The highly developed tonal hues of Wagner's orchestra and the equally highly developed colour/light painting of Monet were to become the fixed stars of Kandinsky's artistic praxis, while the duality of colour and sound became the pivot of his theoretical reflections. In fact, while Paul Klee's gifts at the start of his career were in the field of drawing, Kandinsky was from the outset a colourist, who had to put considerable effort into gradually acquiring the skills of a draughtsman (in 1900 he enrolled, to this end, in the class of Franz von Stuck who, in Kandinsky's opinion, had 'little sensitivity to colour'). And throughout his artistic career colour was Kandinsky's main concern: colours as an independent compositional element, serving not merely to represent objects but 'living an independent life of their own, with all the necessary qualities for further, autonomous existence'.[5] His interest was in colours that can enter into specific relationships with other colours in a painting, that are expressive, that can convey contents to the viewer and that ultimately – in some mysterious way – embody the 'truth' that exists 'behind' familiar, external and tangibly material reality: the reality of the 'inner' or the 'spiritual', to quote two concepts central to Kandinsky's aesthetic thinking. For Kandinsky, the world of colours was the basis and the practical vehicle for his epochal invention: abstract art. It was not from the stylised line (refined by Jugendstil artists) that he developed abstraction, but from the colour figure that had evolved into an independent pictorial element, which – by virtue of its equivalence to the traditional representational figure – meant that representationalism could now legitimately be replaced by another mode.

Kandinsky soon started to formulate his aesthetic thinking and, significantly, chose the title 'Colour Language' (*Farbensprache*) for an early manuscript draft of his main theoretical work, the book *Concerning the Spiritual in Art* (1912).[6] For Kandinsky art is language, its purpose is expression, mediation, communication. He disapproved of *l'art pour l'art*, art as a purely formal exercise or game. His concern was with the mediation of contents, hence his lifelong resistance to any undue emphasis on matters of form, which all too readily come to the fore in any discussion of abstract art. In fact, Kandinsky's 'contents' are not the traditional contents of painting and have nothing to do with classical myths, historical events and political or social posturing. The contents expressed in his art are concerned with the inner, the soul and the spirit – contents that, as he himself has said, set up 'vibrations' in the viewer's soul. In all of this Kandinsky's thinking is powerfully influenced by music, which no doubt accounts for his use of the word 'sounds' with reference to the semantic units and the vehicles that convey the contents of his artistic ideas. Every colour, every line, and even – in representational art – every pictorial motif has (like every other thing in the world) a particular sound, a particular emotional value, one might say, that specifically speaks to the recipient's soul and unleashes a specific reaction. And a painting is an ensemble of sounds (just as a piece of music consists of a myriad sounds), that, depending on its construction and complexity, form the basis of a spiritual experience guided by the artist's intentions. For Kandinsky a work of art is a carefully planned and realised complex of sounds that is intended to generate a very particular spiritual experience within the viewer.

Now, Kandinsky often refers not merely to 'sound', but to 'inner sound'. This reflects his fundamental orientation towards the world of the inner (in his theoretical statements, he is most often concerned with the inner, apart from his concern with abstraction). In fact, abstraction as such is the logical conclusion of this concern with inner matters, in so far as it turns its back on the world of external objectivity.

So Kandinsky uses the term 'inner sound' in order that 'sound' should not be understood as a reference to the direct, sensory impression of an element. For it was his belief that beyond the first, 'rough' sensory impression there is a deeper, finer level of spiritual sensitivity, a level that no words can properly express. And it is this finer spiritual dimension that his art is intended to reach. But the expression 'inner sound' also refers to the inner, spiritual dimension of any object. Every single thing, as Kandinsky sees it, has an inner value, an inner meaning distinct from its conventional meaning. While, for instance, the outward meaning of a chair may consist in its usefulness as something to sit on, and is thus bound up with the value 'sitting', its inner value could perhaps derive from a particular formal or material quality. This inner quality has nothing to do with any external quality, indeed – and Kandinsky often works with just such paradoxes – one can even contradict the other.

Kandinsky felt that, for normal human beings, this inner dimension is generally veiled or hidden, and that the artist has the capacity to make it accessible to the viewer. He makes a particular point of the fact that even artists producing representational works can, through their art, reveal that inner life (and in his writings he named artists who could do this). At the same time, however, he believed that because abstract art refuses at every stage to allow any associations with the outside world, it is particularly well suited to addressing things spiritual and internal.

The Aesthetic of the Colour Patch – Kandinsky's Early Paintings 1896-1908

The basic semantic unit of Kandinsky's content-oriented art is thus the 'inner sound' that generates spiritual vibrations within the viewer. In its simplest form it is conveyed by the painterly elements colour and form, or – in representational art – by pictorial motifs; in more complex manifestations the work of art can be made up of a whole number of different elements. The most important vehicle for that sound in Kandinsky's early work is the colour patch, which – like the Impressionists and Post-Impressionists – he sought to develop as a pictorial element that is as elemental as it is independent. This early phase of Kandinsky's artistic development is dominated by two – concurrently produced – groups of works: the oil sketches and the so-called 'coloured drawings'.[7]

Oil Sketches

In terms of their appearance, the oil sketches (by 1907 there was a total of about 170) form a relatively unified group of works. They are all of landscape themes, generally executed on commercially available, easily transportable canvas boards, measuring approximately 24 x 33 cm – an ideal size for working outdoors. The technique – lines and patches of impasto paint – remains largely unchanged over the years, although the use of the brush or spatula becomes freer and the colours become more intense. Kandinsky rarely exhibited or published his oil sketches and seldom signed them; he did, however, work some of them up into larger paintings executed in the studio. The oil sketches already manifest some remarkable compositional idiosyncrasies that can be elucidated by looking at individual works.

In the oil sketch *Munich – Planegg I* 1901 (fig.1) and in the oil painting *Kallmünz – Stormy Weather* 1904 (fig.2)[8] we see Kandinsky drawing diagonal lines directly from the foreground to deep in the middle ground, giving the compositions a certain dynamism as well as introducing an element of time into these paintings. This dynamic line often leads directly from the lower edge high up into the painting.

The second, closely related characteristic to be observed in these paintings is the raising of the horizon, as in the painting *Holland –*

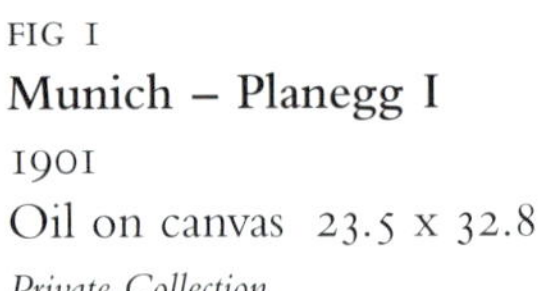

FIG I
Munich – Planegg I
1901
Oil on canvas 23.5 x 32.8
Private Collection

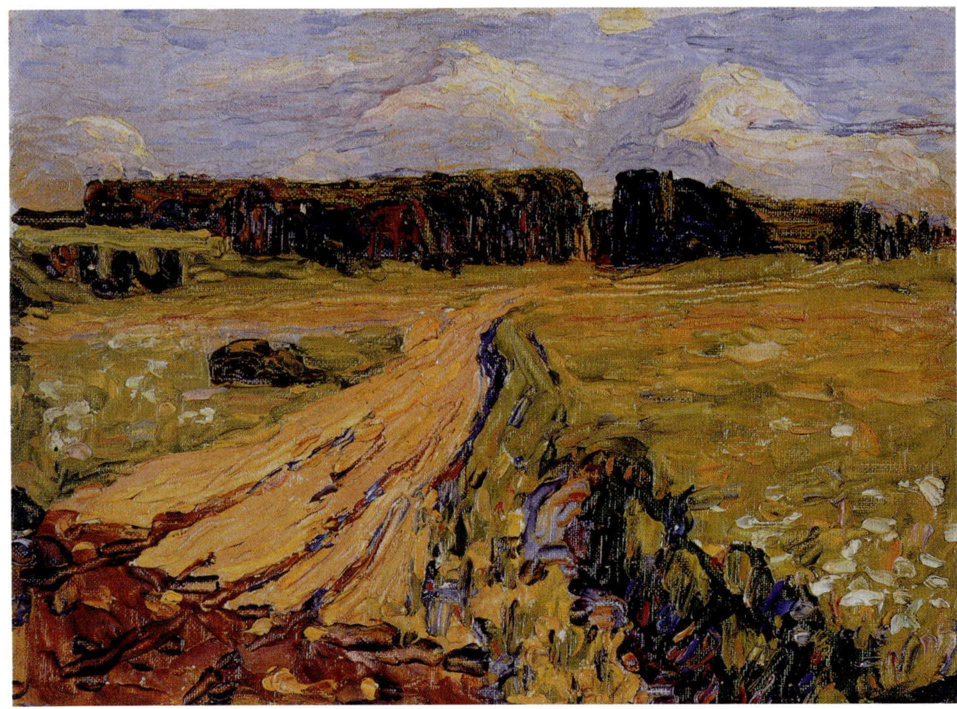

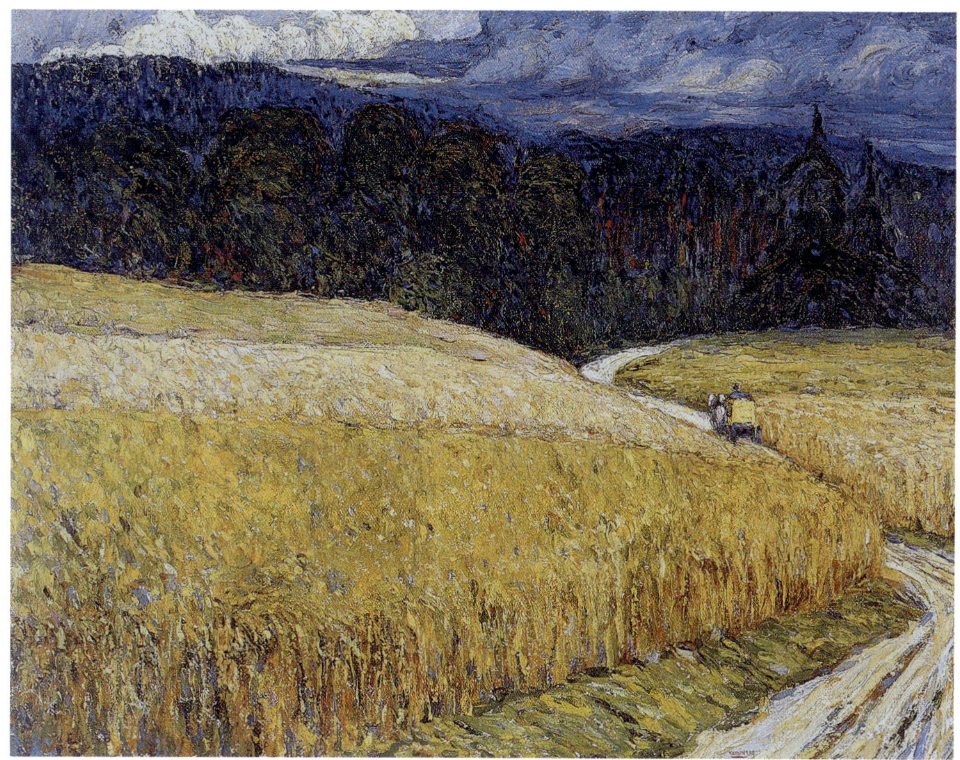

Beach Chairs 1904 (fig.3) and again in the view of *Santa Margherita* in the Bay of Rapallo, painted in 1906.[9] The largest planes in these paintings are occupied by the ground or by water; the architectural motifs are pushed right up towards the upper edge. The raised horizon gives the composition a strikingly planar character, undermining any illusion of space in the conventional sense. This effect is further reinforced by the colour patches covering the whole of the picture surface, which similarly counteract the usual conventions of perspective in paintings.

Now, it may seem that these two compositional features – the depths created by the diagonals and the planarity that tends to bring everything into the foreground – are at odds with each other. It is true that in one sense Kandinsky wanted nothing to do with traditional perspectival spatiality and, by giving greater weight to the picture surface, portrayed perspective as planes. On the other hand, however, he wanted more than just planarity, because he felt that planarity to the exclusion of all else would only take him down the cul-de-sac of mere decoration. He very much wanted to realise a certain form of spatiality in the painting; but he equally wanted to avoid the conventional perspectival spatiality that had become the norm in Western painting since the Renaissance. The simultaneity of these two different compositional

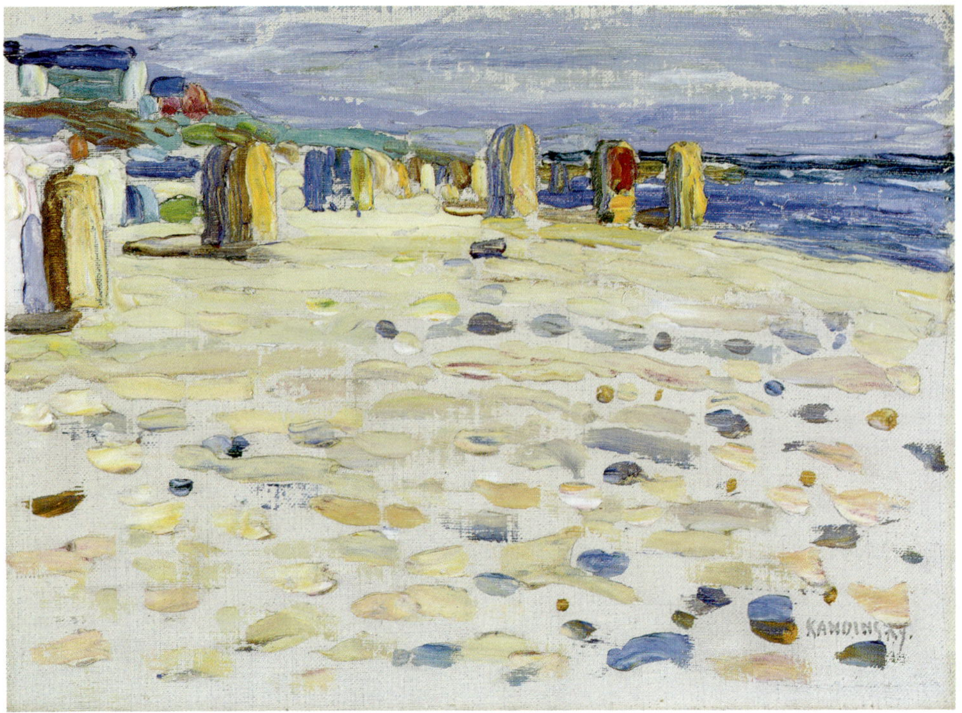

techniques – suggesting depth and planarity at one and the same time – constitute a compositional paradox that was to become one of the essential characteristics of Kandinsky's art and has nothing to do with carelessness or inconsistency.

The third compositional technique often used by Kandinsky involves extreme contrasts between light and dark, as we see for instance in the particularly small oil sketch *Nymphenburg – Large Fountain*[10] of 1901 or 1902 showing a motif from the parklands around Schloss Nymphenburg near Munich, and again in the oil study *Park of St Cloud – Clearing* painted in 1906/7 when he was staying in Paris (fig.4). As he recalls in his 'Reminiscences', these light/dark contrasts go back to the powerful impression Rembrandt's art made on him, and inspired in him two aims: to intensify colour until it assumed a fairy-tale power and to introduce time into the painting, in the sense that the viewer is obliged to explore all the main parts of the painting separately and in succession.[11]

Closely connected to these aims there is a fourth, identifiable compositional technique: in precisely those darker areas of the painting, other, intense colour tones, which are not apparent at first sight but which become powerfully apparent on closer examination. Once again, the intention is to reinforce the colours and to establish

FIG 4
**Park of St Cloud –
Clearing**
1906/7
Oil on cardboard 24 x 33
*Musée National d'Art Moderne,
Centre Georges Pompidou, Paris.
Bequest of Nina Kandinsky 1981*

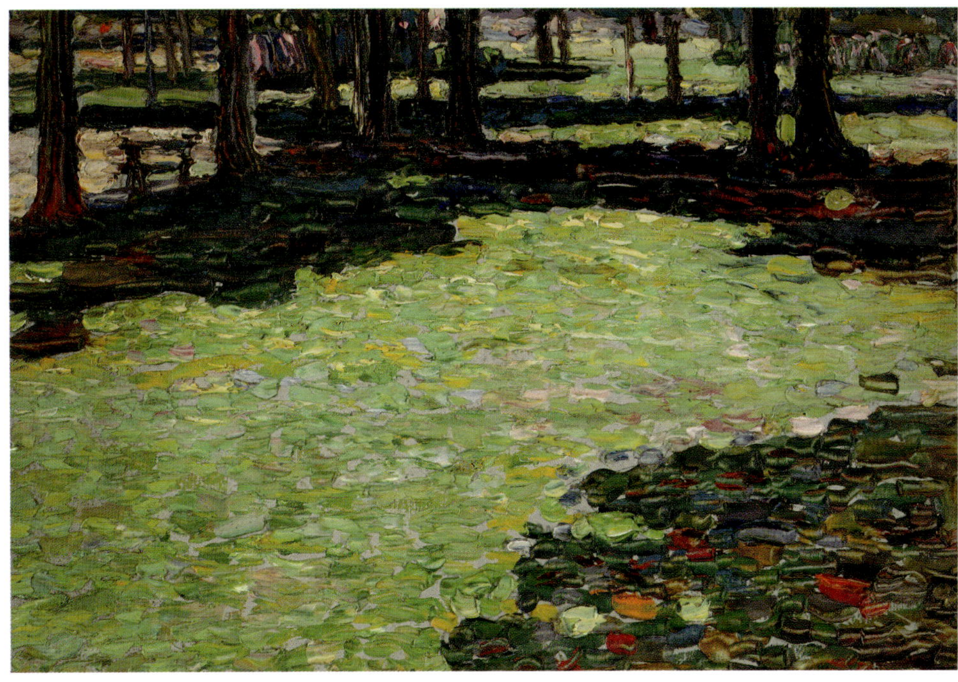

time as a pictorial element. The lower right corner of the view of the parklands at St Cloud is a particularly fine example of Kandinsky's ability to include numerous strong colours in a darker zone, of a density and purity not seen elsewhere in the painting: yellow, orange, blue, green and red, browns and olive tones and a very small dash of white.

The fifth and last compositional technique that should be mentioned here is Kandinsky's frequent use of other kinds of contrast. In the Parisian parkland, for instance, we see not only the contrast of light and dark but also the contrast between the homogenous meadow and the patchwork of the upper section of the painting. And contrast is again used to great effect in the painting *Old Town II* of 1902, of which Kandinsky himself was particularly fond (fig. 5). With diagonals that originate in the lower third of the painting projecting into the pictorial depths (travelling from the lower left to the upper right), there is an unbroken transition from foreground to middle ground, while the raised horizon line is provided by a restless architectural backdrop. The multiplicity and detail of the upper section contrasts with the calmer, larger components lower down. The cubic, straight-edged architecture contrasts with the organically rounded forms and shapes in the lower section. In addition, the diagonals run determinedly in the opposite direction

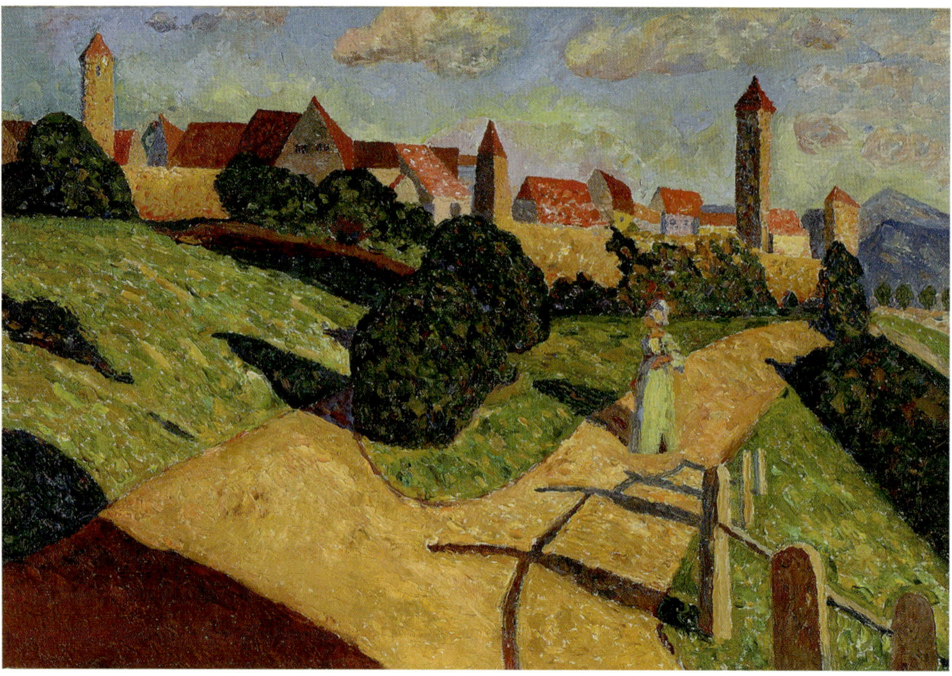

to each other: the paths to the right and the shadows to the left. Once again the spatiality of the painting is defined by paradoxically concurrent suggestions of depth and planarity, which engender an unconventional notion of space, somehow uncertain and suspended aloft.

In effect, these compositional techniques could be reduced to two main issues: ambivalent spatiality and the interplay of contrasts.

Coloured Drawings

The second main group of works to emerge from Kandinsky's early period are tempera works on card or paper, studio pieces rather than sketches. Despite their classification, they are painted, not drawn. Typically patches of paint are applied with a brush to a coloured ground, often in a dark tone, which is itself incorporated into the composition as a whole. Thematically, the pictures are not pure landscapes but genre scenes in various milieus (landscapes and architectural settings), historical themes and fairy-tale scenarios. An important sub-group depicts Russian scenes, which attest to Kandinsky's enduring ties to his homeland. These ties are manifested not only in his thematic interest in Russian history, its fairy-tales and icons, but also in his active contact with Russian artists and references to their art, notably – in this connection – to the fairy-tale illustrations published around 1900 by Ivan Bilibin.

I should like to illustrate this category by looking more closely at an example that also demonstrates the particular type of abstraction Kandinsky achieved in the coloured drawings. Furthermore, there is an interesting comparison to be made here with an oil painting done in a similar technique.

Having spent a few days in Venice, from 6 to 9 September 1903, on his way to Odessa and Moscow, in 1904 Kandinsky made four coloured drawings, *Recollections of Venice 1–4*, based on photographs he had taken in Venice. The fourth work in this series, with the subtitle *Ponte Rialto* stands out more for its 'colour chords' than its design (fig.6). The deep blue of the water, lighter near the sky and with violet tinges in the foreground, is framed and interrupted by the contrasting dual tones of the architecture in black and white, which are in turn warmed by browns and yellows with isolated accents in red. The main formal interest of the composition is the wide span of the Rialto Bridge over the Grand Canal, with its pronounced arc corresponding to the contours of the three boats by the left shoreline. The curves contrast pleasingly with the straight lines of the façades of the buildings lining the canal and the wooden pylons rising up out of the water. Reflected in the water, these various forms dissolve in the choppy, multicoloured waters of the foreground, where an abstract

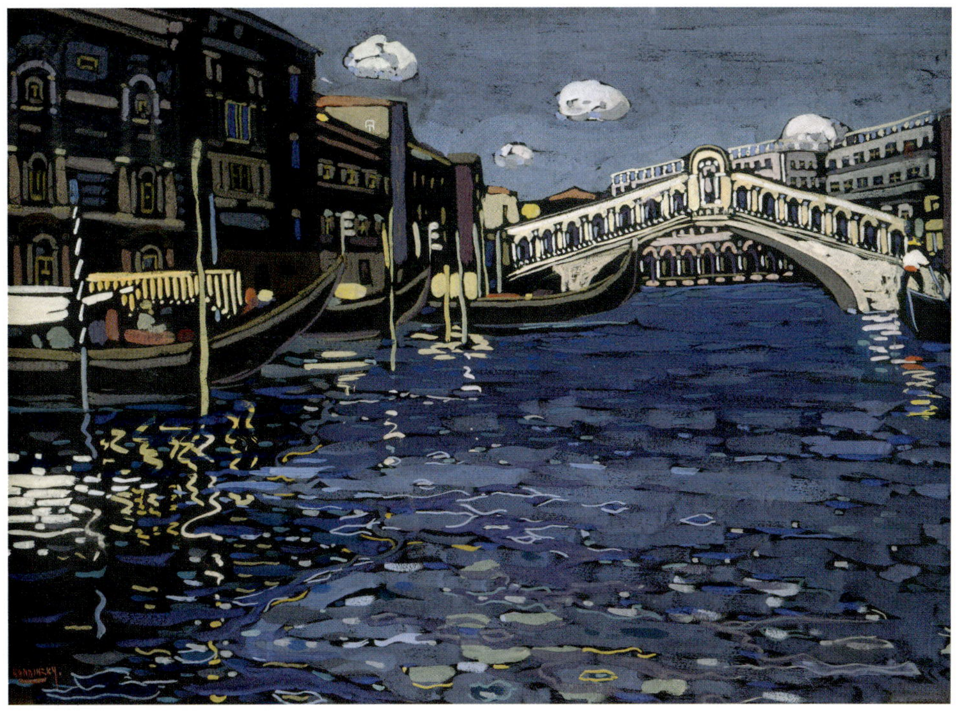

FIG 6
**Recollection of Venice 4
(Ponte Rialto)**
1904
Gouache on cardboard
40.5 x 56
*Musée National d'Art Moderne,
Centre Georges Pompidou, Paris.
Bequest of Nina Kandinsky 1981*

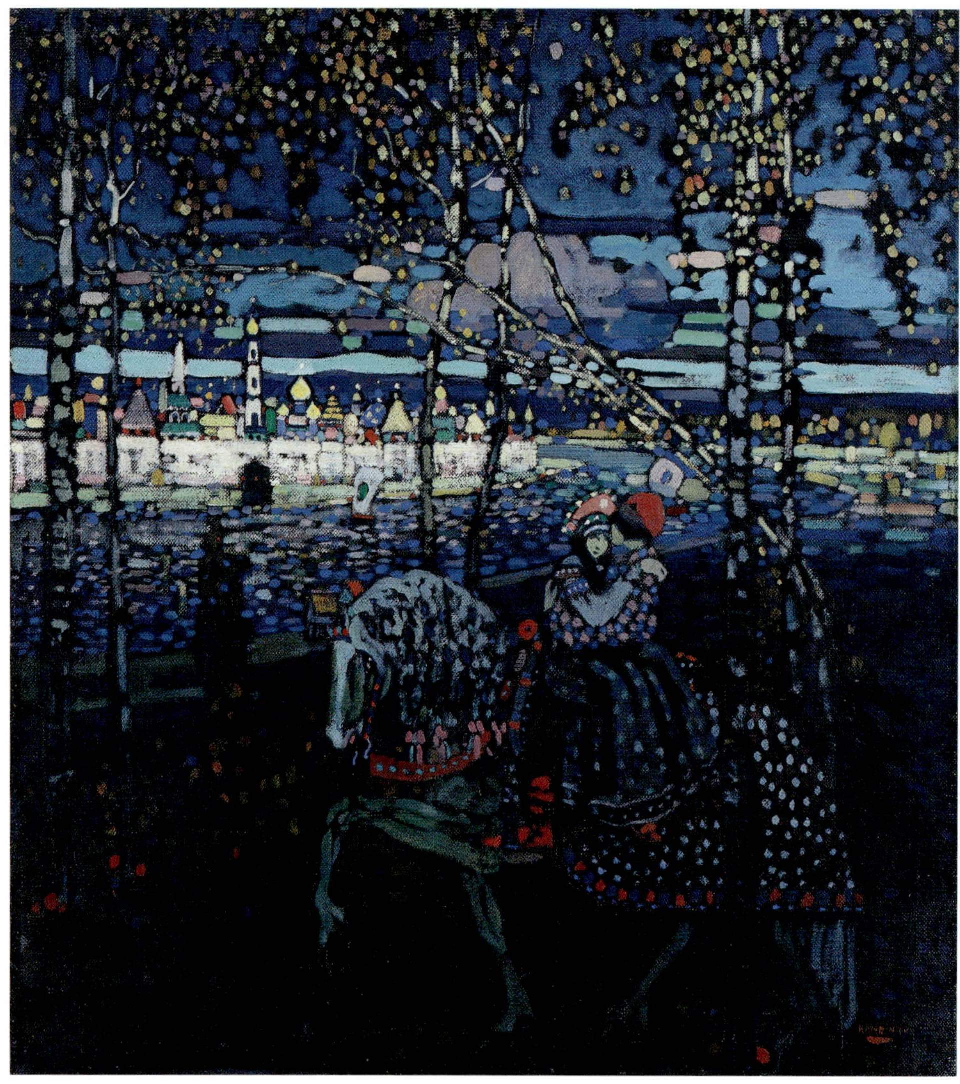

FIG 7
Riding Couple
1907
Oil on canvas 55 x 50.5
Städtische Galerie im
Lenbachhaus, Munich

interplay of lines, short strokes and patches unfolds. This interplay of different forms, which clearly fascinated Kandinsky, had a similar appeal for the French Impressionists, who also relished the confrontation between natural and architectural forms and their shifting, disjointed reflections on water.

I referred earlier to the way in which Kandinsky took a particular delight in adding gleaming coloured tones to the darker areas of his paintings. This is so in this case, only here this particular technique is used all over the painting, which has a black ground onto which are laid small areas of colour. This technique is used to particularly beautiful effect in *Riding Couple* 1907 (fig.7). Although this is clearly a day-time scene, at first sight the dark tones of the black background suggest night-time. As a result the painting creates a very unreal, dreamlike or fairy-tale situation. Against the black background the colours develop a singular luminescence quite distinct from that of colours seen against a white background (as in Impressionist paintings). While colours against a pale background represent natural daylight, colours against a dark background seem to glow from within – and appear all the more intense.[12] The aesthetic of the colour patch is important here: as small isolated patches the colours become precisely those independent living beings, equipped with mysterious powers, that Kandinsky described in his texts. While the shape of the colour patches is still determined by the objects portrayed in the painting, as may be seen on the mane or the legs of the horse, the tendency is for these patches to become non-specific. They tend to form a non-representational configuration of colours and shapes, as in other examples from this category of paintings – witness in the *Arrival of the Merchants* 1905 (fig.8) the mass of human figures streaming out of the town towards the shoreline, which Kandinsky portrayed as a band speckled with glowing spots of colour.

Murnau Landscapes

By about 1906/7 Kandinsky had developed a level of abstraction that could be described as follows: its constitutive component is the colour patch which, in the paintings discussed in the previous paragraph, is distinctly isolated and independent, and has little to do with any object as such. The network of colour patches is an abstract structure, although there is still a connection to the lingeringly representational nature of the painting, even if in parts this connection is a very loose one. However, while the paintings in respect of form still owe much

FIG 8
Arrival of the Merchants
1905
Oil on canvas 92.5 x 135
Miyagi Museum of Art,
Aoba-ku, Sendai

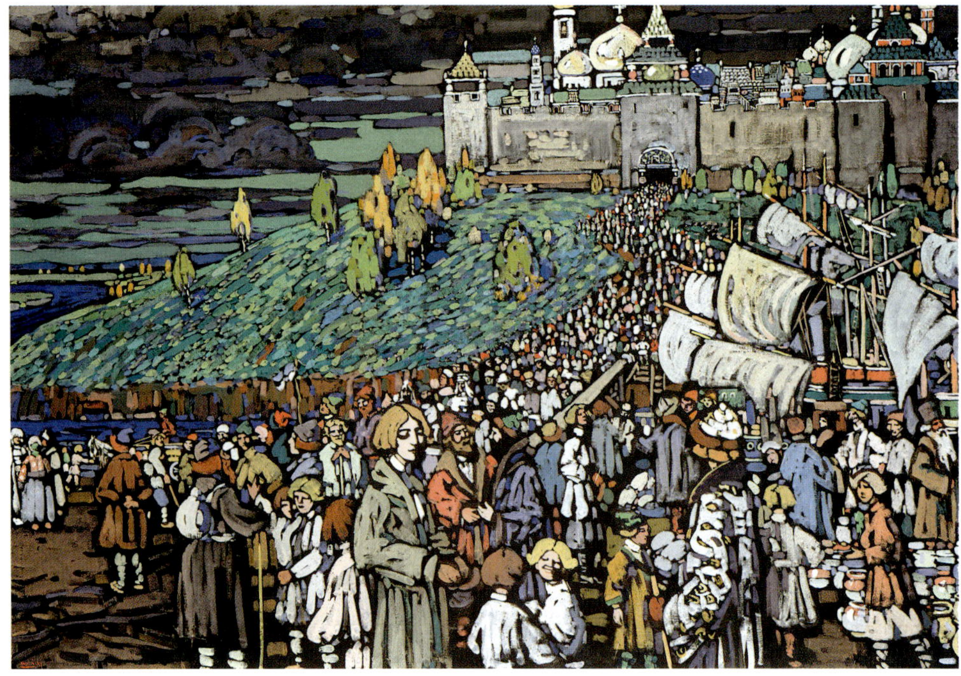

to Impressionism and Neo-Impressionism, the point of colour patches is very different. Kandinsky's interest lies not in the optical mixing of the colour patches in the beholder's eye, but in the independent effect of these patches as the elemental sounds that resonate within the painting.

By the next stage of Kandinsky's path to abstraction, we see the influence of the French Fauvists and the colourist Henri Matisse, with whose work Kandinsky had become familiar during his stay in Paris in 1906/7. At the same time, Kandinsky partly – not entirely, but identifiably so – moved away from Impressionism and the small colour patches. The new technique is evident in the so-called Murnau landscapes, of which Kandinsky painted around 120 between 1908 and 1910. In 1909 another group of works came to the fore, the Improvisations, and in 1910 Kandinsky started work on his Compositions. Having been a constant component in Kandinsky's output, after 1909 the landscape retreated increasingly into the background. However, in the artist's early days in Murnau the landscape still played an important part in the radical changes that were to emerge in Kandinsky's style. In so far as they are finished oil studies, the Murnau landscapes follow in the wake of the oil studies and 'paintings'. As a rule they are larger than the oil studies, with most measuring approximately 34 x 45 cm. Some have also been worked up as 'paintings' in the narrower sense of the term, in which case the format is larger. As in the case of oil sketches, for Kandinsky many of the Murnau landscapes were 'studies' rather than fully fledged paintings. Many were left unsigned.

The canvas *Murnau – Village Street*, painted in late summer 1908 (no.4), is an outstanding example of this new group of works. Kandinsky has abandoned the spatula in favour of the brush alone. The immediate effect is that the restless, almost relief-like surfaces created using the spatula disappear and are replaced by flat brushwork. Nevertheless, this brushwork is to a large extent clearly visible and, with its restless, often staccato textures, crucially contributes to the dynamic effect of the painting, which almost looks like a Van Gogh taken to new extremes. The dynamics of the main forms are also greatly heightened. This is achieved first and foremost by the large cloud which has to be read as the main motif in this painting. While one's attention is actually only on the street, foreshortened due to the perspective and culminating in an unremarkable crossways façade, ultimately the pictorial effect created by the painting is all about centrifugal motion. The cloud, the houses, the street – all seem to be rushing towards the viewer. The dominant yellow with a slight orange tinge pushes forwards, touching the cloud, which therefore cannot remain coolly in the background; by the same token, neither the few white accents in the painting nor the dark sky blue nor the other minimal occurrences of blue are able to lessen the heat of the warm colours. If anything, they raise the temperature by introducing an all too restrained contrast. As in many of the other Murnau landscapes, the main colour chord is composed of the opposites blue and yellow, with the red/green contrast as a secondary element, followed in third place by black and white. A number of features familiar from the older oil sketches are seen again in these paintings: diagonals leading deep into the composition, powerful light/dark contrasts and contrasting geometric and organically rounded forms. And again we see the ambivalent spatial structure: while perspective is used to suggest spatial depth, the grid-like distribution of light and dark together with the uniform colour of the many yellow motifs generates a planarity that pushes itself into the foreground.

Even larger than this is the oil painting *Murnau – Kohlgruberstrasse* 1908 (no.5), which stands as the fully finished version of a normal-sized landscape. The diagonals of the path leading into the pictorial depth and of the high ground on the right are balanced by shadows running in the opposite direction and a number of verticals. Once again Kandinsky combines a dominant yellow/blue contrast with a less important green/red contrast; white, lilac and violet mediate between the contrasts. Despite the use of colour patches in some parts of the painting, the tendency is towards homogenously coloured planes. The brushwork is plain to see: it is varied and flexible – very short brushstrokes adjacent to long ones, straight lines and curves, with all the brushwork being completely free with regard to the direction it takes on the picture plane.

In the course of the continued evolution of this technique, individual elements – ever more stylised or dynamised – increasingly lose any connection with objective natural forms, as we see to great effect in the oil painting *Murnau – Garden II* of 1910 (no.19). Caught up in the dynamic of the movement that sweeps through the painting from the lower left to the upper right, the flowers in the foreground become as one with the houses that are in fact much further in the background, creating a staccato of interlinked colour bodies. Thus, with the gradual disappearance of small-scale patches or dots and the ensuing emergence of more homogenous zones, the pictorial elements themselves become increasingly dynamic; at the same time, the original natural forms start to distort. This makes the new paintings 'less comfortable' for the contemporary viewer – in the previous paintings the forms 'underneath' the patchwork of colours had remained largely untouched. However, these changes also mark considerable progress for Kandinsky on his path to abstraction. Light/dark contrasts also give way to colour contrasts and colour relationships that gain proportionately in importance; yellow/blue contrasts, complementary contrasts and the primary colours red/yellow/blue come to the fore.

Improvisations – The Question of Sense and Meaning

In retrospect, Kandinsky's artistic development from 1908 onwards might seem to progress steadily and inexorably towards complete abstraction in 1913. In reality, however, this process was anything but steady – his first abstract painting (*Picture with a Circle*) is dated 1911,[13] but at first this degree of abstraction remained a one-off, because Kandinsky was not satisfied with the painting. Both form and content underwent change. With the decreasing clarity in the portrayal of objects it became increasingly hard to read the paintings' 'meaning', as is particularly evident in the series of Improvisations and other related paintings. Between 1909 and 1914, Kandinsky produced thirty-five sequentially numbered Improvisations as well as some unnumbered Improvisations, but with a marker of some kind in the title. In his text *Concerning the Spiritual in Art*, Kandinsky describes the Improvisations as 'chiefly unconscious, for the most part suddenly arising expressions of events of an inner character, hence impressions of "internal nature"'.[14] This group of works can be seen as the successors to the coloured drawings, in the sense that they have similar motifs – genre scenes, historical and fairy-tale themes – enriched by architectural and landscape elements. The iconography is difficult to interpret, even intentionally mysterious, although individual motifs such as the rider or the town on a hill can be seen in numerous paintings. Kandinsky himself felt that the inner sound of a work of art can only unfold and take effect when conventional meaning no longer applies; it seems that this is exactly what he was aiming at.

There is a study for the *Painting with Houses* 1909 (no.13), where the representational elements are much easier to identify.[15] In the foreground with two trees it is possible to make out three – evidently female – figures; in the oil painting these are abstracted to varying degrees. On the left and the right there is a crouching figure; in the centre under the trees is a kneeling figure. Clearly identifiable are the hill with a town in the upper right of the painting and the diagonal row of houses with which Kandinsky cites Bavarian folk art.[16] He was interested both in folk art and children's art – in his view 'primitive' artists and children had the capacity to give naive, undisguised expression to the inner life of things.

A greater degree of abstraction is apparent in *Improvisation 10* 1910 (no.29). Nevertheless, there are at least four clearly recognisable motifs. The upright figure with the rounded red shapes at its tip already featured as the main motif in *Improvisation 1*, where Kandinsky described it as a 'cupola tower'.[17] It could be a variant of the hill crowned with a town that appears in so many of Kandinsky's paintings. In the right foreground is a tree – possibly a willow – with branches drooping towards the centre as though in an expression of deep sadness. A very similar motif is seen in the *Sketch for Composition II* (no.21), where it is combined with two rocks and a recumbent figure. In *Improvisation 10* we see, behind the tree trunk, a standing figure with yellow hair streaming out towards the right – a motif, also seen in *Improvisation 5*, which Kandinsky called 'flying hair'.[18] Meanwhile the

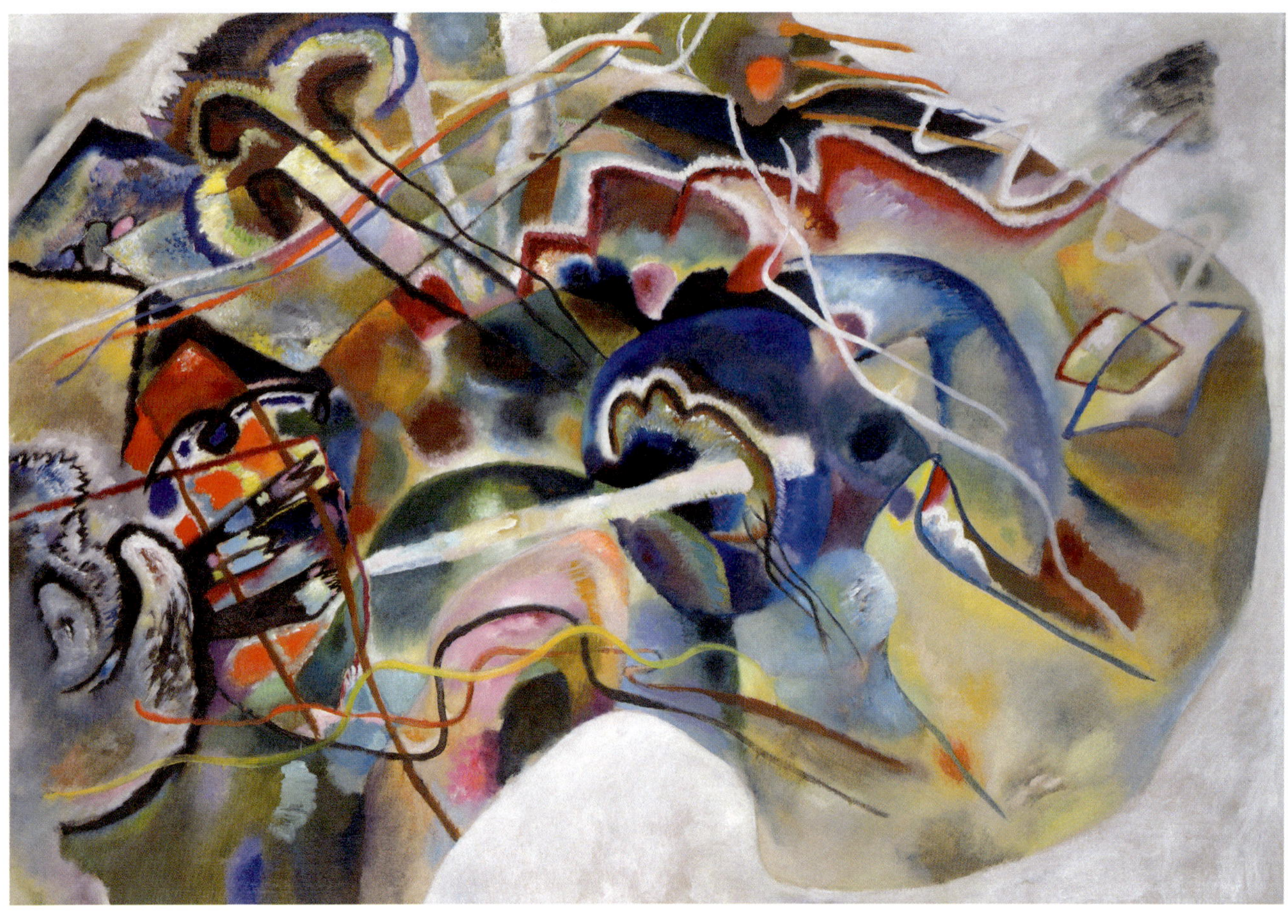

FIG 9
Painting with White Border
1913
Oil on canvas 140.3 x 200.3
Solomon R. Guggenheim, New York

lines leading downwards to the left from the tip of the cupola tower trace the shape of a rainbow – and Kandinsky did name the painting *Rainbow*. Three further motifs can be identified with relative certainty: the flashes of lightning in the shape of jagged lines above the rainbow aiming at the cupola tower; in the left foreground three warriors or guards holding three vertical lances – a motivic connection to *Composition IV* (no.32); and in the lower left corner a crouching figure. One has the sense that this painting derives from a very particular idea or story, but it is hard to reconstruct a logical narrative from the identifiable elements.

The question as to the potential for interpretation offered by pictures of this kind is still very much a bone of contention amongst art historians. From Kandinsky's own writings and statements it is clear that he imagined, in the best-case scenario, the perception of his paintings as being a largely emotional process, during which the inner sound of the colour/form composition would be felt rather then read as the actual content of the composition. In his view an iconographic reconstruction of the painting would shift the perception onto an intellectual level, thereby making it harder for the inner sounds to register. After all, abstraction is specifically about dissolving identifiable representational motifs so that the viewer can no longer 'cling' to these. On the basis of this – perfectly understandable – premise, many art historians have been particularly critical of one such as Rose-Carol Washton Long who set about finding vestiges of Kandinsky's earlier representationalism even in his seemingly completely abstract paintings.[19] Nevertheless, in so far as iconographic elements are in fact present in Kandinsky's paintings – either covertly or openly – they must also be analysed as such and recognised as a positive moment in the work of art.

The dilemma facing the would-be analyst of these works is exemplified in *Painting with White Border* 1913 (fig.9). Although the picture title draws attention to the 'white border', it betrays nothing of the work's contents. However, in May 1913, Kandinsky himself commented at length on this painting and mentioned, amongst other things, that the sketch he made for this painting in December 1912 'was the outcome of those recent, as always extremely powerful impressions I had experienced in Moscow – or more correctly, of *Moscow* itself'.[20] The only representational motif he alludes to is the 'troika motif' in the upper left – a line drawing of a figure based on a trap and three horses. Oddly, Kandinsky says nothing at all about the main motif of the work, easily recognised by any viewer familiar with his visual world: the struggle between St George and the dragon. Bathed in a blue aura, the rider drives his white lance from the centre of the composition towards the multicoloured dragon on the left. The dragon has its limbs extended, trying to ward off its attacker; its long tail is represented by the curved lines below the lance. Despite the high degree of abstraction in this painting, there is another clearly legible motif: an angel flying into the composition from the right, its hair streaming out behind it and bearing a trombone – marked only by an outline – that cuts across the troika motif. The most abstract of the motifs is the princess who also has a part to play in the story of St George and the dragon; she is seen as a rose-coloured figure below the lance. So this painting has a 'dual iconography': the Moscow iconography claimed for it by the artist but not at all apparent to the viewer, and the religious iconography of the struggle with the dragon and the angel of the Last Judgement, readily identified by the viewer but tacitly ignored by the artist.

The *Painting with White Lines* 1913 (fig. 10), which has both motivic and thematic links to the *Painting with White Border*, also attains a high level of abstract representationalism; in this case the viewer can identify a hill crowned with a town and an angel of the Last Judgement. Only the angel's trombone is clearly recognisable; the angel's body has been transformed into a dark streak of green, red and blue. All that is left of the hill is a white outline; the towers have become rising lines against bright flecks of colour.

The Breakthrough to Abstraction

The third and last stage of Kandinsky's path to abstraction starts in 1911 and reaches its destination in 1913 with the almost completely abstract *Composition VII* (no. 52). His progress can be followed in two Murnau landscapes. In 1910, as we see in the painting *Murnau with Church II* (no. 26),[21] Kandinsky's rendering of the motif 'Murnau with Church' (the view from Gabriele Münter's house in Murnau of a hillside with a castle and a church) was only moderately abstract; very much in the Fauvist style, like, for example, *Improvisation 10* 1910 (no. 29). The version painted in 1913 – *Landscape with Red Spots I* (no. 48)[22] – is so abstract that its connection to the earlier painting is not immediately apparent. Anyone who is not aware of its genesis might simply assume

FIG 10
Painting with White Lines
1913
Oil on canvas 88 x 100
Private Collection

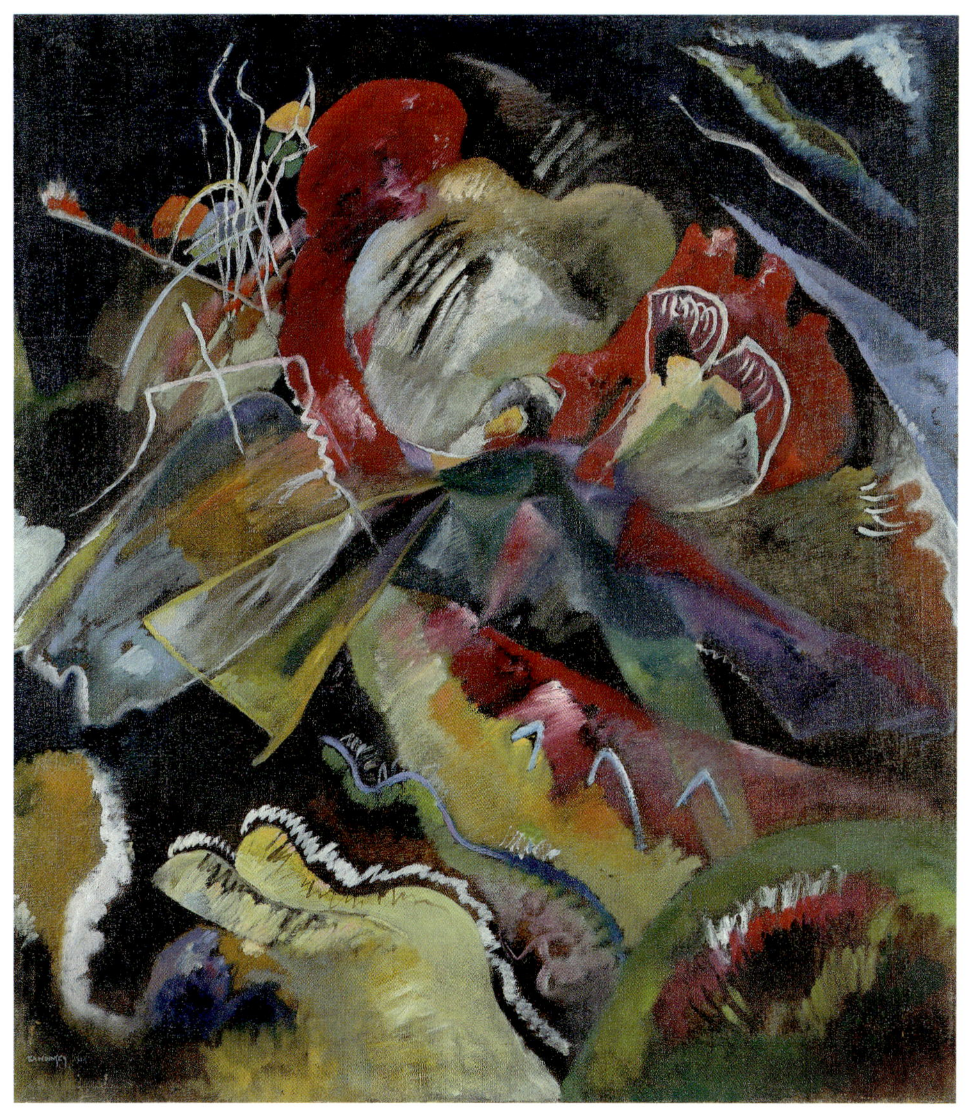

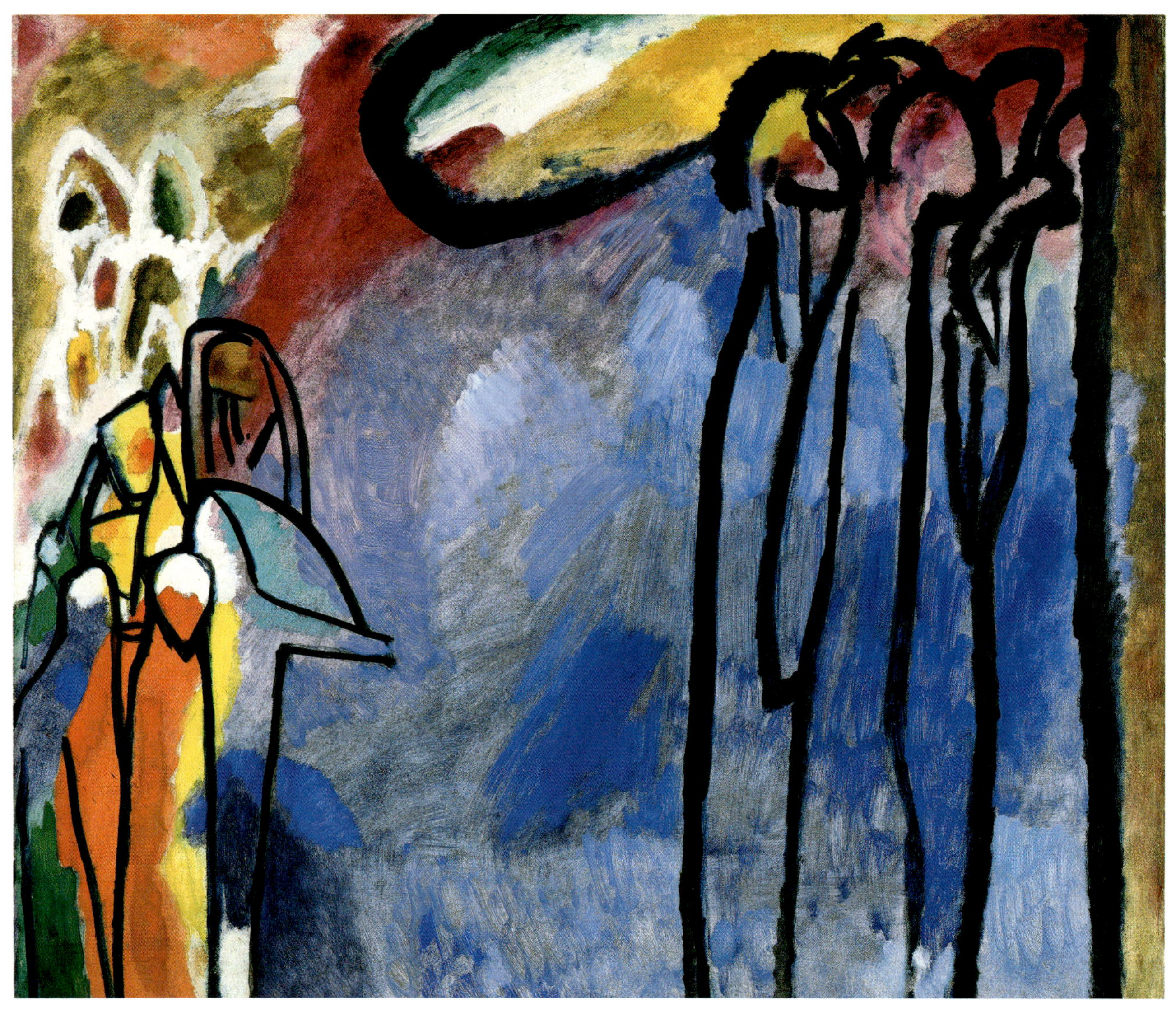

FIG 11
Improvisation 19
1911
Oil on canvas 120 x 141.5
Städtische Galerie im Lenbachhaus, Munich

that the motif had been derived from a hilly landscape. The houses in the lower left, the church façade and tower, and the cemetery, could not be identified if it were not for the comparison with the earlier work. The outlines of the various objects have been conceived anew. In the case of the church façade and tower, the outlines no longer seem to imply solid, stone material – nor do the two adjacent houses in the lower left. And the outline of the crossways roof to the right of the church also seems to have turned into a kind of free-standing structure in the landscape. And, as it turns out, the outline of the mountain plateau can be made out inside this form. The various colour zones have the appearance of free-floating mists or coloured billows of steam; sometimes they look like swathes of cloud – as do the patches of colour along the lower picture edge apparently rising out of the crowns of trees. In this composition matter seems to have shifted into a different physical condition; it is as though it has liquefied, dematerialised.

The increasing self-sufficiency of the outlines of objects, as they become independent of the colour ground, is already seen to impressive effect in two paintings from 1911: in *Composition IV* and *Improvisation 19* (fig. 11). The fortress on the blue hill in *Composition IV* is marked by a strong outline which has no material contents but seems, instead, to float – unattached – above the fluid underground. In *Improvisation 19* there are two differently formed groups of figures, conveyed solely by means of outlines. Again, these outlines do not contain physical forms but lie freely on a colour plane whose internal articulations do not coincide with the shapes of the outlines. Thus the colour planes in this composition are organised independently of the lineature; the two have been 'freed' from each other. An ethereal colour substance seems to fill the pictorial space. Representationalism only lingers on in the black outlines. But these 'objects' have been dematerialised; they have lost their physical presence. The last step in the emancipation of the line was achieved in *Composition V* (fig. 12), which was finished on 17 November 1911. At last the line has achieved the same status as other pictorial elements liberated from representational associations; it conveys content and expression in its own right and is on a par with the emancipated colour patch.

Leaving aside the isolated precursor *Picture with a Circle* 1911, Kandinsky's fully fledged abstract style emerges in the paintings of 1913, most notably in *Composition VII* (no. 52),[23] which was completed on 29 November 1913. Although this painting – at 2 x 3 metres

Kandinsky's largest to date – has its origins in representationalism (it arose from an All Saints' Day painting and a representation of the Last Judgement), its origins are all but completely obliterated. The abstract style achieved by Kandinsky in this painting has four main qualities. Firstly, the line no longer serves to provide the outline for a figure, but has become a free compositional element. Secondly, the role of the bodies, figures and objects in the representational compositions is now fulfilled by all kinds of colour forms – they may be clearly delineated or flow into the surroundings; they may be intrinsically homogenous or complexly structured; they may appear opaque or transparent. Thirdly, the basic nature of the pictorial reality is highly dynamic; the elements in the painting seem to rotate in some kind of vortex – and manifest a tendency to swallow each other up, to superimpose themselves on each other or even to dissolve into each other. The result is an impression of indefinable spatiality. Fourthly, the 'materiality' of the pictorial reality has become immaterial; it seems more reminiscent of coloured mists or clouds that take on almost object-like forms and appear to float above the picture ground.

The third and final stage in the development of Kandinsky's abstract style of painting cannot be explained with recourse to contemporary modes of abstraction either in his immediate or more distant surroundings. Besides his own artistic originality, a crucial role in this development was played by the theosophical and occult notions that he and Gabriele Münter had been intensely preoccupied with for some time. There is no need to go into any great detail here with regard to these influences that have already been thoroughly discussed elsewhere;[24] a brief summary of the salient points should suffice. Broadly speaking, Kandinsky's abstract style is an aesthetic realisation and representation of the 'world of fine matter'.[25] It is as though he were dealing with a 'second level' of reality that is not visible to the normal eye but that can be perceived by those with a heightened sensibility. It is by nature ethereal and manifests itself above all in auras and thought forms – coloured filigree forms with the consistency of clouds or mist, sometimes clearly outlined, sometimes with no distinct delineation and flowing into the surroundings, superimposed on one another or even mingling, now – as auras – spatially connected to the relevant beings (although extending beyond them), now – as thought forms – floating free in the ether. Since these filigree forms correspond to living beings, objects or spiritual entities, they can serve as models for the complete replacement of representationalism by colour/form

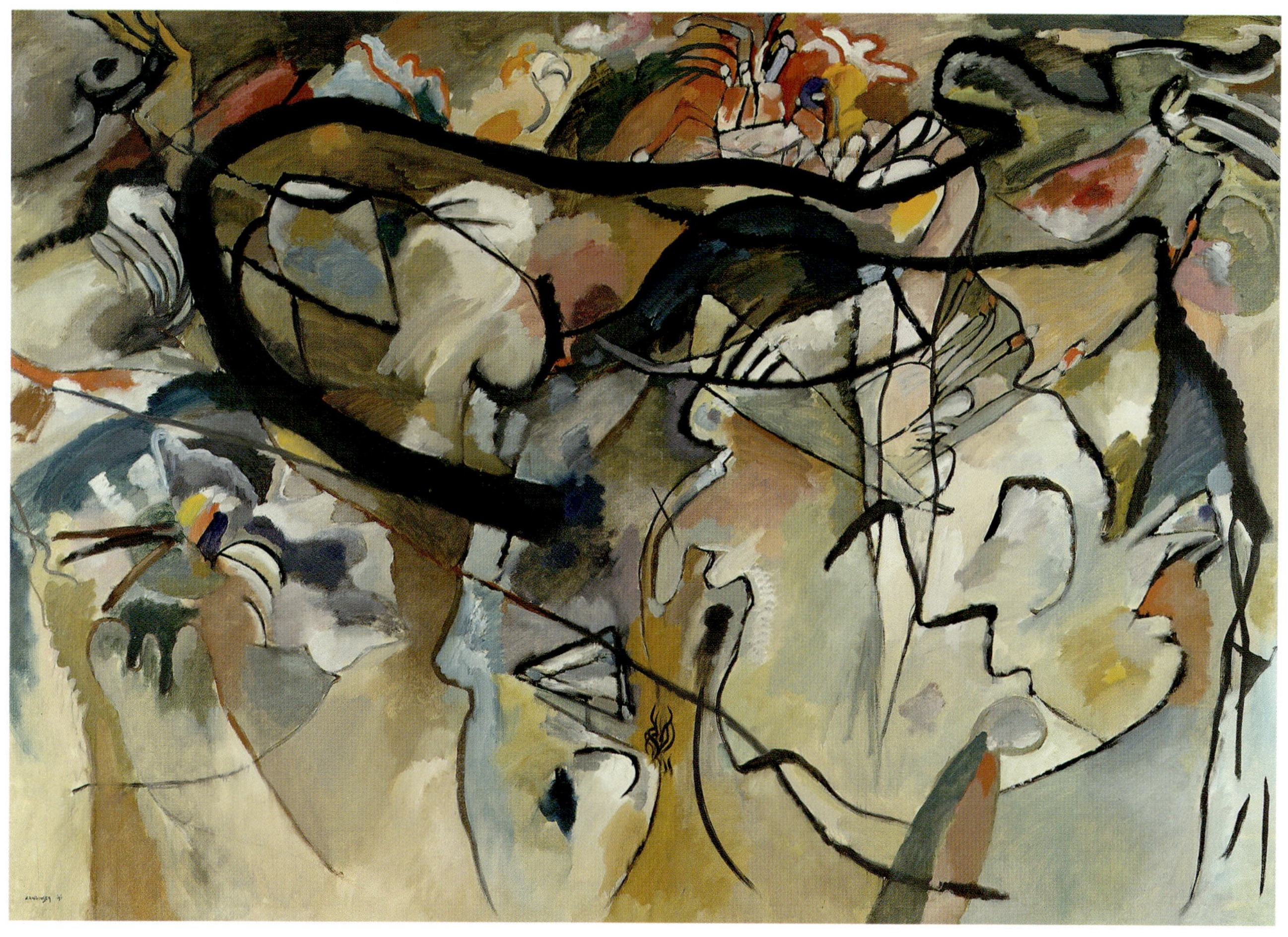

FIG 12
Composition V
1911
Oil on canvas 190 x 275
Private Collection

configurations. And their embedding in an indefinable, ethereal space (which is also home to the paradoxical space of Kandinsky's early works) is in keeping with the artist's occult, theosophical concept of bodies and space.

After 1913 Kandinsky's abstract style in his paintings does not undergo any fundamental change. But there are two distinct tendencies. Not only does the pictorial space become freer, opener and less physically dense, but also the amount of colour is reduced – witness the painting *In Grey* 1919 (no.70). At times the darker tones are reinforced, as in *Grey Oval* 1917 (no.68). The picture titles chosen to suit this mood, such as *Twilight* 1917 (no.66) or *Overcast* 1917 (no.67) would appear to express a pessimistic state of mind. However, not only do brighter tones soon regain the upper hand; it is also not right to assume the superficial pictorial effect is an expression of the inner contents. It is one of Kandinsky's fundamental strategies to 'hide' the actual meaning of the work under its optical surface, with the two relating to each other in a paradoxical, even antithetical manner (which naturally makes it all the harder to interpret his paintings correctly).

For years Kandinsky determinedly developed and honed – one might even say 'thought through' – his abstract style. By virtue of the enormous richness of its aesthetic structure, it stands out from all the many abstract styles developed in the twentieth century. Its opposite pole is the 'protestant', reductionist style of the painter Piet Mondrian. In 1913 Kandinsky had at last reached the goal that he had already described as far back as 25 April 1904 in a letter to Gabriele Münter:

Without exaggerating, I can say that, should I succeed in this task, I will be showing [a] new, beautiful path for painting susceptible to infinite development. I am on a new track, which some masters, just here and there, suspected, and which will be recognised, sooner or later. [26]

Translated from the German by Fiona Elliott

Plates 1905 - 1910

1 **Arab City**

1905

Tempera on cardboard 67.3 x 99.5

Musée National d'Art Moderne, Centre Georges Pompidou, Paris. Centre de Création Industrielle.
Bequest of Nina Kandinsky, 1981

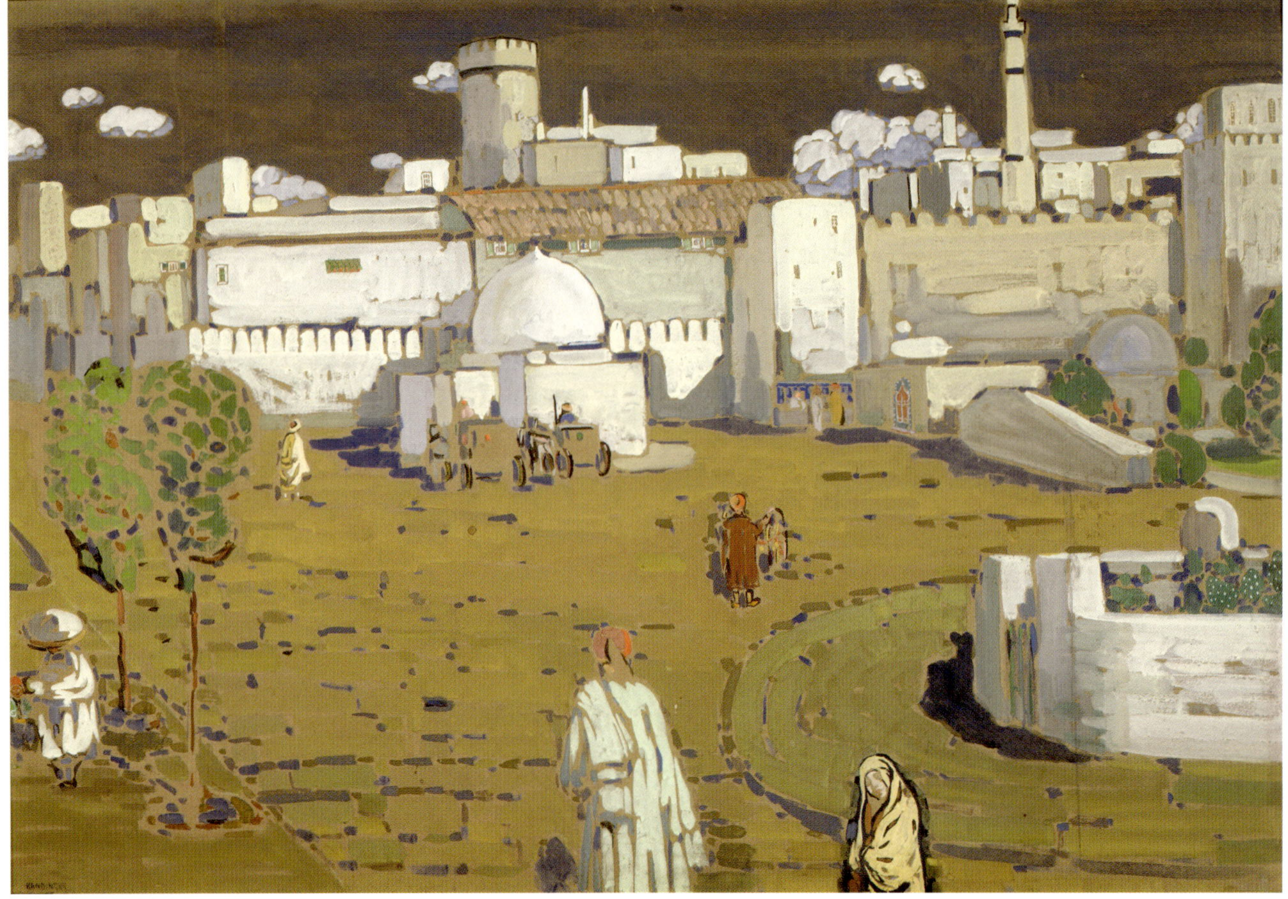

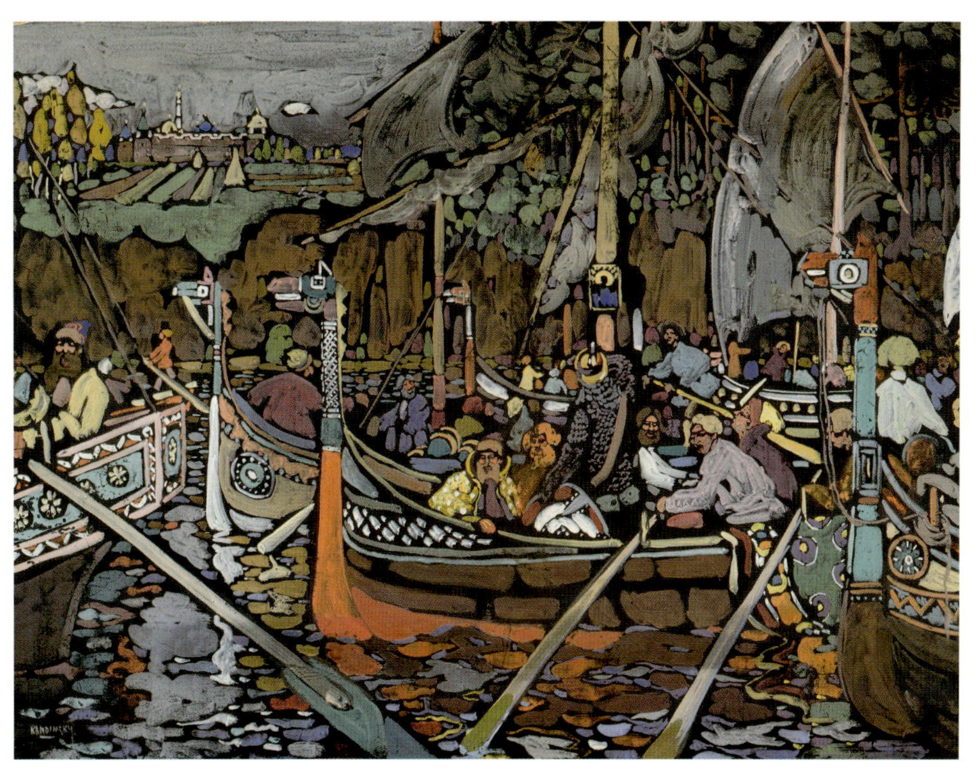

2   **Song**
1906
Gouache on cardboard 49 x 66

Musée National d'Art Moderne, Centre Georges Pompidou, Paris. Centre de Création Industrielle.
Bequest of Nina Kandinsky, 1981

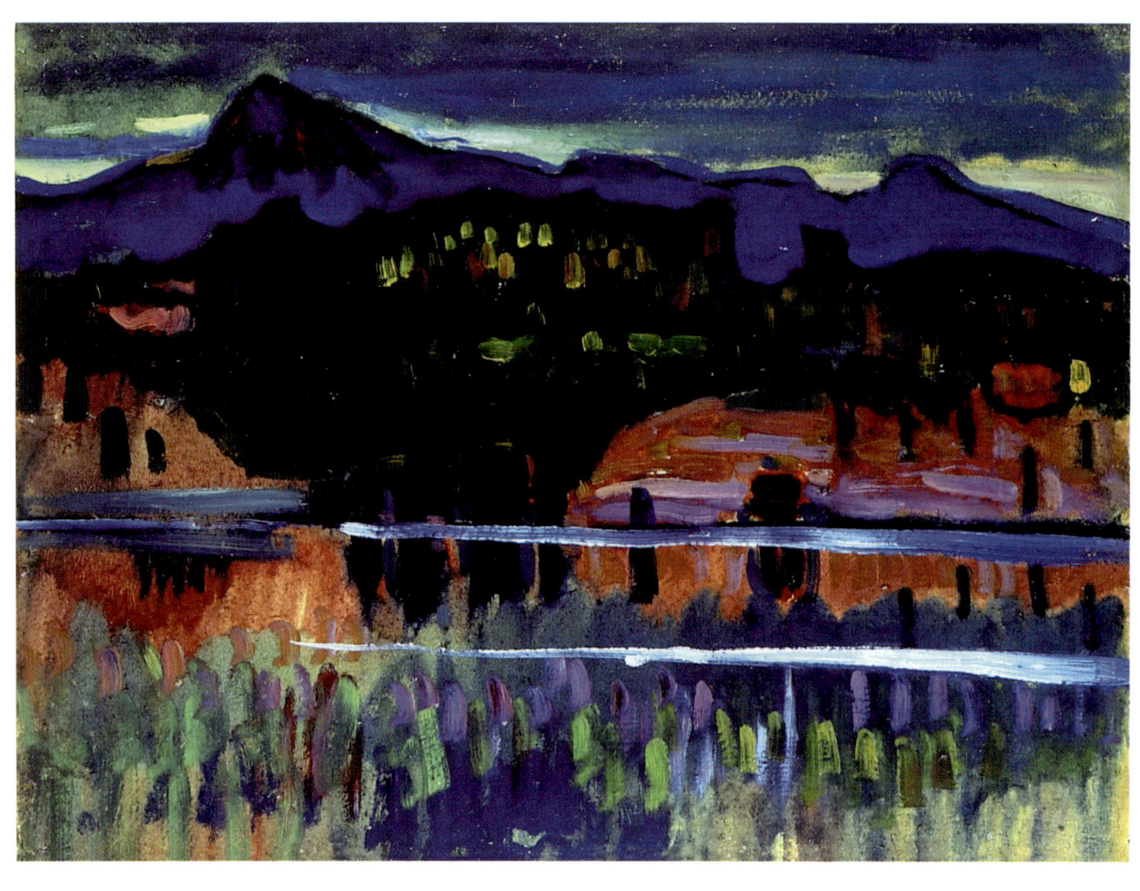

3   **Murnau – Staffelsee I**
1908
Oil on paper laid on board   33 x 40.5
The Ashmolean Museum, Oxford

4   **Murnau – Village Street**
1908
Oil on cardboard, mounted on wood 48 x 69.5
Private Collection, Switzerland

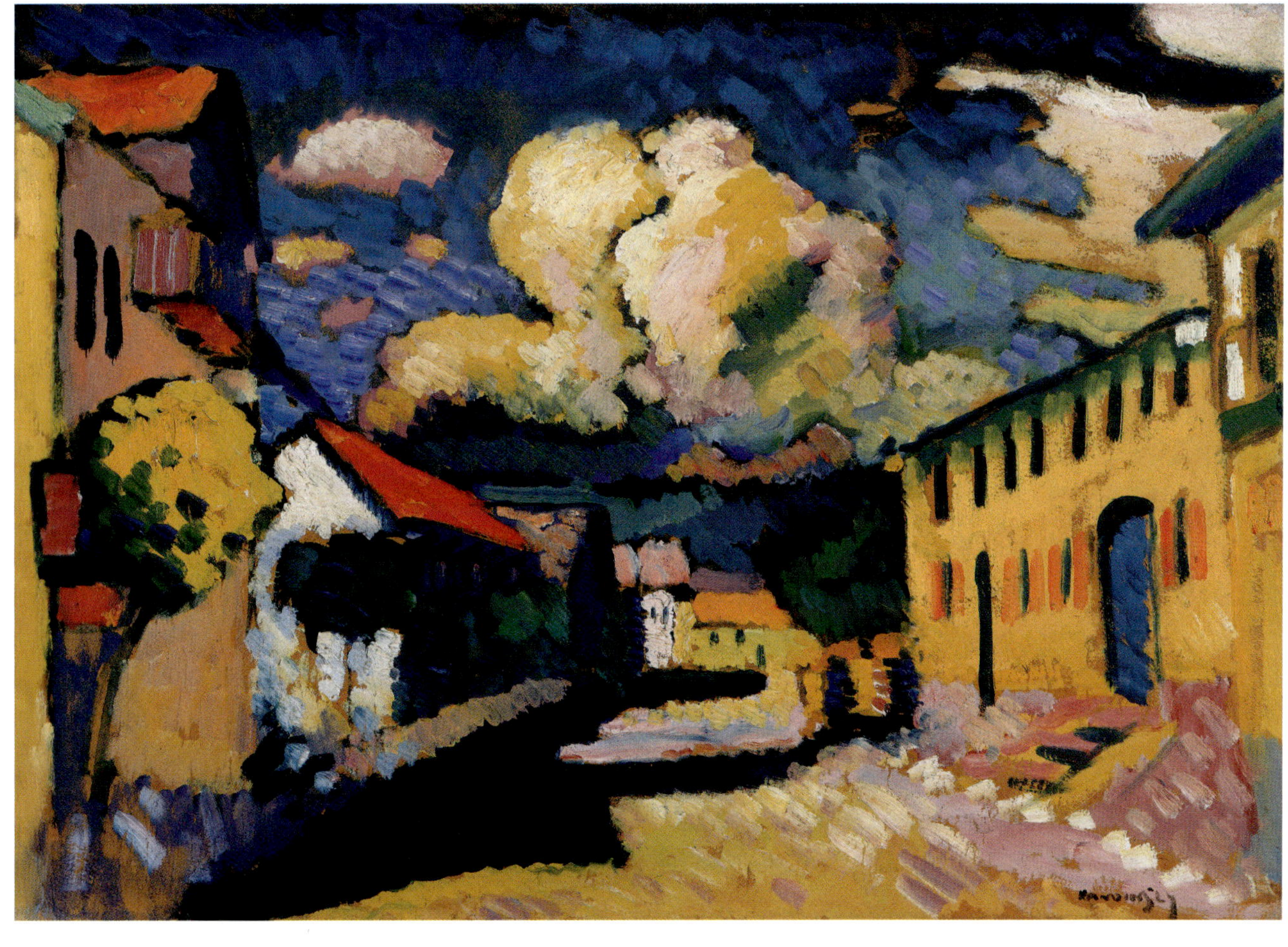

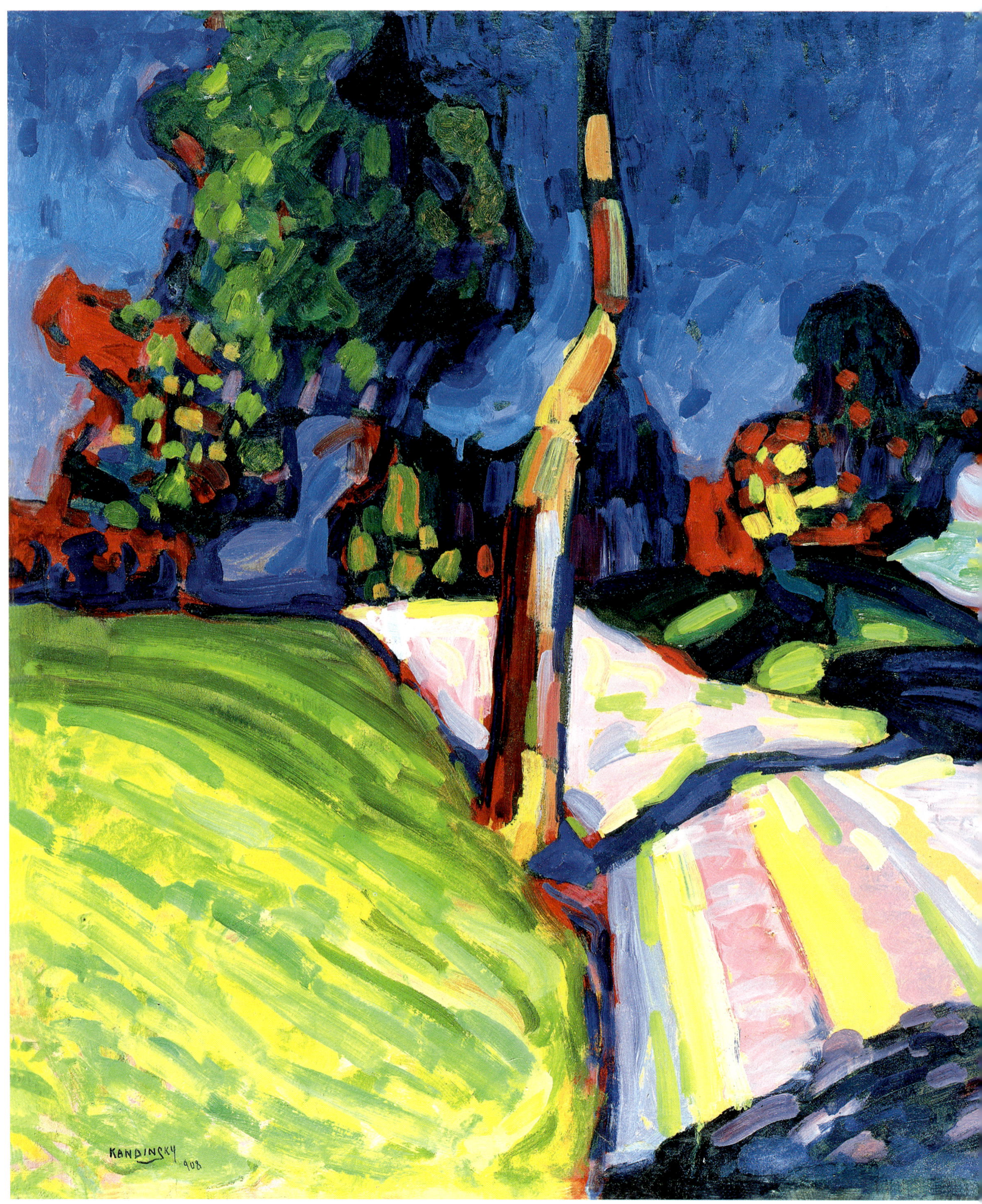

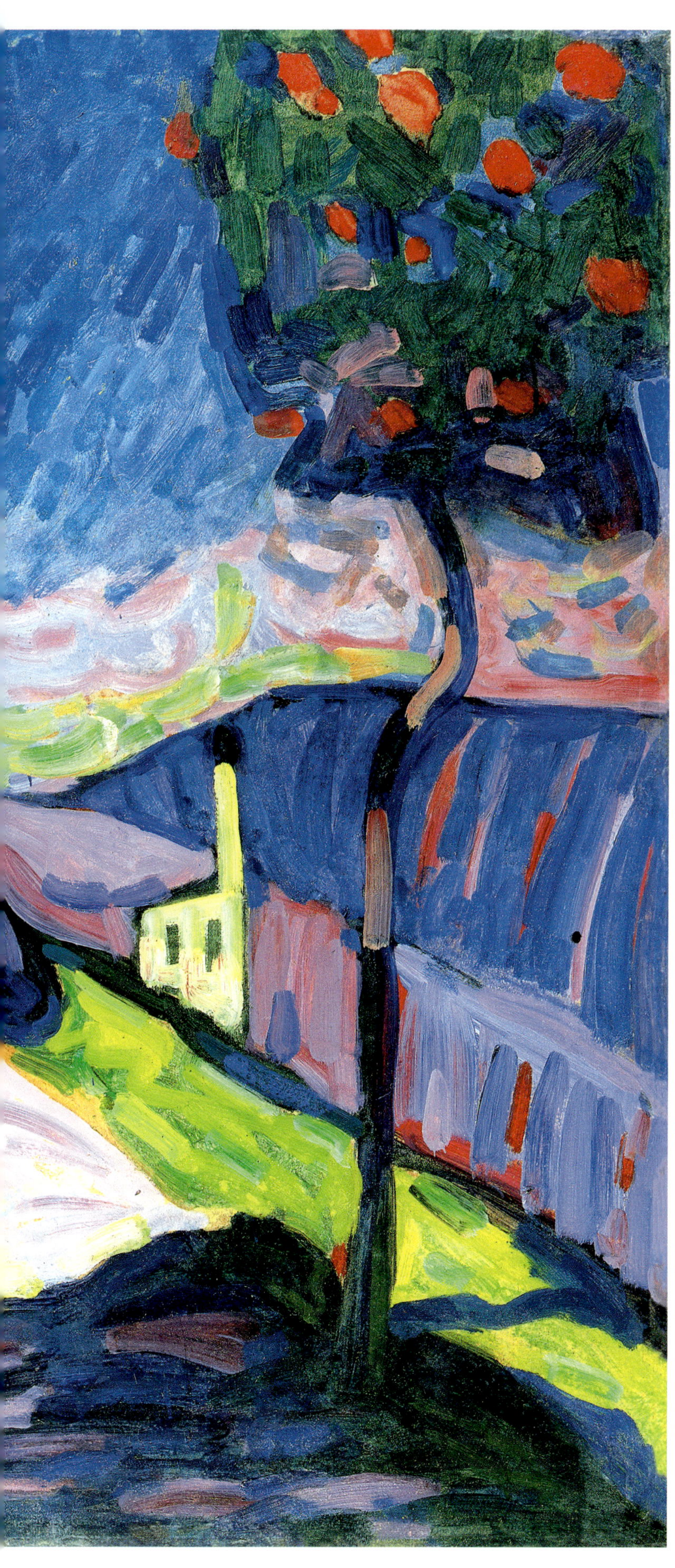

5 **Murnau – Kohlgruberstrasse**
1908
Oil on board 71 x 97.5
Private Collection, Switzerland

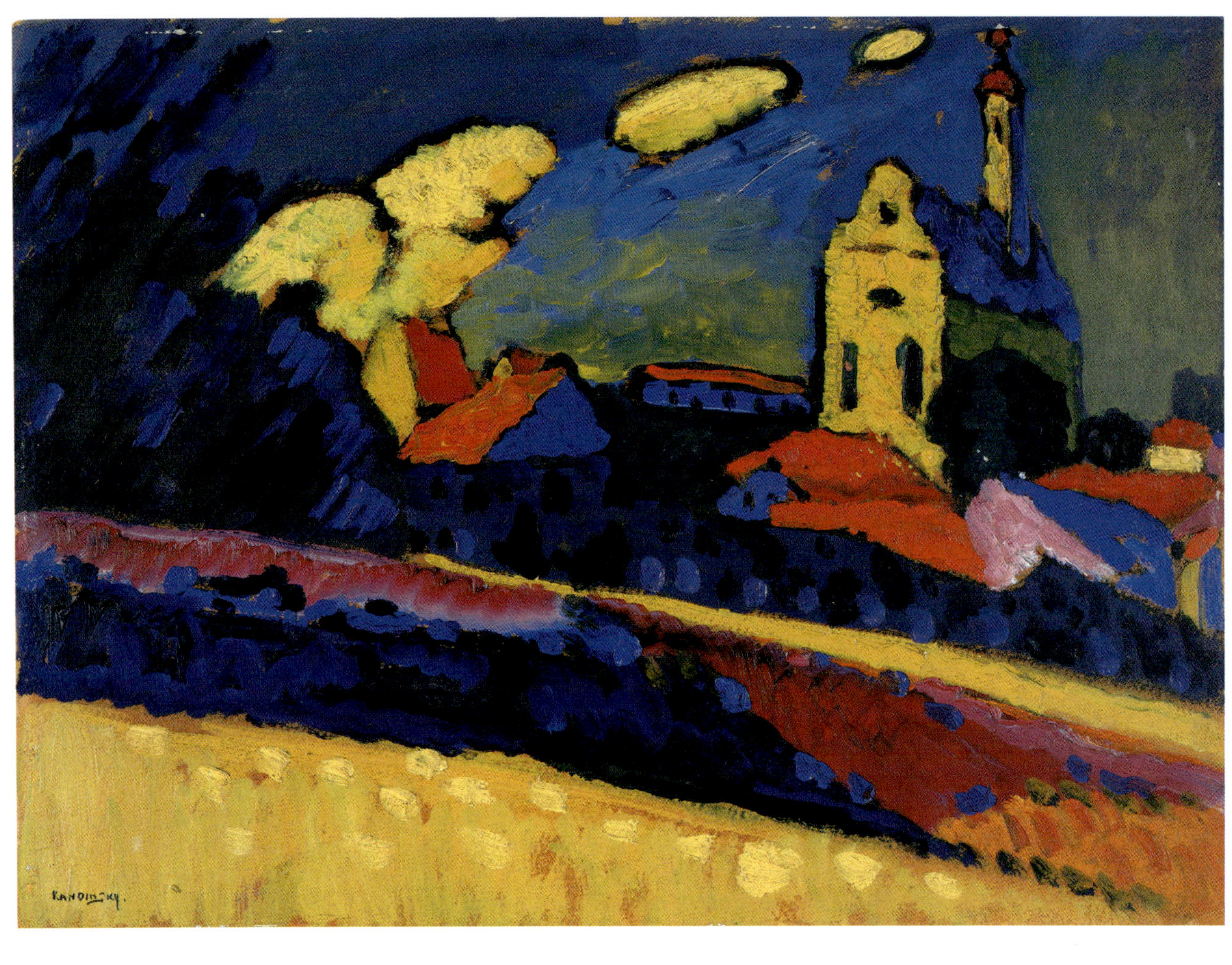

6 **Study for Murnau – Landscape with Church**
1909
Oil on cardboard 33 x 45
Collection Im Obersteg, Basel

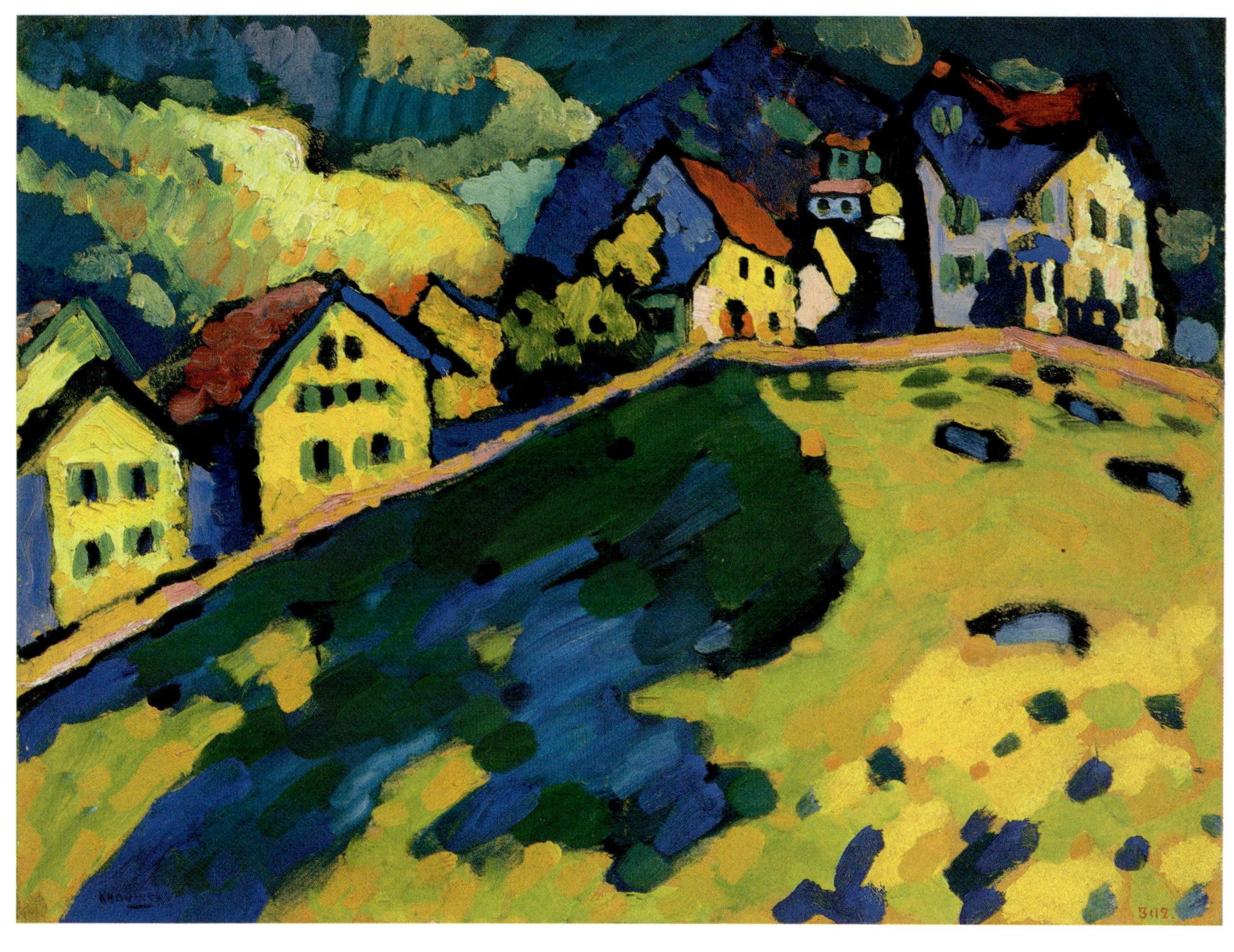

7 **Study for Houses on a Hill**
1909
Oil on cardboard 33 x 45
The State Russian Museum, St Petersburg

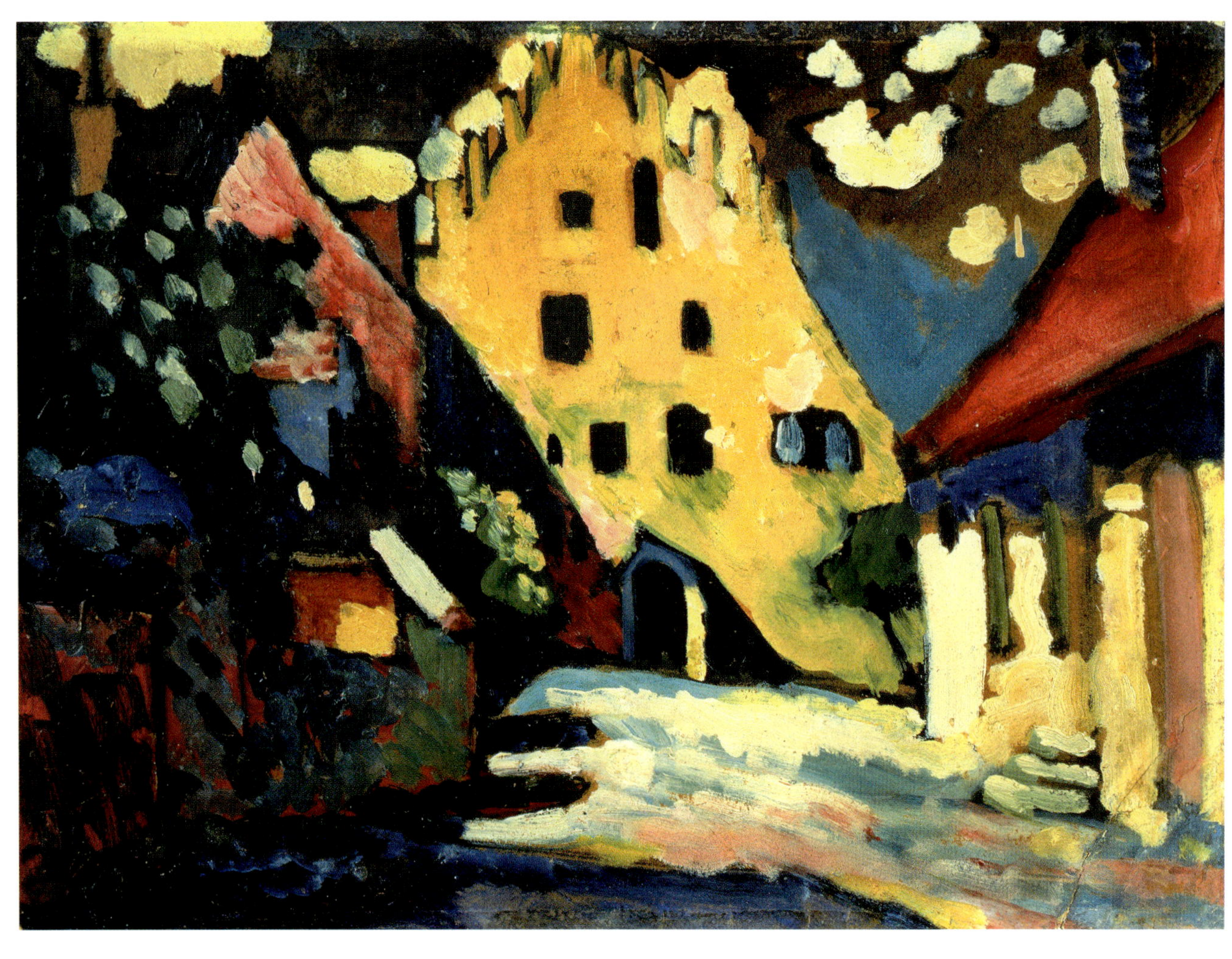

8   **Murnau – Castle Courtyard I**
1908
Oil on cardboard 33 x 44.3
The State Tretyakov Gallery, Moscow

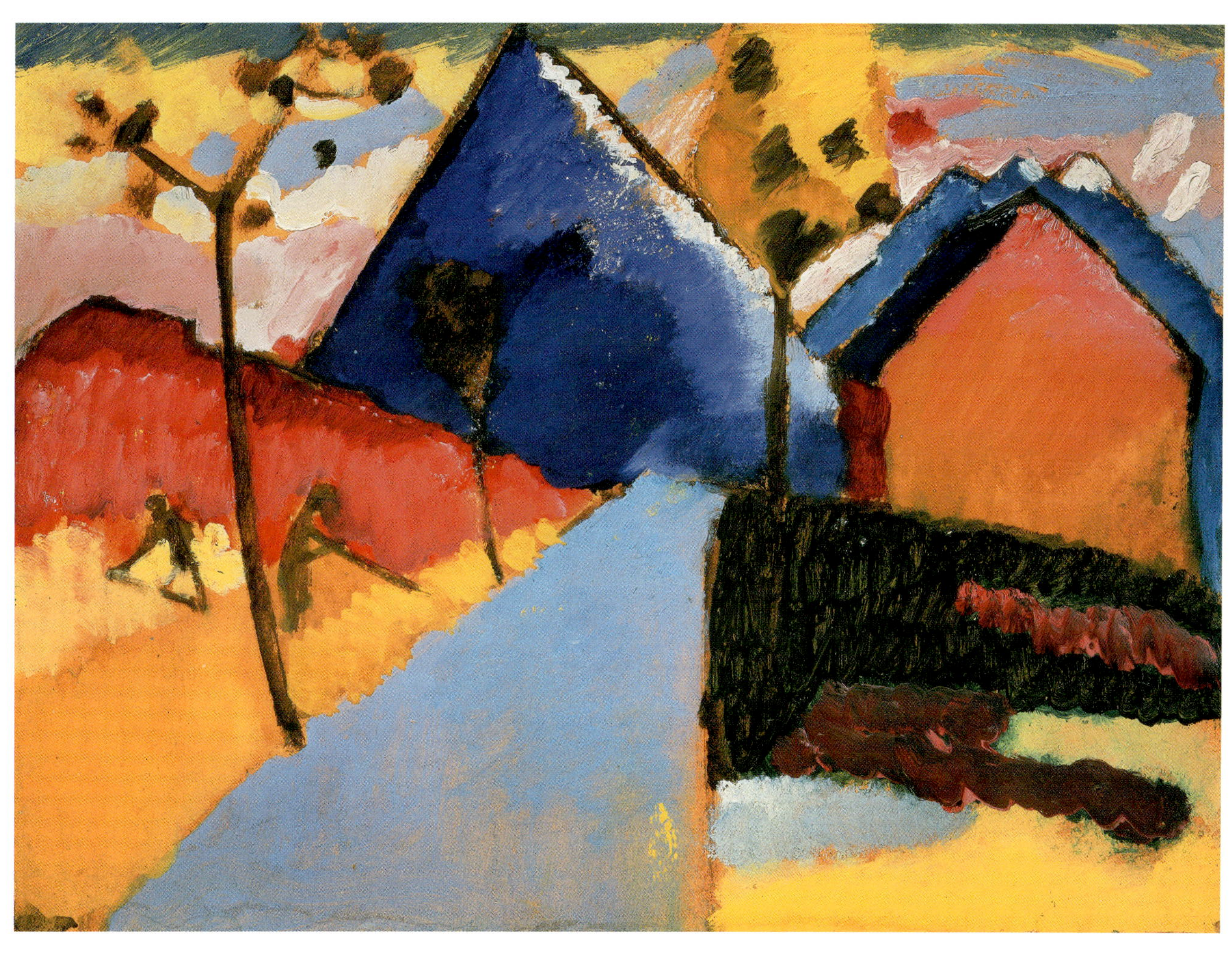

9 **Kochel – Straight Road**
1909
Oil on cardboard 33 x 44.8
Städtische Galerie im Lenbachhaus, Munich

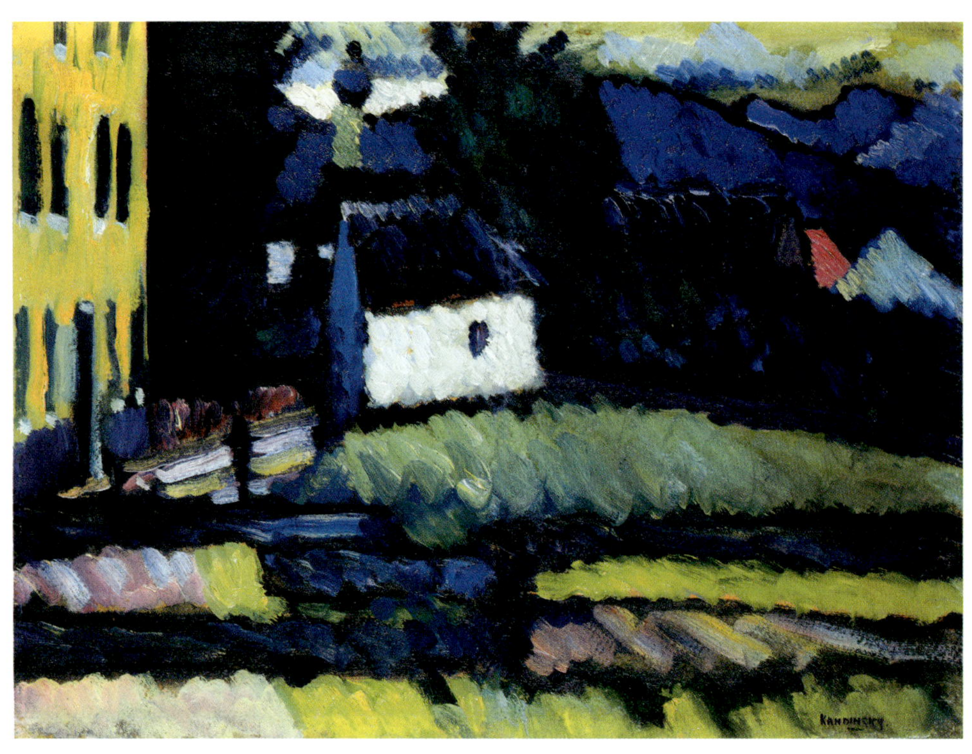

10 **St Peter's Chapel at Murnau**
1908
Oil on cardboard 33 x 43
Private Collection, Hamburg

54

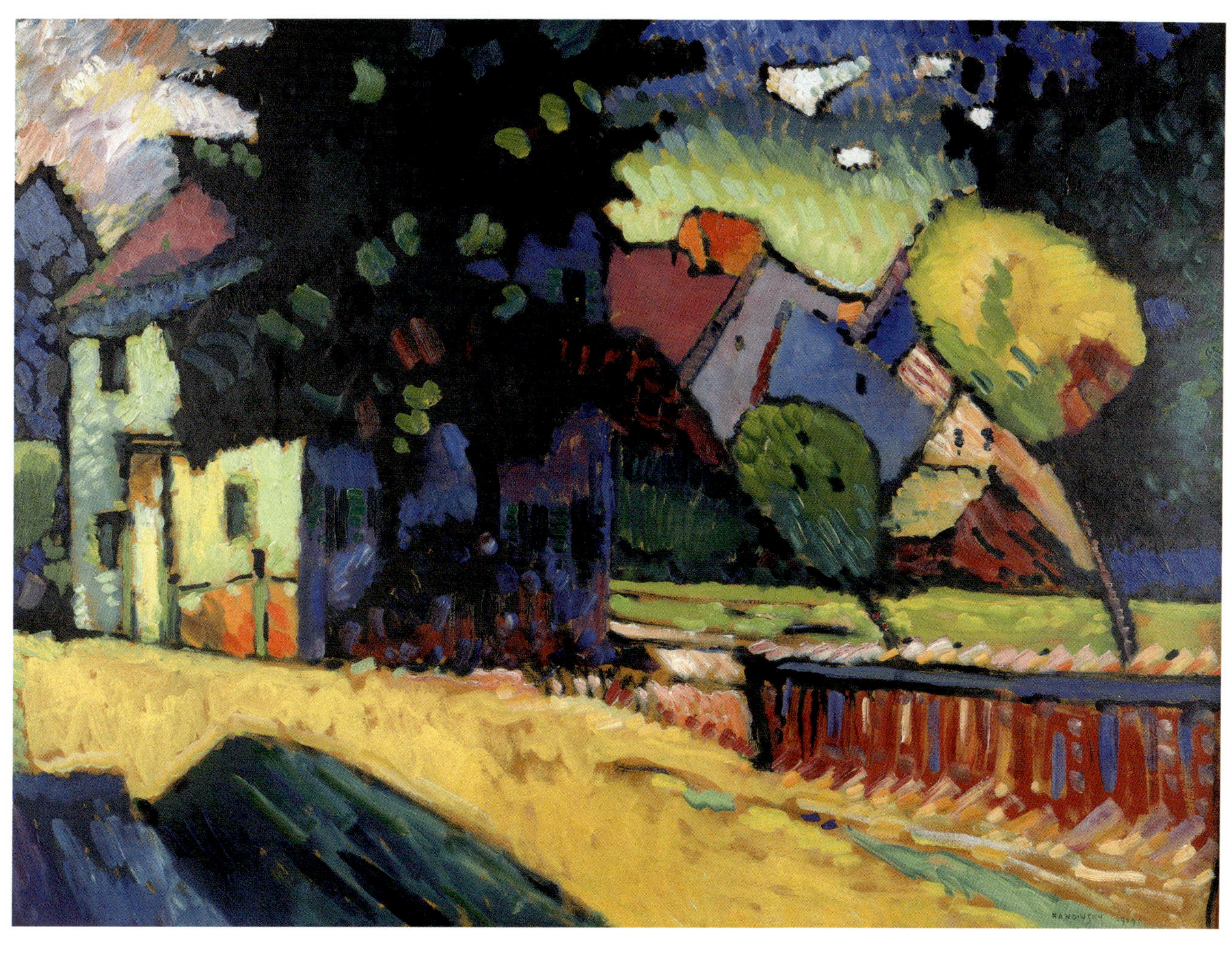

11 **Murnau – Landscape with Green House**
1909
Oil on cardboard 69 x 94
Private Collection, Israel

55

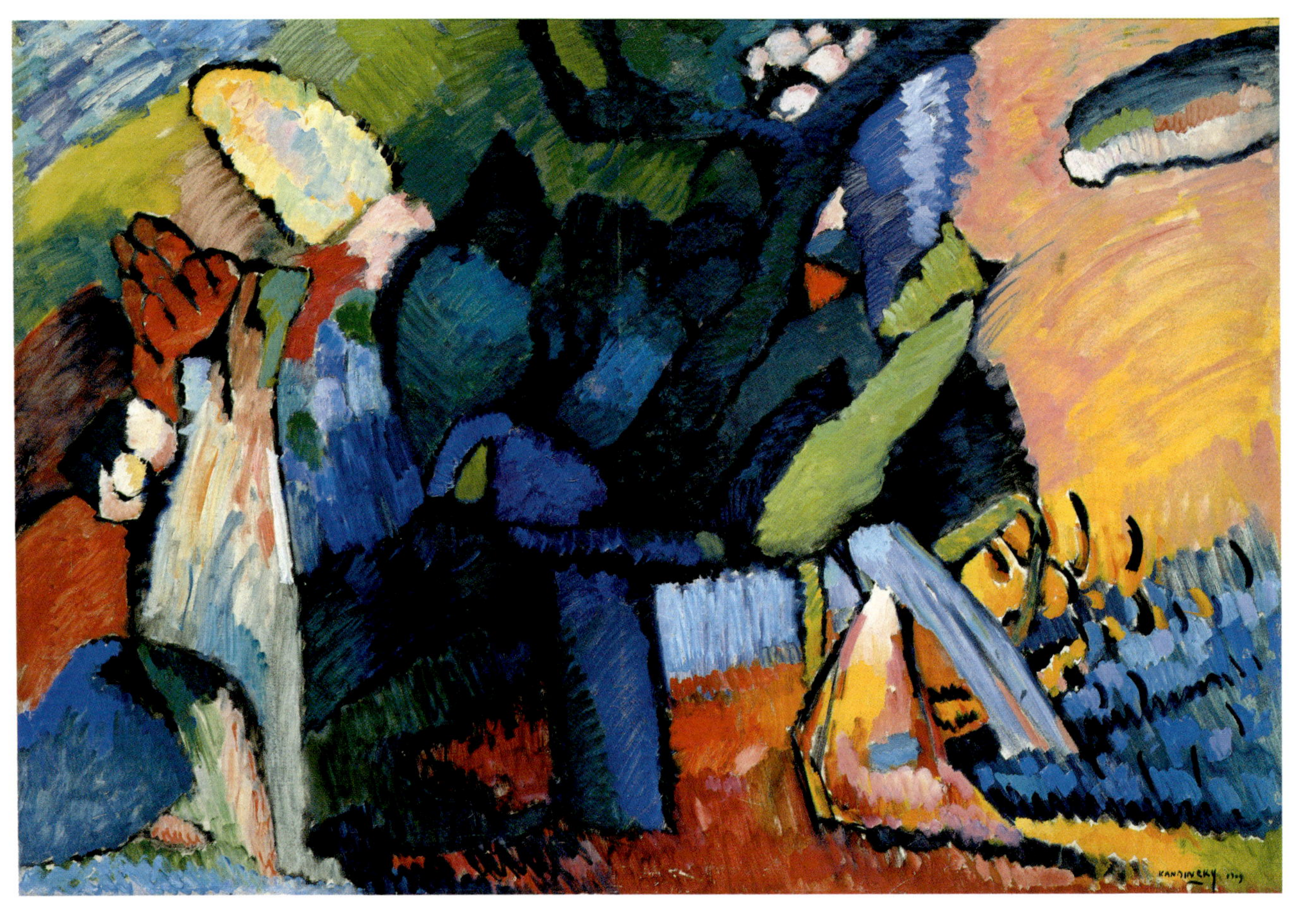

12 Improvisation 4

1909
Oil on canvas 108 x 158.5

State Art Musum, Nizhny Novgorod

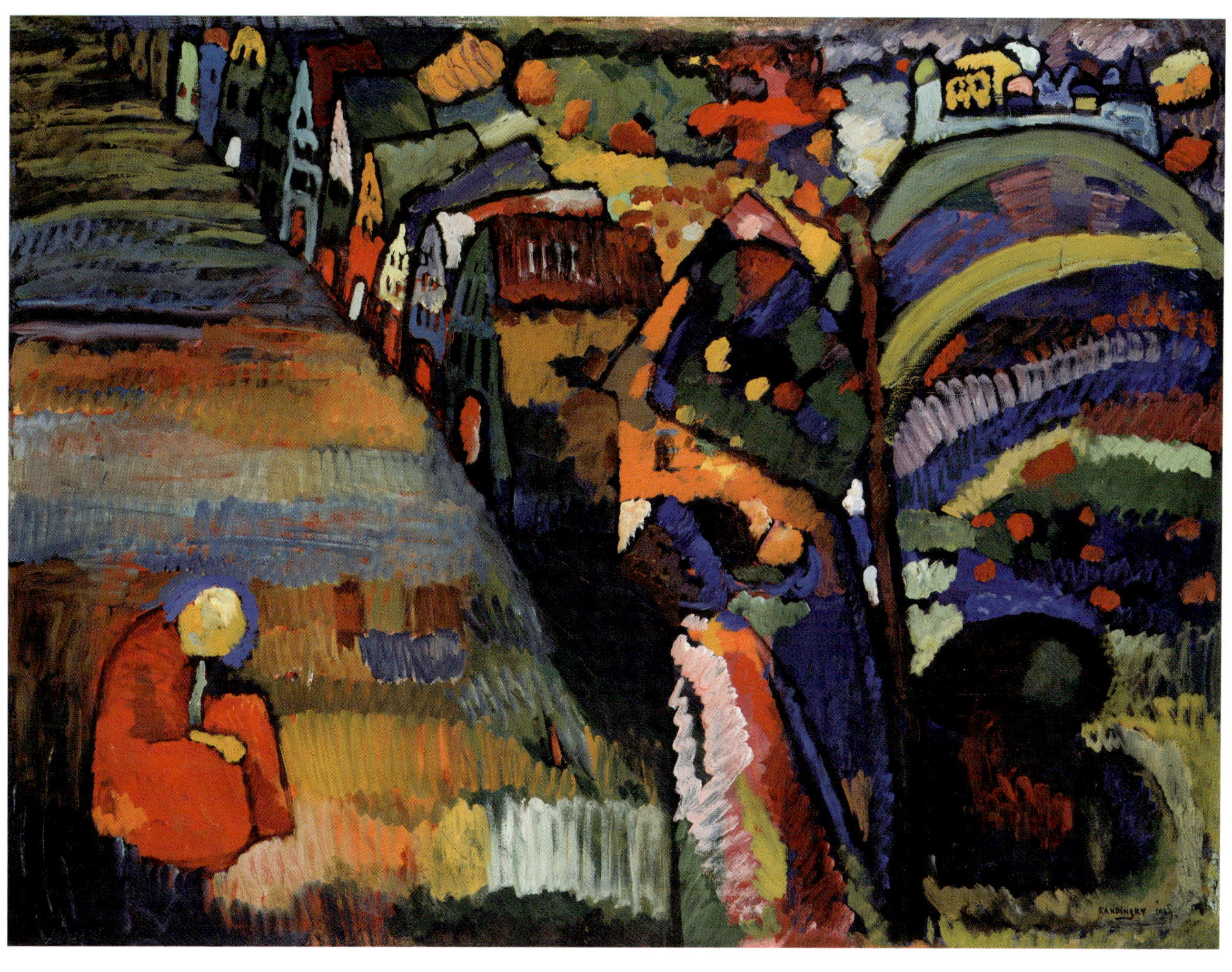

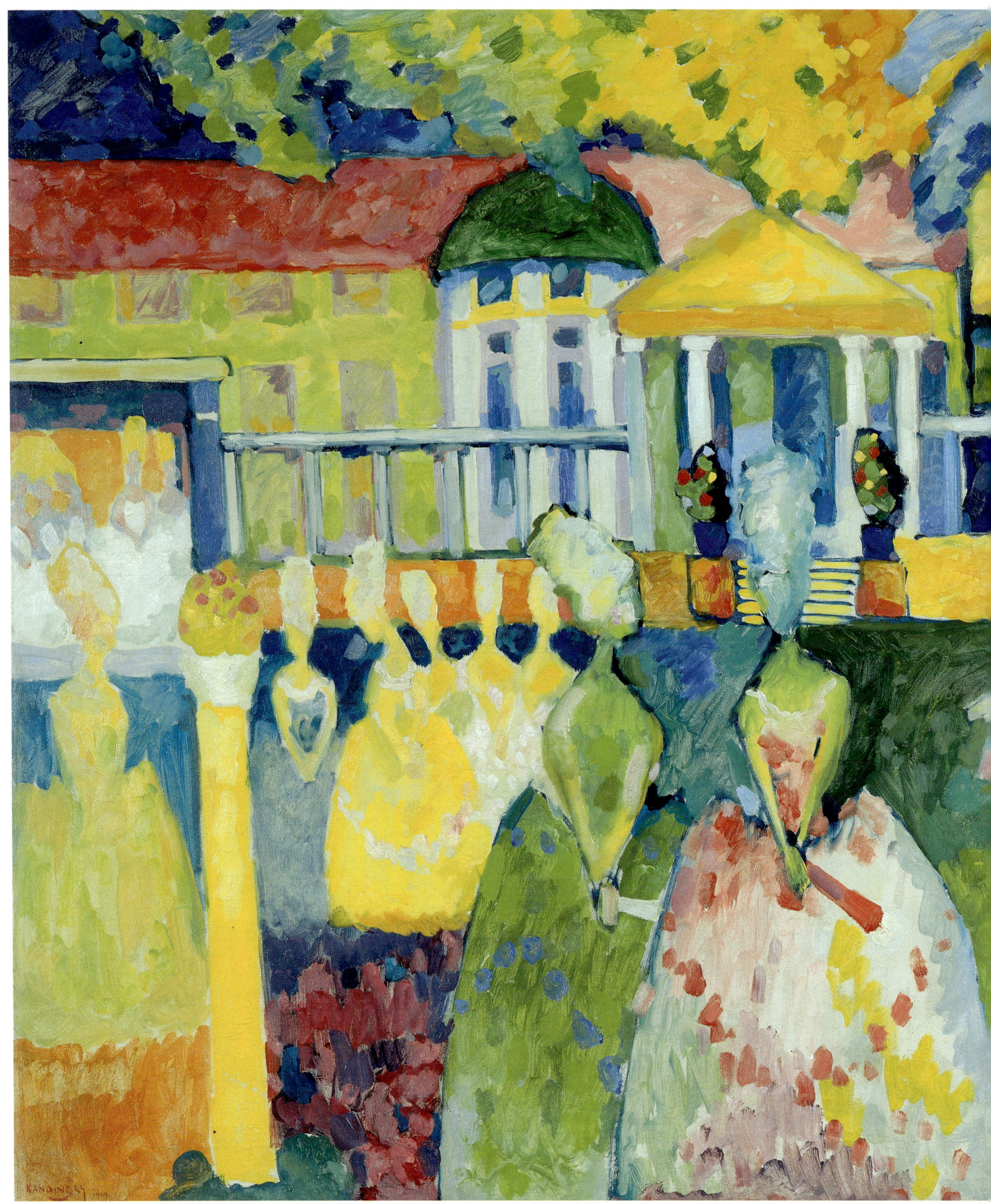

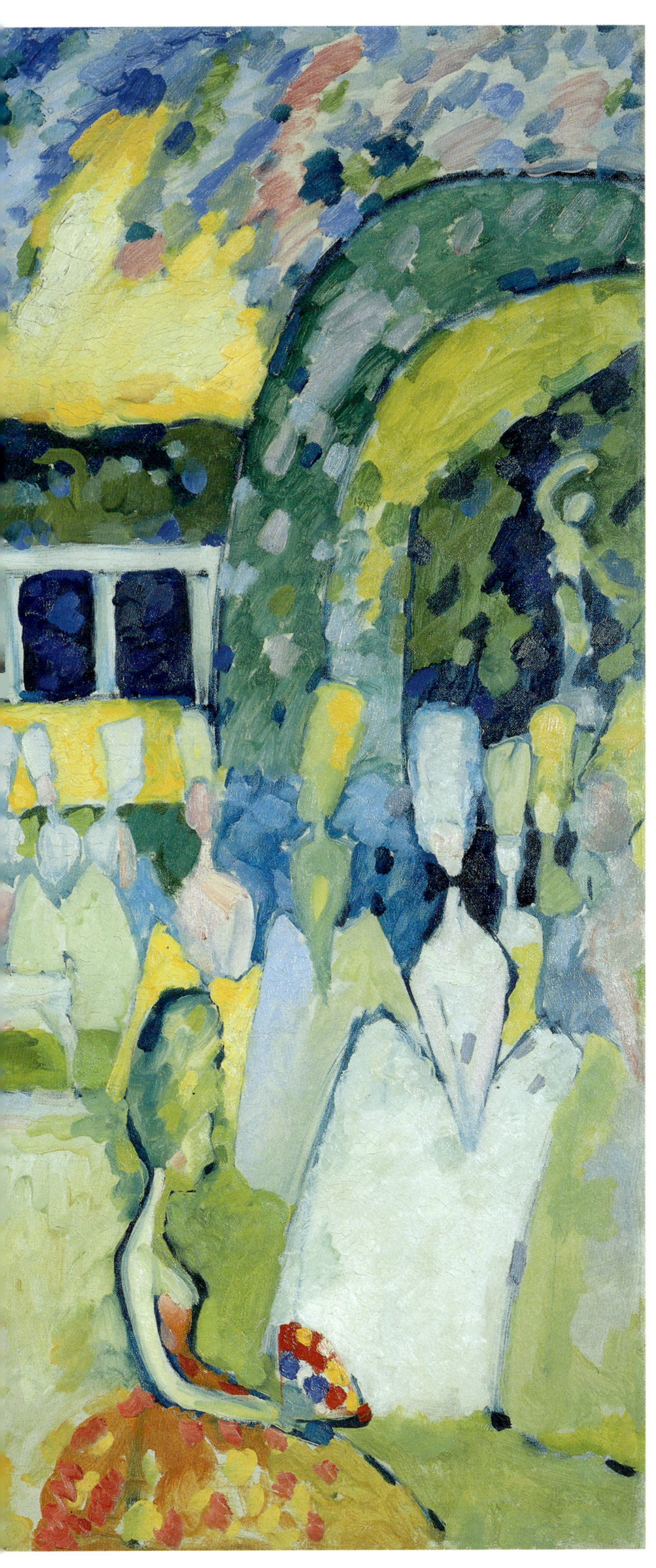

14 **Crinolines**
1909
Oil on canvas 95 x 128.5
The State Tretyakov Gallery, Moscow

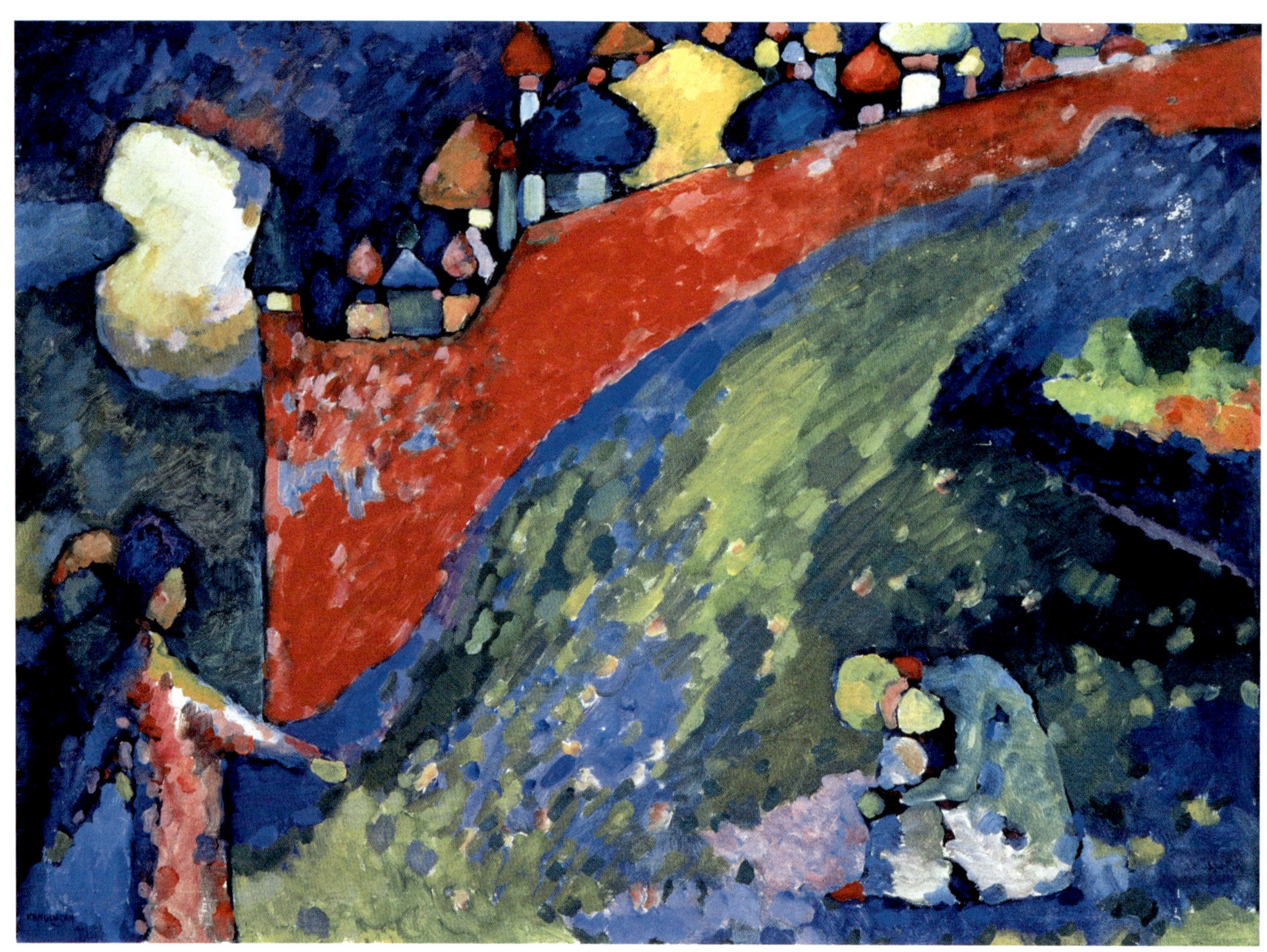

15 **Cupolas**

1909

Oil on cardboard 83 x 116

The State Kustodiev Gallery, Astrakhan

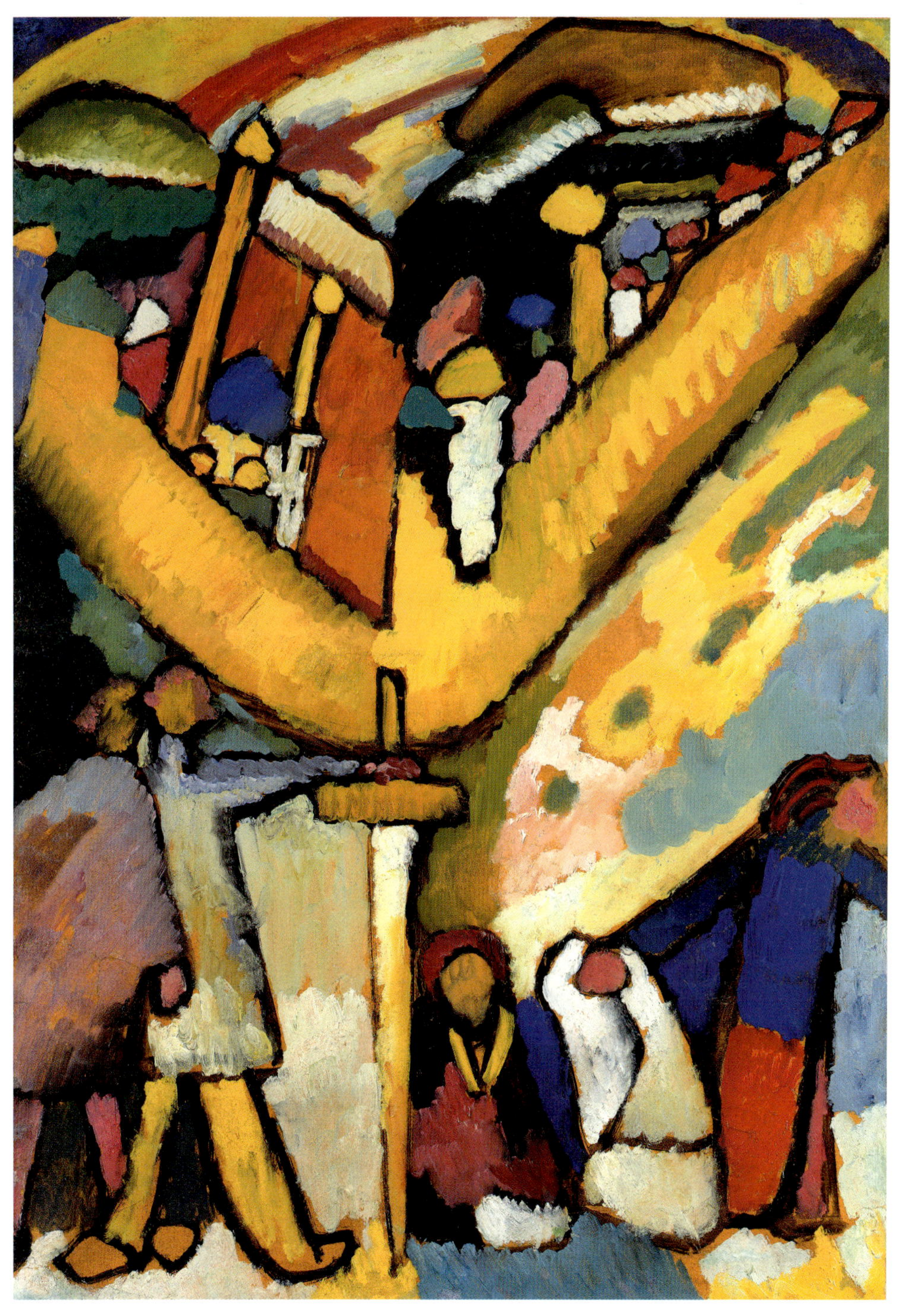

16 **Study for Improvisation 8**

1909

Oil on cardboard 98 x 70

Kunstmuseum Winterthur. Permanent loan of the Volkart Foundation, 1960

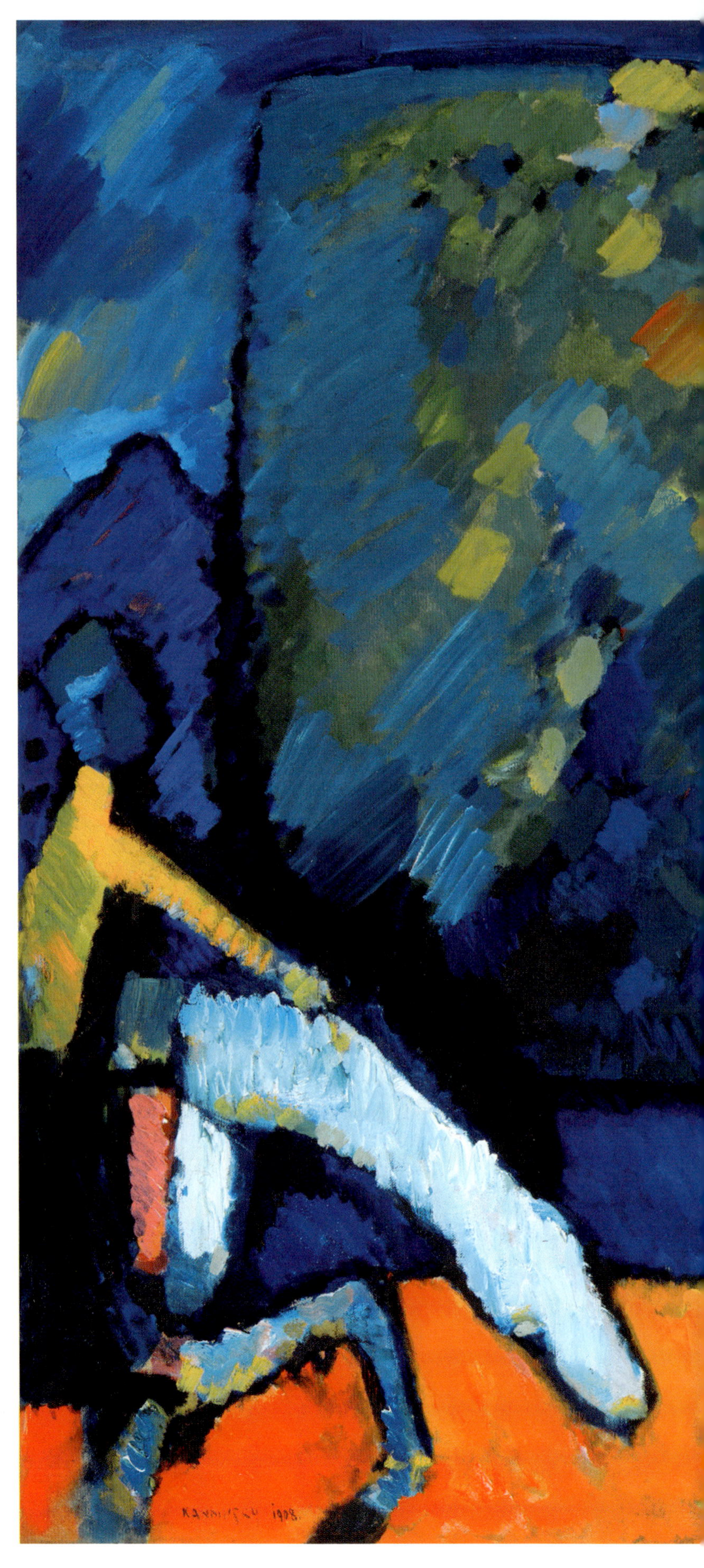

17 **Improvisation 2 (Funeral March)**
1908
Oil on canvas 94 x 130
Moderna Museet, Stockholm

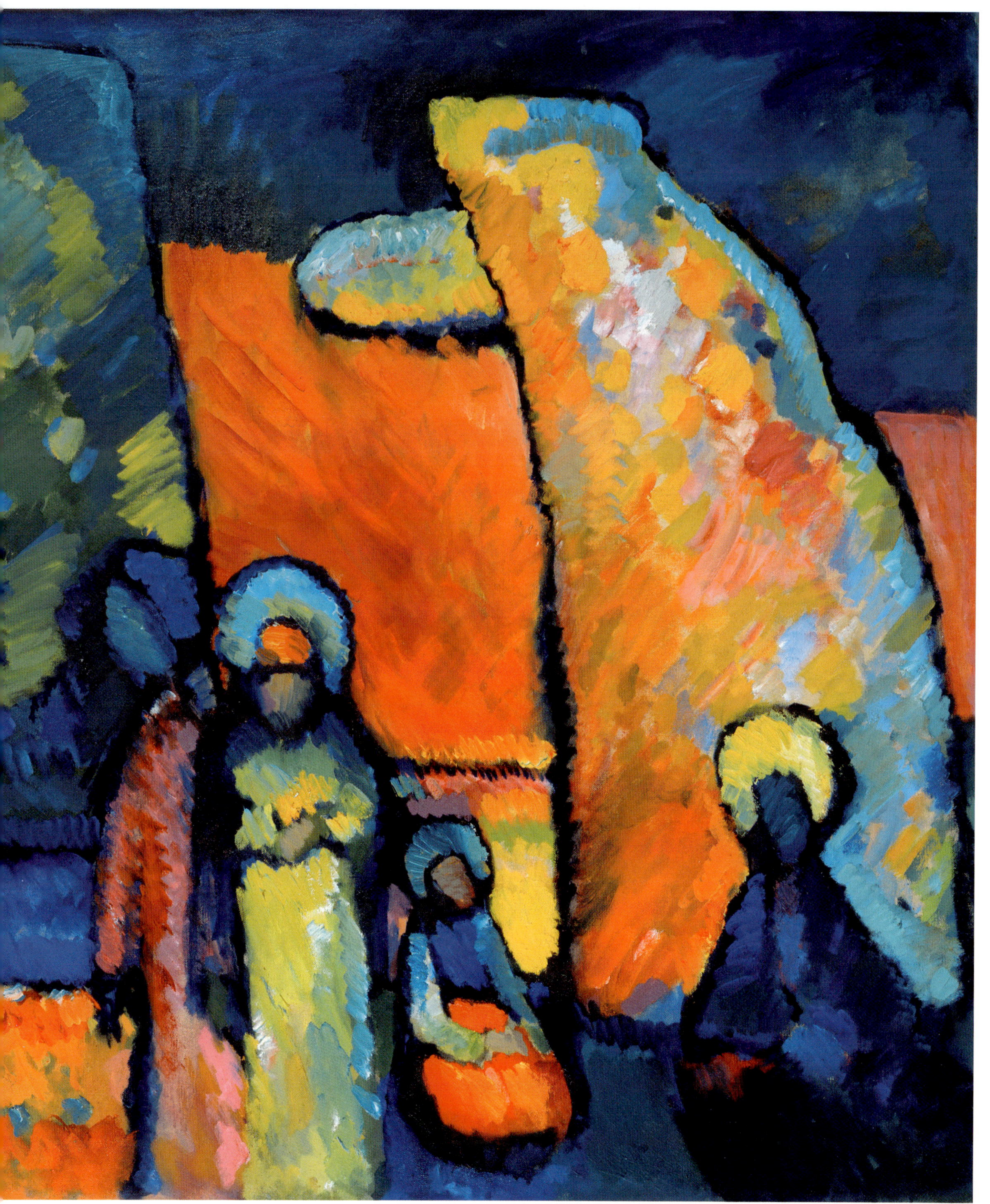

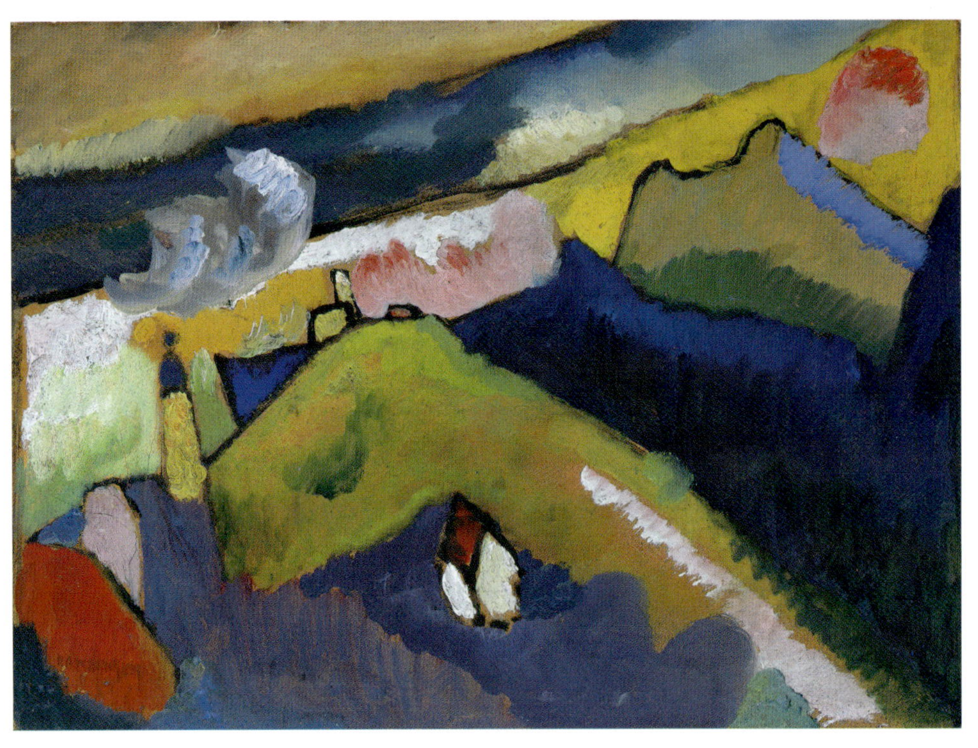

18 **Murnau – Mountain Landscape with Church**
1910
Oil on cardboard 32.7 x 44.8
Städtische Galerie im Lenbachhaus, Munich

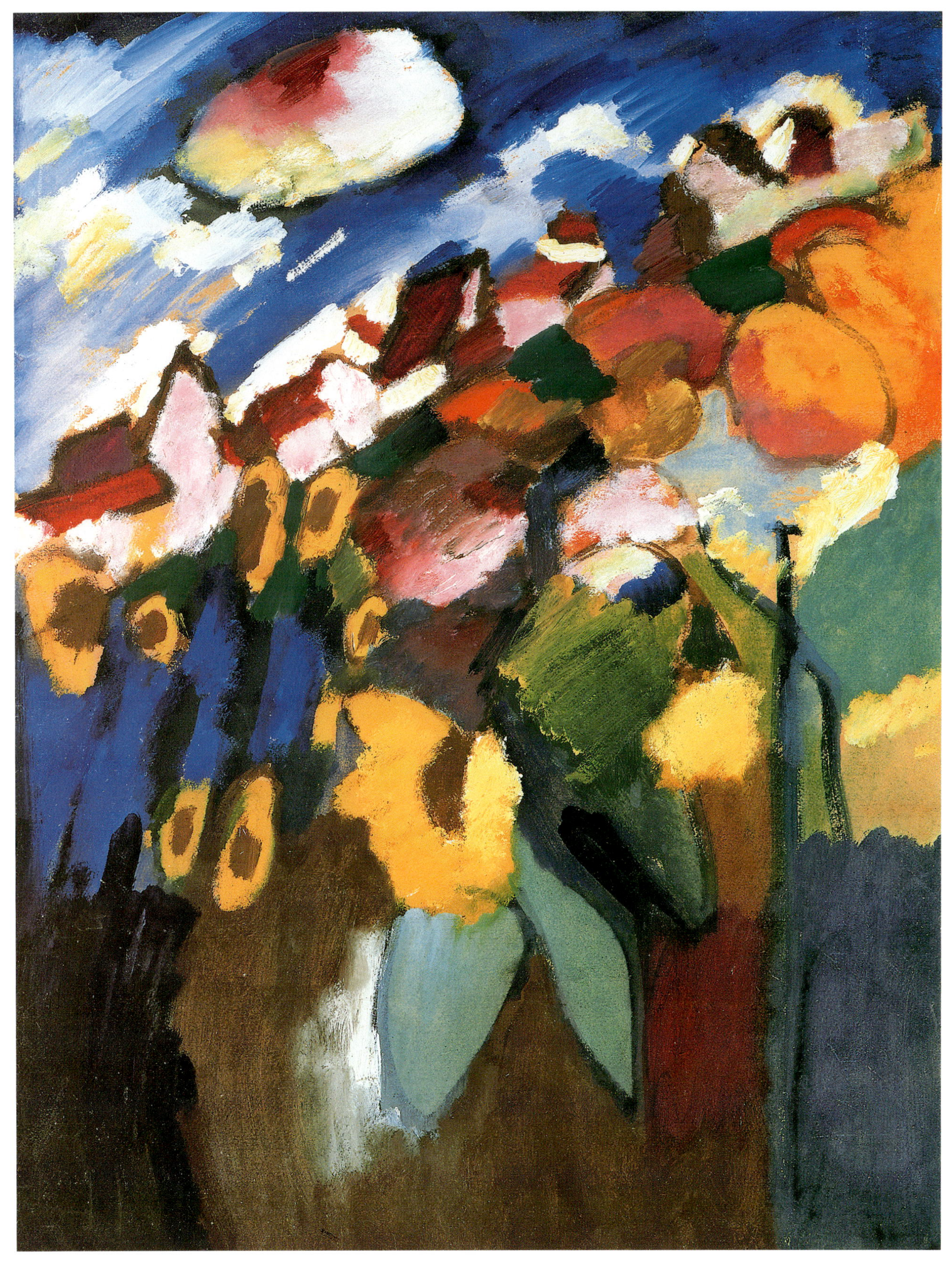

19 **Murnau – The Garden II**
1910
Oil on board 67 x 51
Private Collection, Switzerland

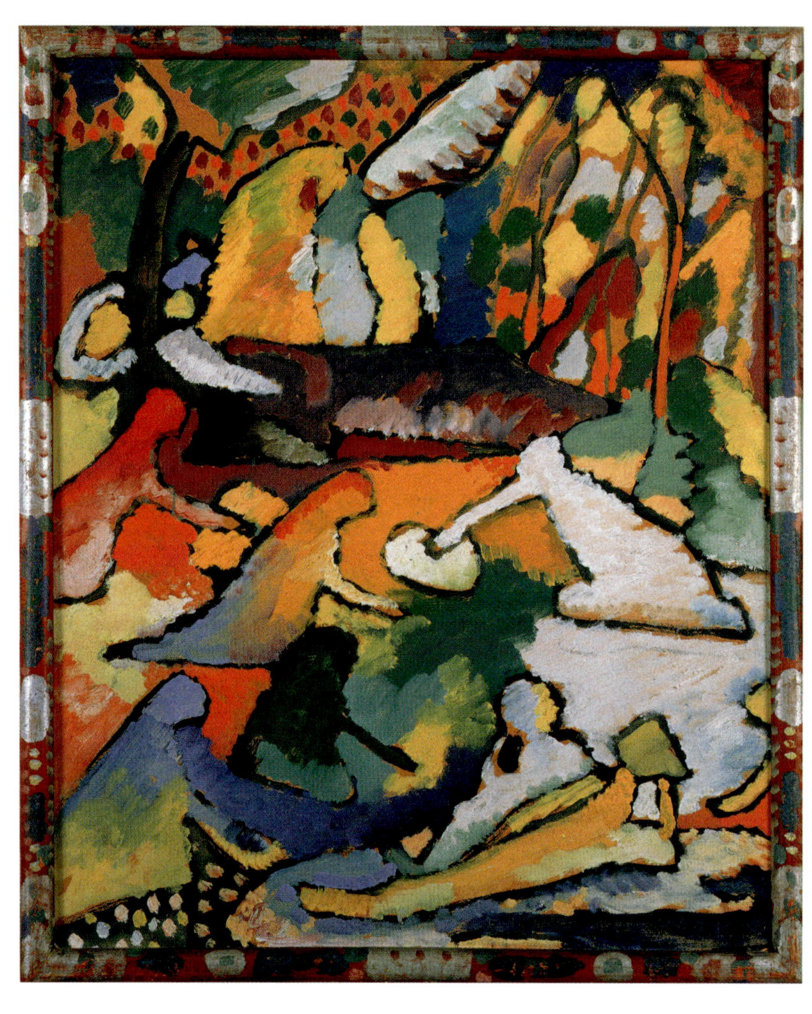

20 **Sketch for Composition II**
1910
Oil on cardboard 57 x 47.5
Private Collection, Switzerland

21 Sketch for Composition II
1910
Oil on canvas 97.5 x 131.2
Solomon R. Guggenheim Museum, New York

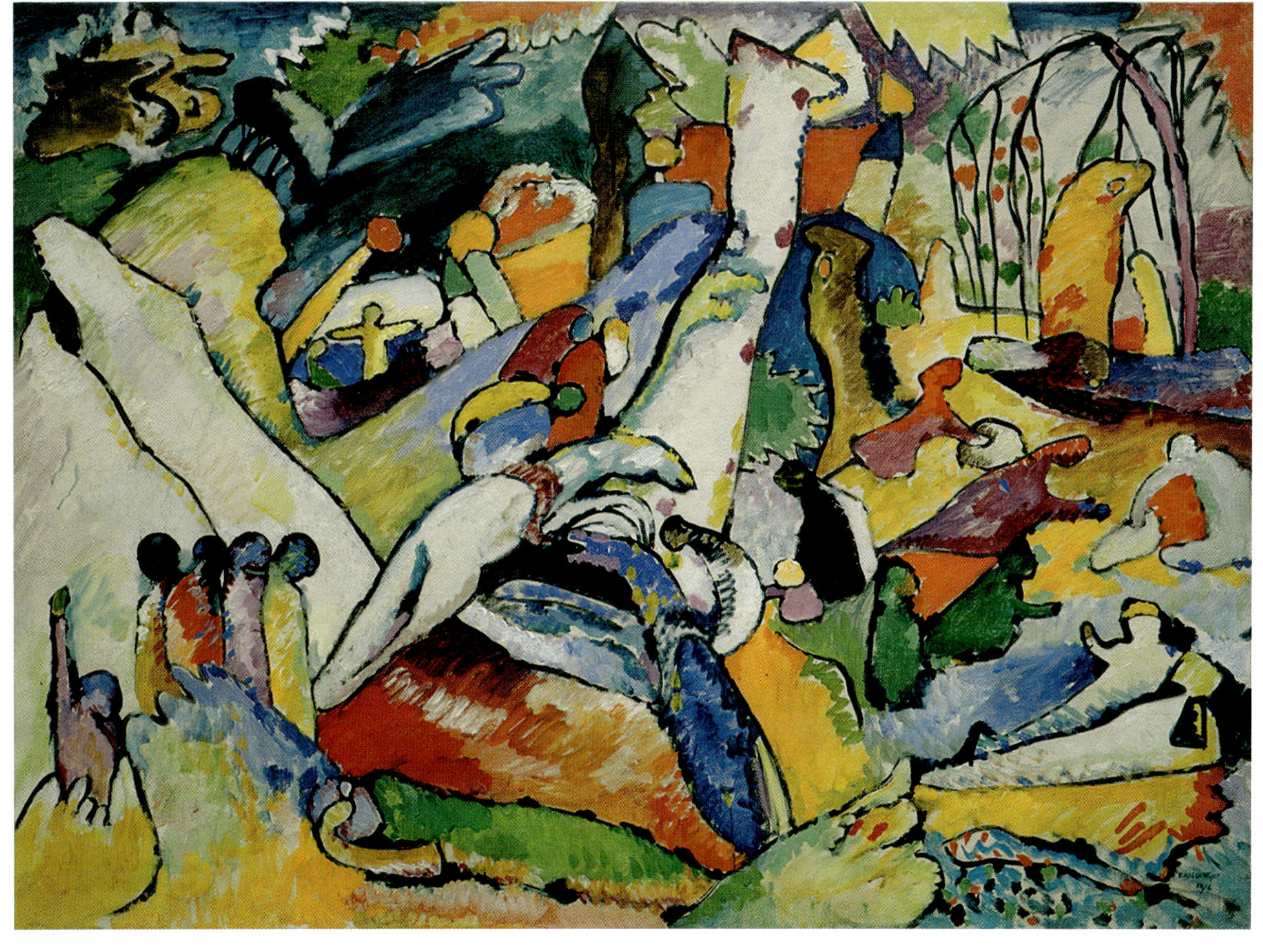

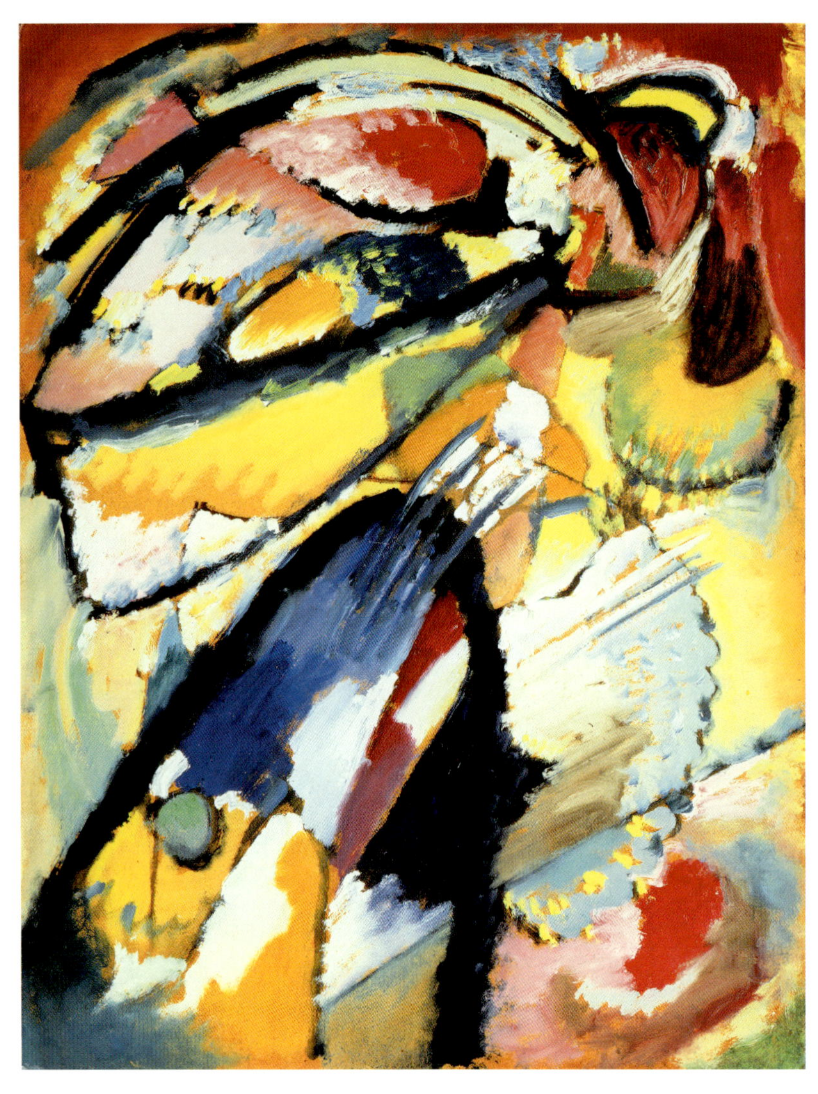

22 Angel of the Last Judgement
1911
Oil on cardboard 64 x 50
Private Collection, Switzerland

23 **The Last Judgement**
1910
Oil on canvas 126.5 x 73

Private Collection.
Courtesy Helly Nahmad

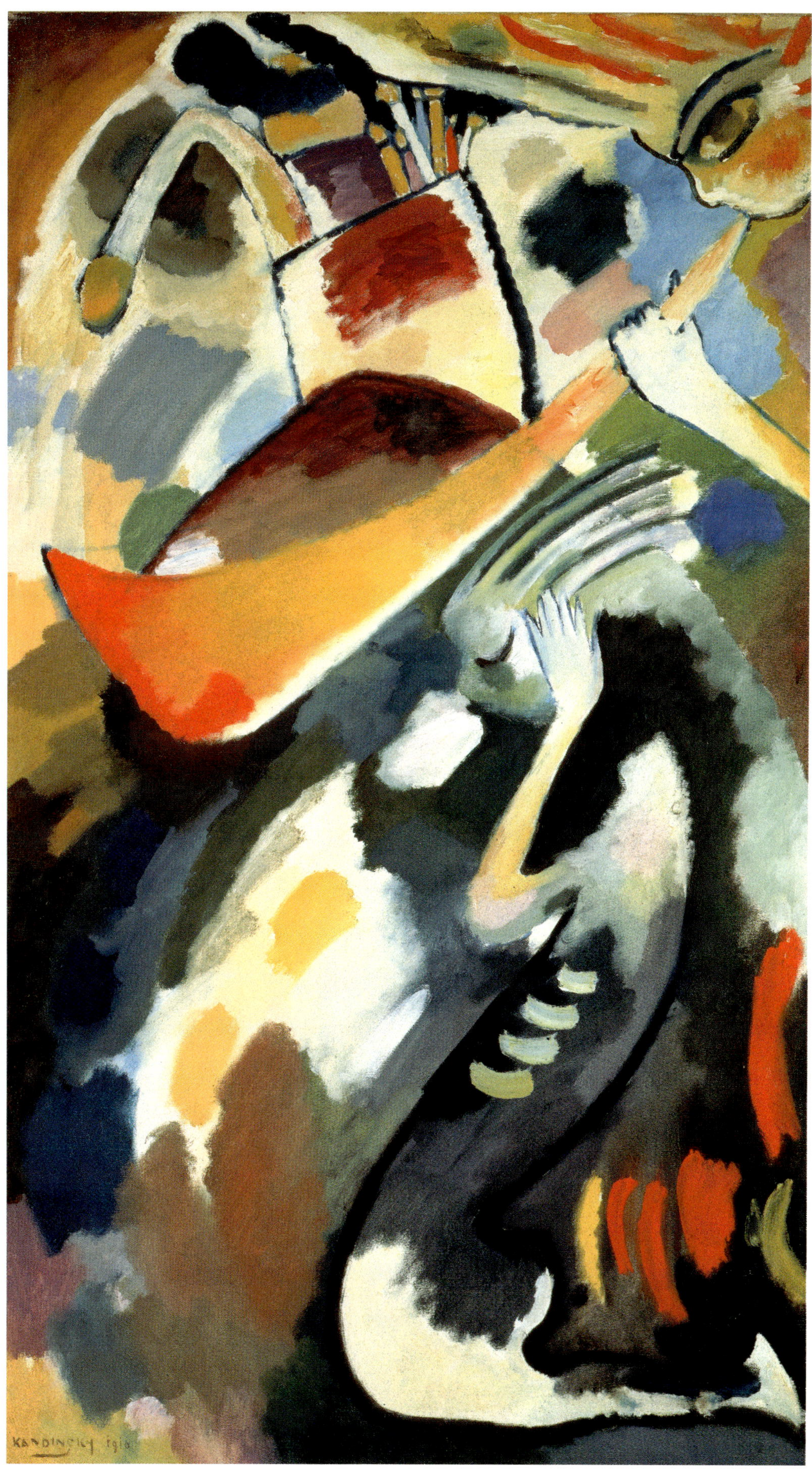

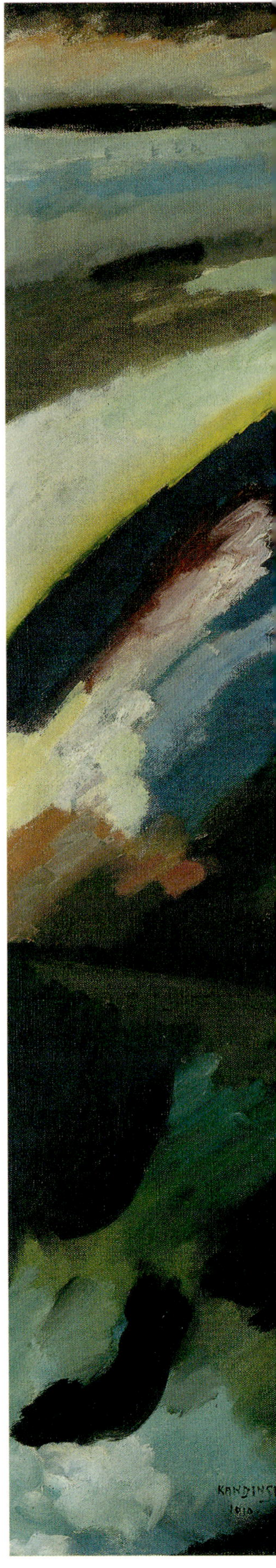

24 **Boat Trip**
1910
Oil on canvas 98 x 105
The State Tretyakov Gallery, Moscow

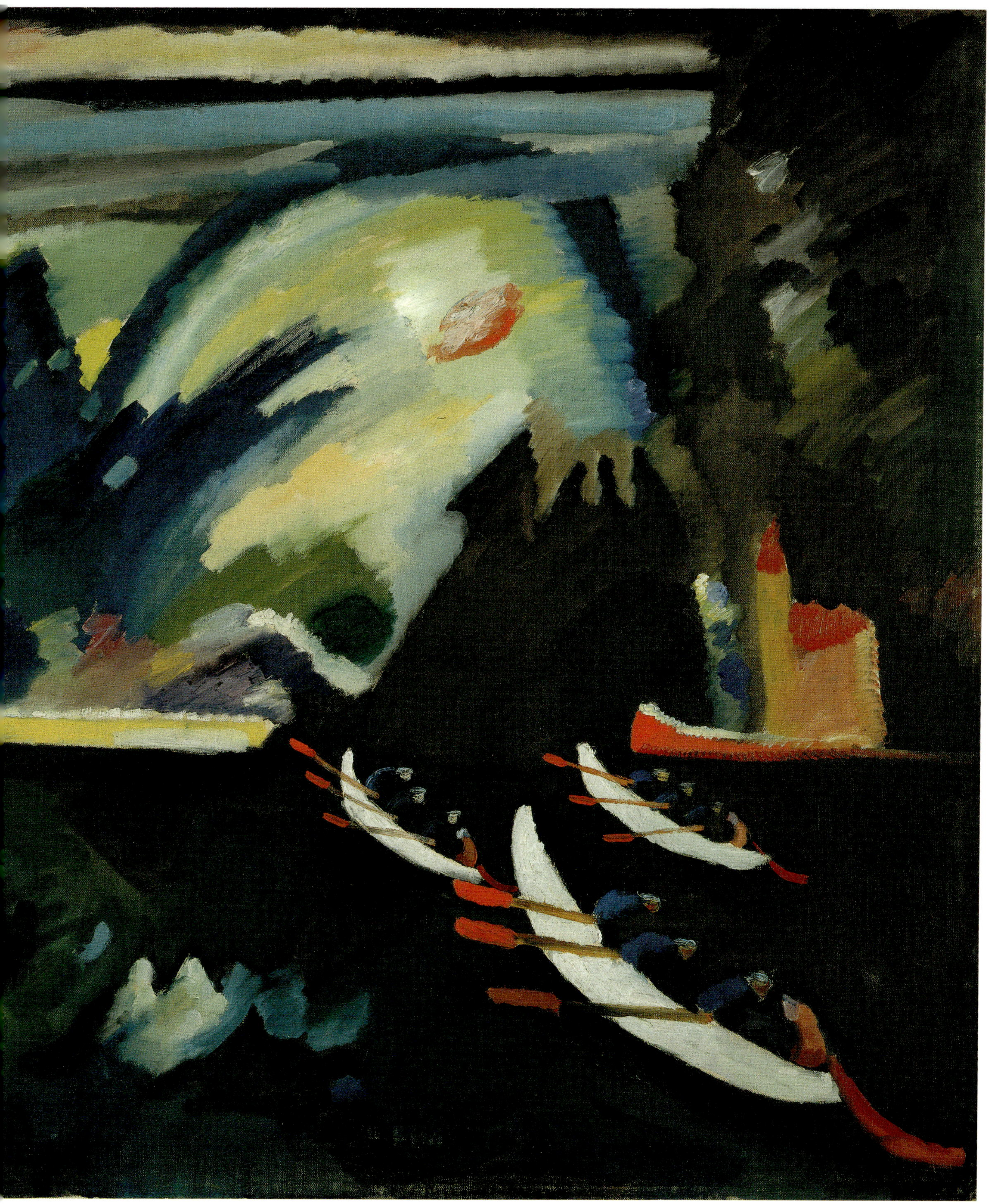

25 **Autumn Landscape**
1911
Oil on canvas 71 x 99

Jan Krugier und Marie-Anne Krugier-Pontatowski Collection
NOT EXHIBITED

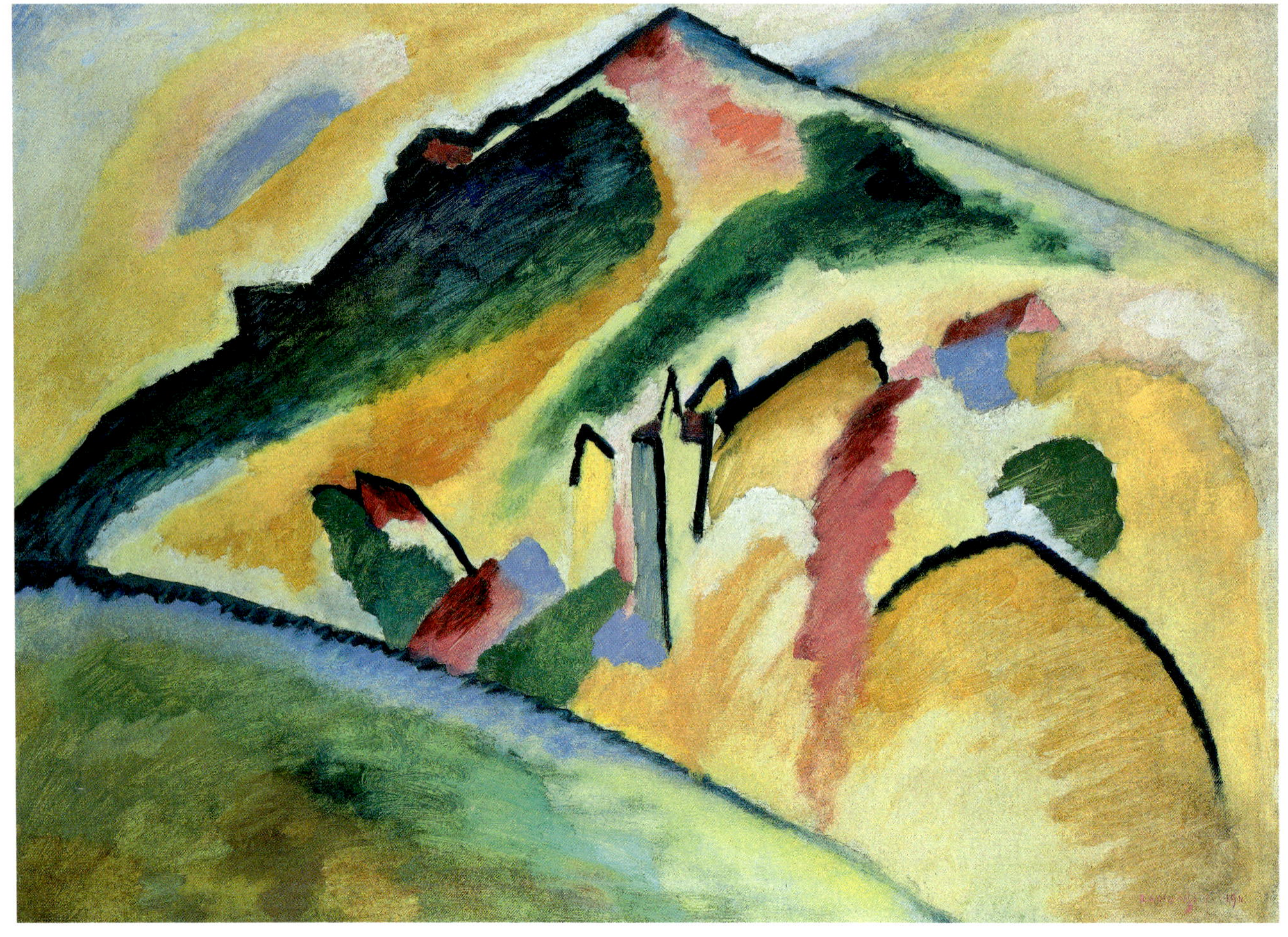

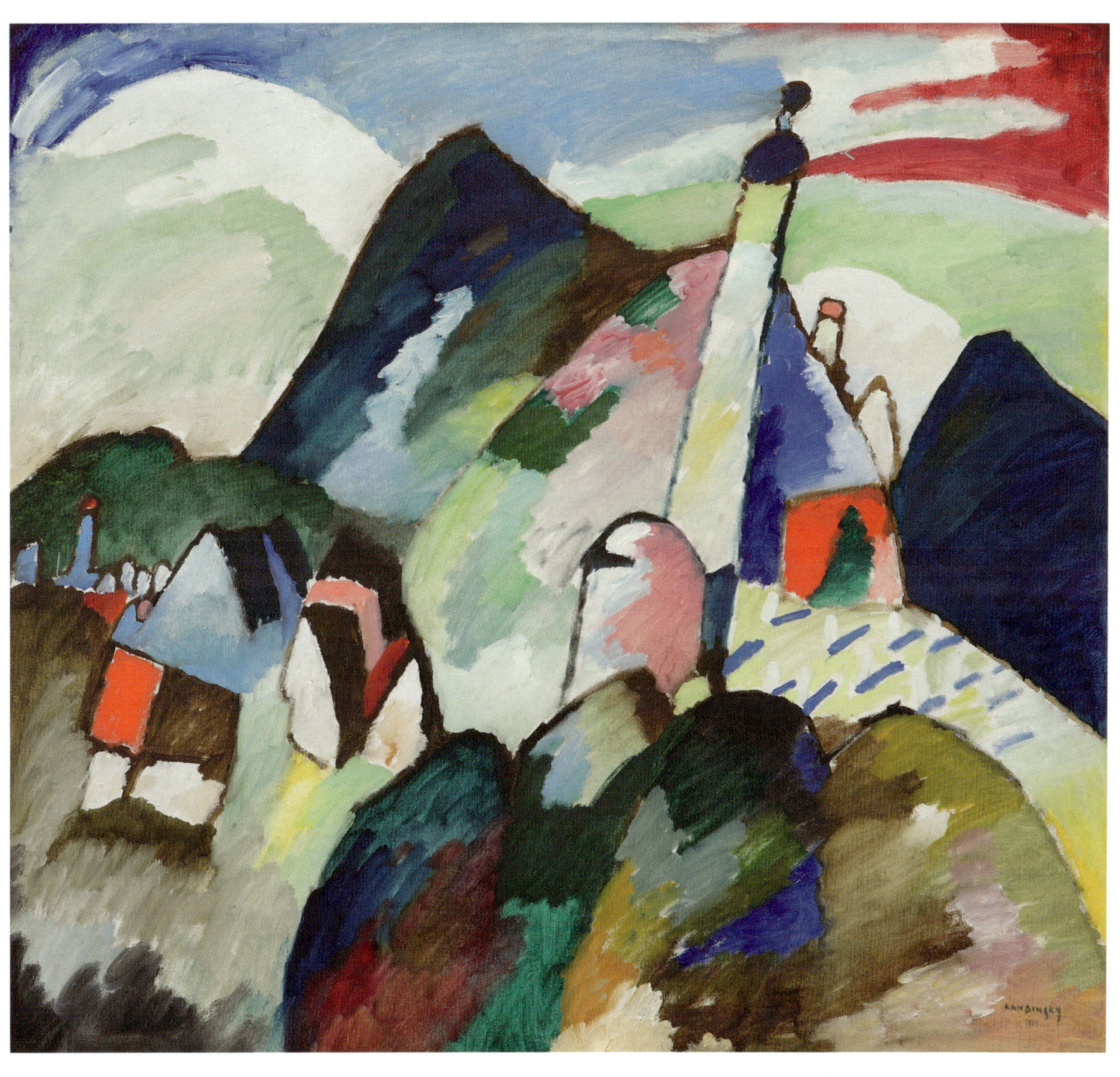

26 **Murnau with Church II**
1910
Oil on canvas 96.5 x 105.5
Collection Van Abbe Museum, Eindhoven

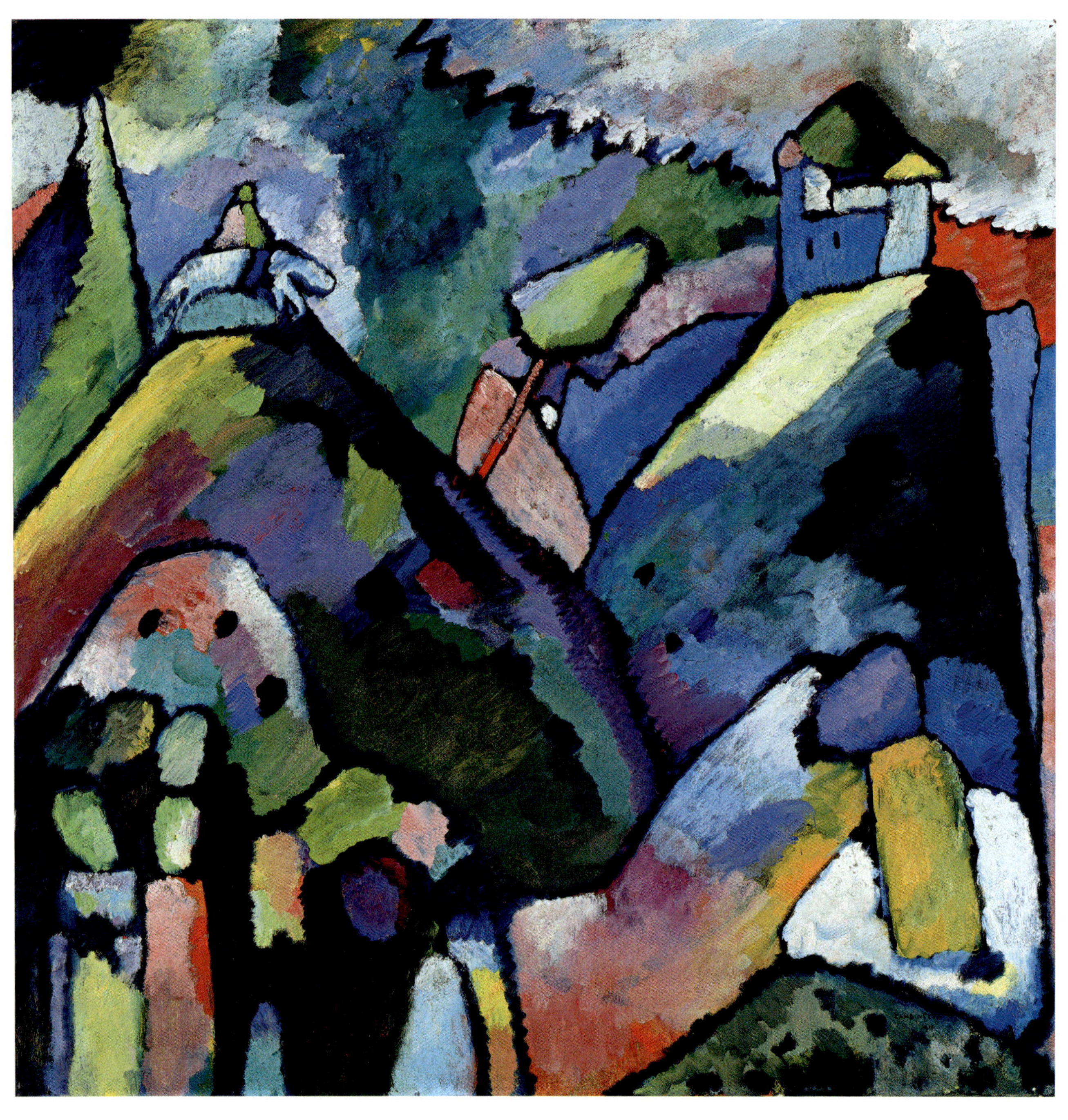

27 Improvisation 9
1910
Oil on canvas 110 x 110
Staatsgalerie Stuttgart

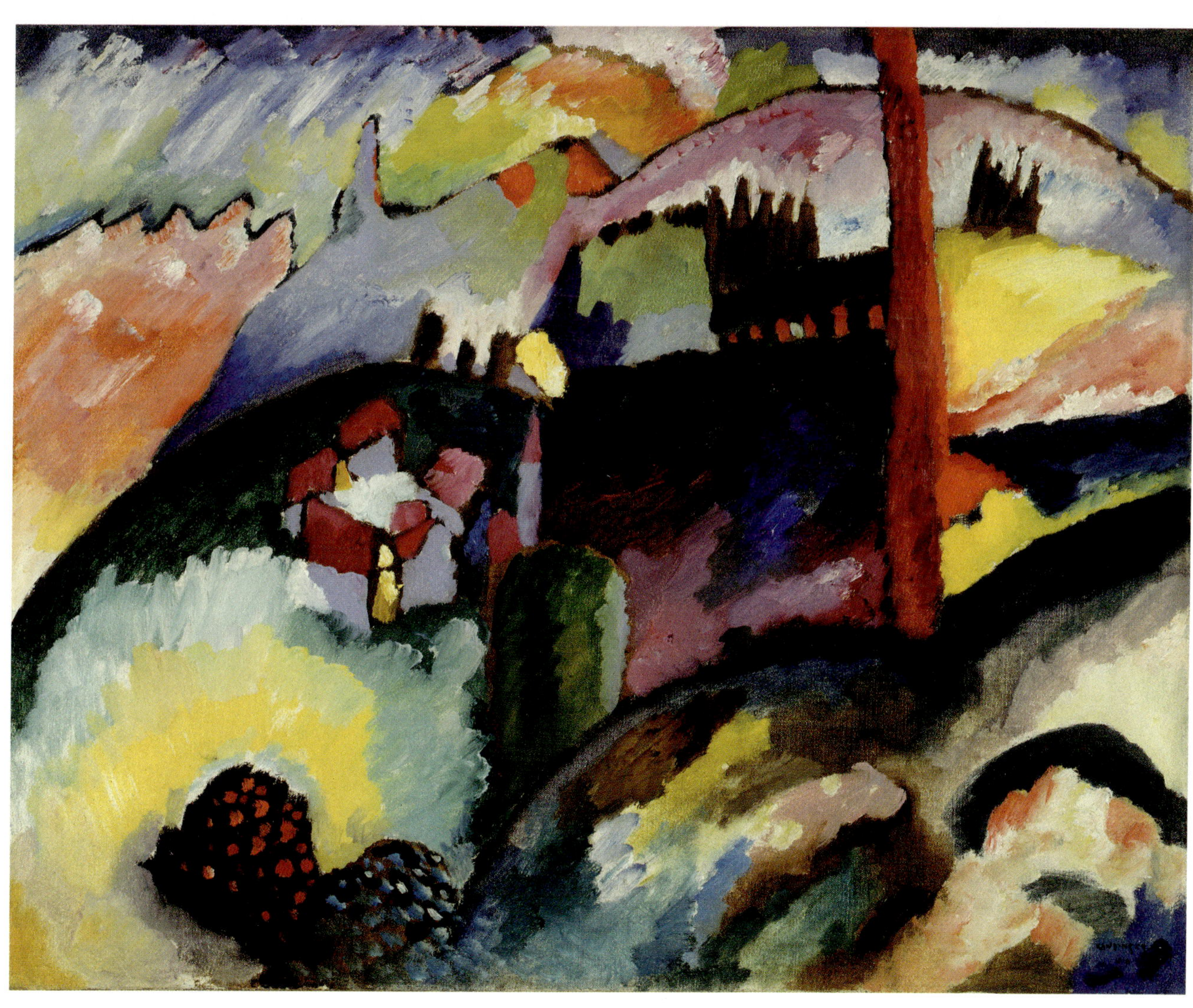

28 **Landscape with Factory Chimney**
1910
Oil on canvas 66.2 x 82
Solomon R. Guggenheim Museum, New York. Gift, Solomon R. Guggenheim, 1941

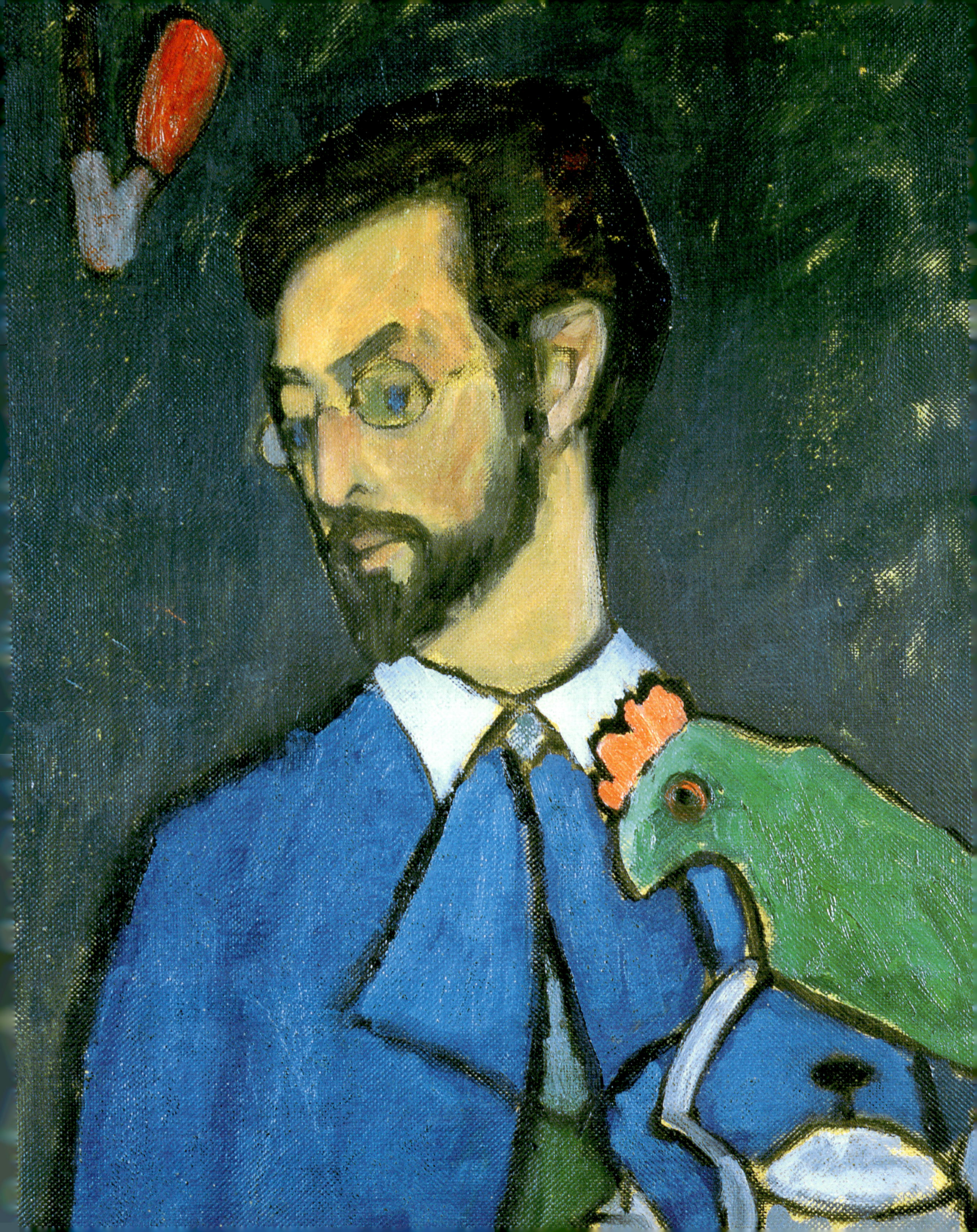

Kandinsky, Münter and Creative Partnership

SHULAMITH BEHR

'It is a pity that one cannot hang Kandinsky's large composition and some others beside the Mohammedan carpets in the Exhibition Park. A comparison would be inevitable and how instructive for us all! … The grand consequence of his colours holds the balance of his graphic freedom – is that not at the same time a definition of painting?'

Gabriele Münter
Kandinsky at the Tea-table
1910
(FIG. 15, DETAIL)

'I am totally in love with Moscow … and it is beautiful, Ellchen, indescribable … Much, much love, my old Paint-Ellchen'[1]

In his correspondence with Gabriele Münter in October 1910, Kandinsky conveyed his intense excitement while on a brief return to the Russian capital after a gap of several years. Following severe critical and public reception of the second exhibition of the Munich New Artists' Association (Neue Künstlervereinigung München, NKVM), Moscow was for him both a 'whiplash' and a 'balm'; indeed he was 'practically delirious' in renewing contact with local avant-garde artists, composers and actors.[2] Typically of émigré experience on returning to their roots,[3] Kandinsky felt 'Russian and yet also un-Russian', hoping he would find the core that he was in search of. Indeed he wondered how the old religious art would affect him. The two poles of his inspiration emerge forcefully in these letters: Moscow '[which] has always been the cornerstone, the leitmotiv, of my art'[4] and his German 'Ellchen' – the diminutive of 'Ella', a pet name for 'Gabriele'.

Eleven years his younger, Gabriele Münter first met Kandinsky in 1902 in the Phalanx school in Munich, where he tutored her in life-classes and *plein-air* landscape painting. However, her initial role as student was succeeded by a torrid love affair which was complicated by Kandinsky's married status. This factor, in addition to the social and religious mores of the time, meant that his extramarital affair was reserved for periods when the lovers travelled. Leading a peripatetic lifestyle from 1904 until 1908, their compatibility was severely tested, no more so than during their sojourn in Sèvres, where they separated briefly while Münter engaged in the Parisian art world. However, their return to Munich signalled the maturing of their partnership; Kandinsky gained public recognition, given his central role in the formation of the avant-garde exhibiting groups the NKVM and Der Blaue Reiter. Münter, for her part, revelled in their collaboration with the Russians Alexei Jawlensky and Marianne Werefkin, particularly in their painting excursions to the Bavarian town of Murnau where Münter eventually purchased a house in 1909.

As can be gauged from their correspondence, the theme of painting as an expression of love and desire is consistent and, characteristic of intimate creative partnerships of the time, Münter's persona was invested with muse-like associations.[5] Yet when compared to Lovis Corinth's eroticised and naturalistic depictions of his former student and wife Charlotte Berend-Corinth, Kandinsky's austere abstractions of Münter

FIG 13
Lady (Gabriele Münter)
1910
Oil on canvas 110 x 109
*Städtische Galerie im
Lenbachhaus, Munich*

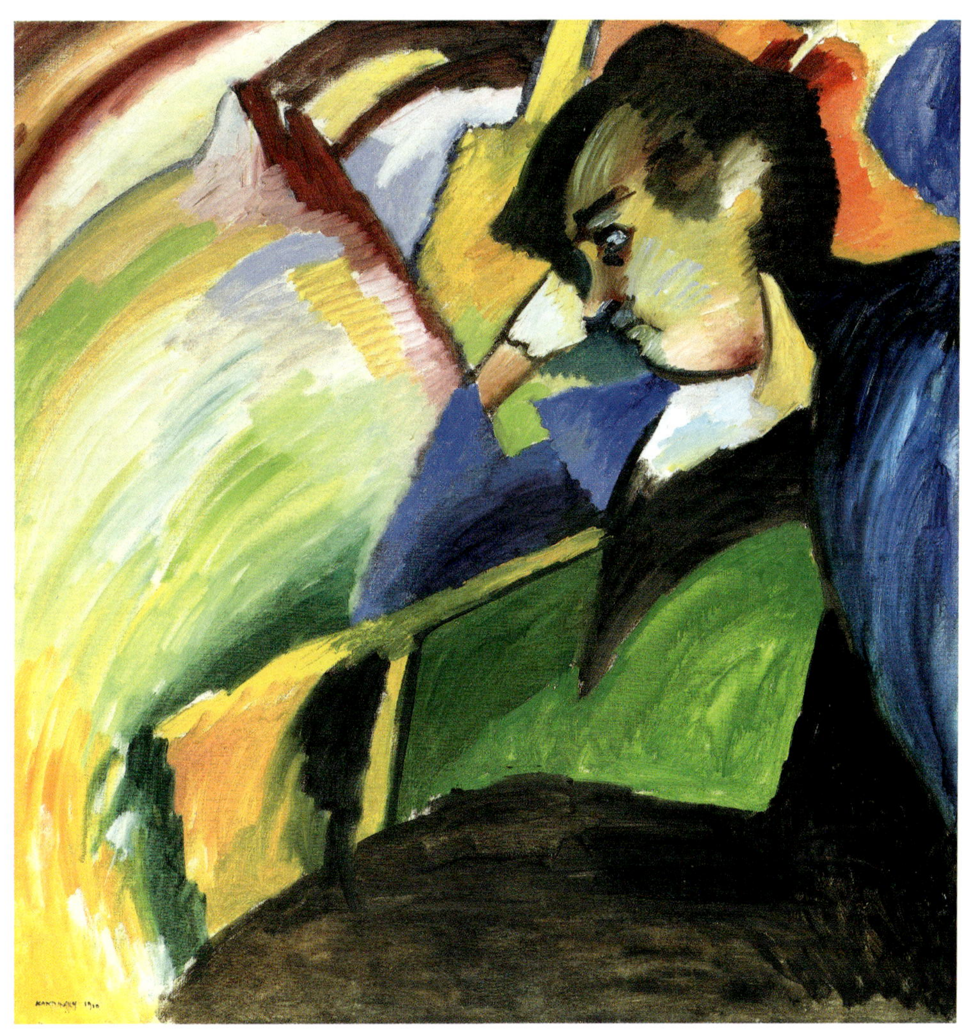

are mystifying and lead us to interrogate the paintings more closely.
In 1910, and before his departure for Russia, Kandinsky painted the
portrait *Lady (Gabriele Münter)* (fig.13), which was an unusual departure
from his more conceptual works of the time – the Impressions,
Improvisations and Compositions – but no less complex. As both
object and subject, the figure echoes his musings on woman and art.
Münter's demeanour is pensive, the head lowered and resting on the
hand reminiscent of the dejected personification of Melancholy as
portrayed in Dürer's *Melencolia I* 1514 (fig.14).[6] In the Renaissance,
as the temperament of genius, Melancholy was said to be possessed
by artists in whom 'Imagination' predominates. Thereby, Dürer's
engraving is often interpreted as an 'oblique', spiritual self-portrait
of the creative genius.[7] Turning our attention to Kandinsky's painting,
can we assume likewise?

FIG 14
Albrecht Dürer
Melencolia I
1514
Engraving 24.1 x 19.2
British Museum, London

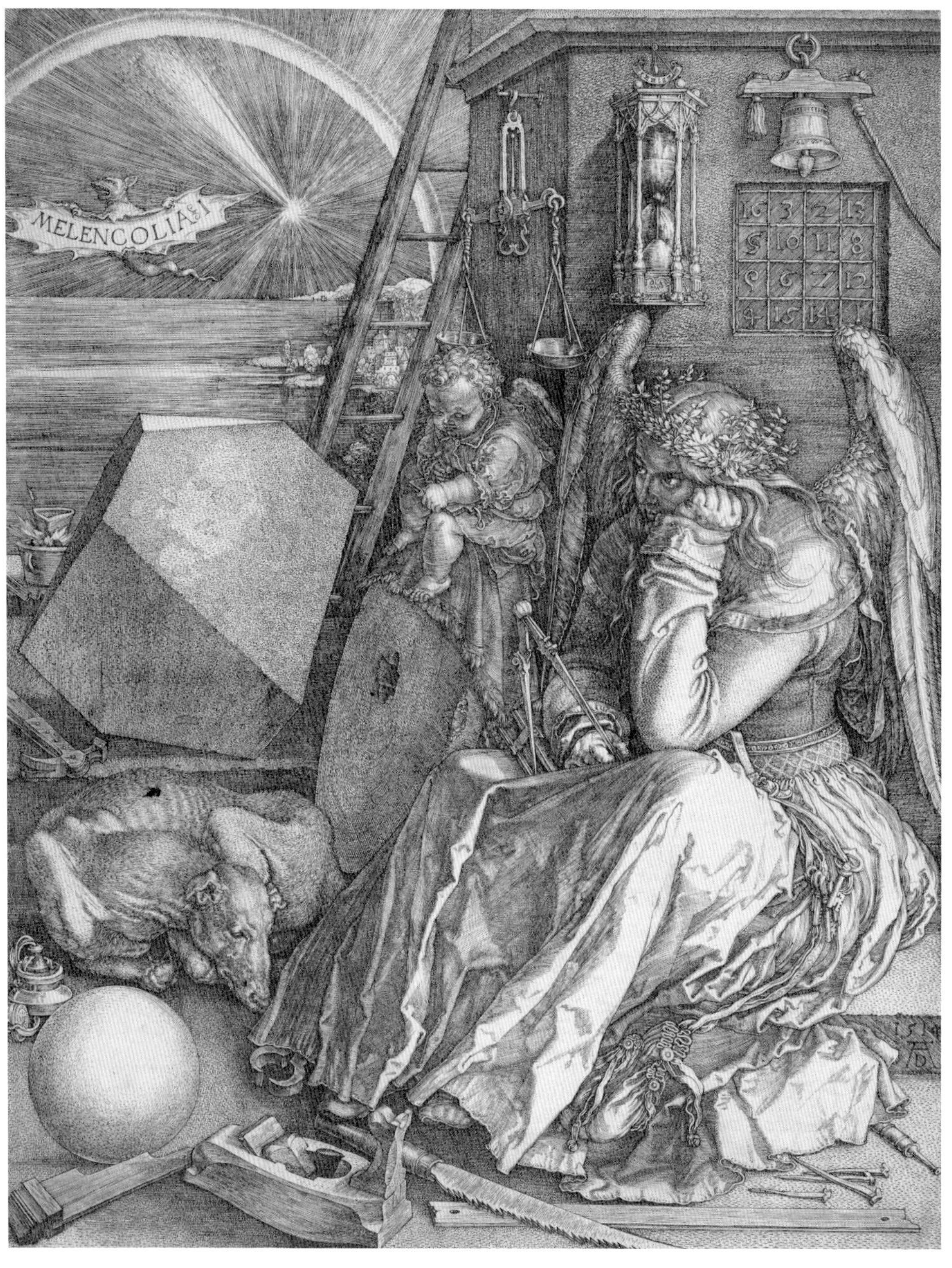

We notice that there is a similar compositional arrangement opening up the domestic *mise-en-scène* to the sublime landscape with comet and rainbow. However, here we find not the symbols of geometry (considered one of the seven liberal arts underlying artistic creation) but quasi-geometric motifs of the Bavarian alpine setting of Murnau as an equivalent. Interestingly, as in the case of *Melencolia*, Münter's open-eye gaze is directed away from the natural world. Critical to the couple's theoretical programme in 1910, nature was considered subservient to the inner and expressive vision of the creative artist. As with many modernists, it was through the impulse of landscape painting that Kandinsky's Murnau works gave way to greater abstraction in order to achieve this inner vision. Hence the portrait, though bearing resemblance to Münter, is also self-referential in advancing Kandinsky's ideas regarding the spiritual in art. Just as in the case of Dürer, who had access to occultist sources,[8] so the artist couple were greatly taken with contemporary esoteric beliefs like Theosophy.[9] Instructively, the manuscript of Kandinsky's major treatise of the pre-war years – *Über das Geistige in der Kunst* (*Concerning the Spiritual in Art*, 1912) – in which he highlighted Theosophy 'as the new torch-bearer of the truth' was lodged with a publisher for consideration.[10]

Yet Münter was more than handmaiden to Kandinsky's febrile imagination and, in the quotation above, we detect how he conjoined 'Mal' – 'mark' or 'sign' – with 'Ellchen', thus associating her name with the act of painting. Concurrent with the above-mentioned portrait, Kandinsky produced a work, *Gabriele Münter Painting Outdoors in Front of an Easel*, which is similarly abstracted.[11] Echoing the painterly handling of the surrounding landscape, her figure is shown leaning forward and absorbed in applying colour while balancing the palette in the crook of her elbow. In addition to investing her with the attributes of the muse Pittura (Painting), Münter's femininity is integrated with 'masculine' agency.[12] Although the mere existence of innumerable sketchbooks from all periods attests to her systematic reliance on preliminary studies for her final paintings, it is evident that Münter painted very quickly, often completing one or more large-format pictures in a single afternoon.[13] The apparent effortlessness with which she achieved her stark compositional arrangements and bold coloration was a source of high regard for Kandinsky and became the departure for his writing on the subject. Ironically, since there are few portraits or photographs of Kandinsky that portray him in the act of painting, it is to the representations of his muse that we turn for elucidation of this process.[14]

Hence the biographical drama of Kandinsky's and Münter's fourteen-year relationship belies a close and 'critical' friendship, a partnership that questions the enshrined separateness of the creative act and focuses on issues of collaboration around gendered relationships and difference.[15] Concentrating on Kandinsky's works, this essay initially considers whether such interchanges can escape the limitations imposed by social and psychological constructions of gender that identify separateness with masculinity, connectedness and domesticity with femininity.[16] Understandably, the value of artistic partnership is not always mutual from the perspective of the woman practitioner. Since Münter was first his student, most commentators dwell on this given relationship and the homogeneity of the time-span rather than on exploring nuances and the explanatory potential of other forms of evidence. While declaring that 'she was hopeless as a pupil' – since her talent was 'instinctive' – Kandinky's didactic methods were spurred by their contact and Münter's precociousness.[17] Moreover, Annegret Hoberg, editor of Kandinsky's and Münter's published correspondence, goes so far as to say that the desire for an artistic partnership and the stimulus it provided was one of the main reasons that Kandinsky left his wife Anya Shemyakina (a cousin and the companion of his university days) for Münter.[18] From the outset, their mutual interest in the reforming principles of Jugendstil, as the Arts and Crafts movement was articulated in Germany, prepared them for their fruitful experimentation in various media and fascination for Russian and Bavarian folk art.

However, from 1911 onwards, the dynamics of their collaboration was altered by the linkage of Kandinsky's name with that of Franz Marc, co-editor of the almanac *Der Blaue Reiter*. Within a short period Kandinsky's correspondence with Marc reached an intensity that was comparable to the exchange of letters with Münter.[19] Though much of this was dedicated to the planning of the almanac and exhibitions, there was meaningful communication regarding their current artistic theory and practice. As in the case of the pre-war relationship between Picasso and Braque, though maintaining the integrity of their distinctive statements, Marc and Kandinsky forged a path based on mutual recognition of each other's talent. Whether Münter shared in this 'doubling of masculine creativity'[20] is open to question and forms part of the consideration of this essay. Notwithstanding constant insecurity owing to the absence of marital commitment following Kandinsky's divorce from Anya Shemyakina in 1911, Münter continued to chronicle his oeuvre. Moreover, there has been little acknowledgement of her photography in constructing Kandinsky's artistic and public persona, studio practice and engagement in the Munich avant-garde milieu. Whereas their relationship formally ended in Stockholm in 1916, their names were bound together for posterity. Before illuminating the consequences of Marc's entry into their circle, the following section explores those moments where Kandinsky's and Münter's interests converged and one can talk of a collaborative and creative partnership as well as revealing differences in their artistic direction.

Murnau, convergence and divergence

Resettling in Munich in June 1908, Münter and Kandinsky made excursions to the Staffelsee, a lake near the town of Murnau. They recommended the area to their friends and fellow artist couple Marianne Werefkin and Alexei Jawlensky who, after following their advice, invited Kandinsky and Münter to join them in mid-August at the guesthouse Griesbräu. This initiated a period of interaction that involved their testing of the limits of painting within the landscape genre, while intensifying an engagement with notions of primitivism through their encounter with folk art of the region.

Located in the south Bavarian Alps, Murnau was a market town with a predominantly agrarian and Catholic population. Being close to Oberammergau, celebrated for its Passion plays, Murnau was easily reached by train from Munich and attracted many visitors over the summer months, particularly in that it had a developed infrastructure of guesthouses with large hotels located near the Staffelsee. Hence city and country debates informed the Bavarian interludes of this community of artists, Kandinsky seizing the opportunity to don lederhosen and leather sandals when going 'native'. However, their allegiance to notions of 'rural authenticity' belied the modernisation of the town, a programme that was overseen by the well-known Munich architect Emanuel von Seidl. This entailed the restoration of vernacular architecture and a regeneration of local craft traditions as part and parcel of its contrived reinvention.[21]

Of the group of artists, Werefkin was the most concerned with themes exploring the impact of modernity on the changing economy of the region. Her focus on the social topic of labour initially arose from her Russian background; she trained privately with the realist

Ilya Repin before attending the Moscow Academy between 1883 and 1886. In 1896 she followed Jawlensky to Munich, where she refrained from painting in order to devote her time to promoting his career. Acting as muse and supporter of her errant and more intuitive partner, Werefkin nonetheless recorded her theoretical concerns in an extensive journal *Lettres á un inconnu* (*Letters to an Unknown*, 1901–5) before resuming painting in 1906.[22] Her Murnau landscapes, informed by the school of Pont Aven, consisted of the silhouettes of darkly clad peasant women, burdened by washing, in the alpine setting.[23] The severity of her style, steep perspectives and elongated figures also evoke Munch's works, which were frequently exhibited in Munich in the early twentieth century.[24]

The foursome otherwise explored similar motifs, views from the guesthouse windows and, from 1909 onwards, the outlook over the town from Münter's so-called 'Russian House'. Beyond the cultivated lowlands, the environs offered the expanse of the Murnau moors, the largest living moorland in southern Germany. Bordered by woodlands and the range of Bavarian Alps, the vivid panorama was compelling – as was the quality of light peculiar to the region in exposing the planar divisions between these different components. As the most conversant with the French avant-garde, Jawlensky adopted the term 'synthesis' from Synthesist and Symbolist aesthetic theory to apply to a radical simplification of form and colour, bound by line, so as to avoid anecdotal content and strengthen the autonomous qualities of the work of art.[25] This led him to use the dark contours of *cloisonnisme* to signal the horizontal planes of the moors, mountains and sky as well as the boundaries of differently coloured areas.[26]

Certainly in their landscapes between 1908 and 1910, Kandinsky's and Münter's paintings developed in tandem. Since their painting excursions to Kochel in 1902, Kandinsky had encouraged Münter to make extensive use of the palette knife, commenting in a letter: 'It is a source of the greatest delight to me that you have had so much success and enjoyment with the spatula.'[27] However, in Murnau, encouraged by Jawlensky's example, they gave up the use of the palette knife in favour of broad short-haired brushes and unprimed canvas boards so as to retain the freshness and spontaneity of direct colour application. Employing an unusual palette, they also bound the diverse surfaces and facture of their vistas with strong contour. An essential change in Kandinsky's style of painting was the preference for unvarnished surfaces, a characteristic that renders the colour effects of these paintings,

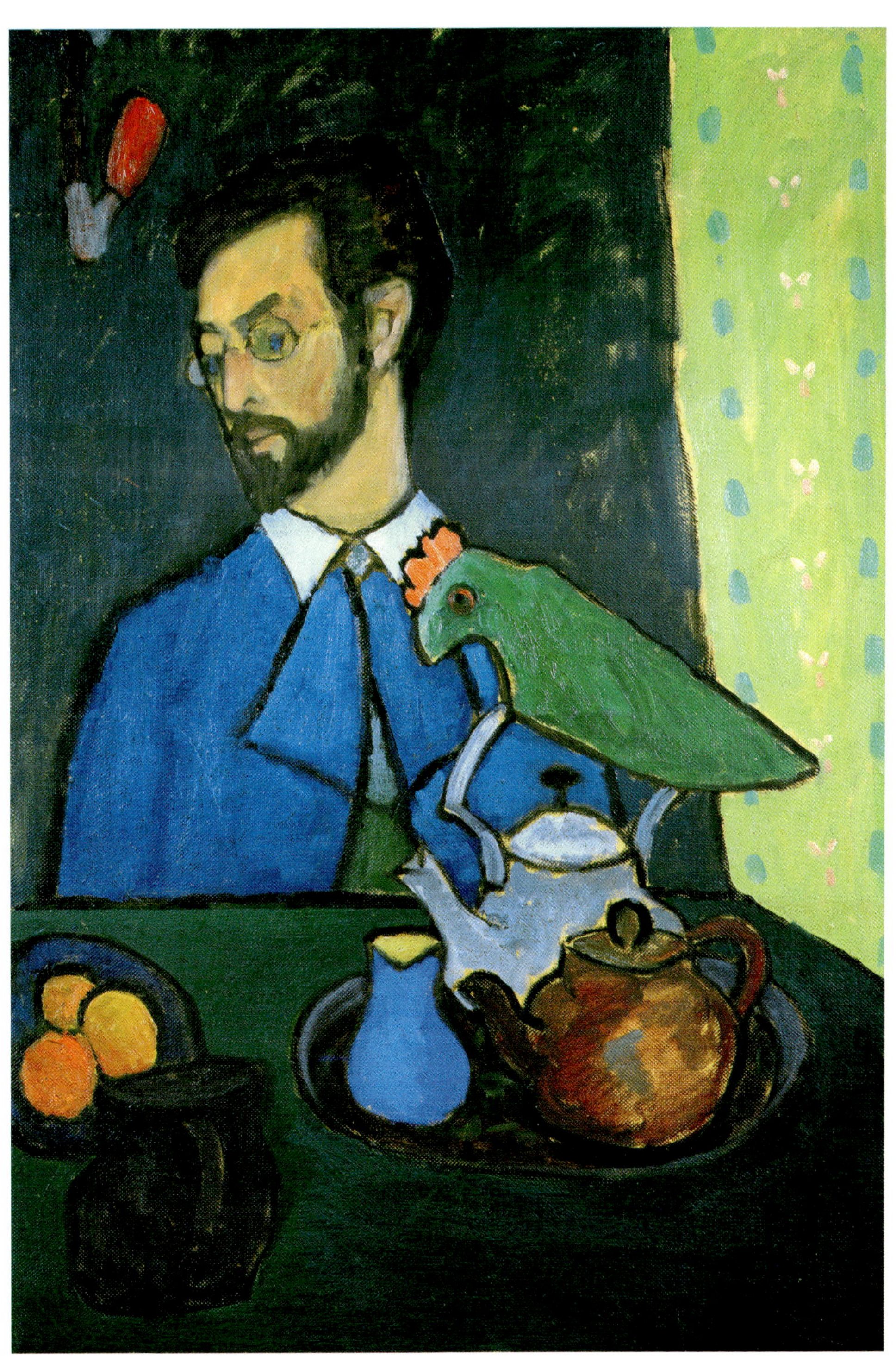

FIG 15
Gabriele Münter
Kandinsky at the Tea-table
1910
Oil on canvas 98 x 103
The Israel Museum, Jerusalem. Gift of Billy Wilder, Los
Angeles, to American Friends of the Israel Museum Collection

even nowadays, 'completely fresh'.[28] These small-scale oils on board, measuring roughly 33 x 44 cm, served as an increasing stimulus for technical radicalism as the artists sought to negotiate a path between Jawlensky's Matisse-linked modernism and the inspiration of folk art.

On occasion, while pursuing similar themes, Kandinsky's and Münter's paintings diverged. In 1910 both submitted works entitled *Boat Trip* to the second exhibition of the NKVM.[29] The scale of Kandinsky's work (no.24) as well as the iconicity of the motifs suggest that he had come to regard the landscape genre as worthy of a fully worked-up 'painting', rather than a mere 'sketch' or 'study'. He deals expansively with the landscape, stressing the Romantic elements, the distant mountains commingling with the hovering red sun, surmounted by blue and lemon yellow striations. The progress of the small regatta-like boats, set at steep angles to the lake, appears arduous given the primal and overpowering forces of nature. In contrast, Münter's painting, one of three in the series, portrayed a leisure outing on the Staffelsee, the company – attired in urban and fashionable clothing – including Andreas (the son of Jawlensky) and Marianne Werefkin.[30] They are depicted frontally, seated between a rear-view self-portrait of Münter, who is shown rowing the boat, and the standing figure of Kandinsky at the stern. Here Münter has modified the boating theme, so favoured among the Impressionists for its suggestion of informal enjoyment, into a group portrait set against an emblematic landscape.

In general, therefore, Münter's oeuvre does not conform easily to modernist paradigms of autonomy and painterly abstraction.[31] Her depiction of the portraits of the community of artists of the NKVM and Blauer Reiter groups, juxtaposed with images of folk art in rural interiors, may suggest the domestic, a 'connectedness' as distinct from the separate masculine practice of high art. However, as has been observed, it is precisely in such spheres of femininity that women artists' articulation of space is central to the iconography of modernity.[32] In the portrayal of *Kandinsky at the Tea-table* 1910 (fig.15), Münter's orientation of all the elements of the composition to the vertical format and the compression of space add to the paradoxes of the painting. The depiction of the still-life objects is freer and more animated – as in the amusing parrot-handle of the teapot – when compared to Kandinsky's stiff pose, his awkwardly 'trapped' countenance questioning an assumption of masculine control of domestic and private spaces.

Intriguingly, such works and the communal atmosphere in the

FIG 16
Interior (with Two Ladies)
1910
Oil on cardboard   50.5 x 65
Museum of Fine Art, Bern.
Livia Klee Donation

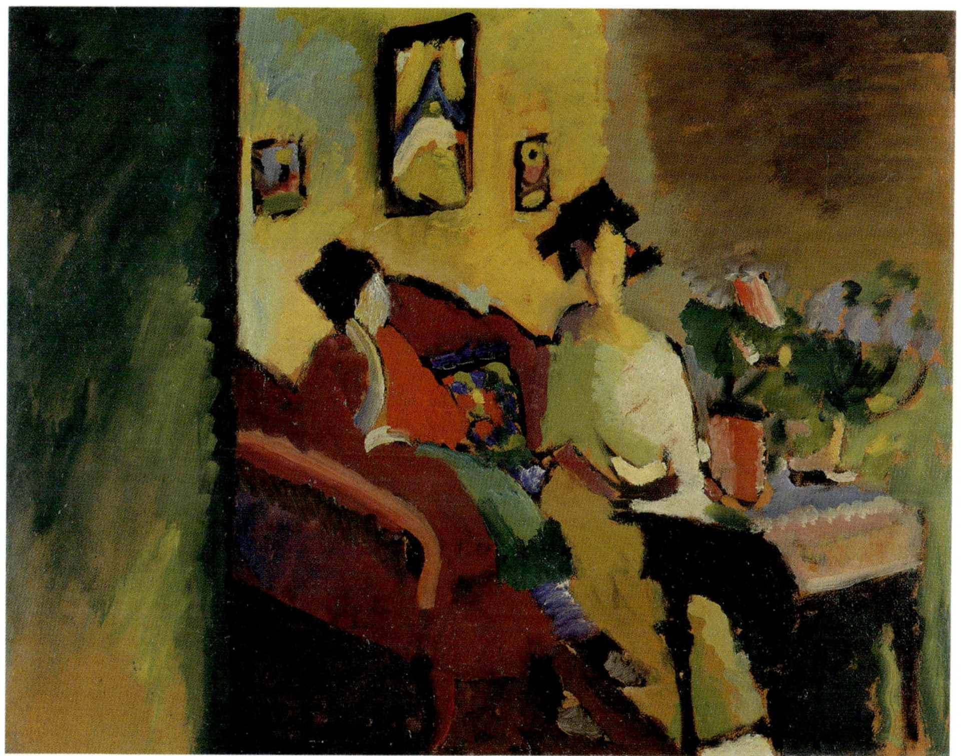

Murnau house may have spurred Kandinsky to broach the interior genre, as in his *Interior (with Two Ladies)* 1910 (fig.16), portraying Münter and Werefkin in conversation and seated on a sofa in the parlour. The spatial arrangement is more inviting, the diagonal from left to right leading the eye to the two protagonists. Notwithstanding their faceless appearance, we are able to detect the psychological coordinates from their demeanour, the languor of Münter's pose contrasting with Werefkin's tautness. The furniture and floral display are subordinate to the scale of the figures, and the saturated use of colour – as in the splash of red over Münter's left shoulder – is contained by the overall yellow glow. Here one can usefully refer to Kandinsky's theories of colour in *Concerning the Spiritual in Art*, where he maintains that 'a picture painted in yellow gives out a spiritual warmth'.[33] As conveyed in Münter's concurrent photograph of the setting (fig.17), Kandinsky also deployed their collection of original artefacts to crown the composition, the *Hinterglasmalerei* (painting behind glass) contributing to the ethos of the rustic interior.

Apparently, it was Jawlensky who first drew their attention to Bavarian and Bohemian glass painting – a substantial collection was owned by a local brewer in Murnau, Johann Krötz – and Münter

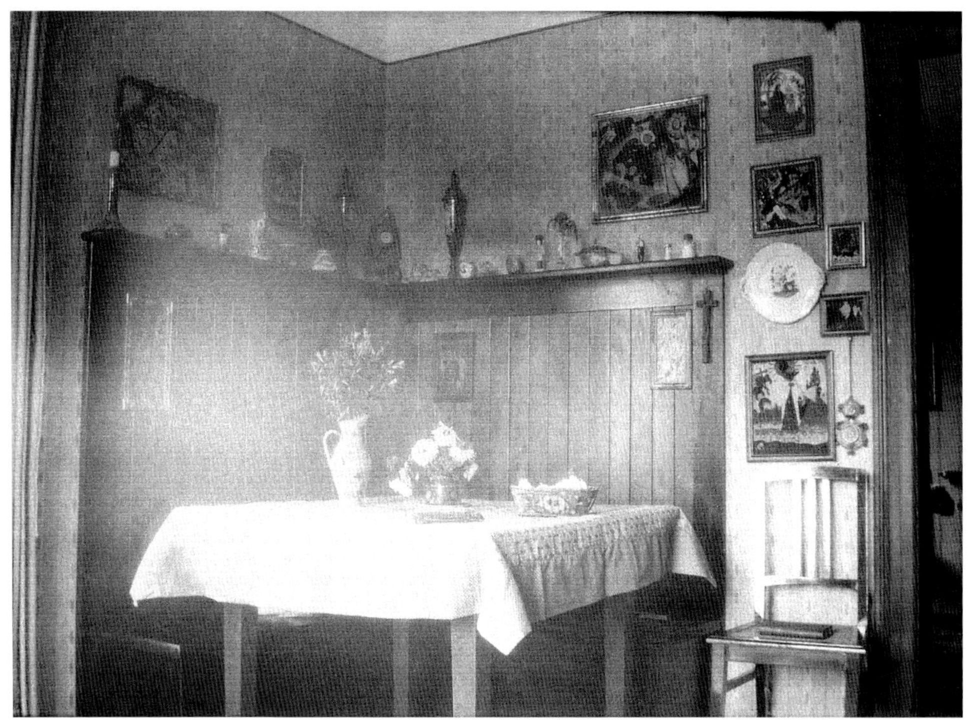

learnt the technique from a glass painter, Heinrich Rambold, who was still active at the time.[34] Kandinsky also immersed himself in the technique, which involved much ingenuity and skill in superimposing patches of brilliant and unmixed colour on the reverse of the glass without having recourse to the form-defining contours beneath. Beyond this, he was attracted to the purported 'naïve' directness of the religious iconography – patron saints, images of the Madonna, the life of Christ. More so than Münter's works in this vein,[35] Kandinsky's painting *Interior (with Two Ladies)* conveys the intimacy of a conversational piece, the traditional *Hinterglasbild* of a *Pietà* enhancing the Marian overtones of ideal womanhood to which mortals could aspire. Unexpectedly, it is Kandinsky's interpretation of this genre that reinforces a 'connectedness' in the domestic sphere, the homely atmosphere belying spiritual associations immanent in the motifs and formal elements.

Münter's ironic and, at times, subversive depictions of this genre, while divergent from Kandinsky's, were no less admired for their difference. In an introduction to the catalogue of her retrospective exhibition, which was held in the Kunstsalon Dietzel in Munich in 1913, Kandinsky praised her 'original' and 'truly female' talent, maintaining that her colours resembled that of medieval stained-glass windows, her drawing was close to the old, 'primitive' German masters and her sensitivity similar to that still alive in German popular music and poetry.[36] But, for Kandinsky, who had specialist training in Russian peasant law and ethnography,[37] the local folk art and its environs in Murnau held further national resonances. That the Bavarian experience rekindled memories of Russia can be ascertained in his autobiographical essay 'Rückblicke' or 'Reminiscences' (1913). Here he deliberately negated chronological time by interspersing the narrative of his recent training in Munich, as well as the future prospects of his oeuvre, with memories of his childhood artistic experiences and student ethnographic expedition (undertaken in 1889) to the remote province of Vologda in Russia. Writing of this *in situ* encounter with Russian folk art, Kandinsky seized on the impact of the living room of the great wooden houses (*Wunderhäuser*): every object was covered with 'brightly coloured, elaborate ornaments' that were 'so strongly painted that the object within them became dissolved'.[38] His receptiveness to intense colour relationships and the concordant dissolution of form was strengthened by such examples that evoked the 'spiritual' values of pre-industrial communities. Indeed, he concluded this section with a comparison of the interiors of Russian churches and Bavarian chapels.

When I next visited these churches [in Moscow] after my journey, the same feeling sprang to life inside me with total clarity. Later, I often had the same experience in Bavarian and Tyrolean Chapels. Of course, on each occasion the impression was differently coloured, being formed by quite different constituents. Church! Russian Church! Chapel! Catholic Chapel![39]

Kandinsky's literary mechanisms as outlined above allow insight into the complex processes of recollection and reinvention in émigré artistic identity. In this process, memory is constitutive of the present as well as the past and serves as the tool for purposes in the present and future.[40] Such strategies of temporality were similarly at work in his concurrent paintings, where his aesthetic response to domestic and religious interiors seemingly infiltrated his handling of the contemporary Bavarian landscape that included themes of Old Russia.

By 1910 Kandinsky was working in three parallel modes, which he called Impressions, Improvisations and Compositions, dependent on the degree of reference to the outer world. Clearly, the Compositions were his most intensively researched works, comparable in musical terms to symphonic structure. Although *Composition II* is known only from a black and white photograph (it was destroyed in Allied bombing during the Second World War),[41] the fully worked-up oil sketch in the Guggenheim Museum collection (no.21) allows for consideration of its major components. The Murnau environs serve as the locus for a bewildering narrative in which faceless and unidentifiable figures occupy indeterminate zones, given the intensity of the figure–ground relationships and inconsistent horizon line. A Russian hill-top city with toppling towers, rocky outcrops as well as the dramatic features of the composition – riders leaping in opposite directions and tempest blotting out the light in the upper left – further add to a non-perspectival reading of space. As for the iconography, do the groups of figures – some reclining and straining their necks, several pointing upwards – represent the theophany of the Revelation of St John and the riders the breaking of the Seven Seals?[42] Washton Long suggests that the composition incorporates dual notions of apocalypse and redemption in line with the theosophist Rudolf Steiner's interpretation of the Book of Revelation.[43] Or are these figures, as Peg Weiss claims, manifestations of the autochthonous beliefs of the Zyrian tribe whom Kandinsky studied during his expedition to Vologda?[44]

Whatever our conclusion, the synthesis of Christological symbolism and pagan myth, what Weiss refers to as *dvoeverie* or 'double faith', characterised Kandinsky's endeavour to heal a tired civilisation through the teachings of the so-called 'primitives'. His primitivism, one which was to become a well-tried avant-garde strategy, involved the construction of a Utopian vision of a future made possible only by reference to a past; in Kandinsky's case mythical conceptions of natural, intuitive laws were textually mediated by eschatological writings. Interestingly, Münter's experimentation with abstraction arose within the genres of landscape and still life but it was in her interiors, particularly within the paintings *Nach dem Tee I* and *II* (*After Tea*, 1912) and the resultant *Abstraktion 25.4.1912*, that she harnessed the concepts of memory and experience to the creative process.[45] Although the departure for *Abstraktion 25.4.1912* was inspired by her recall of actual events – the visit of the art dealer Hans Goltz and his wife to Kandinsky's residence in Munich – the final composition excludes the protagonists, focusing instead on a linear, intersecting framework and planes of modulated colour. Unlike Kandinsky, who transformed a phenomenological reading of the landscape into one that is controlled by colour and cosmic/biblical connotations of light and dark, Münter retained the sensate experience of the interior space, differentiating her excursion into 'absolute painting' from his practice.

By this time, however, their immediate circle had dramatically expanded to include the young Munich artist Franz Marc and his future wife, the artist Maria Franck, as well as the Bonn-based couple August and Elisabeth Macke, among others. The public profile of the exhibiting group Der Blaue Reiter had also displaced that of the NKVM. What consequences these events in the art world bore for creative partnership is explored in the section below.

The Marc factor, Blauer Reiter and framing Kandinsky

It is a pity that one cannot hang Kandinsky's large composition and some others beside the Mohammedan carpets in the Exhibition Park. A comparison would be inevitable and how instructive for us all! … We have no decorative work in Germany, never mind a carpet, to which we may juxtapose it. If we try it with Kandinsky's compositions – they will stand this dangerous test, and not as carpets, but as *'pictures'* … The grand consequence of his colours holds the balance of his graphic freedom – is that not at the same time a definition of painting? [46]

How fascinating that, in defending the second exhibition of the NKVM from hostile, critical reception, Marc compared Kandinsky's painting *Composition II* with a 'Mohammedan carpet'. [47] Indeed in his 'Letters from Munich', destined for a Russian audience, Kandinsky reported enthusiastically on the exhibition *Meisterwerke muhammedanischer Kunst*, a spectacle that additionally held great significance for Henri Matisse. [48] However, Marc sought to retrieve Kandinsky's composition from accusations of the 'decorative' and the 'ornamental' by establishing a genealogy in the anti-materialist tradition of Paul Gauguin and the group of Pont Aven. Here Marc revealed his familiarity with Symbolist aesthetic theories, in particular with Maurice Denis' essay 'Définition du néo-traditionalisme' (1890) wherein it was famously stated, 'remember that a painting – before being a war horse or a nude woman or any kind of anecdote – is essentially a flat surface covered with colours assembled in a certain order'. [49] So as to distinguish Kandinsky's practice from 'lesser' feminine, craft-like associations, Marc instated the now familiar modernist paradigm of the *tableau objet*, ascribing a new 'definition of painting' to the formal components of Kandinsky's work.

Clearly, Kandinsky and Marc shared interests in the realm of ideas; rejecting principles of descriptive aesthetics, they turned to German Idealist notions in Arthur Schopenhauer's treatise *Die Welt als Wille und Vorstellung* (*The World as Will and Representation*, 1819). Here they found justification for responding to the emotional and driving forces of the 'Will', Marc in particular stressing his preference for the world of the irrational, unreasoning animal in contrast to the corrupt world of man.[50] Kandinsky was taken as well with the priority the philosopher gave to music's ability, above all the other arts, to transcend the world of 'Representation', Schopenhauer's *Über das Sehn und die Farben* (*On Vision and Colour*) of 1816 being one of the many sources to inform the artist's complex and synaesthetic theories of colour.[51] Interestingly, prior to meeting Kandinsky formally on New Year's Day 1911, Marc had independently arrived at a mystical, symbolic and gendered interpretation of the primary and complementary colours, expressing cynicism with the vagueness and impracticality of the musical analogy.[52] Just a few weeks later, having attended a Schoenberg concert with Kandinsky, Marc shifted his position, as conveyed in his correspondence with Macke:

Could he [Macke] think of any music in which tonality (and also the content of the key) is dismissed? I must think of Kandinsky's large Composition in which nothing remains of traditional tonality … and also of Kandinsky's 'springing spots' when I listen to this music, in which each tone is sounded, is allowed to speak for itself (a kind of *white canvas* between the colour spots).[53]

Hence, of all contemporary accounts, Marc's was the most empathetic in conveying an enthusiasm for Kandinsky's theories regarding the correspondences between colour and sound and the consequences that this bore for an abstract style.

Through 1911 their relationship gathered pace and, in the summer, Kandinsky invited him to collaborate on an almanac, which would possibly be entitled *Die Kette* (*The Chain*): 'There we will bring an Egyptian beside a small Zeh [drawings by the children of Munich architect August Zeh], a Chinese beside a Rousseau, a folk print beside a Picasso and such like, still even more!'[54] A few days after this invitation, on 24 June, Münter photographed *Kandinsky in his Home at Ainmillerstrasse 36, Munich* (fig.18). The nucleus of his programme in which the book would provide 'a connecting link to the past and a beam into the future' can be found therein. On the wall, displayed alongside his works from left to right are crucifixes, child art, Russian *lubki* and old German prints, a veritable showcase of artefacts selected from Europe and Russia's so-called 'primitives'. As we have seen, Kandinsky sought not only to break down the barriers between different visual cultures but also to synthesise the arts – poetry, music, painting and theatre. Instructively, while a Bavarian votive figurine is positioned level with Kandinsky's eyes, he is shown examining a proof of one of his woodcuts that was destined for publication in a book of his poetry and graphics. [55] Kandinsky evocatively entitled this collection *Klänge* (*Sounds*), experimenting with words and syntax in just as audacious a manner as his abstracting of form and colour in the prints. The

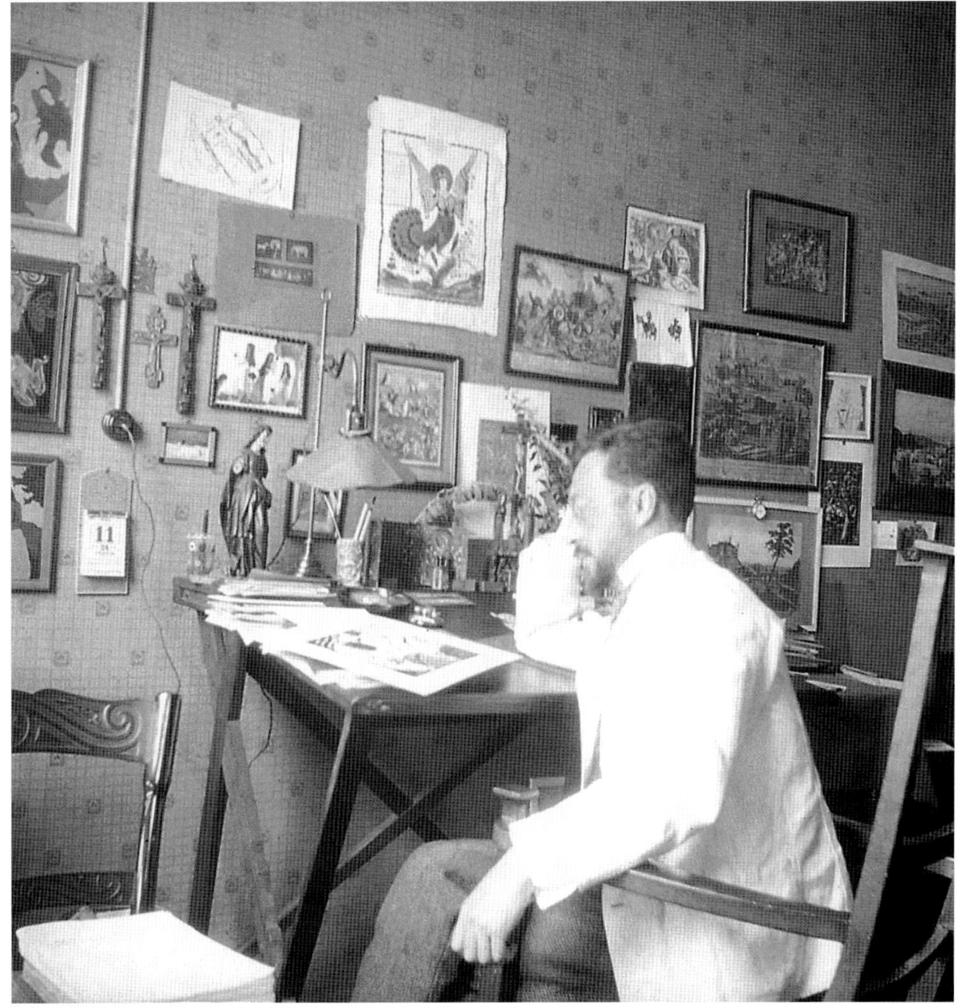

FIG 18
Gabriele Münter
Kandinsky in his Home at Ainmillerstrasse 36, Munich
24 June 1911
Gabriele Münter-and Johannes Eichner-Foundation, Munich

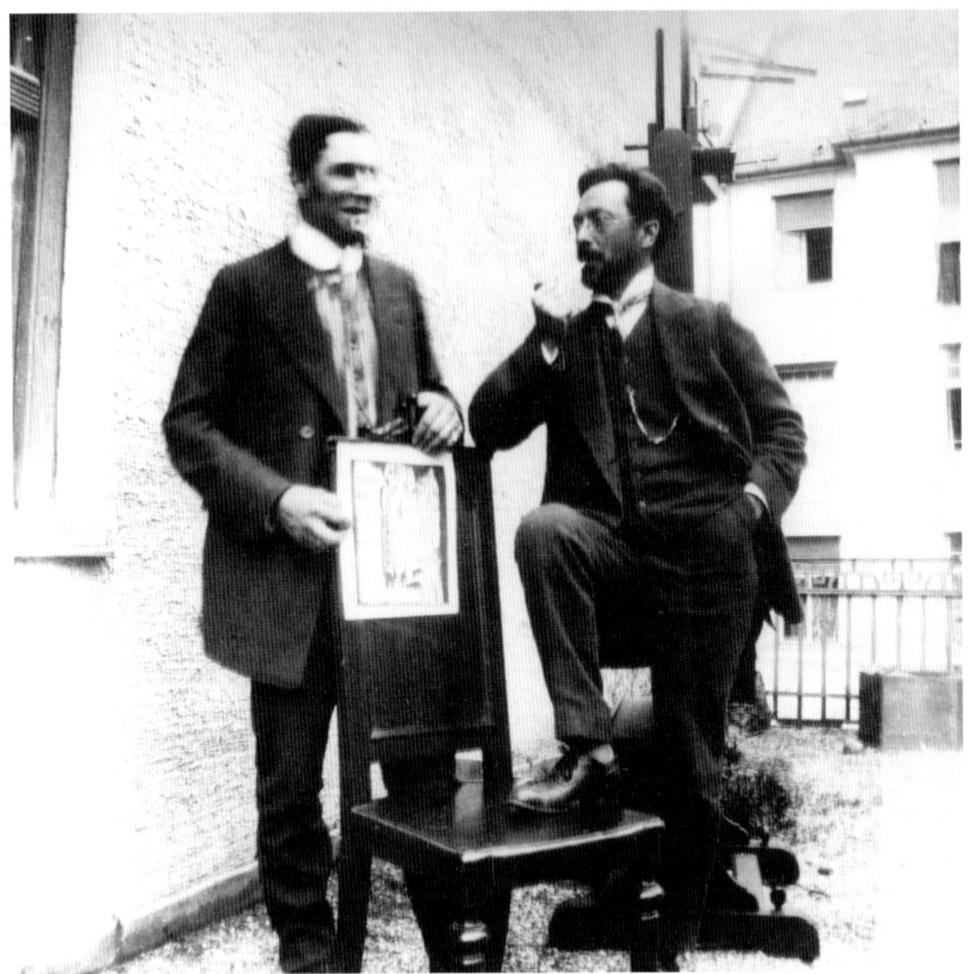

FIG 19
Photographer unknown
Kandinsky and Marc standing on either side of a woodcut for the cover of the almanac *Der Blaue Reiter*
1911–12
Gabriele Münter-and Johannes Eichner-Foundation, Munich

photograph discloses the manifold range of his activities as painter, graphic artist and poet, the phenomenon of the *Doppelbegabung* (double talent) in the early twentieth century by no means being restricted to Kandinsky.[56]

While collating and editing material for the almanac – a sequence of essays on art, music and theatre interspersed with illustrations of child and folk art, tribal masks, medieval sculpture, old German graphics and contemporary art – the title altered to *Der Blaue Reiter*. How this came about is somewhat ambiguous. In later years, Kandinsky gave a rather anecdotal account of its origins as arising from a coffee-table discussion with Marc and his wife Maria: 'We both liked blue: Marc – horses, I – riders.'[57] However, the colour blue, invested with spiritual associations by both artists, and the rider motif were richly evocative symbols. They signified a range of meanings, from the masculine virtues of charging medieval knights and Christian warrior saints, to the generative libido of the male artist. [58] Eventually published in May 1912, the almanac's cover featured Kandinsky's woodcut image of St George, patron saint of Murnau and Russia, as emblematic of the artists' spiritual mission. The posed photograph (fig.19), where the editors are shown standing on either side of the proposed woodcut cover of the almanac, bears testimony to their personal investment in and the significance of the rider motif.

Although women artists were welcome in the two exhibitions of the 'Editors of the Blaue Reiter', their role was peripheral to the centrality of Kandinsky's and Marc's collaborative enterprise, notwithstanding the fact that the possibility of a 'Reiterin' (woman rider) was entertained in correspondence between the poet and writer Else Lasker-Schüler and Marianne Werefkin. [59] If Münter was merely spectator to a new and evolving male artistic partnership, then this could partially explain her slackened production from 1912 onwards. Her personal and artistic crisis is also attributable to a worsening relationship with Kandinsky, in which mutual tensions and disappointments arose over his lack of commitment to marriage. [60] Yet it didn't deter her from cultivating Kandinsky's oeuvre and persona in other ways, Münter continuing to make maximum use of her Kodak Eastman Camera (No.2) which she acquired as a birthday gift while visiting cousins in the United States at the turn of the century. For the travelling photographer or amateur, this model was recommended over all other since it was based around Eastman's invention of paper-roll film. Indeed, in their earlier careers, Münter and Kandinsky at times drew on photographs interchangeably with *in situ* sketches as part of the creative process. [61]

Interestingly, if not for Münter's photographic interventions, we would have no visual documentation of the installation of the landmark exhibition of the Blaue Reiter. On the jury's rejection of Kandinsky's *Composition V* 1911 (fig.12, p.41) for inclusion in the third exhibition of the NKVM, Kandinsky, Münter, Marc and Alfred Kubin resigned from the association. Immediately, efforts were made to organise the first exhibition of the Blaue Reiter, held from 18 December until 1 January 1912 at Thannhauser's Modern Gallery. In view of the limited time which they had to arrange this, the name was adopted from the project of the almanac. Selecting three major works drawn from his Impressions, Improvisations and Compositions, Kandinsky's choice of exhibits was intentionally programmatic. In the first room, Münter captured a section of the painting *Impression II (Moscow)* (fig.20); notwithstanding the bold use of an abstract grid, the spectator can still decipher the various components of the urban landscape within an overall fluidity of the expressive mark.[62] As a document of curatorial practice as well as of a painting destroyed during the Second World War (it was in the Berlin collection of the well-known manufacturer and patron Bernhard Koehler), Münter's recording of this moment is invaluable in historical terms alone.

Yet her close involvement in archiving Kandinsky's oeuvre was ongoing. During the earlier years (1900–8), Kandinsky listed a relatively small number of his pictures chronologically. Sometimes he noted the place where the painting was done and in many instances he added a minute shorthand sketch of the painting's main features. However, during the period 1909 until 1916, in a sketchbook containing Münter's writing, it is clear that she was responsible for itemising and updating Handlist III.[63] Following Kandinsky's practice, she accompanied these with a 'shorthand' sketch; measurements are always noted, the size of the frame sometimes being added. Apart from the title, Münter also provided a short description, signalling that the more abstract Kandinsky's compositions, the more intervention was required on his behalf. *Improvisation 12* 1910 (fig.29, p.151), for example, which features a pattern resembling a bunch of bananas, was indeed subtitled 'Bananen'.

These subtitles reveal a friendly banter, a dialogical relationship between the couple since they evidently arose from Kandinsky's and Münter's studio jargon. Chronicling his oeuvre therefore went beyond mere cherishing of his efforts and involved interpolation in the creative process. Nowhere is this more evident than in Münter's decision to photograph Kandinsky's major abstract painting of the pre-1914 years, *Composition VII* (no.52), at four critical stages of its evolution (fig.22). Interestingly, he made more preliminary studies for this composition than any other – over thirty drawings, watercolours and oil sketches. Nonetheless, in relation to its two-month gestation, it was painted comparably quickly; according to Münter's pocket calendar it was started on 25 November 1913, when the canvas (2 x 3 metres) was delivered, and completed three days later.[64] The photographs provide us with enduring testimony and insight into his working methods; we can ascertain that the full composition was sketched out on the canvas and that it progressed from the central section to the right-hand corner before consolidating on the other parts. It is clear too that he painted the lightest white areas that emphasise the material

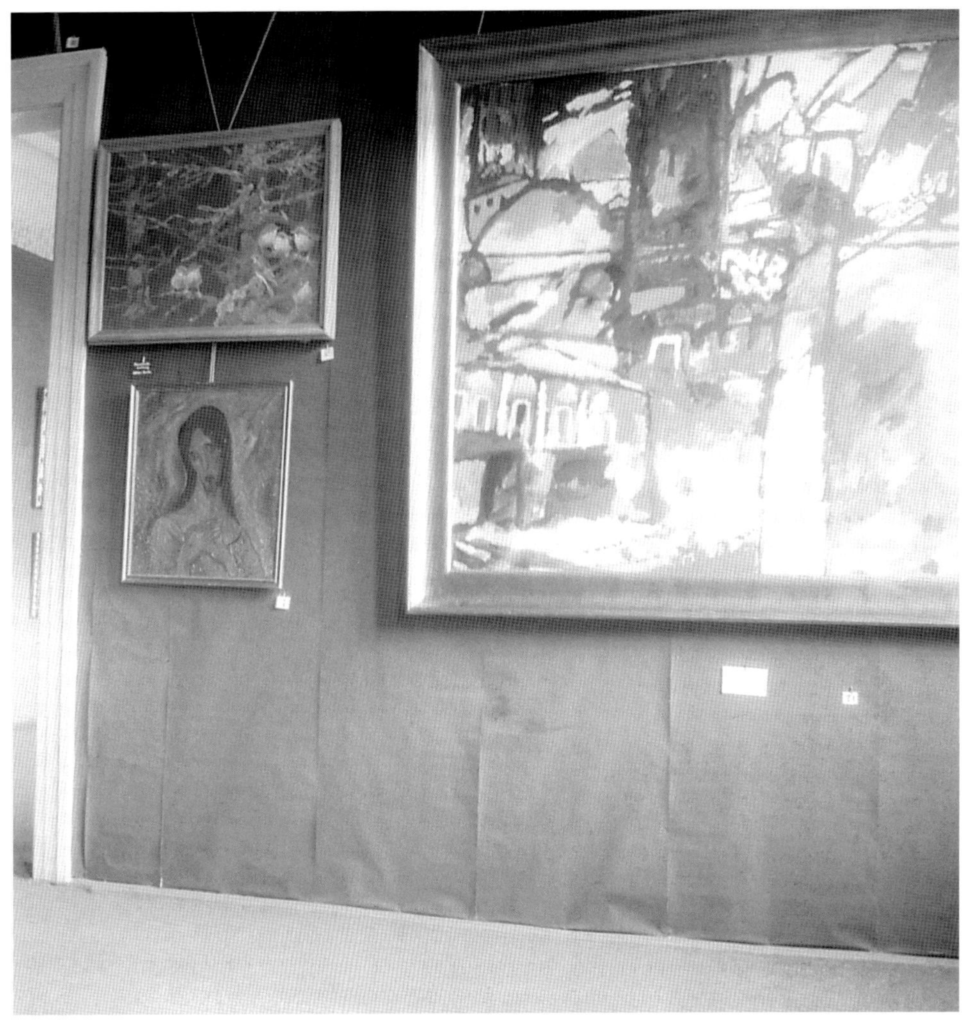

plane of the canvas while developing the linear elements. Through superimposition, as well as varying the thickness and colour of line, he retained the ebb and flow of pictorial depth. There is no evidence, moreover, of changes of mind or 'pentimenti', confirming Kandinsky's definitive vision of the work that he had in mind.

Whereas the final painting appears to be totally non-figural (no.52), its iconographic departure is highly complex. In a now famous tract known as his 'Cologne Lecture', Kandinsky stated that: 'I calmly chose the Resurrection as the theme for *Composition V*, and the Deluge for the sixth. One needs a certain daring if one is to take on such outworn themes as the starting point for pure painting.'[65] Although he provides no explicit title for *Composition VII*, the painting bears an indexical relationship to apocalyptic themes in his oeuvre – Deluge, Last Judgement, Resurrection and Paradise – and Münter's photographs

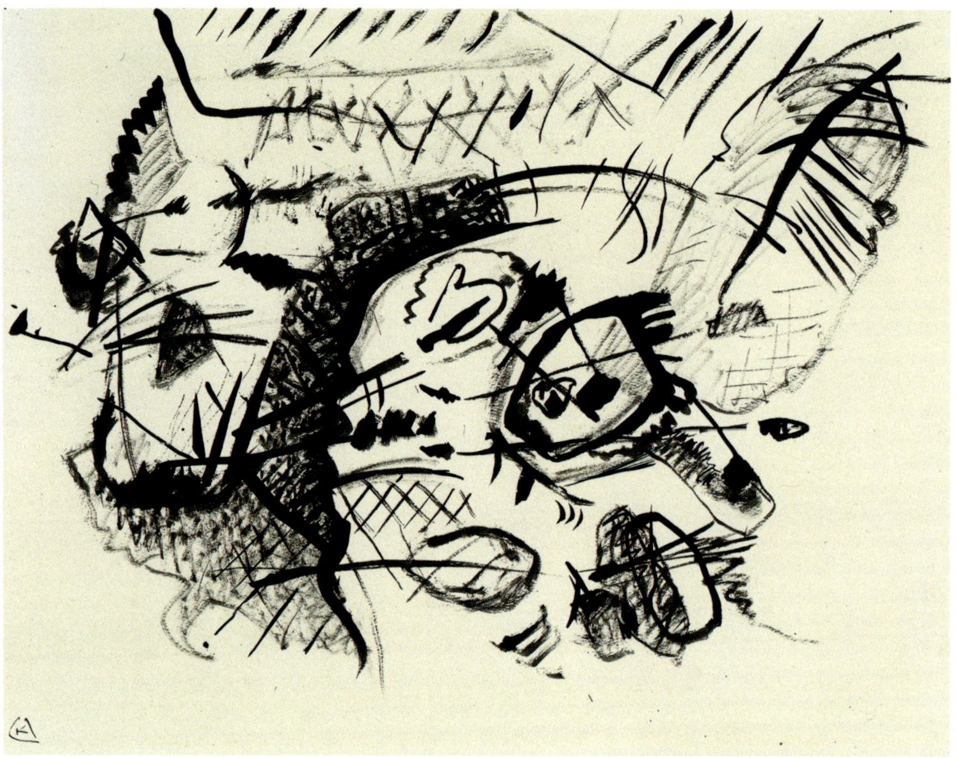

assist us in decoding Kandinsky's deliberate 'veiling' of ostensible motifs. [66] Consistent through the four frames is the prominence of the boat and oars motif of the Deluge in the lower left corner, the arcs of the enigmatic centre and, on the right-hand side, the intersecting enclosed configurations representative of Paradise. Indeed, it is his redemptive interpretation of eschatological texts that suggests a biographical reading of the composition; the intertwined oval shapes symbolising the reclining couple in the Garden of Love. This motif was invested with Utopian associations, the physical union of two lovers connoting the desire for transcendence and the divine. [67] It appears as though it was in these significant creative 'moments' in the studio – witnessed and framed by Münter – that their partnership was at its most intense, transcending the tempest of their far from ideal relationship in the real world.

With the outbreak of the First World War in August 1914, the artist couple left for Switzerland, Kandinsky departing for Moscow soon thereafter. In 1916 they effected a brief reconciliation in Sweden and, though their correspondence was fraught with bitterness, Münter nonetheless hoped to marry Kandinsky. However, Münter's and Kandinsky's separation became permanent when he married the

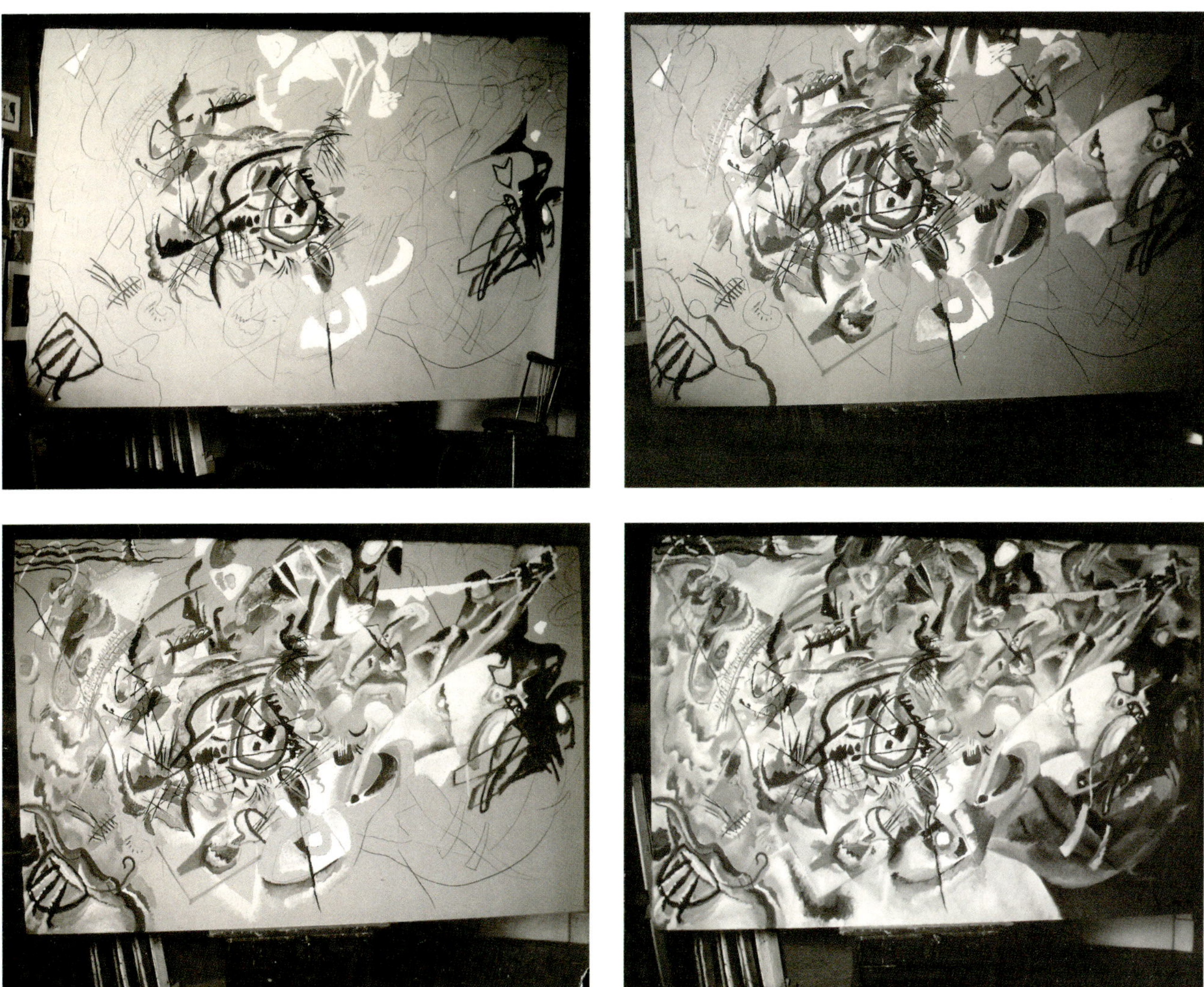

younger woman Nina Andreyevskaya in Moscow in 1917. This essay reveals how aspects of their collaboration can be retrieved from the vicissitudes of their biographies. That Kandinsky benefited from a partnership with a younger woman practitioner is evident given his role as tutor and lover. That he grew to regard her as more than a muse and apprentice is clear from his intense regard for 'Ellchen's' talent, their interests converging in particular in their Murnau landscapes. Their divergences in the handling of the interior genre are instructive, Kandinsky's treatment conveying a 'connectedness' more symptomatic of feminine domesticity when compared to the satirical streak in Münter's paintings. Beyond her practice, her documenting of his oeuvre and creative use of photography lend credence to the positive benefits of intimate creative partnership.

However, Kandinsky's drift away from her following his return from Russia in December 1910 was inevitable. He displayed an intensifying concern for events in Russia and expressed a 'never-waning longing for Moscow … the soil out of which I derive my strength'. [68] That Kandinsky's expatriate identity and growing allegiance to things Russian could have set the course for their eventual estrangement are factors that aren't necessarily acceded to in the literature. Indeed his intense collaboration with Franz Marc was superseded by another coupling of Kandinsky's name with the Serbian writer and activist Dimitrije Mitrinovic in the preparation of a second almanac along the lines of *Der Blaue Reiter*. [69] Münter's investment in the relationship was at a considerable loss to her own career, hence it is understandable that she held on to Kandinsky's pre-1914 oeuvre, notwithstanding his return to Germany in 1921. The legal wrangle continued into the late 1920s, Kandinsky securing a mere fraction of his output. [70]

Whereas, on the one hand, we can be grateful that Münter protected his works from the vagaries of Third Reich confiscations of so-called 'degenerate art', on the other hand, it provokes various art-historical questions relating to Kandinsky's overall development as to whether lack of access to his formative oeuvre compelled him to reinvent himself.

Plates 1910 - 1914

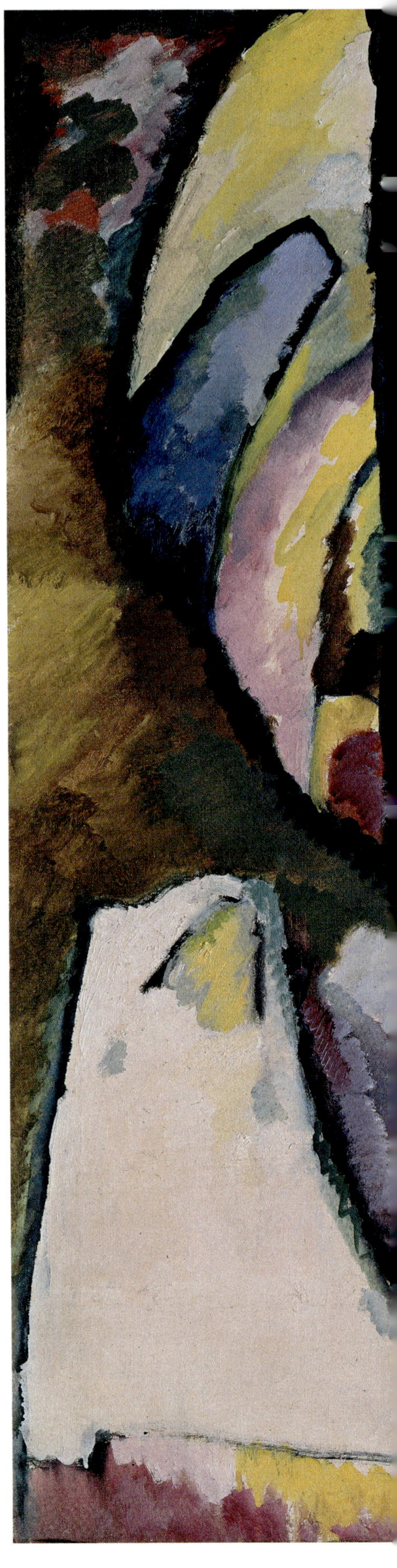

29 **Improvisation** 10
1910
Oil on canvas   120 x 140
Fondation Beyeler, Riehen/Basel

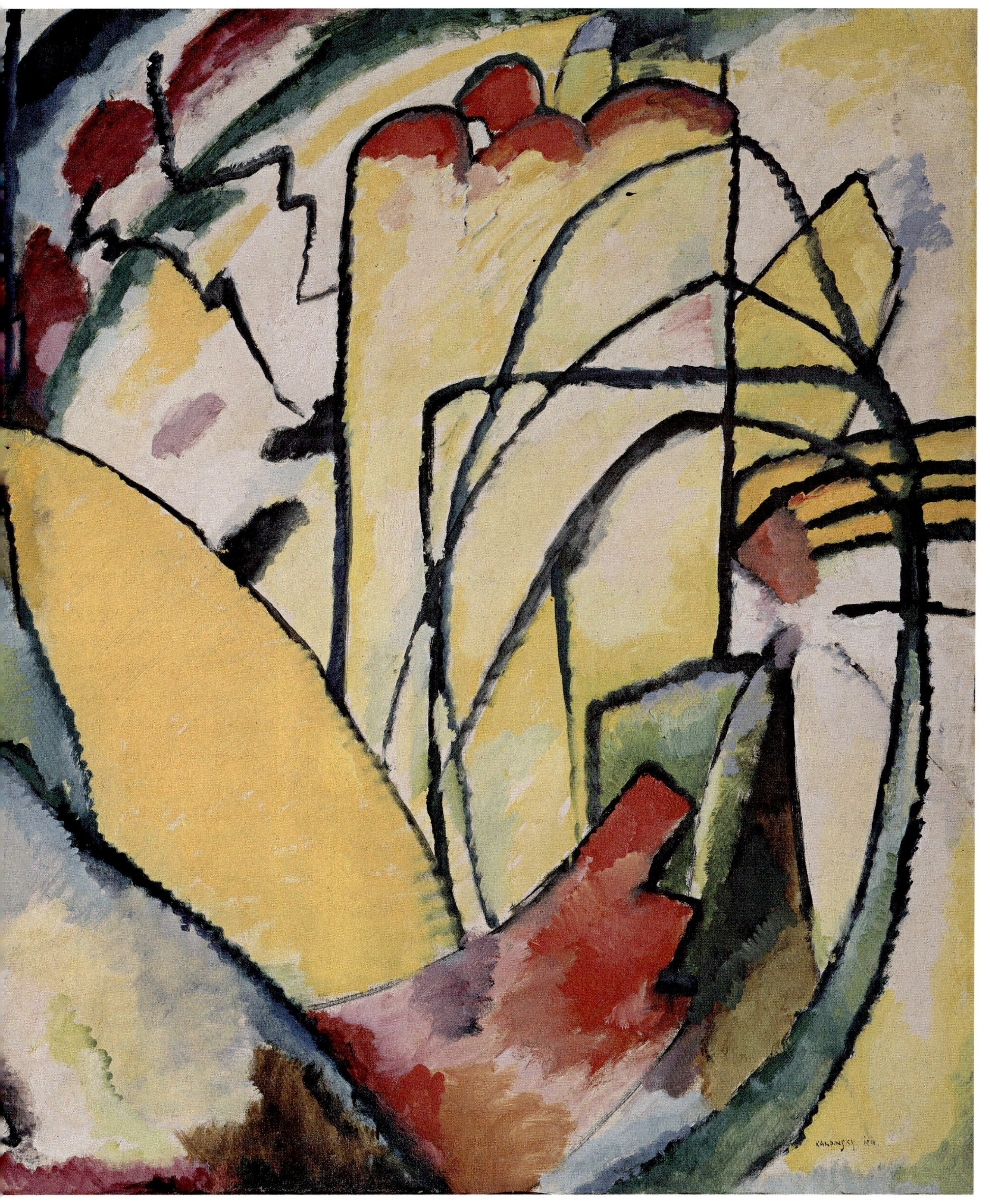

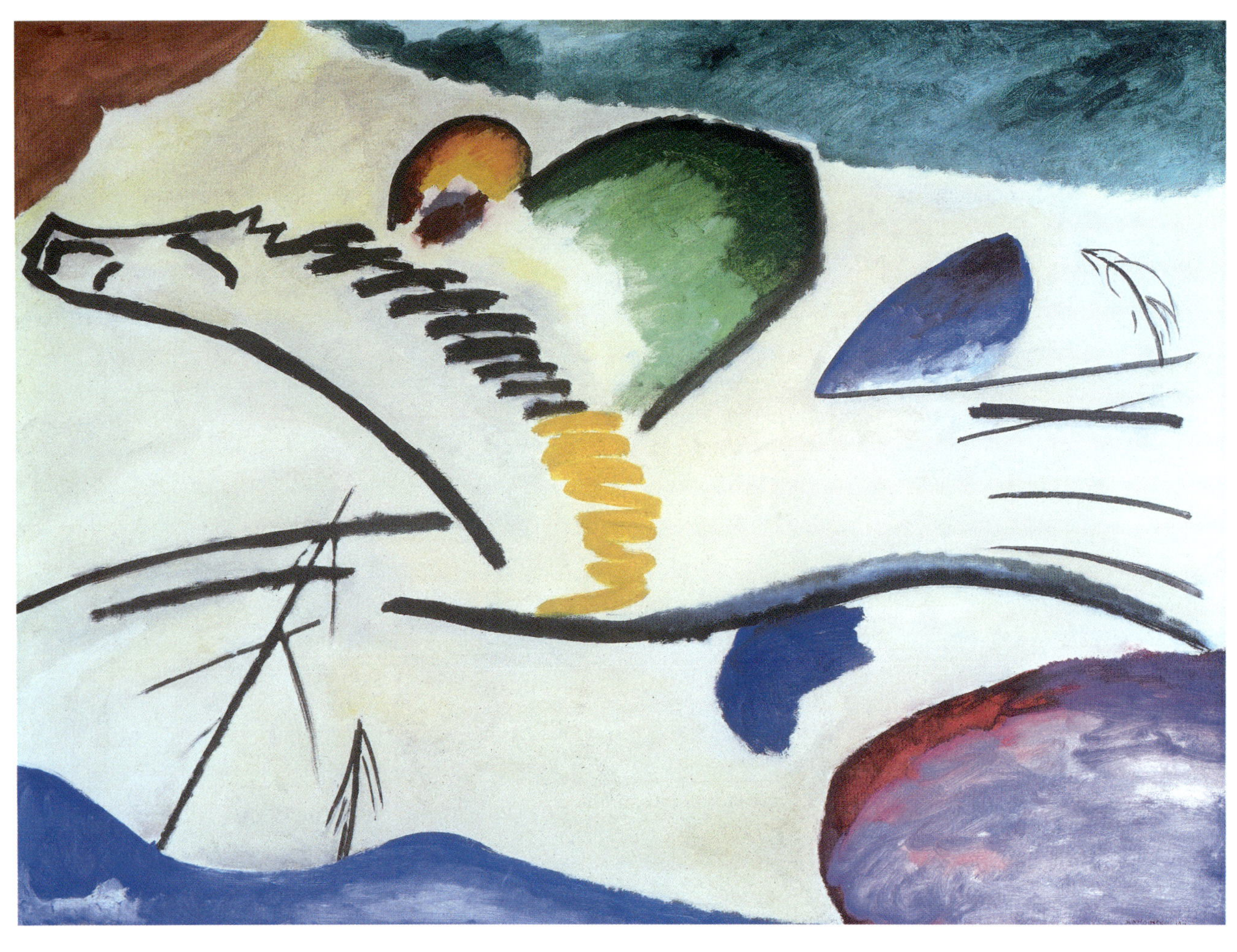

30 **Lyrically**
1911
Oil on canvas 94 x 130
Museum Boijmans Van Beuningen, Rotterdam

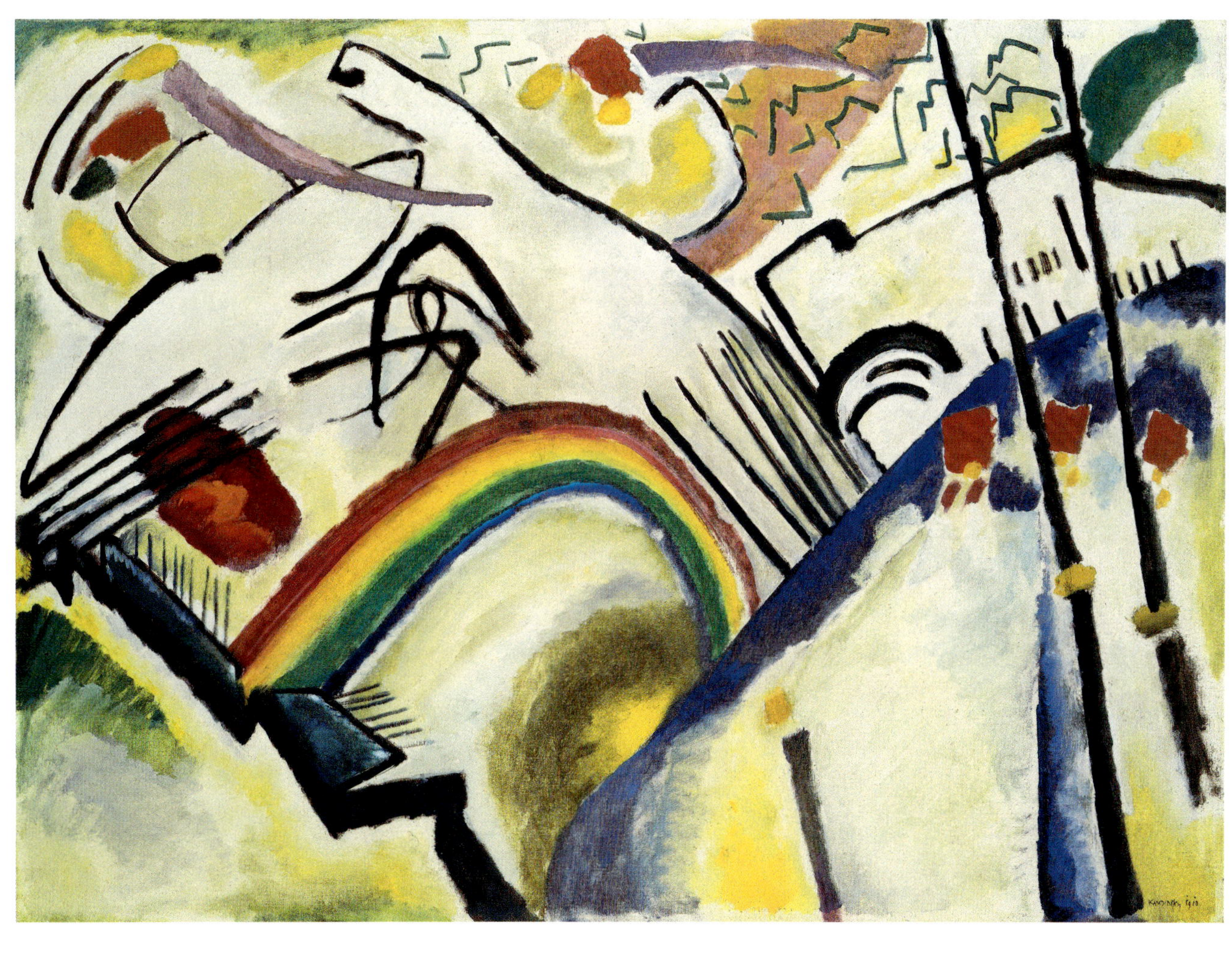

31 **Cossacks**

1910–11

Oil on canvas 94.6 x 130.2

Tate. Presented by Mrs Hazel McKinley 1938

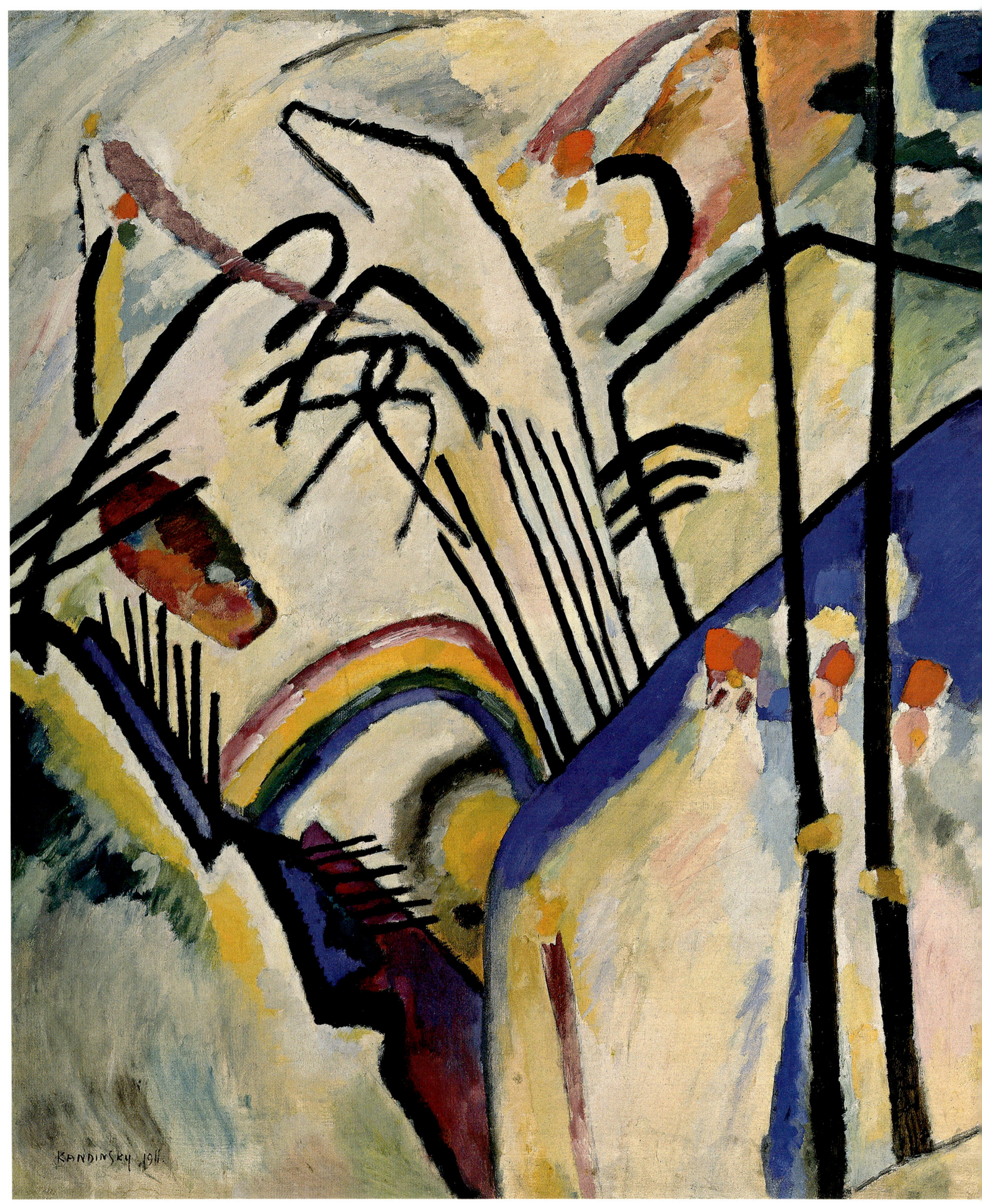

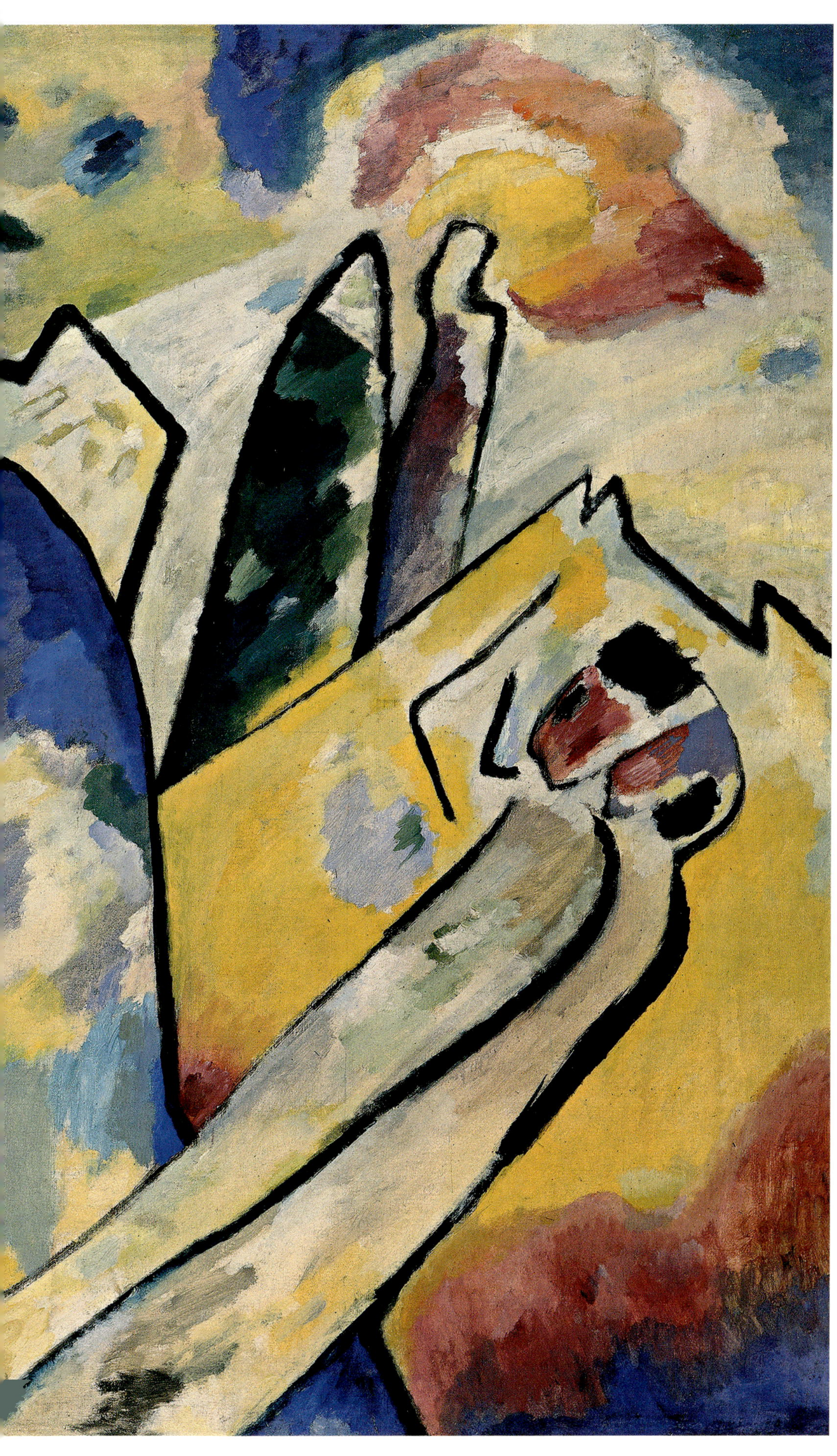

32 **Composition IV**
1911
Oil on canvas 159.5 x 250.5
Kunstsammlung Nordrhein-Westfalen,
Düsseldorf
NOT EXHIBITED

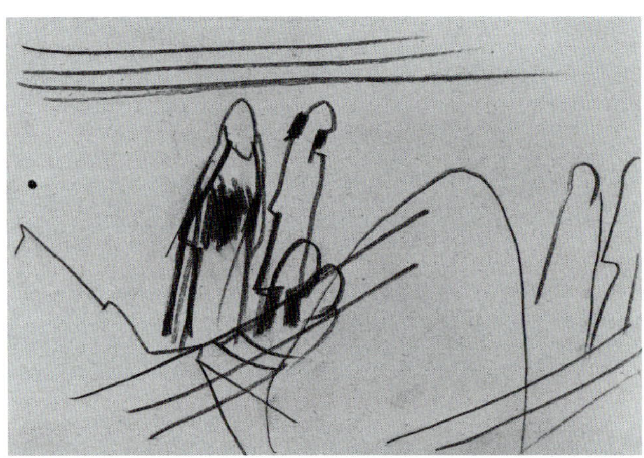

33 **Untitled, Study for Composition IV**
1911
Charcoal on paper   10 x 14.9
Musée National d'Art Moderne, Centre Georges Pompidou, Paris.
Centre de Création Industrielle. Bequest of Nina Kandinsky 1981

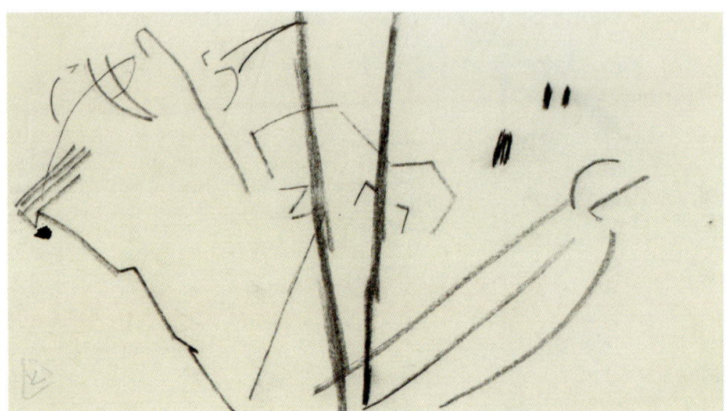

34 **First Sketch for Composition IV**
1911
Pencil, charcoal and Indian ink on paper   10.2 x 20
Musée National d'Art Moderne, Centre Georges Pompidou, Paris.
Centre de Création Industrielle. Bequest of Nina Kandinsky 1981

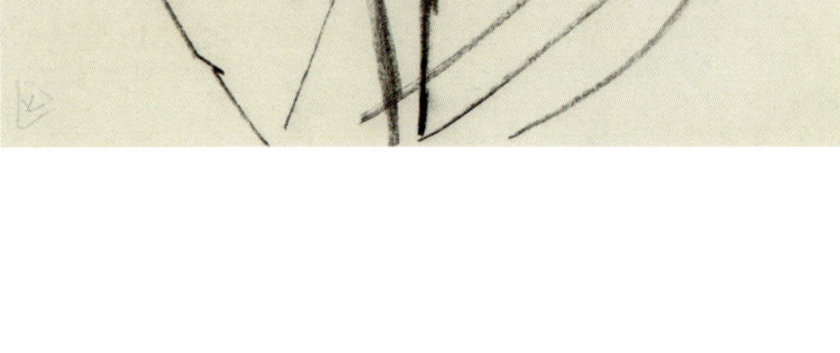

35 **Untitled, Sketch for Composition IV**
1911
Charcoal on paper   10 x 14.9
Musée National d'Art Moderne, Centre Georges Pompidou, Paris.
Centre de Création Industrielle. Bequest of Nina Kandinsky 1981

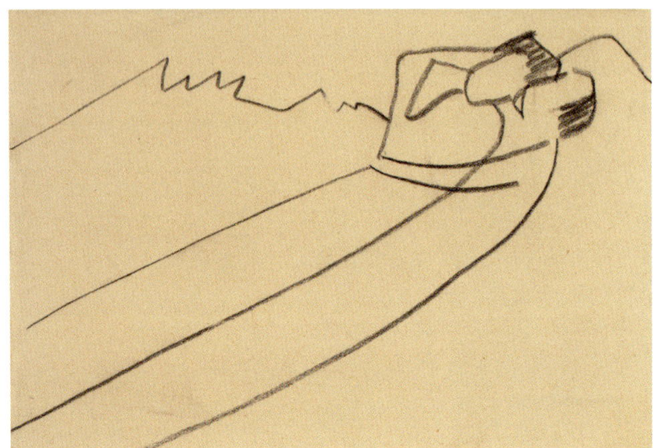

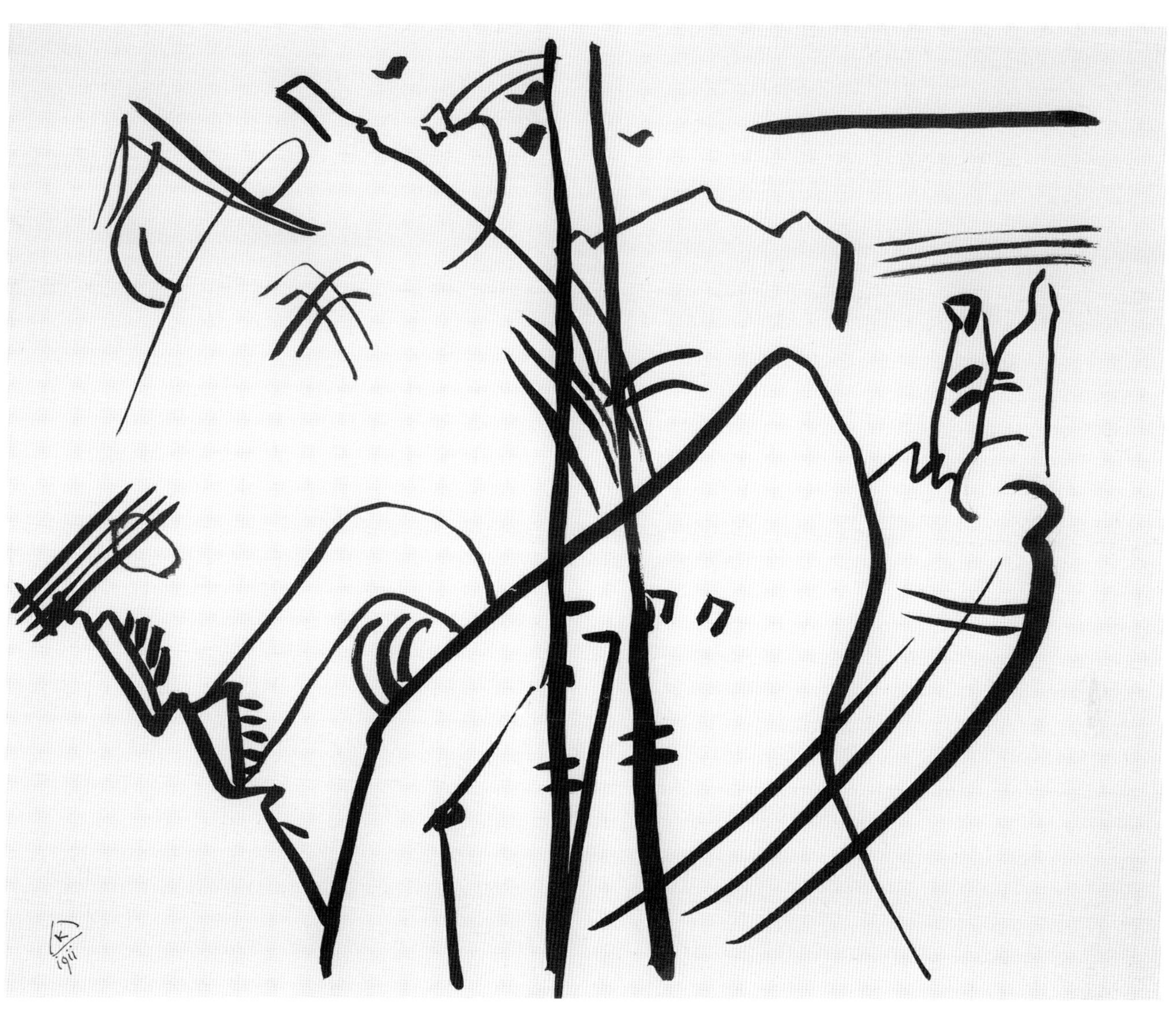

36 **Study for Composition IV**
1911
Pencil and Indian ink on paper 24.9 x 30.5
Musée National d'Art Moderne, Centre Georges Pompidou, Paris.
Centre de Création Industrielle. Bequest of Nina Kandinsky 1981

37 **Study for the Cover of *The Blue Rider* Almanac**
1911
Watercolour, gouache and Indian ink on paper 29 x 21
Musée National d'Art Moderne, Centre Georges Pompidou, Paris.
Centre de Création Industrielle. Donated in 1994

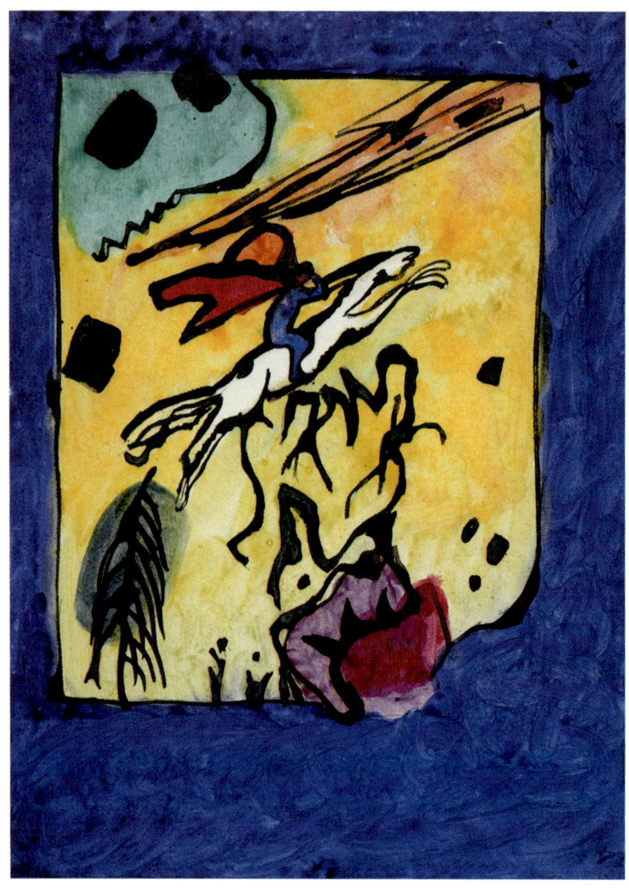

38 **Nude**

1911

Oil on canvas   147.3 x 99

Private Collection

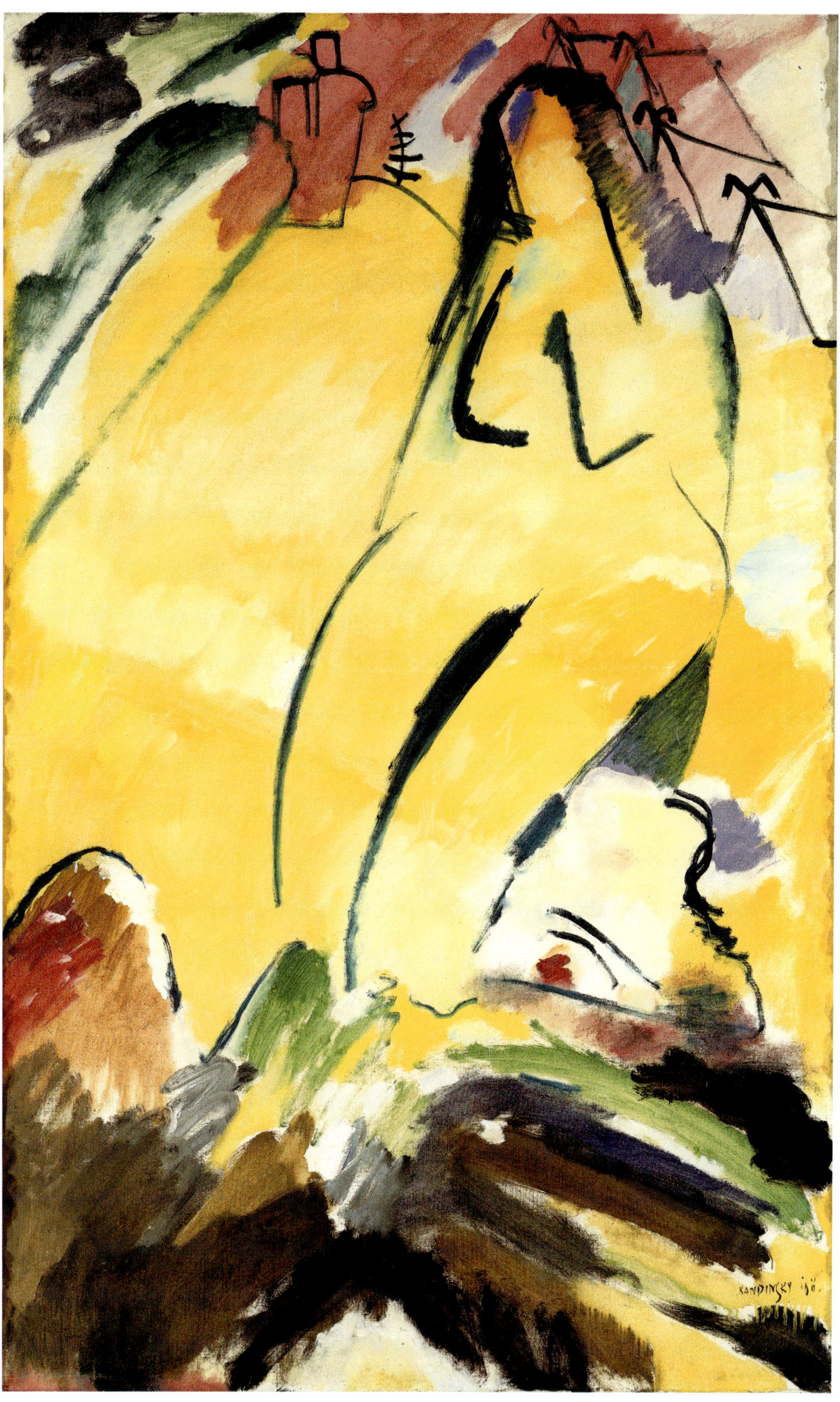

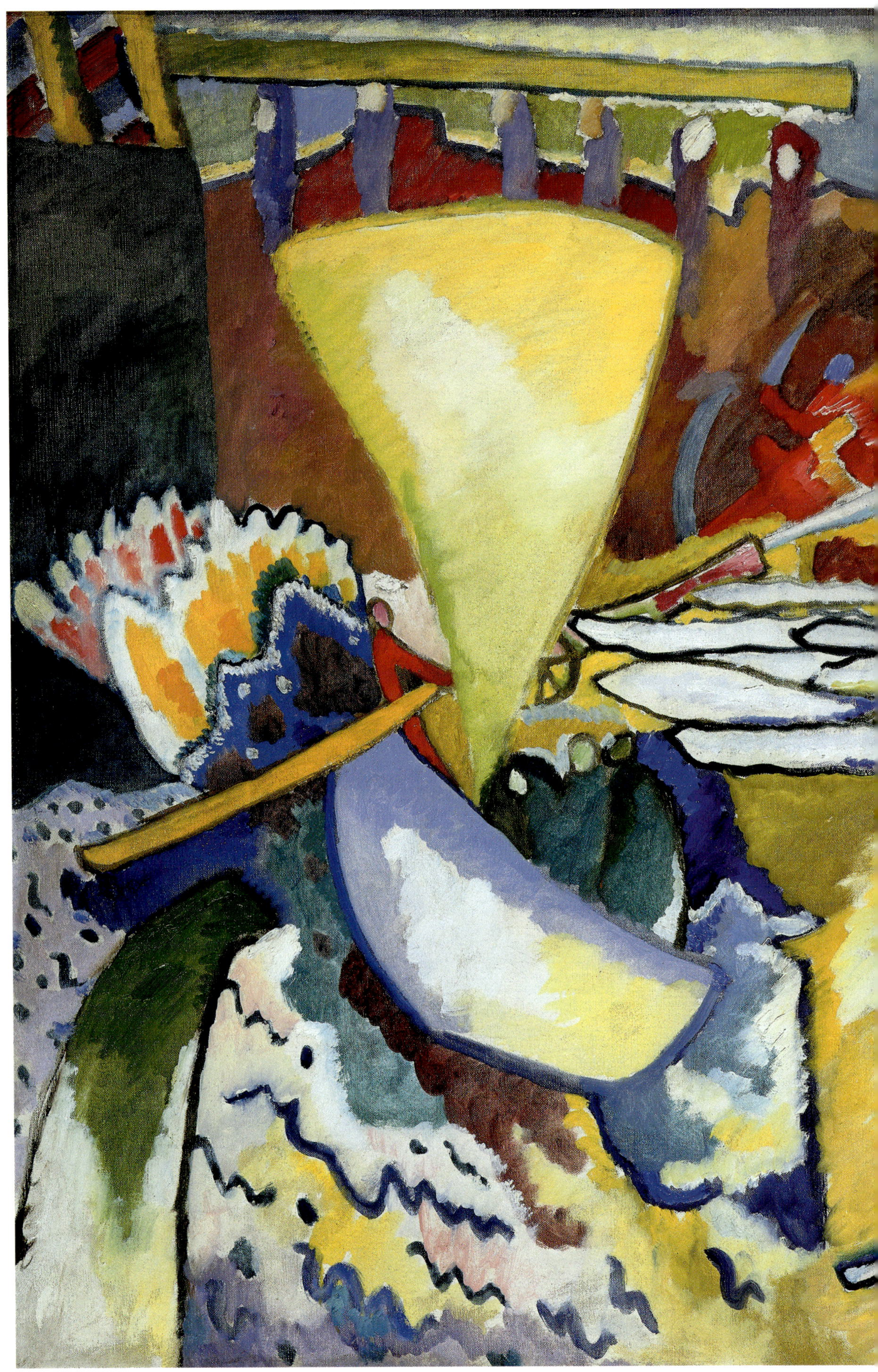

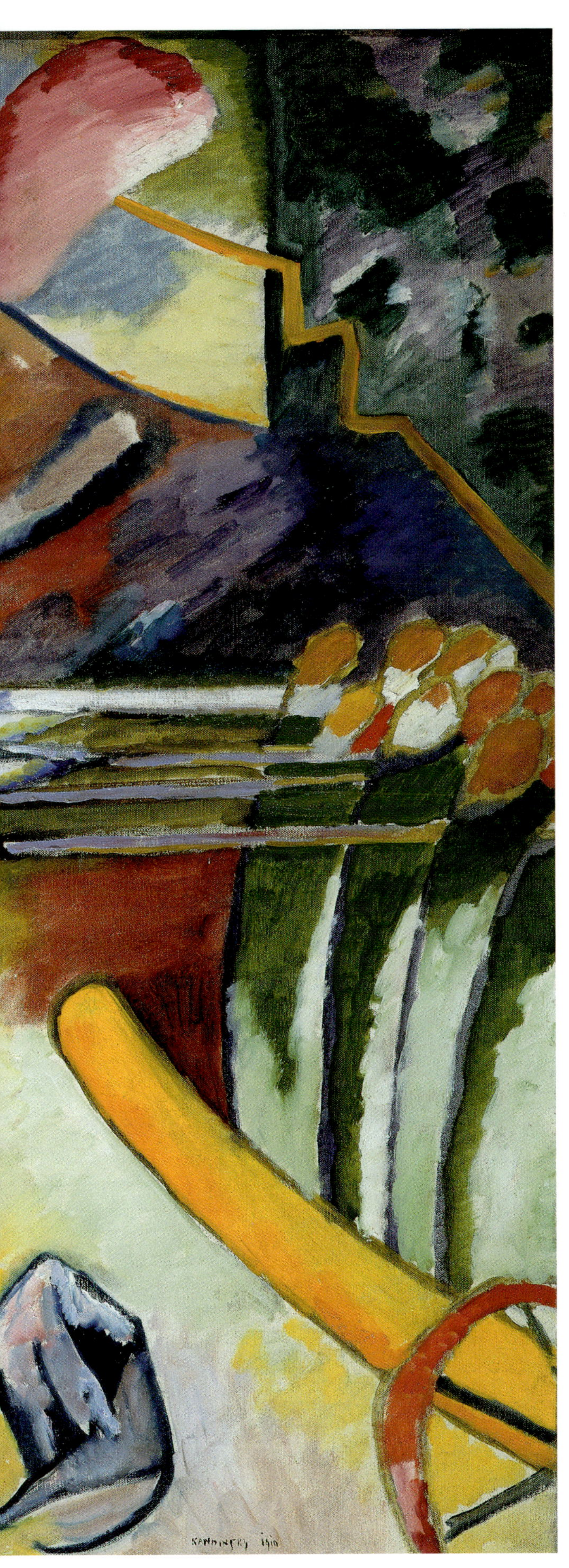

39 **Improvisation 11**
1910
Oil on canvas 97.5 x 106.5
The State Russian Museum, St Petersburg

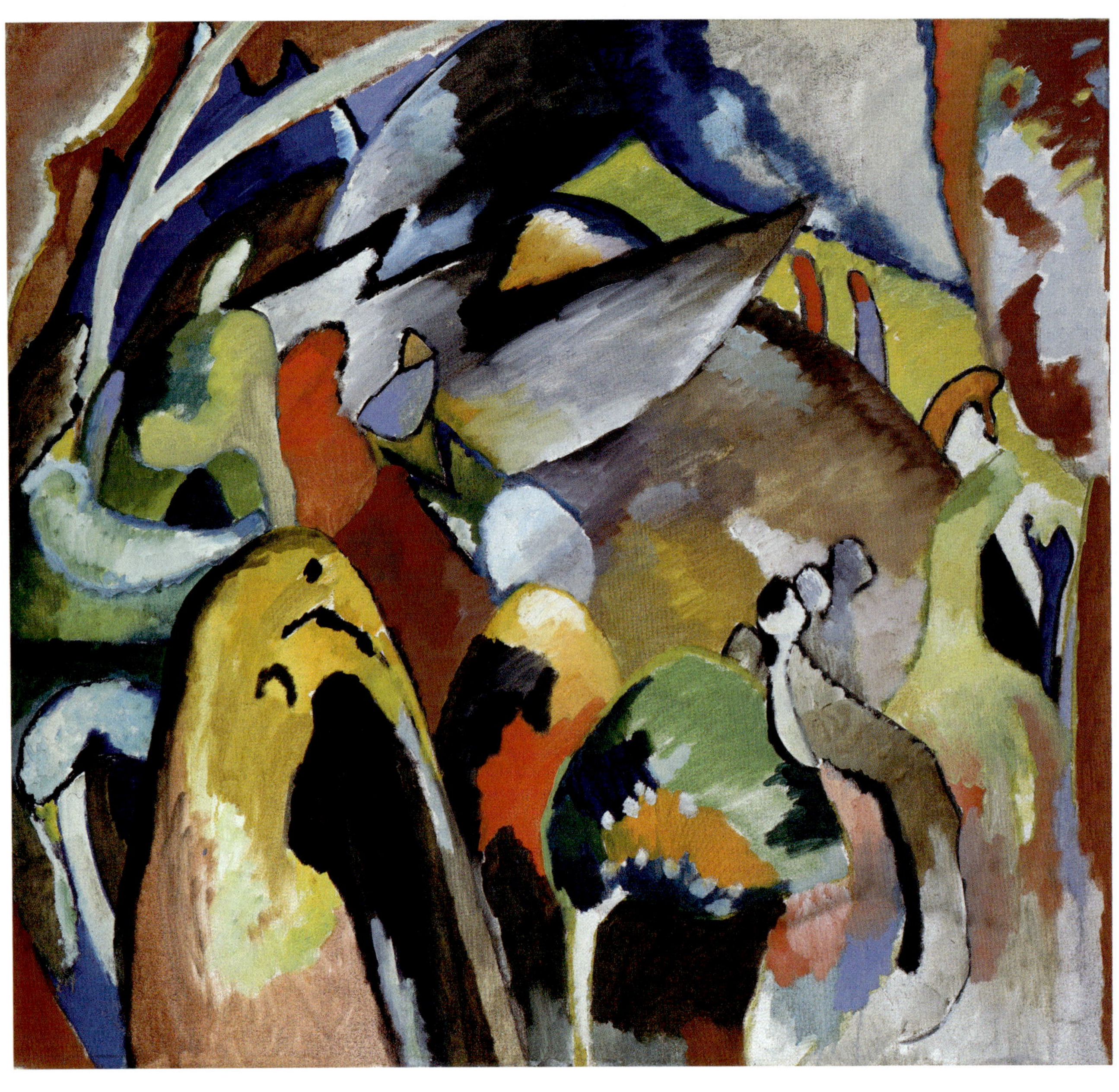

40 **Improvisation 19A**
1911
Oil and gouache on canvas 97.2 x 106.4
Städtische Galerie im Lenbachhaus, Munich

41 Improvisation 20
1911
Oil on canvas 94.5 x 108
The State Pushkin Museum of Fine Arts, Moscow

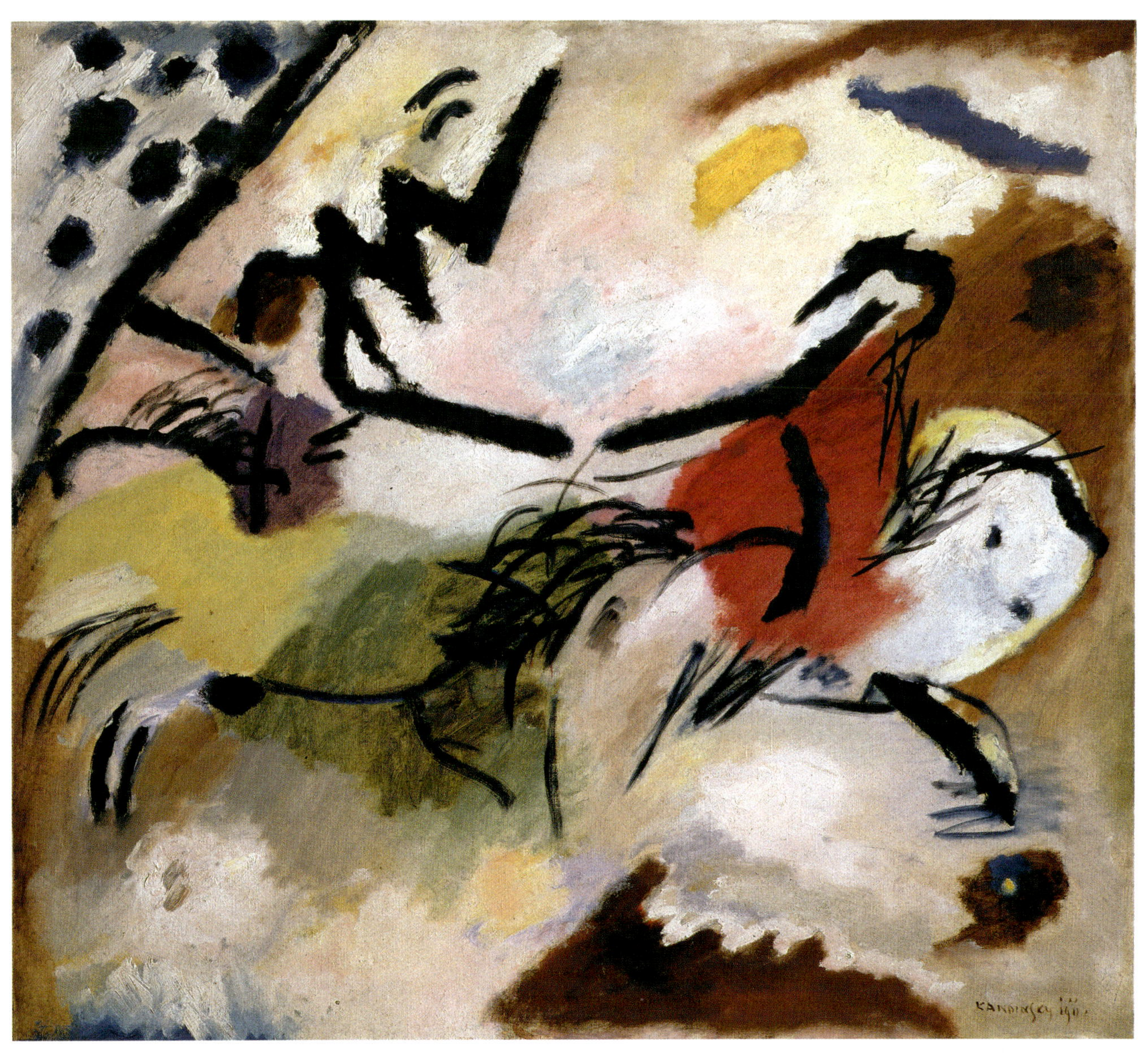

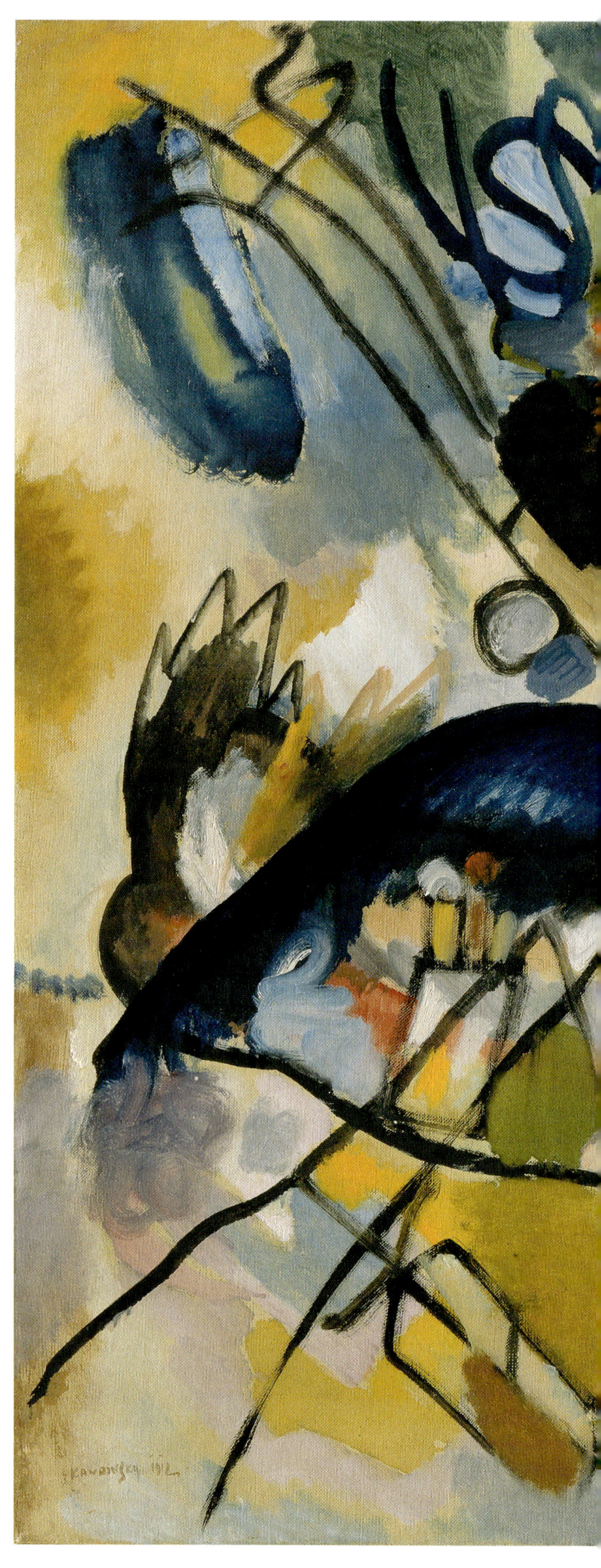

42 **Black Spot I**
1912
Oil on canvas 100 x 130
The State Russian Museum, St Petersburg

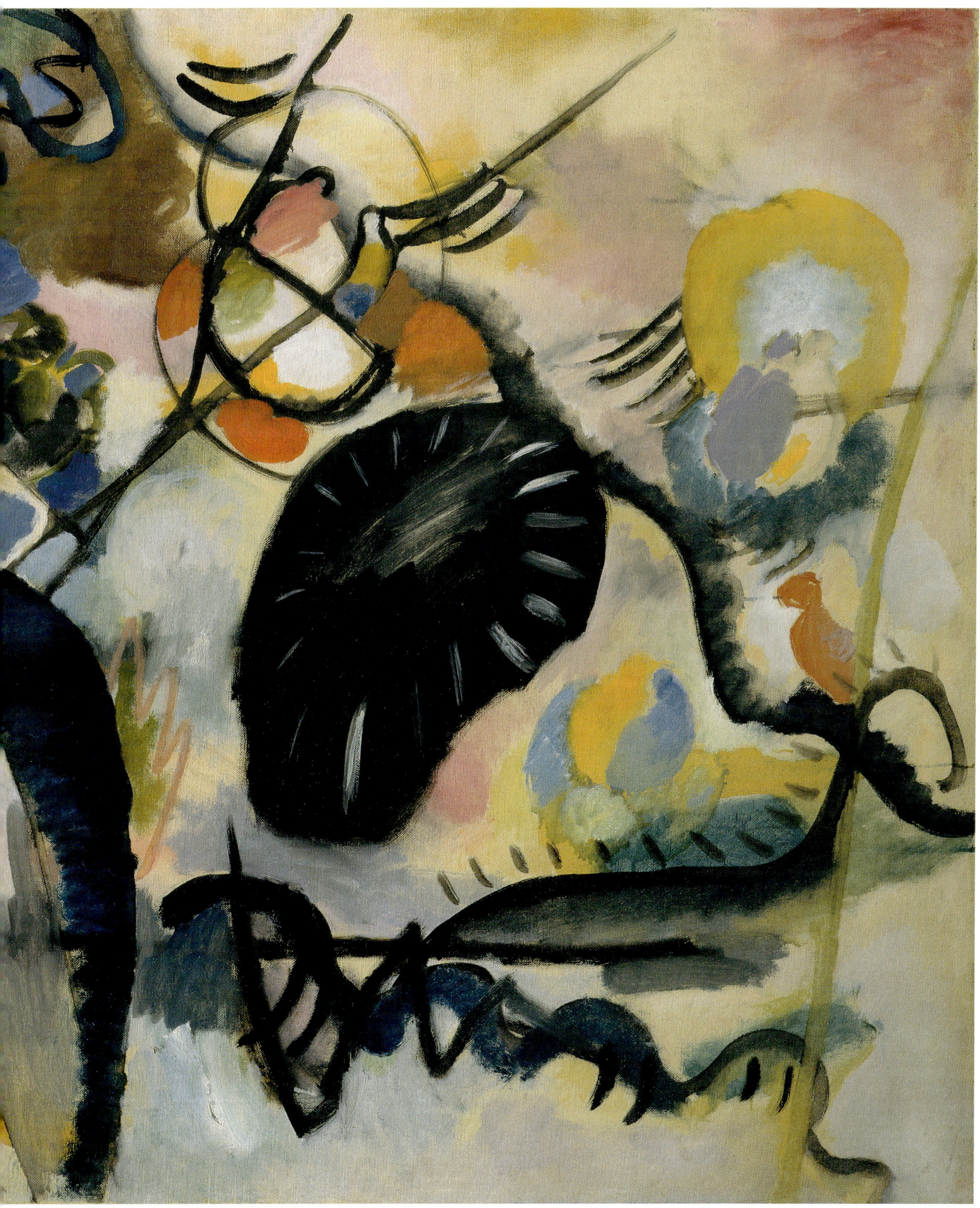

43 Improvisation 28 (Second Version)
1912
Oil on canvas   111.4 X 162.1

Solomon R. Guggenheim Museum, New York. The Hilla Rebay Foundation, 1970

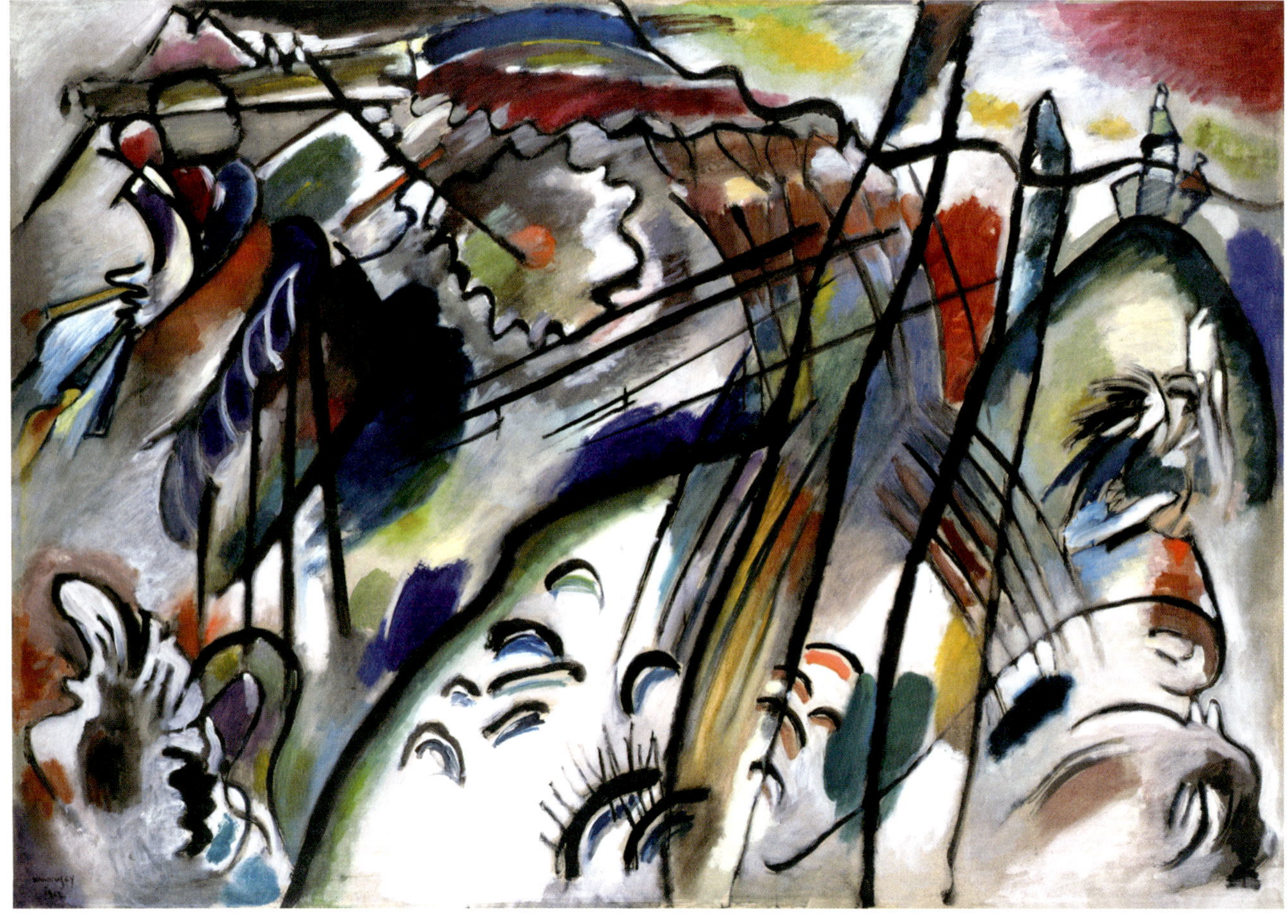

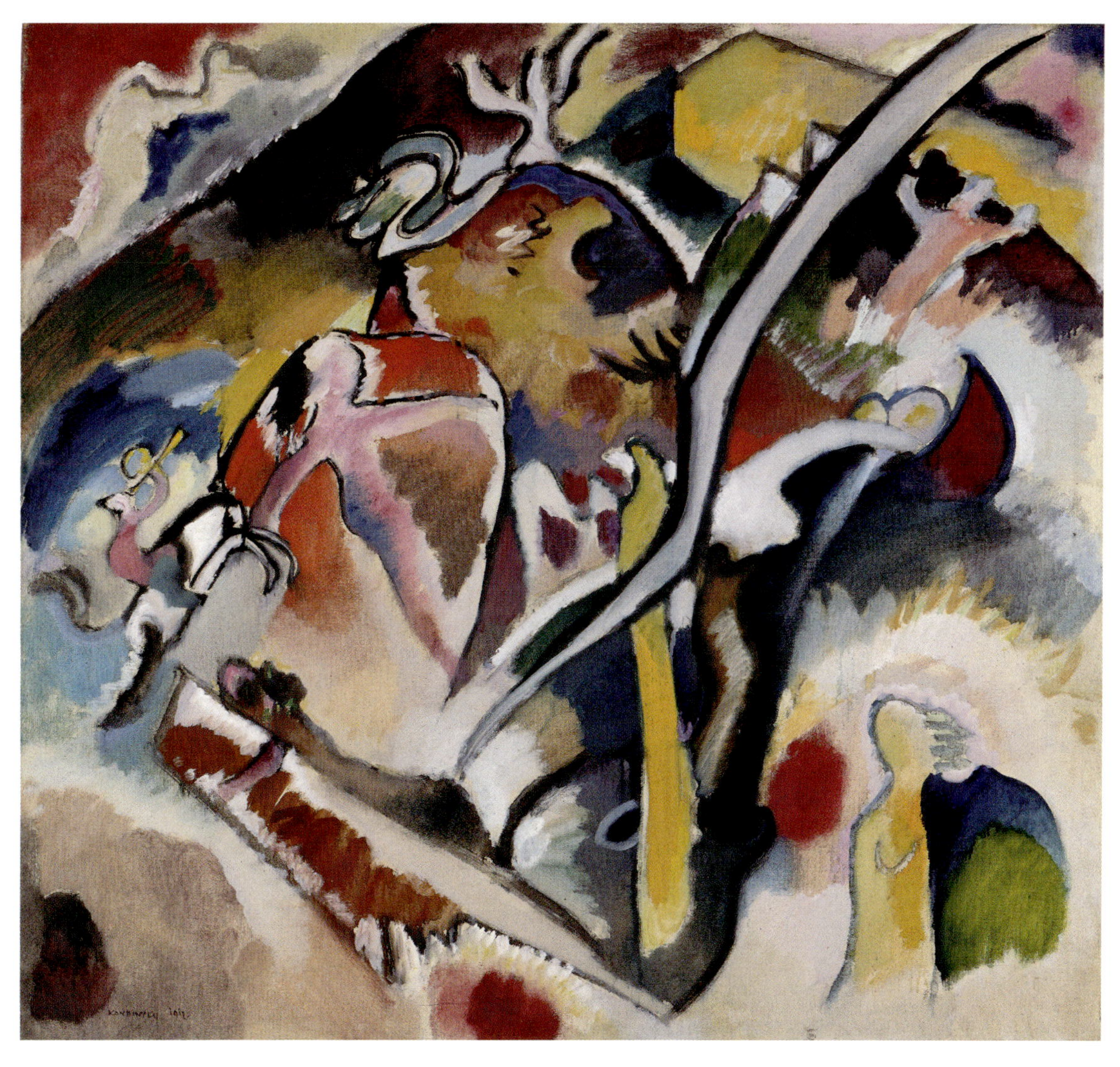

44 **Deluge I**

1912

Oil on canvas   100 x 105

Kaiser Wilhelm Museum, Krefeld

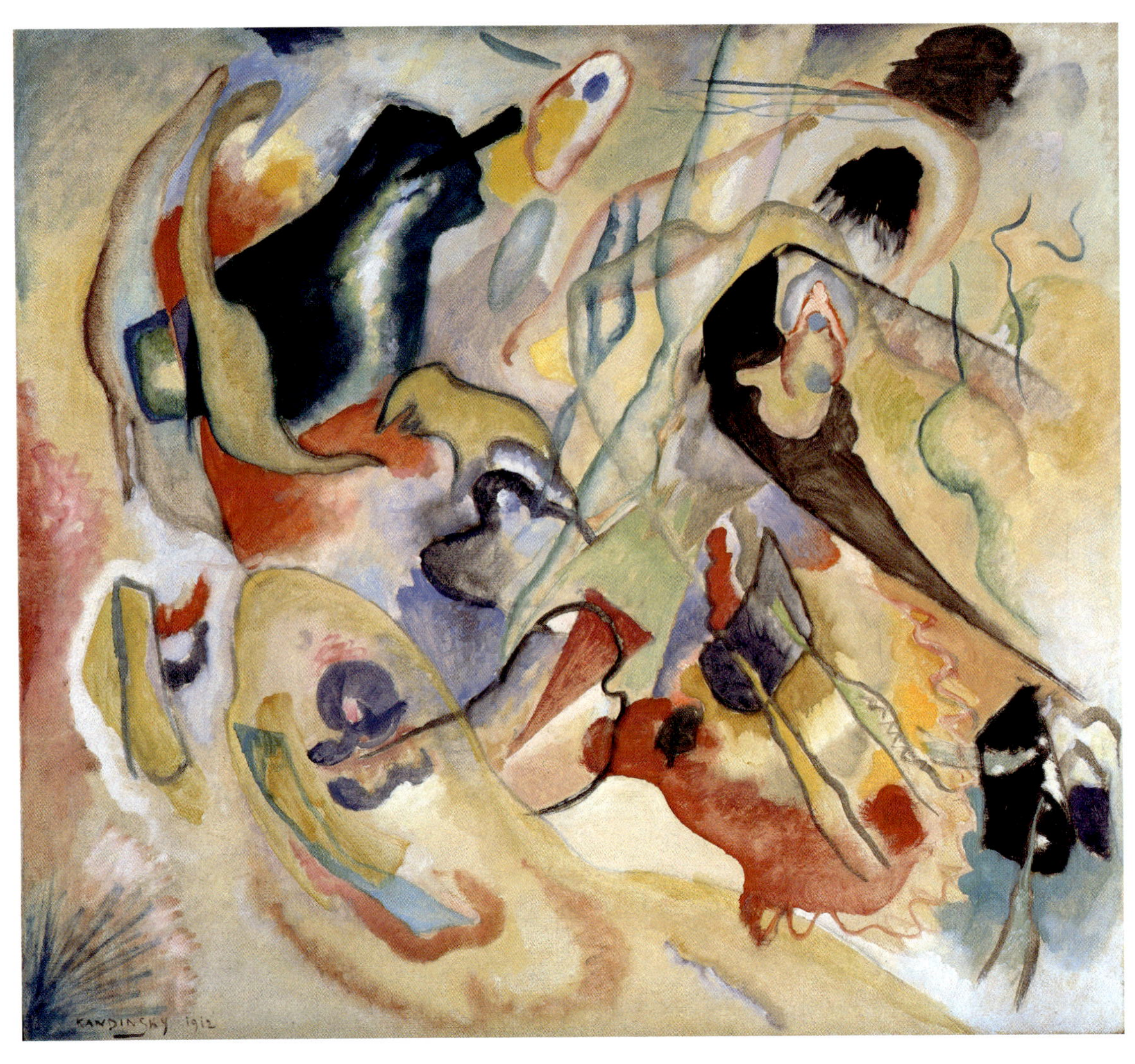

45 **Sketch for Deluge II**
1912
Oil on canvas 95 x 107.5
Acquavella Galleries, Inc., New York

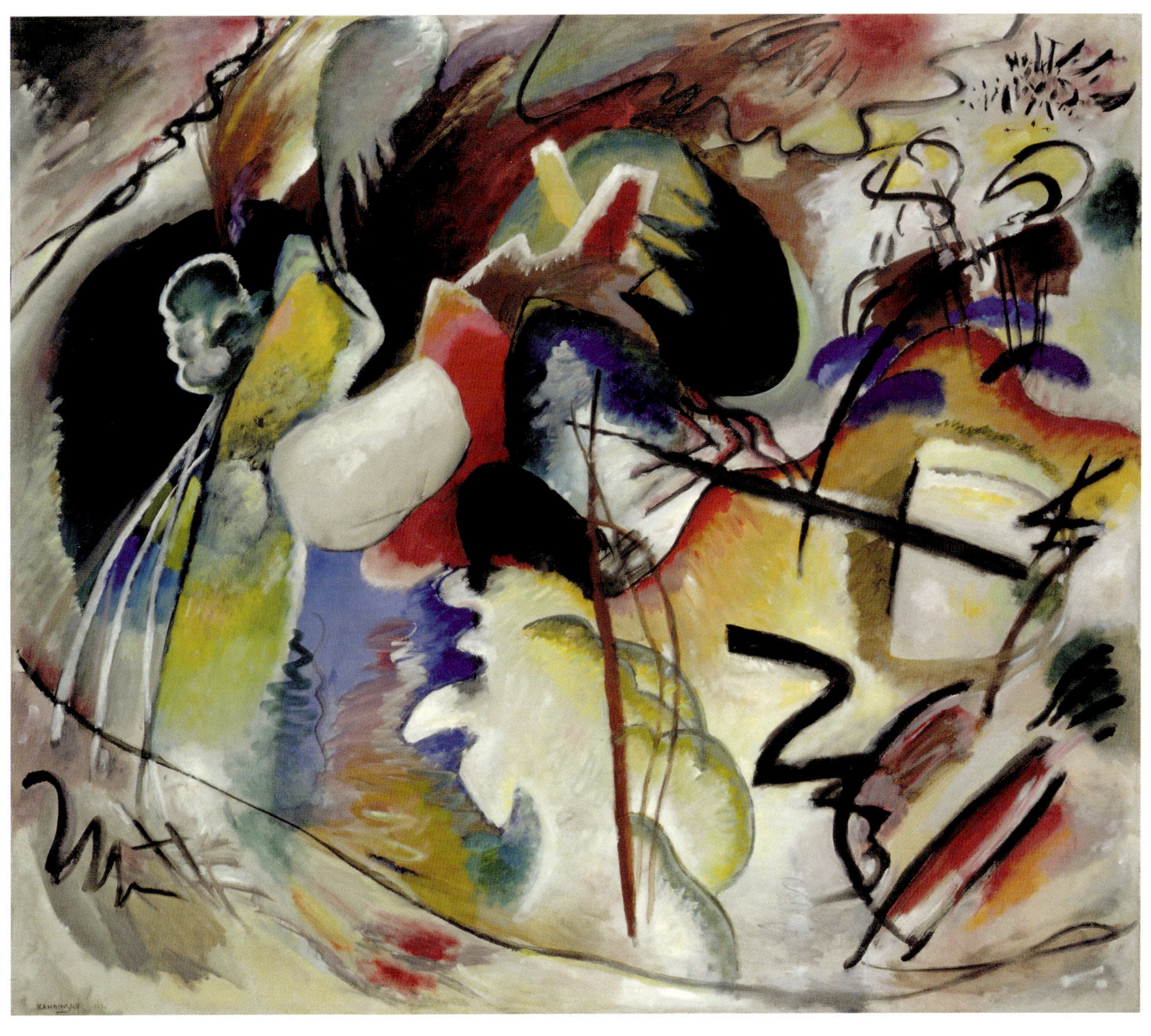

47 Improvisation 34 (Orient II)
1913
Oil on canvas 120 x 140
The State Museum of Fine Arts of Tatarstan

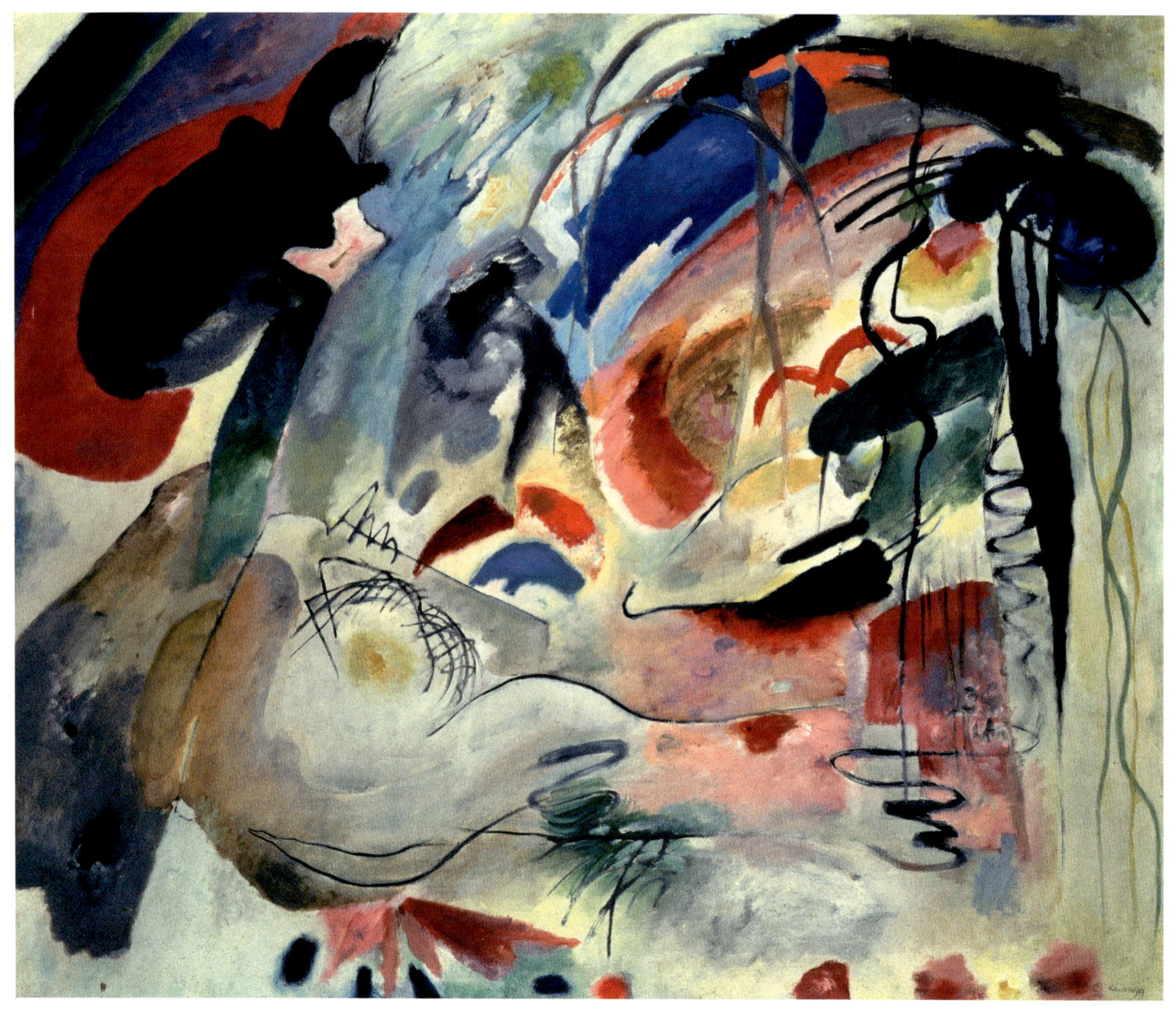

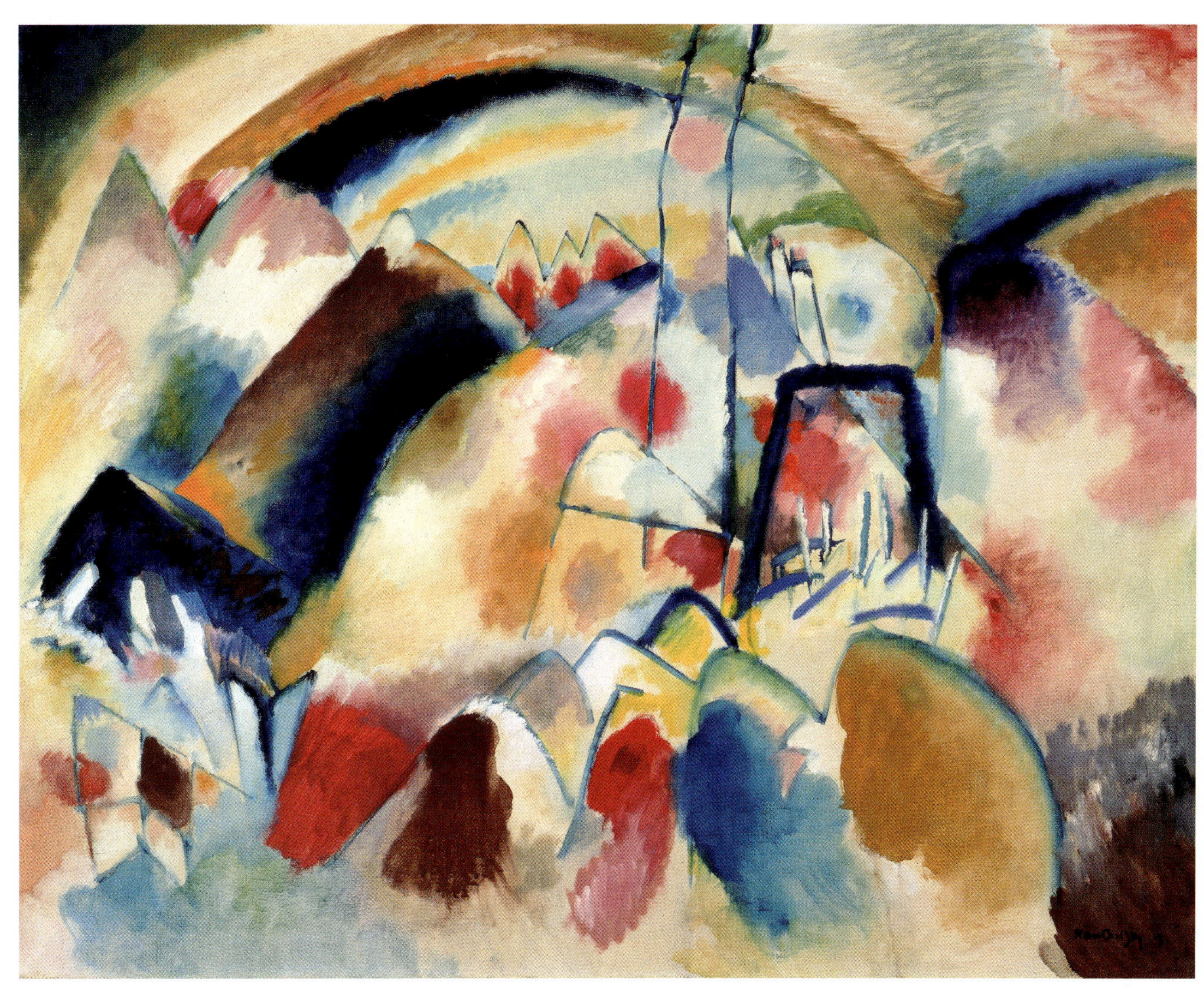

48 **Landscape with Red Spots I**
1913
Oil on canvas 78 x 100
Museum Folkwang, Essen

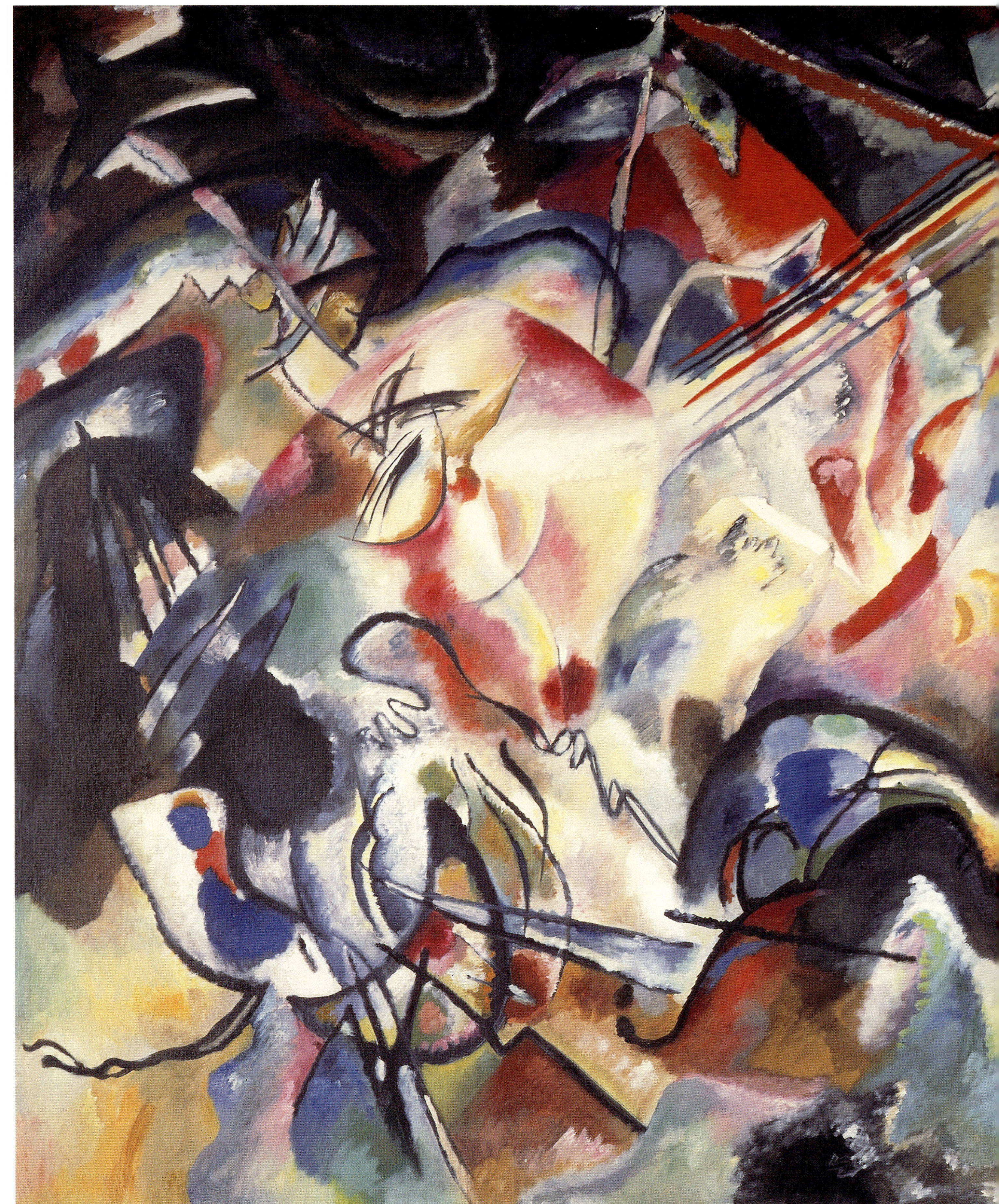

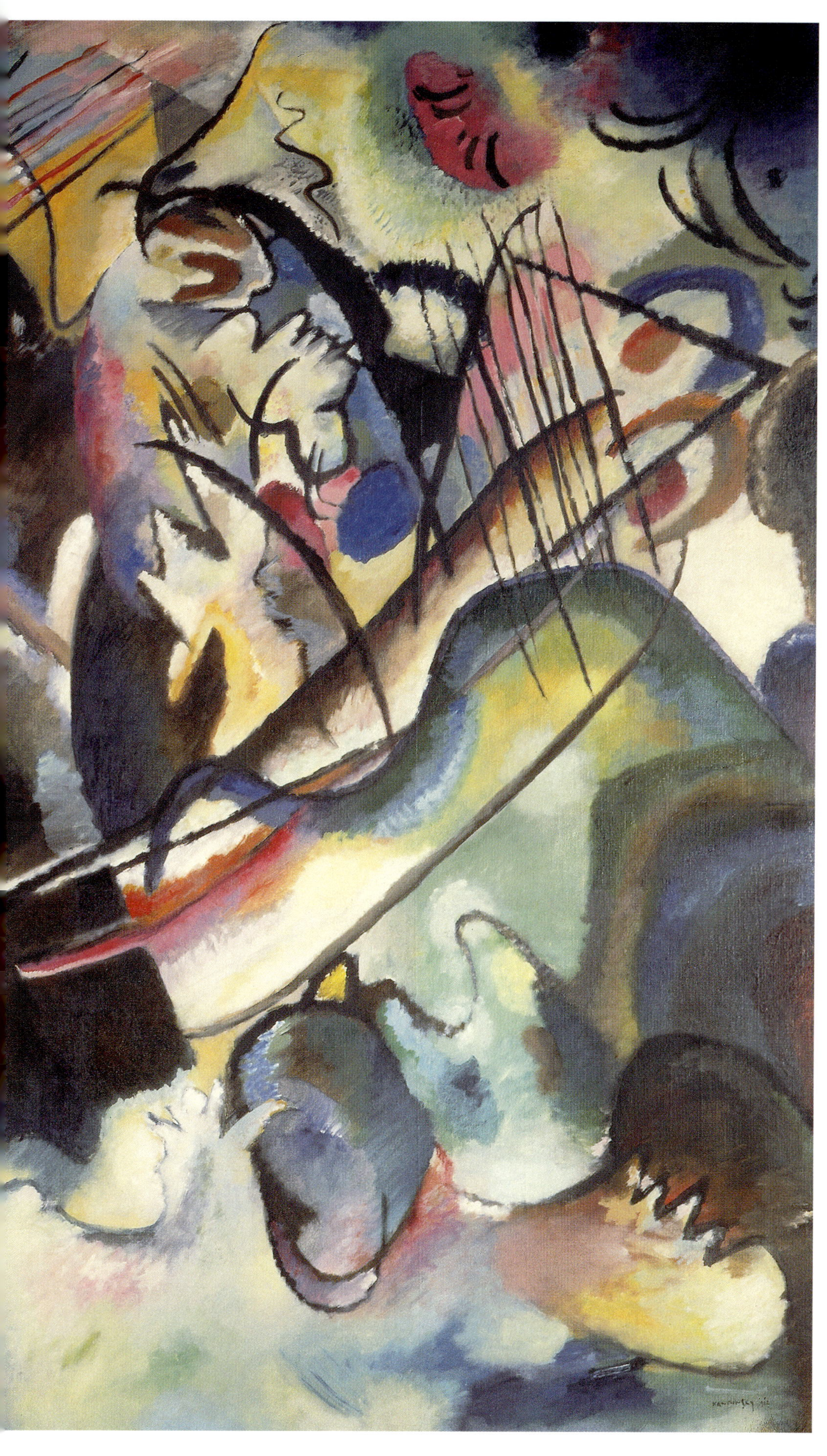

49 **Composition VI**
1913
Oil on canvas 195 x 300
State Hermitage, St Petersburg

125

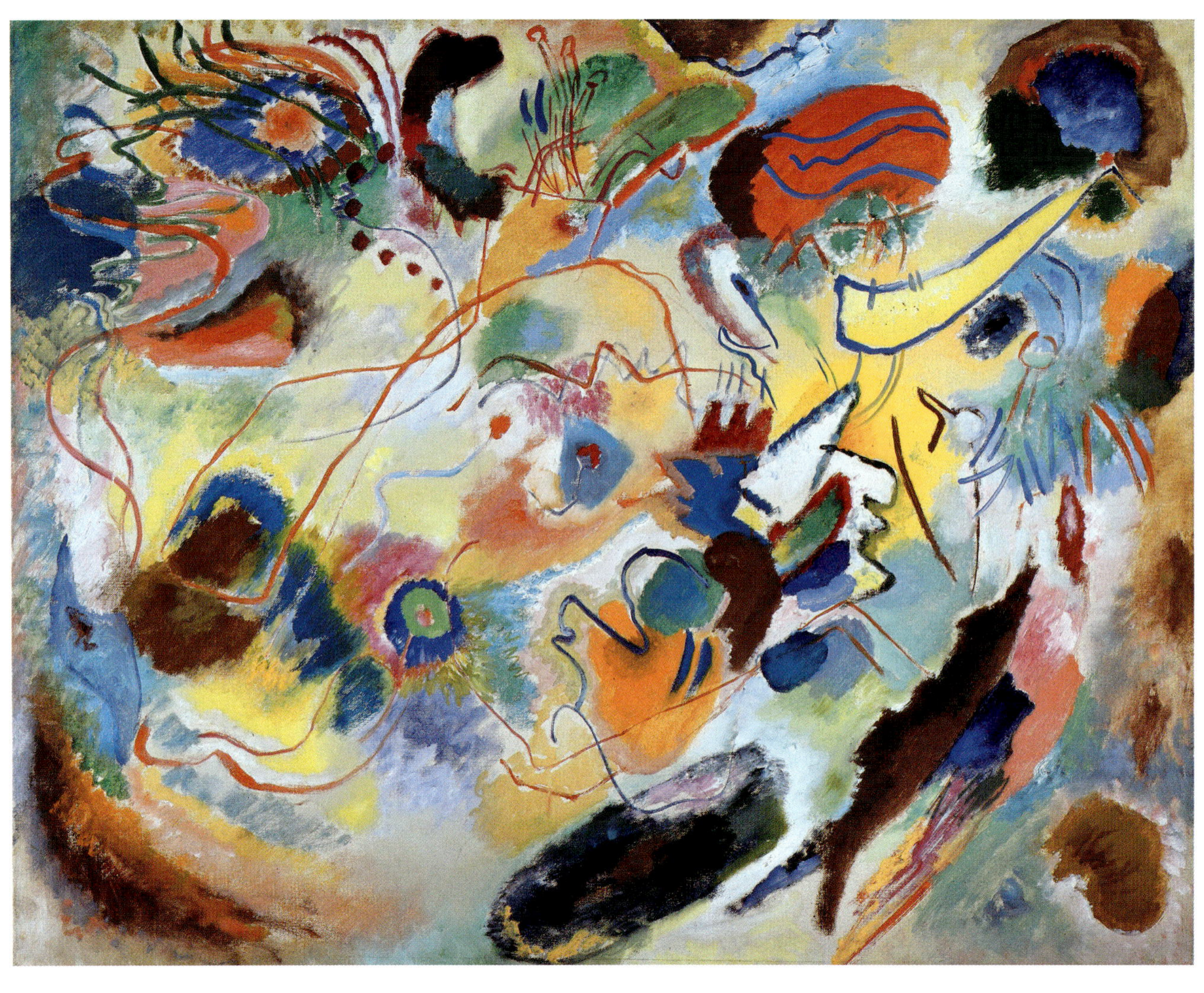

50 **Study for Composition VII**
1913
Oil and tempera on canvas 78.5 x 100.5
Städtische Galerie im Lenbachhaus, Munich

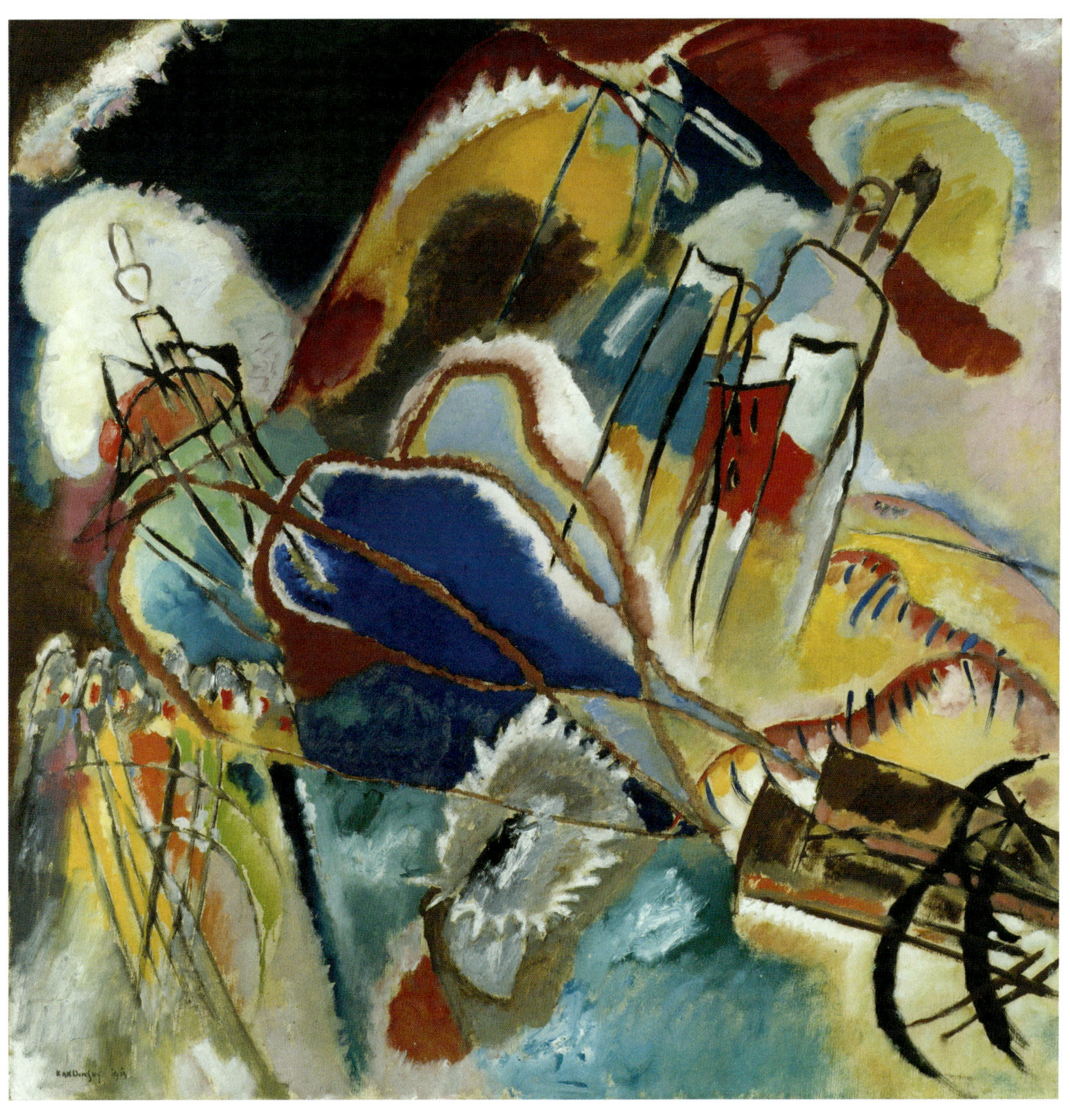

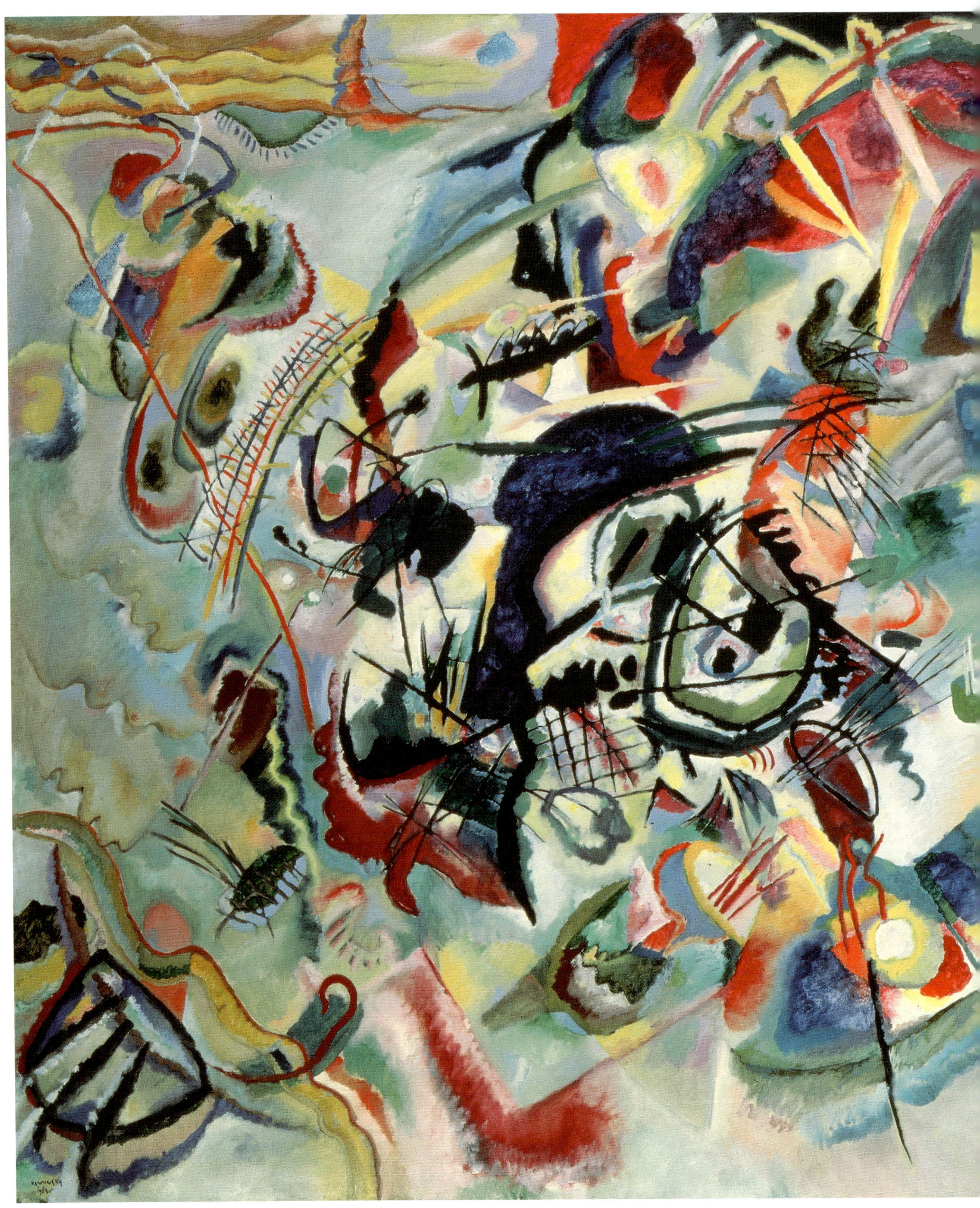

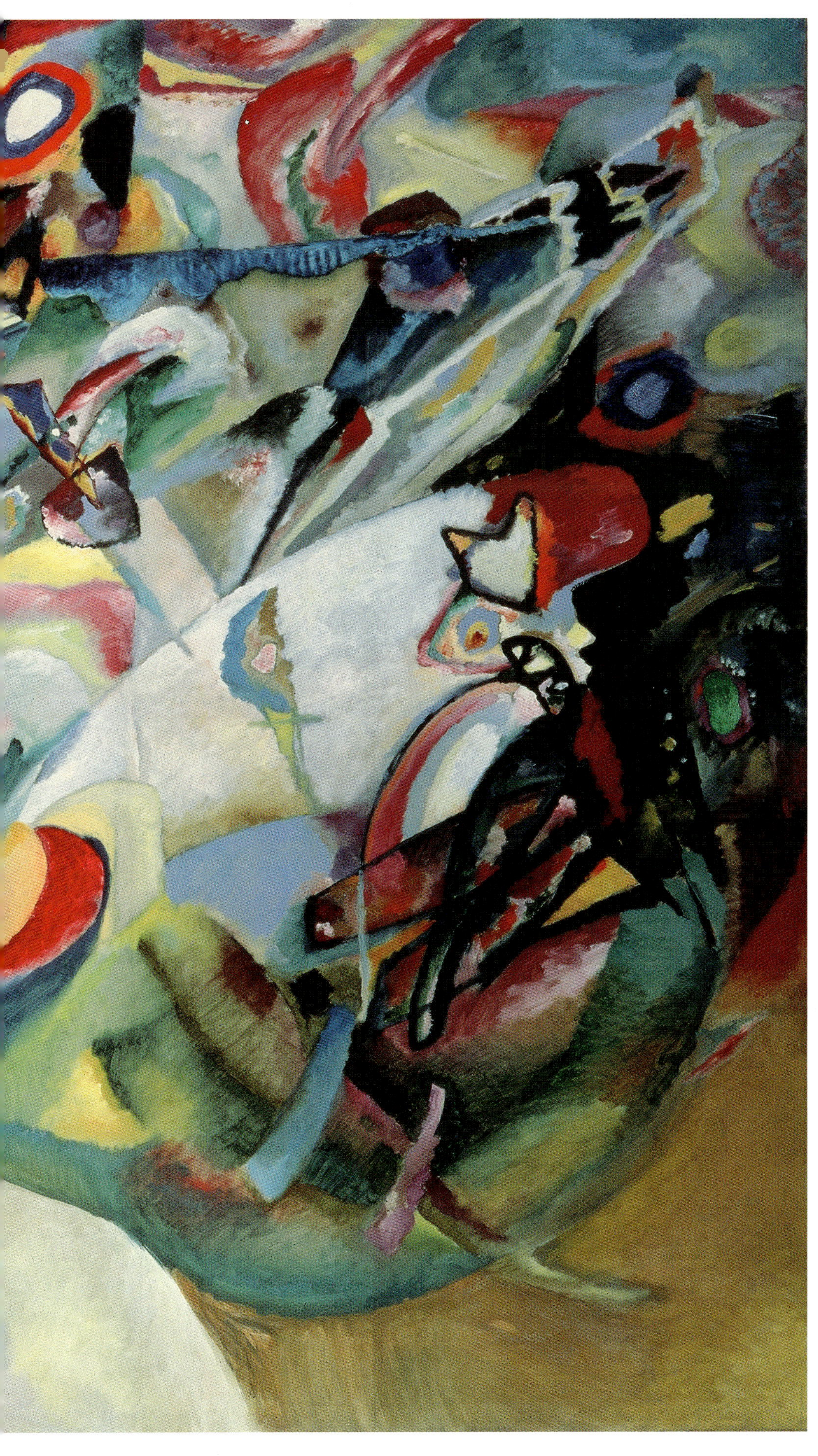

52 Composition VII
1913
Oil on canvas 200 x 300
The State Tretyakov Gallery, Moscow

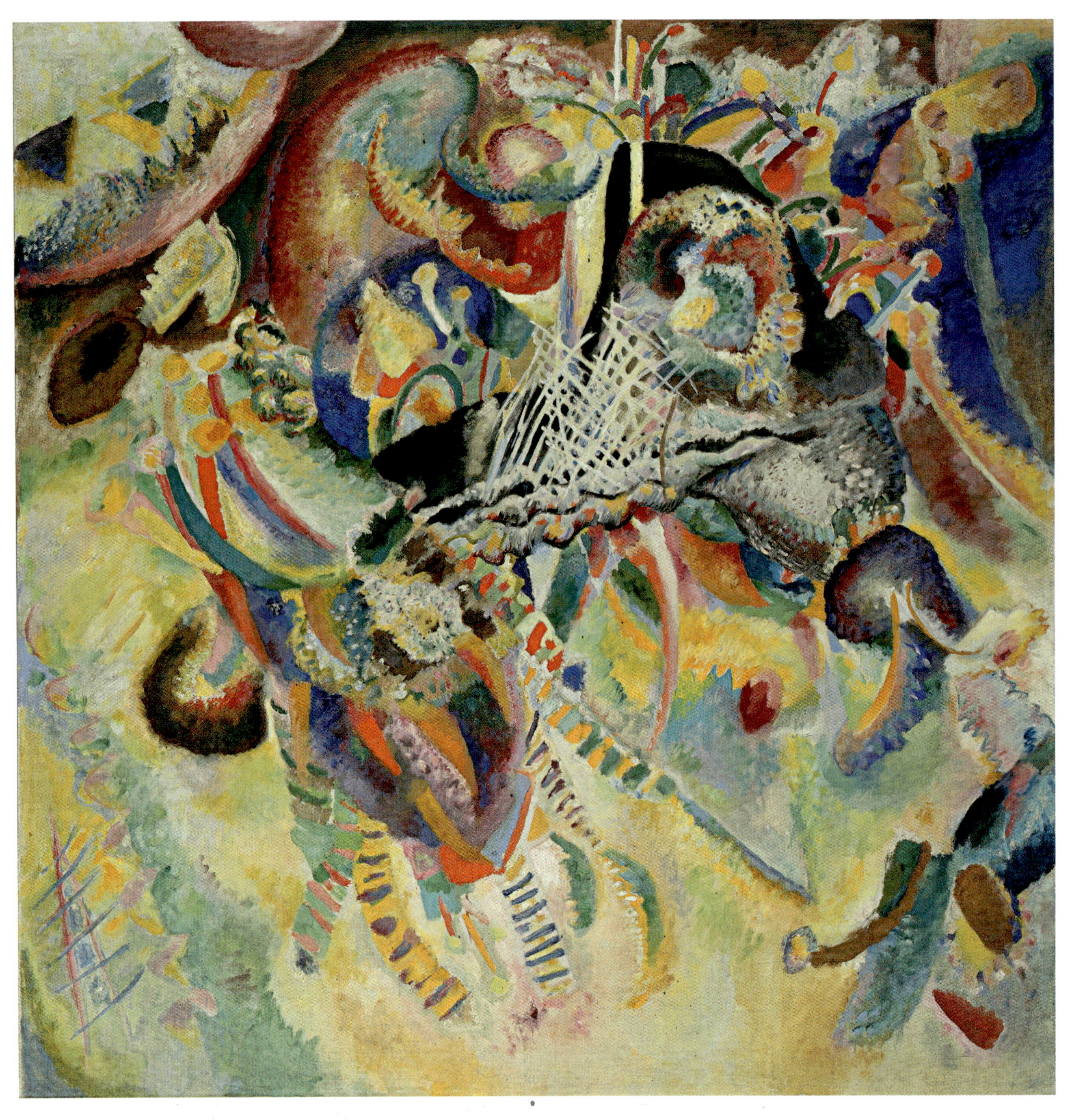

53 Fugue
1914
Oil on canvas   129.5 x 129.5
Fondation Beyeler, Riehen / Basel

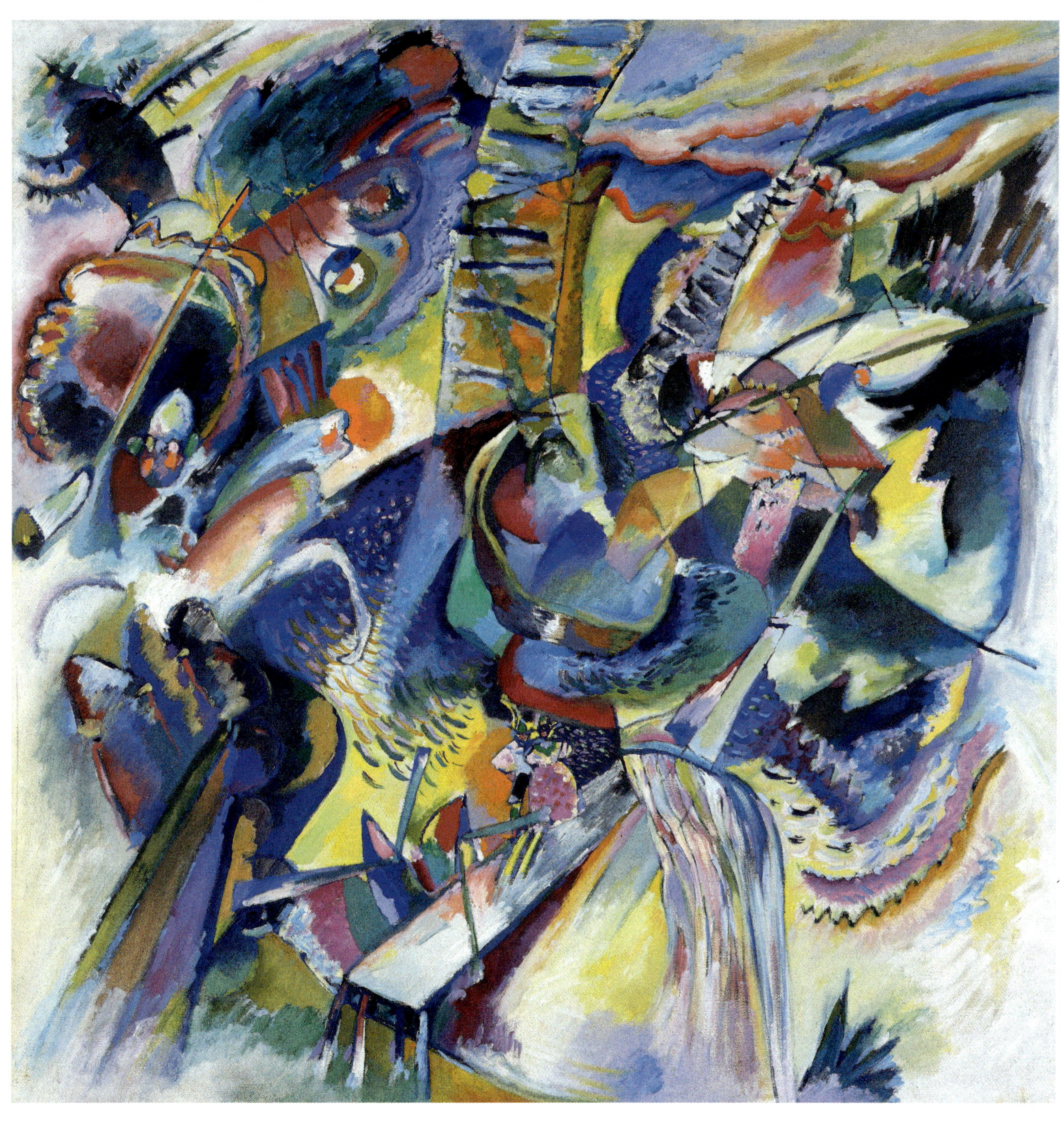

54 **Improvisation Gorge**
1914
Oil and gouache on canvas 110 x 110.3
Städtische Galerie im Lenbachhaus, Munich

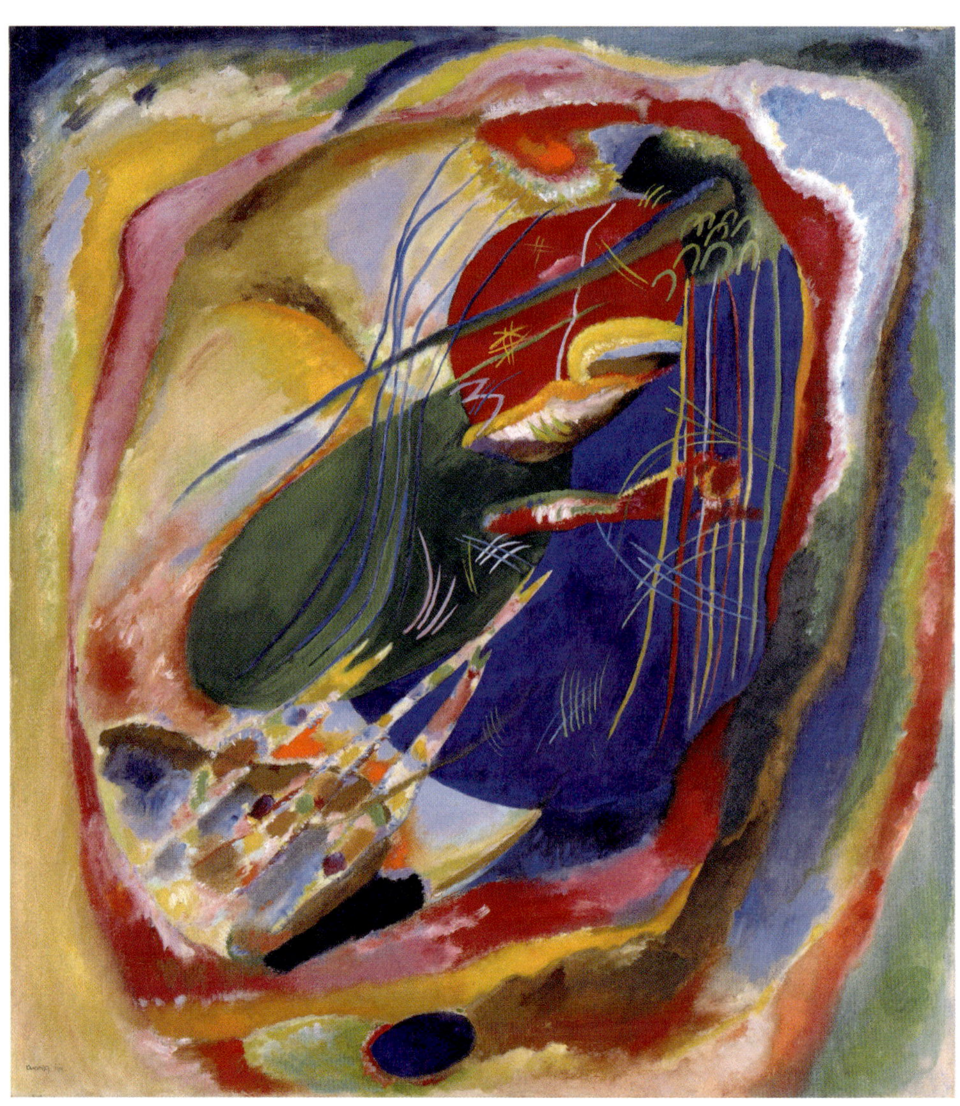

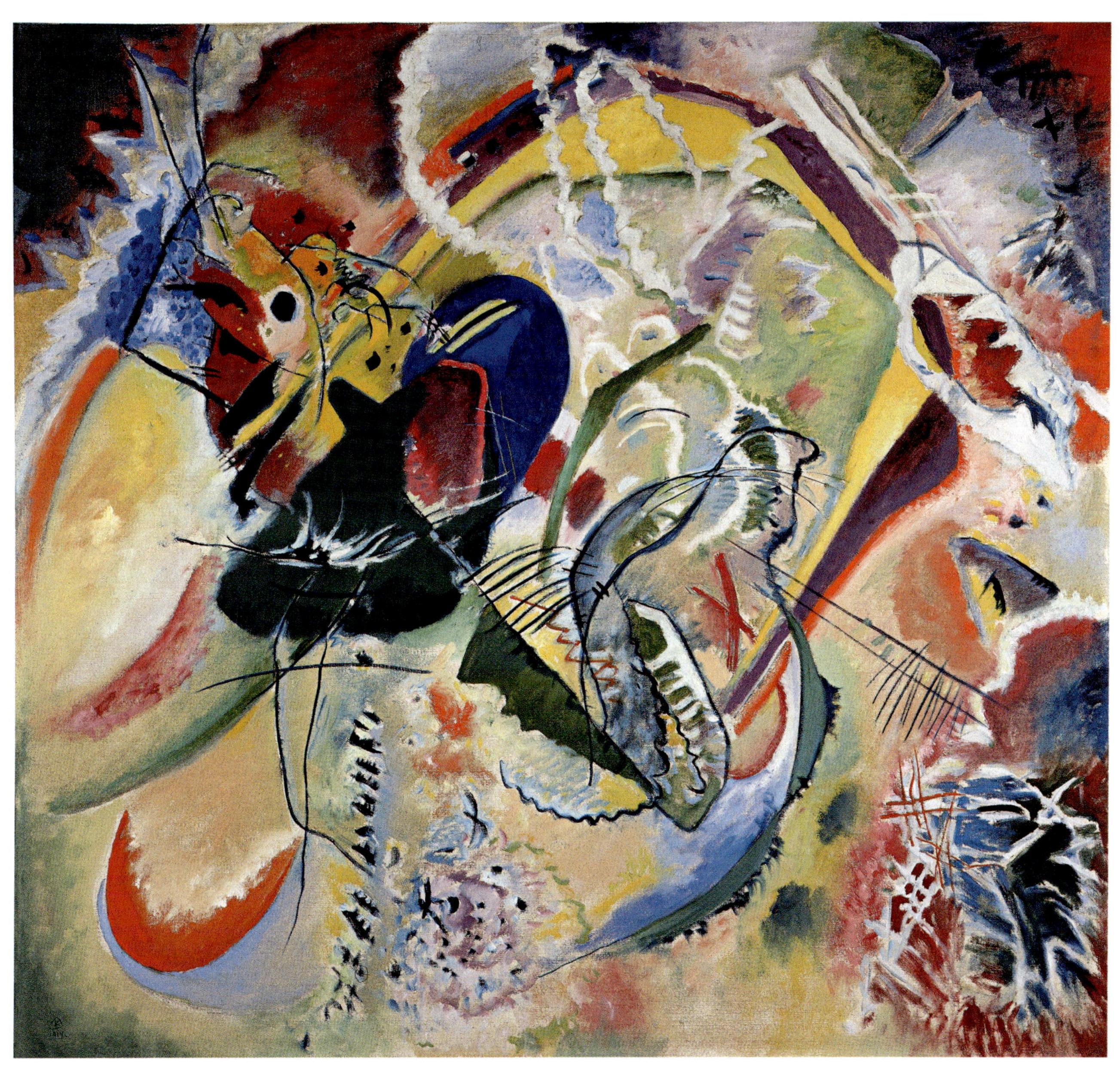

56 **Improvisation 35**

1914
Oil on canvas 110.5 x 120

Kunstmuseum Basel

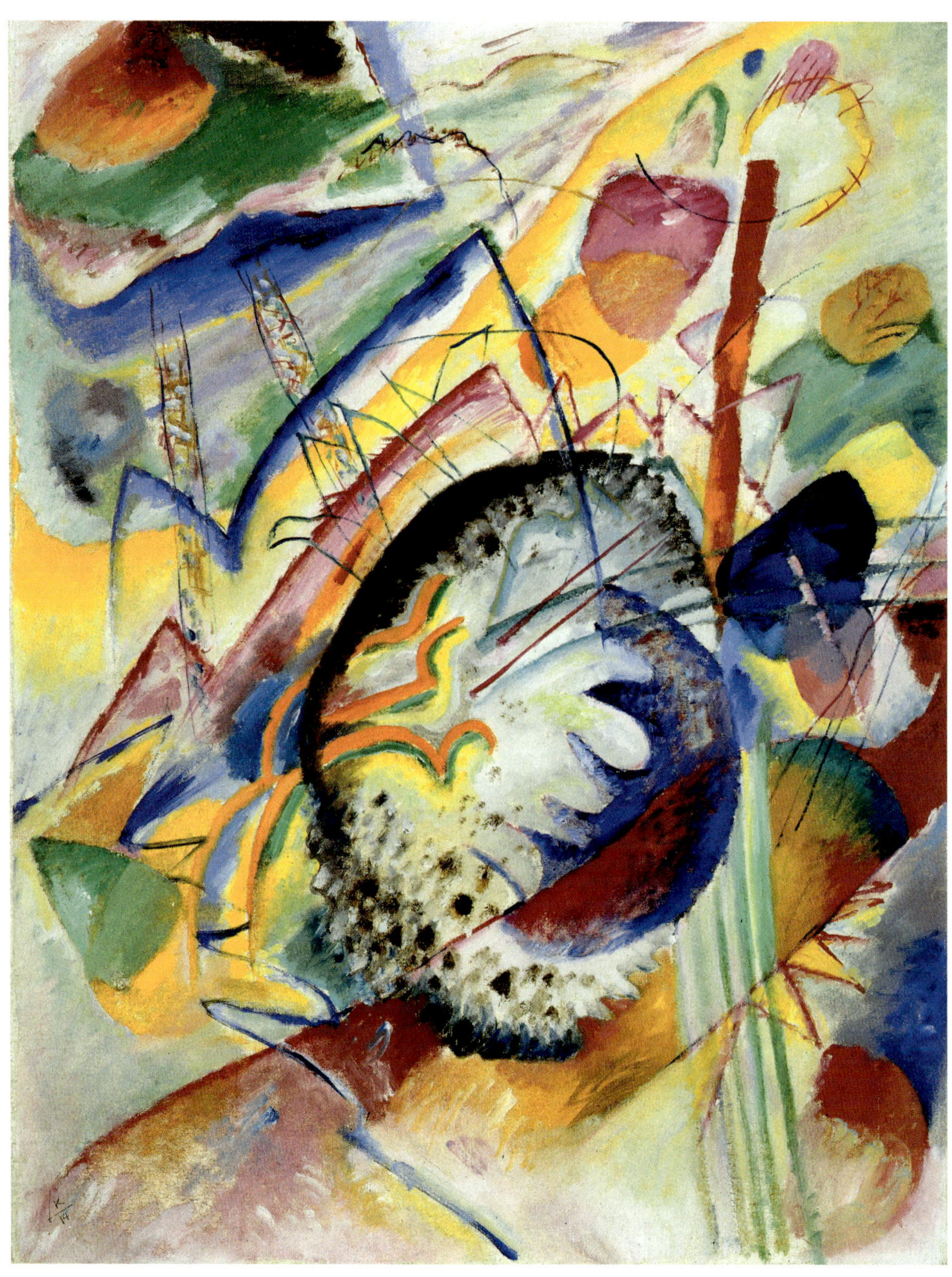

 Improvisation with Cold Forms
1914
Oil on canvas   120 x 140
The State Tretyakov Gallery, Moscow

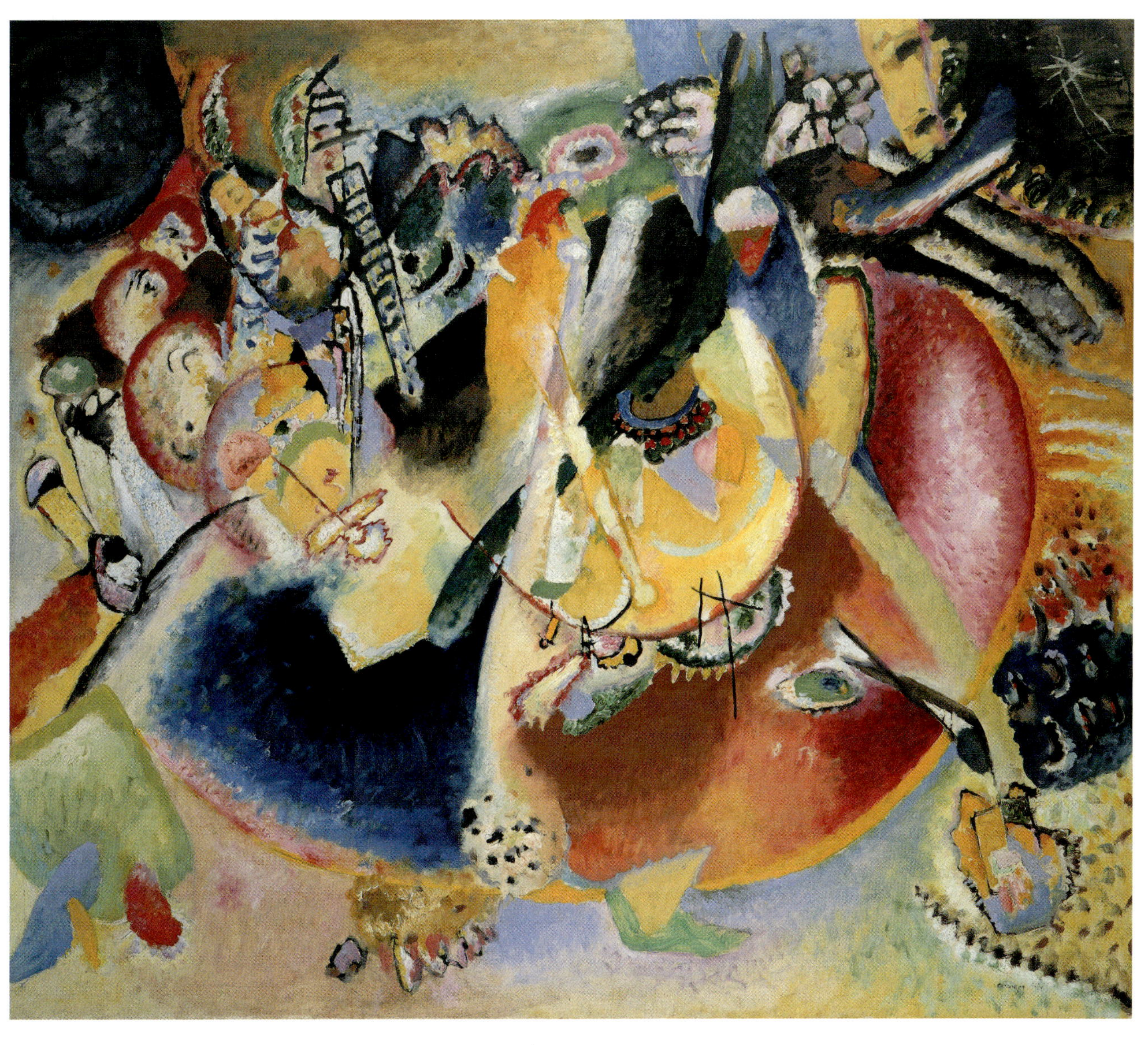

59 **Painting with Red Spot**
1914
Oil on canvas   130 x 130

Musée National d'Art Moderne, Centre Georges Pompidou, Paris.
Centre de Création Industrielle. Donated by Nina Kandinsky 1976

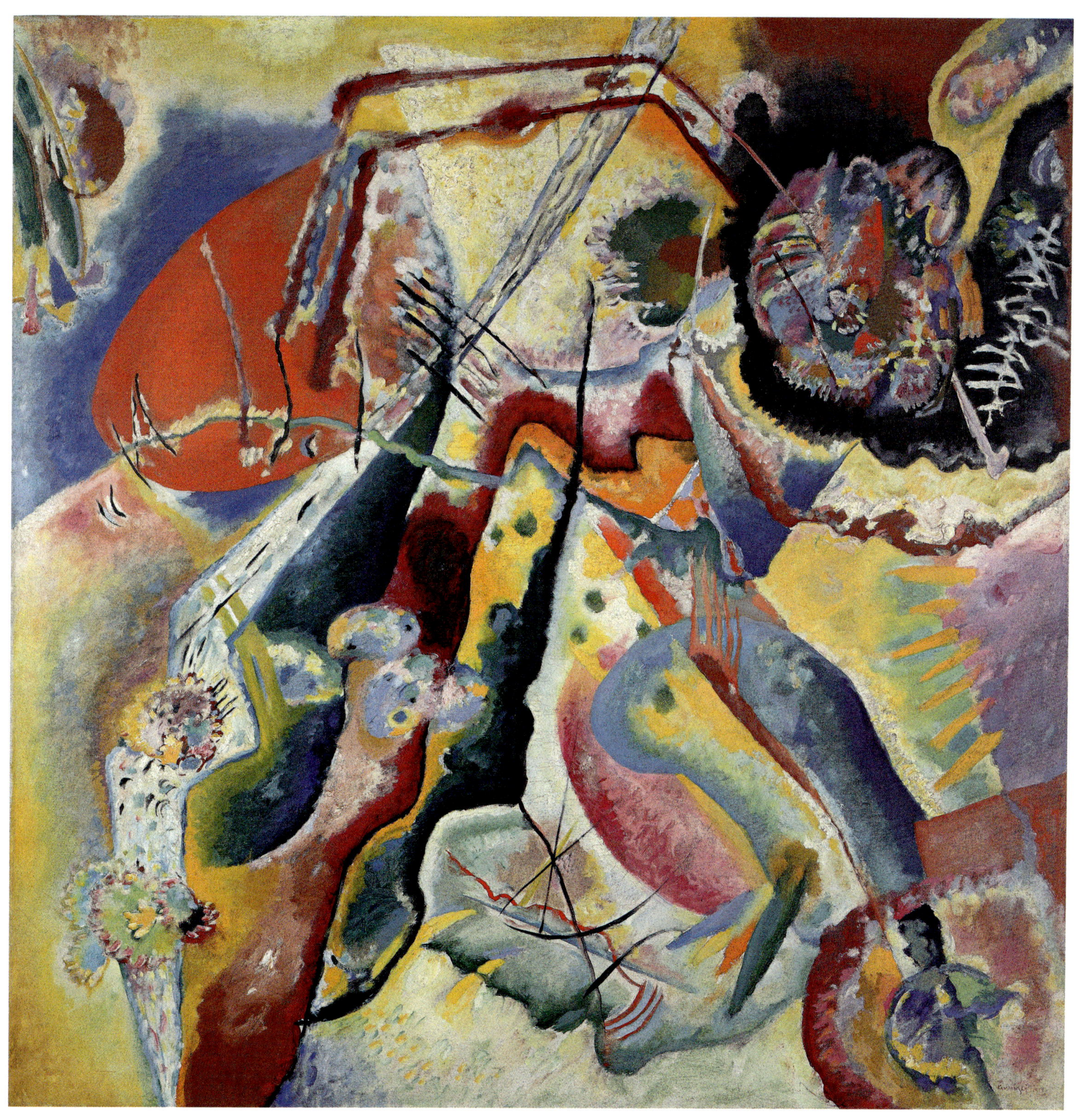

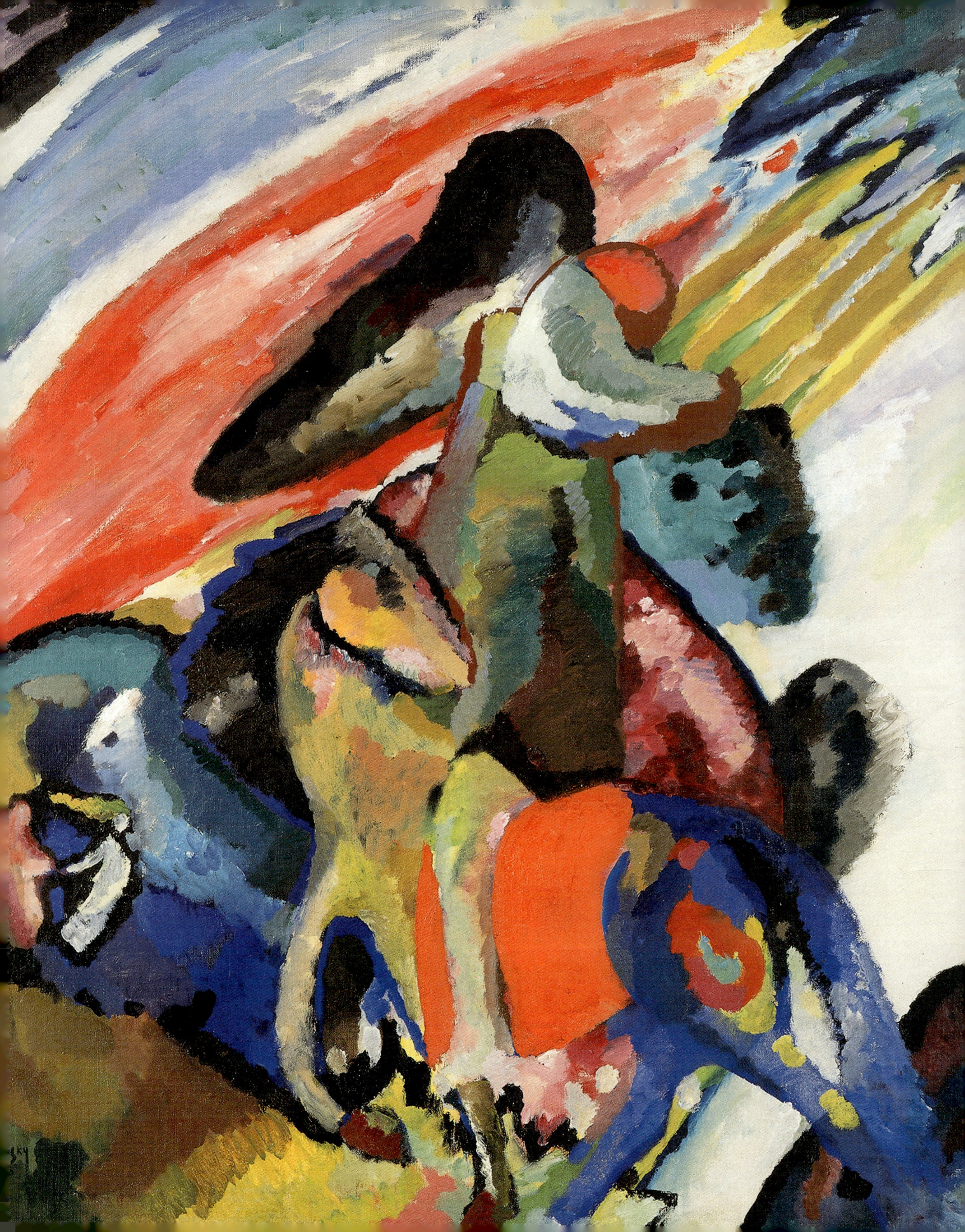

Kandinsky – Resurrection and Cultural Renewal

NOEMI SMOLIK

'I calmly chose the Resurrection as the theme for *Composition 5*, and the Deluge for the sixth. One needs a certain daring if one is to take such outworn themes as the starting point for pure painting. It was for me a trial of strength, which in my opinion has turned out for the best.'

Improvisation 12
1910
(FIG.29, DETAIL)

'We will include some reports on the Russian religious movement in which *all* classes participate. For this I have engaged my former colleague Professor Bulgakov (Moscow, political economist, one of the greatest experts on religious life).'

THIS PROUD DECLARATION OF INTENT COMES IN A LETTER FROM Wassily Kandinsky to his friend and colleague Franz Marc on 1 September 1911.[1] At the time they were working on a new almanac, *Der Blaue Reiter*, which was to be published in Munich by Piper & Co. in May 1912.[2] Besides contributions from the two editors and their mutual friend August Macke, the almanac also had an essay by Leonid Sabaneyev[3] about the Russian composer Alexander Skriabin (1872-1915) and articles about contemporary music by Arnold Schoenberg and the Russian composer Thomas von Hartmann, who was himself in contact with Sergei Diaghilev (1872-1929), the artistic director of the Russian Ballet. But there was no article by Bulgakov. Instead the editors published a text about contemporary Russian art by Vladimir Burlyuk, a friend of Kasimir Malevich. In this article Burlyuk, an artist like his brother David, vehemently distanced himself from the Realism favoured by the 'Peredvischniki'[4] and even revealed that he regarded the term *peredvischniki* (itinerant painters) itself as little short of an expletive.

The new almanac was remarkable for its unusual wealth of illustrations which ranged well beyond the established canon of styles and epochs: medieval prints rub shoulders with African masks, Russian folk art, Bavarian glass paintings, Classical reliefs and paintings by Paul Cézanne, Henri Rousseau, Paul Klee and Vladimir Burlyuk. Only one other European art journal of the day was as richly illustrated: *Mir Iskusstva* (*The World of Art*), published in St Petersburg by Diaghilev. Not only did the almanac and the journal take the same 'democratic' approach to works from very different epochs and cultures, they both championed the work of Skriabin. This is perhaps not surprising in view of the fact that Kandinsky was personally well acquainted with the Russian journal. He himself wrote on contemporary art in Munich for *Mir Iskusstva*, and in his own paintings there are motifs that clearly allude to works by Mikhail Vrubel (1856-1910), Ivan Bilibin (1876-1942) and Nicholas Konstantinovich Roerich (1874-1947) that were reproduced in *Mir Iskusstva*.[5] But let us return to Kandinsky's letter to Marc and his wish to engage the services of his former teacher and future colleague Professor Bulgakov as a contributor to the almanac. Who was Bulgakov? And was he part of any 'movement'?

Sergei Bulgakov (1871–1944), like Kandinsky, studied law at Moscow University. While he was still an undergraduate, he started to study the writings of Karl Marx and was immediately won over. He devoted his time to researching economic and social structures and jurisdiction in rural settlements which operated as communes or 'mirs'. Following the abolition of serfdom in 1861, the communes had attained a greater degree of autonomy in matters of administration, jurisdiction and education. In the second half of the nineteenth century the prevailing legal system in the mirs was not structured according to the same principles as the Western-oriented system based on Roman law that applied in the tsarist towns and cities. However, after 1880 the tensions that arose from the existence of two separate legal systems in one country prompted leading Russian lawyers, trained in Roman law, to lobby for a single jurisdiction that would apply in both town and country. The supporters of harmonisation had a prominent spokesman in the highly regarded lawyer and member of the Russian Academy, Vladimir Danilovich Spasovich (1829–1906). In the opposing camp was Fyodor Dostoevsky (1821–81), who defended the peasants' legal system and their right to autonomy. Dostoevsky was convinced that, when it came to apportioning guilt and meting out punishment, the peasants' legal procedures – which addressed each case individually – were superior to Roman law, which took a purely normative approach to the assessment of guilt.[6] Indeed, Dostoevsky suggested that those in favour of harmonisation should undertake a detailed study of the peasants' legal system rather than condemning it from on high as 'outmoded'; he proposed instead that the more Western system operating in the towns and cities should be extended to accommodate a similar flexibility. Bulgakov was one of the first to take this demand seriously, and went in person to the countryside to see the different system for himself. He was soon followed there by his student Kandinsky.

As his understanding of rural economic, social and legal structures grew, Bulgakov became increasingly sceptical of the absolute universalist claims of Marxism, which took no account of the cultural and historical differences and particularities he found in the village communes. In his significantly titled book, *Ot marksizma k idealizmu* (*From Marxism to Idealism*), published in Moscow in 1903, which traces his own intellectual development, Bulgakov presents Marxism as an ideology that has already been overtaken by developments in Russian society. In his view the materialist principles of Marxism had been invalidated not only by the living example of the Russian peasants but also by the latest advances in scientific research. Bulgakov felt it was not materialism that would shape the already emergent knowledge base of the future, but the latest findings by scientists in Western Europe and Russia, combined with centuries-old ideas handed down from one generation to the next in the Russian countryside. He saw on the horizon a new depth of understanding that would supersede the 'one-dimensionality' of the materialist positivism of Marxism, a new post-idealist idealism that would pave the way for Russian culture to become a force in its own right, free of the clutches of the Western European hegemony.

Bulgakov's contemporaries took his book as evidence of a turning point in Russian cultural politics and it was very well received by his disciples. In 1915, when Malevich was looking for a title for the manifesto that was to accompany the showing of his *Black Square* at the *Last Futurist Exhibition*, he came up with *From Cubism and Futurism to Suprematism*,[7] which alluded to Bulgakov's book.

Around 1900 Bulgakov joined forces with Nikolai Alexandrovich Berdyaev (1874-1948). Having also originally studied law (in Kiev), Berdyaev had been banished to Siberia in 1898 for his contacts to socialist groups. In Siberia he started to study the writings of Dostoevsky and Vladimir Sergeyevich Solovyov (1853-1900). According to his own account of the time, this effected a fundamental change in his thinking.[8] On his return from Siberia, he met Bulgakov (who had been teaching political economy at Moscow University since 1887) and supported him in his struggle against materialist positivism which, by the late nineteenth century, had taken hold in many Russian universities as an obscure faith of sorts which served many Russian intellectuals as a 'substitute' religion. In 1905 Bulgakov and Berdyaev founded the journal *Novye Puti* (*New Paths*), which supported the idea of a distinctively Russian path not only in art, music and literature, but also in the sciences. Its main criticisms of the status quo were directed against materialism as an ideology that was intrinsically alien to the traditions of Russian culture. At the same time, the journal promoted the idea of a reconciliation of city-dwellers' ideas and the much more religious thinking of the rural population. This may be the reason why the movement they had established was often

FIG 23
Colourful Life
1907
Oil on canvas 130 x 162.5
Städtische Galerie im
Lenbachhaus, Munich

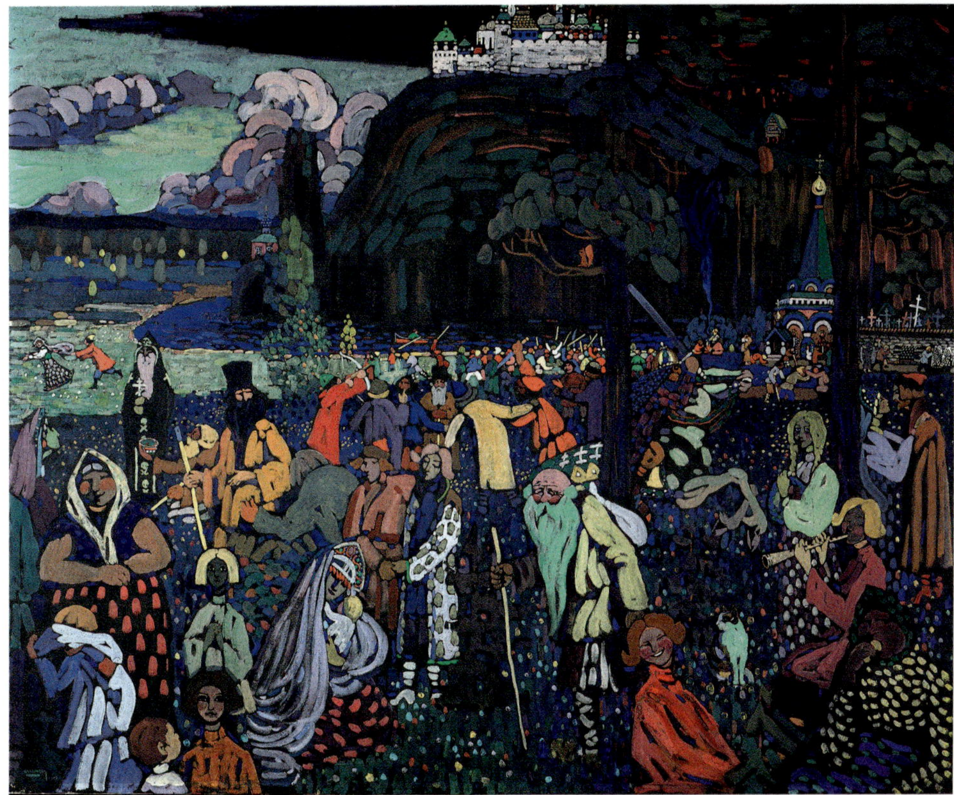

misguidedly accused of having religious aspirations. In fact Bulgakov
and Berdyaev were interested in preserving and advancing a different,
non-Western European culture, which means that Kandinsky's
association of the name of Bulgakov with a 'religious movement' was
somewhat misleading. Not by chance, however, he does specifically
emphasise the fact that 'all' levels of Russian society participate in this
movement.[9] This is in itself an important point in that it is the first
time since Tsar Peter the Great set Russia's sights firmly on the West
that intellectuals – who had enjoyed a Western education – were
seeking to forge closer links with the traditions of rural Russia.
This turning point in certain intellectuals' attitudes to their own
cultural traditions led to the emergence of a movement whose
protagonists like to compare it with the earlier Renaissance in Western
Europe. Consequently some started to refer to it as the 'Russian
Renaissance', while others – including Diaghilev and his followers[10] –
even described it as a 'Russian Resurrection'. In the years after 1900
this movement attracted numerous academics from the fields of law
and economics, from philosophy and theology – as well as those
artists, writers and musicians who, at Diaghilev's side, had already

committed themselves to raising the status of their 'own' culture. They took heart from the debate, instigated by Bulgakov and Berdyaev, concerning the future direction of Russia, seeing it as an affirmation of their own efforts which had so far been conducted outside the universities. In 1909 the champions of a more self-sufficient, Russian culture, untouched by materialist positivism, came together in the almanac *Vechi*, edited by Mikhail O. Gershenzon, later a friend of Malevich.[11] The very title – meaning 'milestone' – is programmatic, and the almanac's appearance was to set an important marker in the striving for a Russian cultural identity and self.

Like his teacher Bulgakov, once he had graduated in law and national economics, Kandinsky spent some months in the country. He stayed in Vologda, an area largely unaffected by Western influences, situated some 460 kilometres (285 miles) north of Moscow. He, too, observed the rural legal system and studied the art and the religious customs of the region. On his return to Moscow he talked in admiring terms of the self-sufficiency of peasant communities, which the majority of intellectuals of the day could only regard with some envy. As Kandinsky wrote later:

After the 'emancipation' of the serfs in Russia, the government gave them control of their own economy, which to the surprise of many people made the peasants politically mature, and their own courts, where within certain limits judges chosen by the serfs from among their own number resolve disputes and may even punish criminal 'actions'.[12]

In 1889 Kandinsky published the results of his research in Vologda. In his 'Contribution to the Ethnography of the Sysola and Vychegda Zyrians. Their National Deities'[13] he describes the pagan practices of the Zyrians (who no longer exist as a distinct ethnic group). In his report 'On Punishment as Meted Out in Peasant Courts in the Moscow District'[14] he presents an impartial account of the court system operating in the mirs, which – as he later writes in his 'Reminiscences' – 'commanded my deepest respect'.[15] By contrast, his assessment of the judicial system (influenced by Roman law) of the tsarist administration would ultimately never satisfy him 'because of its far too cold, far too rational, inflexible logic'.[16] And, as he adds:

> Here, in particular, the people have devised the most human principle, punishing lesser guilt severely and greater offences leniently or not at all. The serfs have their own expression for this: 'according to the man'. Thus it was not a stiff code of law that was established (as, e.g., Roman law – especially the *jus strictum!*), but an extremely free and flexible form, determined *not by the external*, but *exclusively by the internal*.[17]

With these words Kandinsky unmistakably declares his allegiance to Dostoevsky, Solovyov and Bulgakov.

Kandinsky's investigations into the customs of the Russian serfs were not to be without consequences for his future academic path. Significantly, his time in the country ultimately led him to doubt the supposed superiority of the knowledge he had gained at university: 'After six years, however, I began to notice that my earlier belief in the beneficial value of the social sciences and, ultimately, in the absolute rightness of positivistic methods had seriously diminished. Finally I decided to throw overboard the results of many years' work.'[18] He decided to become an artist, despite having completed his dissertation for the Faculty of National Economy, 'On the Legality of Workers' Wages', and despite having been offered an academic post at the University of Dorpat (Tartu, Estonia).

It was only later that he fully realised the crucial influence that these early researches into the peasants' courts were to have on his artistic development and even on his approach to concept of image as such. In Moscow, looking back on his years in Munich, he came to an important conclusion: 'I realised that this vision of art has its origins in the true Russian soul, as it is expressed in the primitive forms of peasants' law, in contrast to the Western European principles of jurisdiction which have their roots in heathen-Roman law.'[19]

Even after he had moved to Munich, Kandinsky's allegiance to life and events in Russia never weakened. This is evident not only from the articles he wrote for Diaghilev's *Mir Iskusstva* and later for Makovsky, editor of the journal *Apollon*, but also – and most importantly – from his own artistic development. After 1903 his paintings increasingly include motifs from the world of old Russian fairy-tales, songs and stories. Mention has already been made of their affinity to the work of Vrubel, Bilibin and Roerich, who had been incorporating Russian traditions into their paintings for some years now. In Kandinsky's paintings after 1903 we therefore find landscapes with old Russian churches, similar to those in Bilibin's compositions, the brightly coloured vessels of the Varangians (the first settlers on Russian soil), taken from paintings by Vrubel and Roerich, and fairy-tale figures like the Firebird or the Rider – favourite motifs in Russian folk art which repeatedly figured in the pages of *Mir Iskusstva*. In the early 1900s the colourful Firebird, a descendent of the Sirens of Antiquity, was an inspiration not only to Russian painters; in 1909 it spurred Igor Stravinsky on to compose one of his most famous scores.

Colourful Life (fig.23), painted in 1907, brings together a whole number of motifs from Russian folk art, including the witch Baba Jaga with her revolving house on chicken's feet. We see here for the first time two saints, whom Kandinsky as it were situates in everyday scenarios, the brothers Boris and Gleb. As the sons of Grand Prince Vladimir of Kiev (978-1015), who were canonised as early as 1071, they soon took their place amongst the patron saints of the Russian people (fig.24). Henceforth Boris and Gleb, and other saints, would

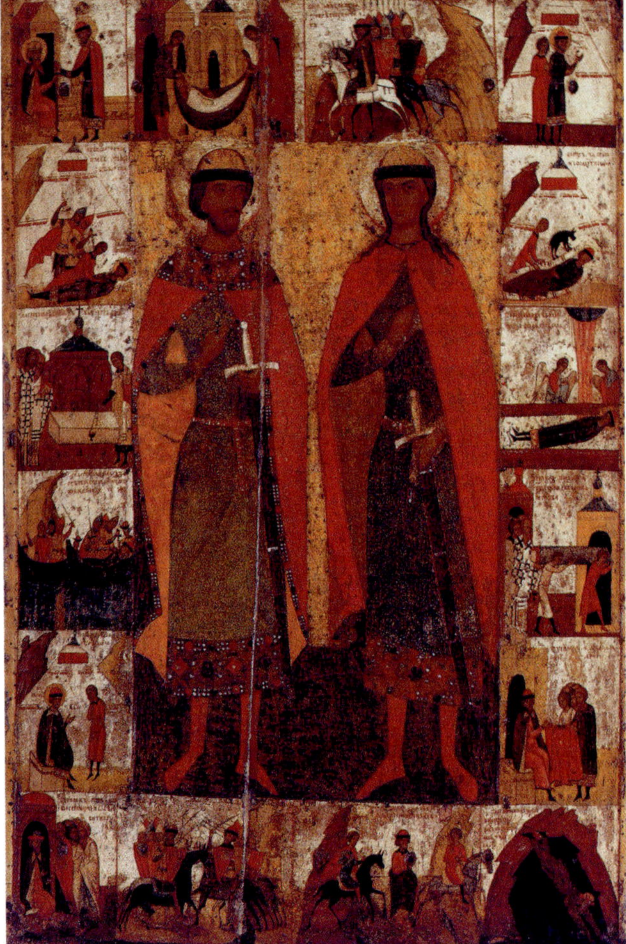

FIG 24
Boris and Gleb with Scenes from their Lives
14TH CENTURY
Tempera on panel 134 x 89
State Tretjakov Gallery, Moscow

FIG 25
All Saints II
1910
Oil on canvas 86 x 99
Städtische Galerie im
Lenbachhaus, Munich

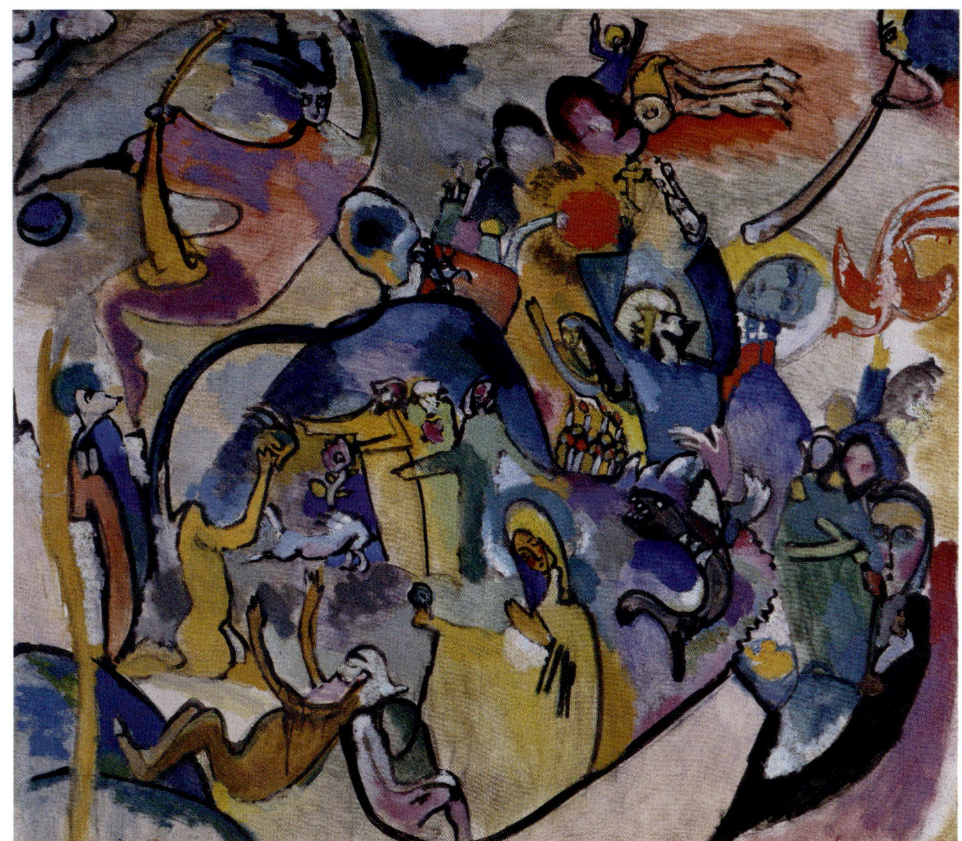

accompany Kandinsky's striving for Abstraction, which culminated in 1913 in his *Composition VII* (no.52).

Over thirty sketches and studies for his large-scale *Composition VII* have survived. In some we can already see a number of strategies that form part of the final version, including a number of clearly defined forms in the centre. Unlike the final version, which is purely abstract, in some of the studies we can make out, besides more indefinable forms, a mountain and a rider. We also find a mountain with a town and a rider in the studies for *Composition IV* 1911 (nos.33–6) and again in the centre of the painting *All Saints II* 1910 (fig.25). Here we discover, too, figures borrowed from Russian icon painters. In front of Grand Prince Vladimir and a model of the Hagia Sophia in Kiev are his sons Boris and Gleb who, until the early twentieth century, were standard figures in the repertoire of the icon painters. At the foot of the mountain in *All Saints II*, a celestial army stands ready to assist the brothers. According to legend this army resides within the mountain, at the ready to save the Russian people and their patron saints in times of need. Our attention is also drawn to the three Cappadocian Fathers of the Orthodox Church – John Chrysostomos, Basileios the Great and Gregory Nazianzus – who, standing together at the foot of the mountain, embody different rhetorical gestures.

The (beheaded) kneeling figure on the right in *All Saints II*, holding his head in his hands, and the standing figure behind him – with a head more like that of a dog – are also stock figures in Russian icons (fig.26). John the Forerunner (also known as John the Baptist), Jan Predteča, represents the belief in the guarantee of resurrection through baptism, while St Christopher behind him, with the dog's head of an ancient kynokephal, also fits in the same world. According to one legend, St Christopher had been baptised in an especially miraculous way. His battles to establish Christianity are as legendary as his ultimate martyrdom. Consequently Kandinsky depicted both of these 'heroes' in a glass painting with the Russian title 'Voskresenie' (*Resurrection*; fig.27). Kandinsky adopts these saints as key figures in Russian icon painting. Hence, in *All Saints II*, the Old Testament figure of the prophet Elijah in his chariot of fire, on the left of the composition, also fits perfectly in this scenario. As he ascends into heaven in his chariot of fire, Elijah – who goes back to the pagan sun god Perun – prefigures Christ's ascent into heaven.

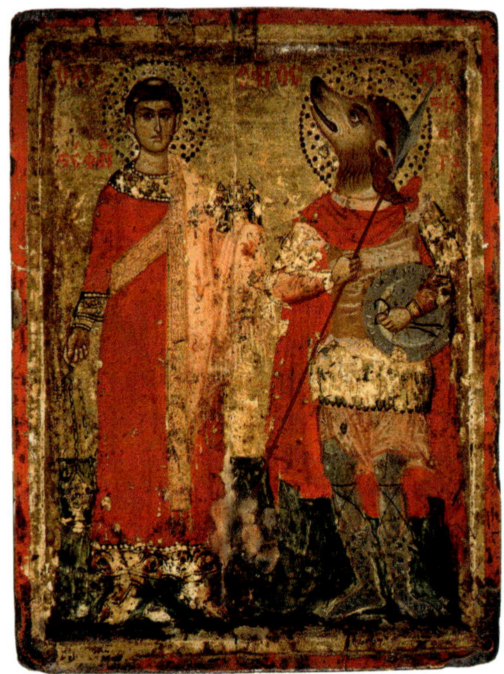

FIG 26
Stephanos and Christophoros
EARLY 18TH CENTURY
Tempera on wood
20.6 x 15.8 x 1.7
Ikonen-Museum, Recklinghausen

FIG 27
Resurrection
1911
Paint on glass 21.7 x 11.6
Städtische Galerie im
Lenbachhaus, Munich

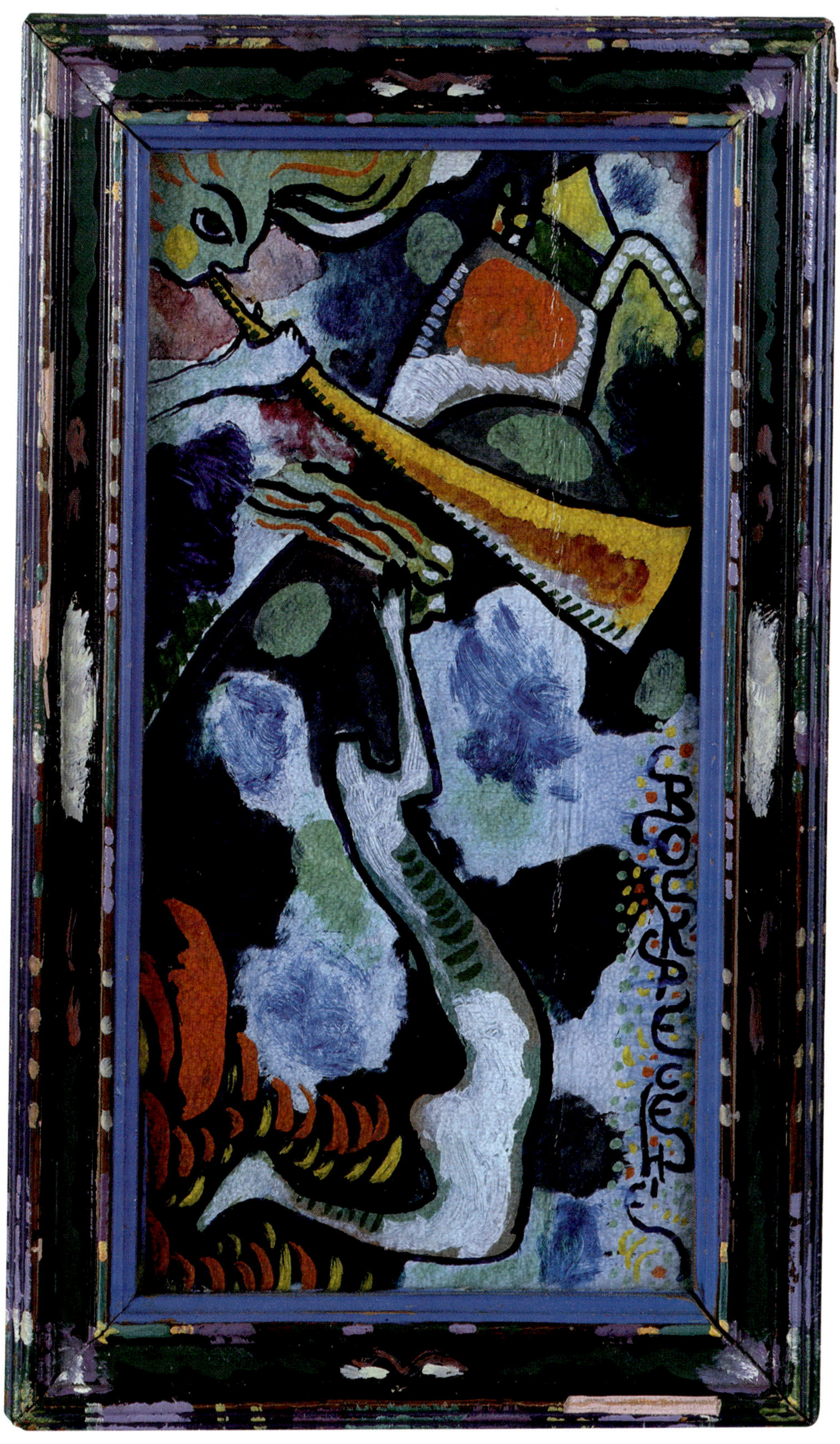

Two riders in *All Saints II*, one disappearing over the crest of the mountain, the other at the foot of the mountain, are also recognisable leitmotifs. The rider on the crest of a mountain is a familiar figure in Kandinsky's paintings between 1910 and 1913, witness the cover of his theoretical text *Concerning the Spiritual in Art,* published in Munich in 1912 and a seminal text in the development of Abstraction. And the cover illustration for the almanac *Der Blaue Reiter* is of course dominated by a rider (fig.31). Even in the later figurative paintings – which followed the abstract *Composition VII* of 1913 – we see the rider again.[20] In fact, in the paintings Kandinsky made between 1911 and 1913 no other motif occurs as frequently as the rider. It is all the more astonishing, then, that its origins have never been systematically researched.

Without doubt the motif of the rider has its roots in Russian icons. Of central importance in this connection is the figure of St George (fig.28). To this day, the many variants of the legend of St George all in essence relate that he prevented a princess from being sacrificed to the fire-breathing dragon, by heroically slaying the beast. The obvious similarities between this legend and the widespread folk tales in which a hero fights to save a princess no doubt account in part for the status enjoyed by St George. However, the notion of killing a dragon – and thus conquering evil – goes far beyond the figure of St George. The Archangel Michael, for one, also slayed a dragon. According to the Book of Revelation, it is St Michael, as the leader of the celestial

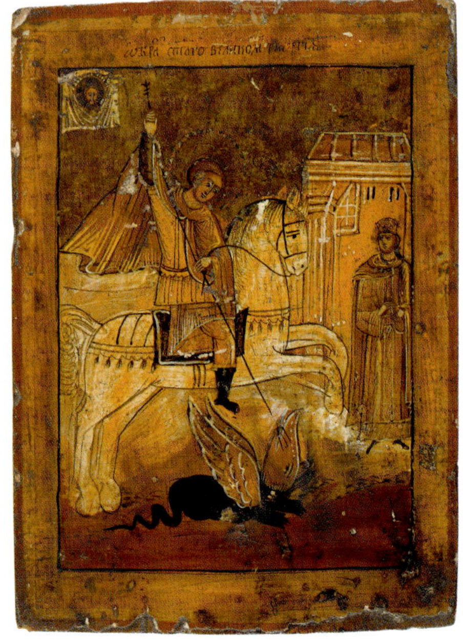

FIG 28
**St George on Horseback
Slaying the Dragon**
19TH CENTURY
Paint on wood
29.5 X 21.5 X 2.3
*Musée National d'Art Moderne,
Centre Georges Pompidou, Paris.
Bequest of Nina Kandinsky, 1981*

Improvisation 12
1910
Oil on canvas 97 x 106.5
Städtische Galerie im
Lenbachhaus, Munich

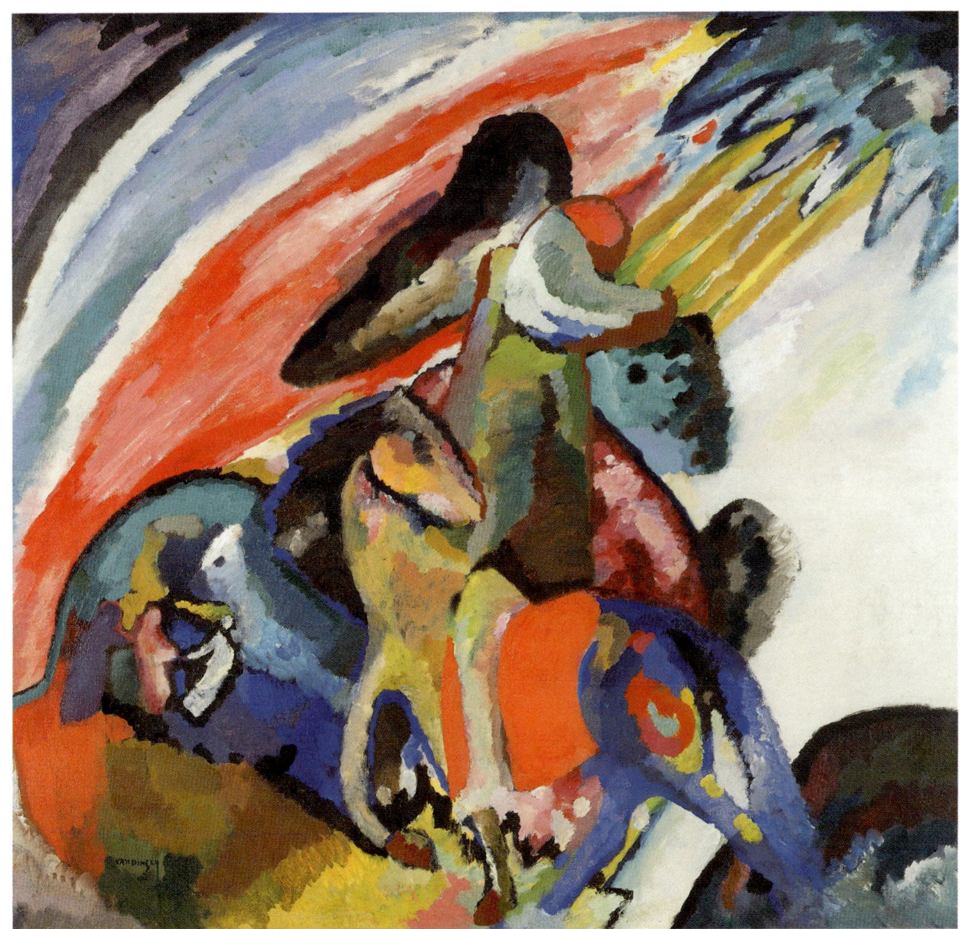

army, who sounds the trumpet on the Last Day, awakening the dead and leading their souls to judgement. Both saints are represented on countless icons. St George, for instance, appears on a white horse outside the city gates, fighting with a serpent-like dragon, while the princess, the *carevna*, watches from a safe distance.

In the painting *Improvisation 12* 1910 (fig.29) Kandinsky again includes a multitude of details that confirm his familiarity with the traditions of Orthodox iconography. St George is riding a white horse, and he is clad in red and armed with a round shield; even the colours of the shield – yellow, red and green – are in keeping with those used by the icon painters.

The Archangel Michael, who heralds the dawn of a new age with his trumpet, is sometimes seen on a fiery steed in a sky-blue circle filled with golden stars, an aureole borne aloft on either side by angels (fig.30). The image of the apotheosis of the saint portrays him as a powerful figure whose ultimate triumph is the slaying of the dragon.

The book, the Holy Scriptures, and the lance crowned with the sign of the Cross denote the triumph of Christianity over evil. A rainbow spans an arc above his hands. The trumpet heralds the conqueror's procession which will culminate in the 'epoch of the great spiritual'. According to Orthodox tradition, the sounding of the trumpet also marks the beginning of this other, spiritual world. Kandinsky's recourse to the traditions of the Orthodox icon is doubly significant. Crucially, the Orthodox view is that the saints depicted on icons are not likenesses as such, for the saints themselves are present in the image, as it were. Consequently, icons are in effect an interface – a physical link – between the materiality of the present and the world of the spirit. They guide us from the visible to the invisible. And the invisible will ultimately

FIG 30
The Archangel Michael
Russian icon
Whereabouts unknown

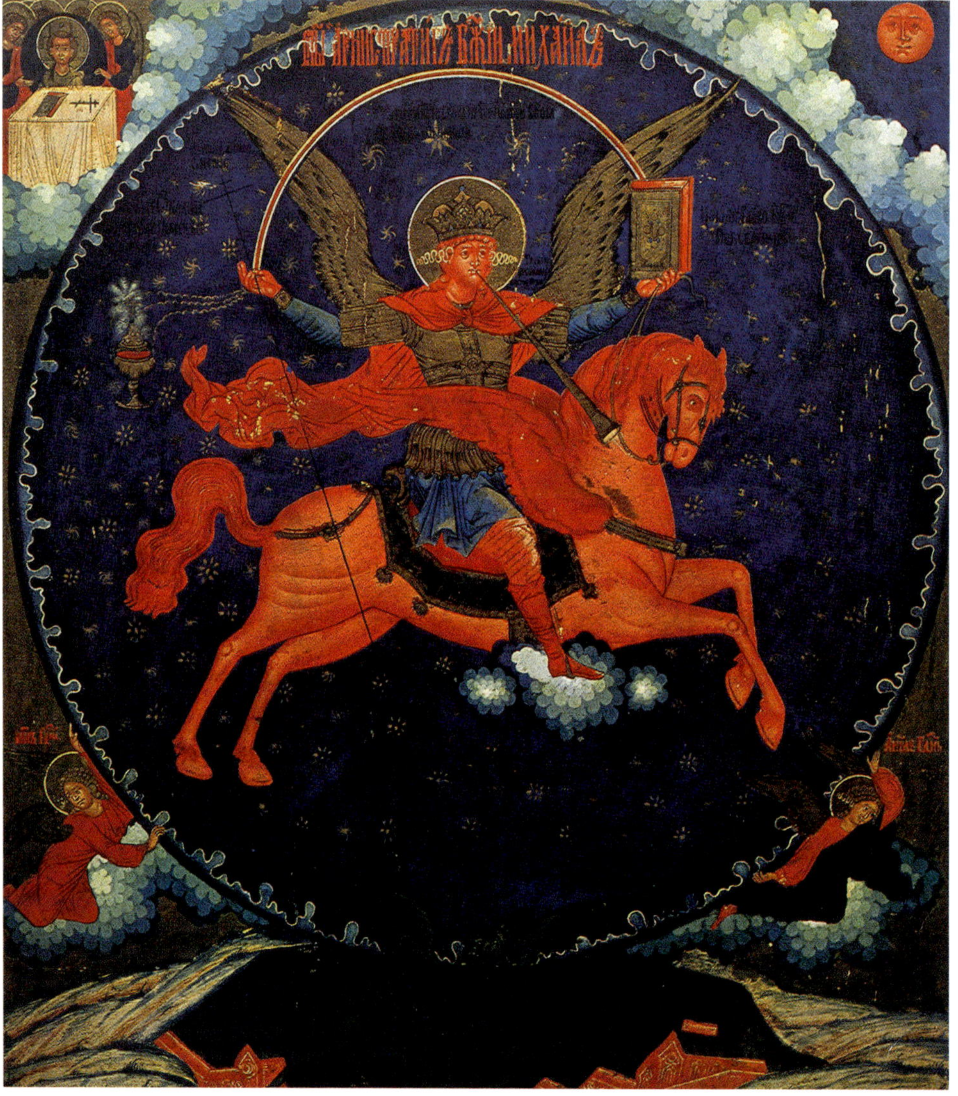

FIG 31
Sketch for the cover of the *Blue Rider Almanac* (*Almanac Der Blaue Reiter*)
1911
Watercolour and pencil
27.7 x 21.8
Städtische Galerie im Lenbachhaus, Munich

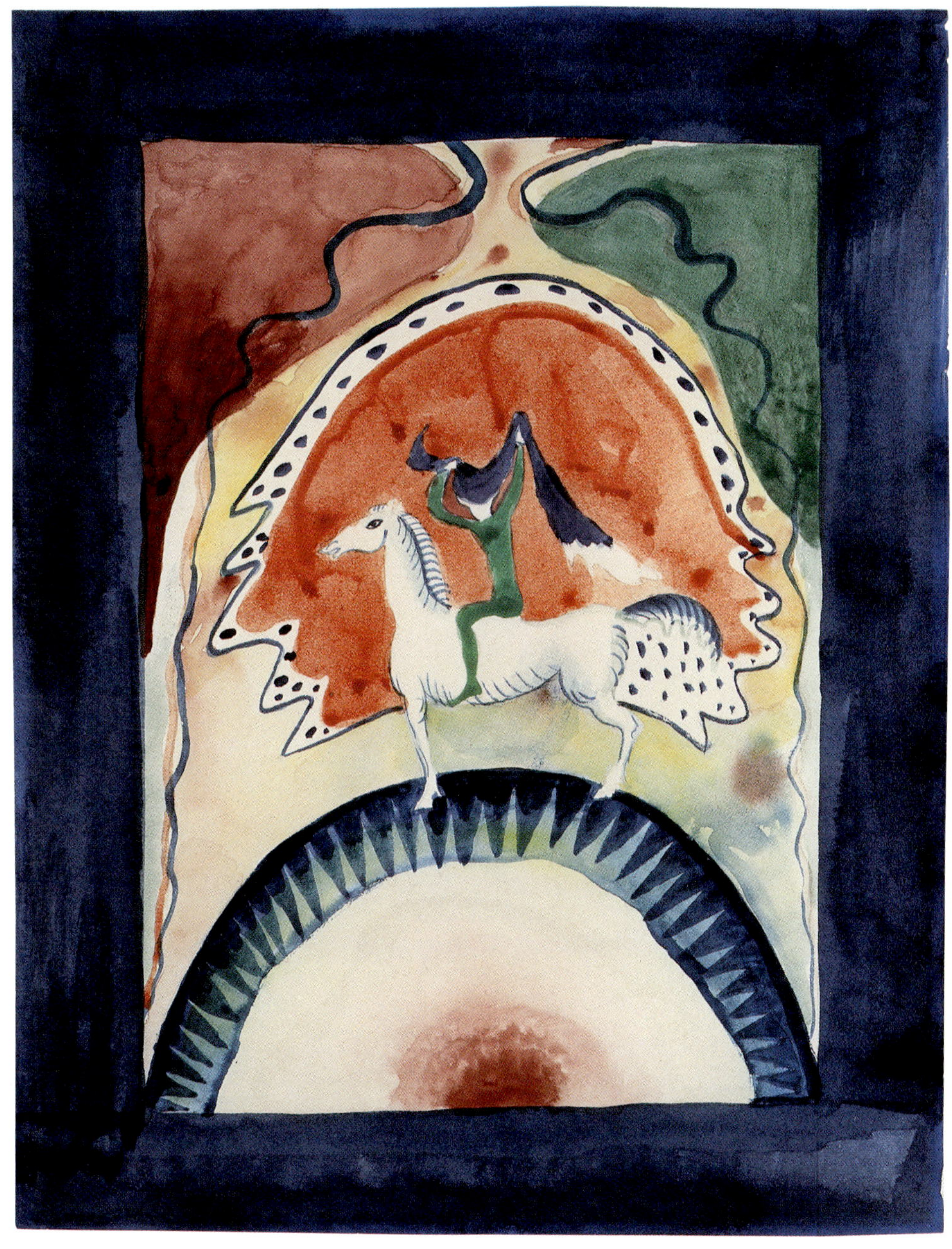

be fully revealed to us at the end of time when our souls are resurrected. St George, and even more so the Archangel Michael, are seen as mediators between this world and the spiritual. Filled with a desire to create an art that would cast off the shackles of representationalism (and hence of 'the material'), it was only natural that Kandinsky would turn to a tradition that from time immemorial had been informed by its belief in the presence of the spiritual in the painted image.

On a sketch for the dust jacket of the *Blue Rider Almanac* of 1911 (fig.31) we see a rider with his hands raised; the semi-circle spanning the distance between his two hands recalls the rainbow above St Michael. Like Michael, the leader of the celestial army, this rider is raised up above the earth. On the cover of *Concerning the Spiritual in Art* the rider stands in a triumphant pose on the crest of a mountain. Whether leaping, hovering or standing, in the examples mentioned here the horse and rider are always portrayed on or above a mountain. Once again, this is not by chance, for in Orthodox iconography – in depictions of the Holy Trinity or of the transfiguration of Christ – the mountain always symbolises the 'Ascent of the Spirit'.

Looking at the sum total of the motifs that, so to speak, accompany Kandinsky on the path to Abstraction, one cannot help but be struck by the fact that these motifs are taken almost exclusively from the iconography of the resurrection or the elevation of the spirit (portrayed as the rider). Moreover, there is a significant instrumentalisation of the archangels Michael and Gabriel, as we have already seen in *All Saints II*, with which we opened our observations. The archangels not only frame the composition with their trumpets; while one is directing the sound of the trumpet towards the centre of the picture, the other is sweeping dynamically towards the same point from the other side of the composition. Bearing in mind their traditional functions, we may assume that all the saints have assembled here at the sound of their trumpet calls. And it is as though the massed saints in the centre of the composition were caught up in some kind of maelstrom. Kandinsky is literally calling on a tradition that tells of the new beginning of a world of the spirit which will ultimately be heralded by these same protagonists. The same trumpets are seen again in two works from 1911, which portray the archangels with the kneeling figures of Jan Predteča and St Christopher: a glass painting entitled *Large Resurrection*, and a watercolour entitled *Sound of Trumpets (Large Resurrection)*.[21]

In the sketches and studies for *Composition V* (fig.12, p.41) and *Composition VII* (nos.33–6), once again we predominantly find motifs associated with the Resurrection and not with the Day of Judgement. [22] As he expressly says in the 'Cologne Lecture':

Composition 2 is painted without theme, and perhaps at that time I would have been nervous of taking a theme as my starting point. On the other hand, I calmly chose the Resurrection as the theme for *Composition 5*, and the Deluge for the sixth. One needs a certain daring if one is to take such outworn themes as the starting point for pure painting. It was for me a trial of strength, which in my opinion has turned out for the best. [23]

No mention here of the Day of Judgement, nor is there any reference to it elsewhere in his writings.

The vision of the Resurrection, which also follows the Deluge, was always alive to Kandinsky as he carved out his path to Abstraction. Several of his paintings from 1912 are entitled *Deluge*. In one of these (no.44) we see a mountain crowned by a tree. Around it are figures defying the waves; a streak of lightning cuts through the picture from the upper right to the lower left. Here, too, Kandinsky's imagery is surprisingly close to that of Russian Orthodox icons, as seen, for instance, in the frescos in the eighteenth-century Church of the Prophet Elijah in Jaroslawl on the River Volga (see also fig.32). The precursor to this image is visible in *Sketch for Deluge I*, [24] which formed the basis of *Composition VI* 1913 (no. 49). This means that not only *Composition V* and *Composition VII* (no.52) have close links with Orthodox iconography, but that the same can also be said of *Composition VI* (no.49) as an image of the Deluge, or of the demise of mankind, which precedes the Resurrection.

But why does Kandinsky return so persistently to the Resurrection? This question is of prime importance in so far as this is Kandinsky's preferred theme during the phase of his work that eventually led to fully fledged Abstraction. His interest in this theme owes much to the debate on 'Russianness' that was largely instigated and directed by Dostoevsky, Solovyov and Diaghilev. They had a vision of cultural rebirth which, as we have seen, was described at the time as a 'Russian Renaissance' or – alluding to the Russian Orthodox tradition – as a 'Resurrection'. This vision has its roots in the desire of Russian artists and academics – as Kandinsky was before he left the country – for their own cultural identity. That this identity was to be defined through a critical questioning of Western modernism and

FIG 32
**The Ascension of the
Prophet Elijah in a
Chariot of Fire**
19TH CENTURY
Paint on wood
26.9 x 22.7 x 2.5
*Musée National d'Art Moderne,
Centre Georges Pompidou, Paris.
Bequest of Nina Kandinsky, 1981*

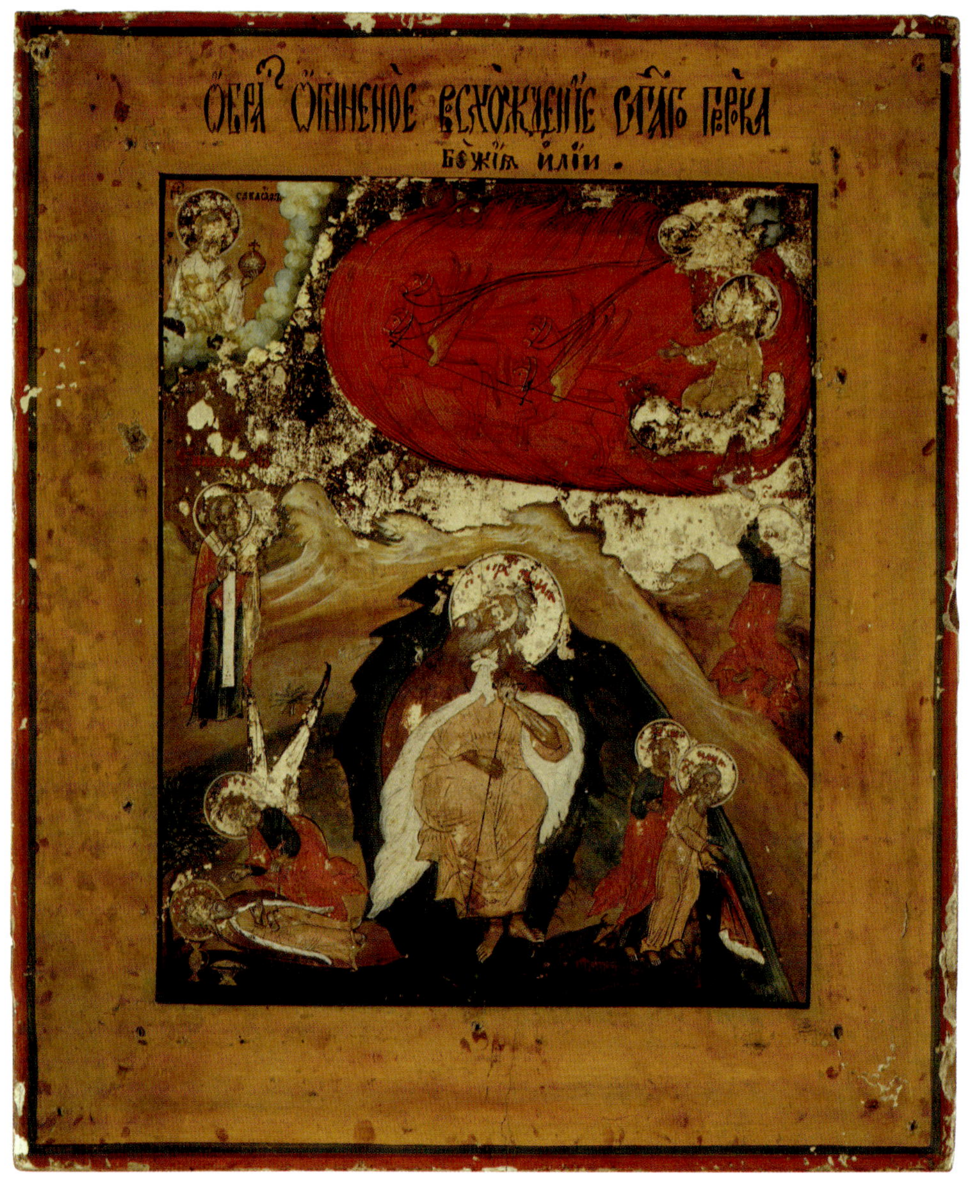

the concomitant scientific epistemology, on one hand, and, on the other hand, by a re-evaluation of innately Russian thinking (untouched by modernism and hence dismissed by the champions of modernism) was a view shared by many Russian artists and academics around 1900. The same players were also convinced that at that time in Russia there were moves under way that would open up new, undreamt-of vistas in the arts and wider human understanding. It was Solovyov who used the image of the Resurrection to express this widespread vision of imminent cultural change. And this image was taken up by Diaghilev and those around him, who saw it as a turning point that would affect every area of Russian life. As he said in a lecture delivered in Moscow in 1905 and published in the journal *Vesy*, in which he described with characteristic pathos a journey he had recently undertaken through his native Russia: 'This was what finally convinced me that we are living through a time of terrifying upheaval, that we are condemned to die so that a new culture may be resurrected.[25]

Since 1905 the journal *Vesy* had regularly been publishing articles under the rubric *Na perevale* (*At the Crossroads*) addressing cultural issues by Diaghilev's friend and comrade-at-arms, the theoretician Andrey Bely (1880–1934). In these articles Bely repeatedly talks of the imminent 'resurrection', of the need for a 'spiritual resurrection', and of the 'resurrection of a new culture'. And he openly points to the spiritual fathers of this vision: Dostoevsky and Solovyov. Moreover, in Bely's writings, this vision is also closely associated with the resurrection of a new art, which will have its roots in the traditions that still pertain in rural Russia. And, as the art critic and contemporary of Bely, Georgy Ivanovich Chulkov (1879–1939), wrote, 'At present there are also other signs of a cultural resurrection. Young artists are learning with passionate energy from our own folk art – treating their own work and the creative work of the people as one and the same thing, they are searching for a new realism'[26] – that other 'realism' that Malevich would talk of in his 1915 manifesto *From Cubism and Futurism to Suprematism*.

Kandinsky, too, was fired by this vision of cultural renewal that would have its roots in Russian soil. This is not only evident in the final sentence of *Concerning the Spiritual in Art* in which he looks forward like the philosopher Solovyov to the 'epoch of the great spiritual',[27] but above all in his own translation into Russian of his 'Reminiscences'.

This gradual emancipation of the spirit – the good fortune of our time – explains the profound interest and increasingly prominent 'belief' in Russia that more and more frequently possesses those elements in Germany capable of independent sentiments. During the last years before the war, I had increasingly frequent occasion to receive in Munich representatives of the young, unofficial Germany, which had previously been unknown to me. They manifested not only an intense inward interest in the essence of Russian life, but also a firm belief in 'salvation from the East'. [28]

Translated from the German by Fiona Elliott

Plates 1916 – 1921

60 **Moscow, Red Square**
1916
Oil on cardboard   51.5 x 49.5
The State Tretyakov Gallery, Moscow

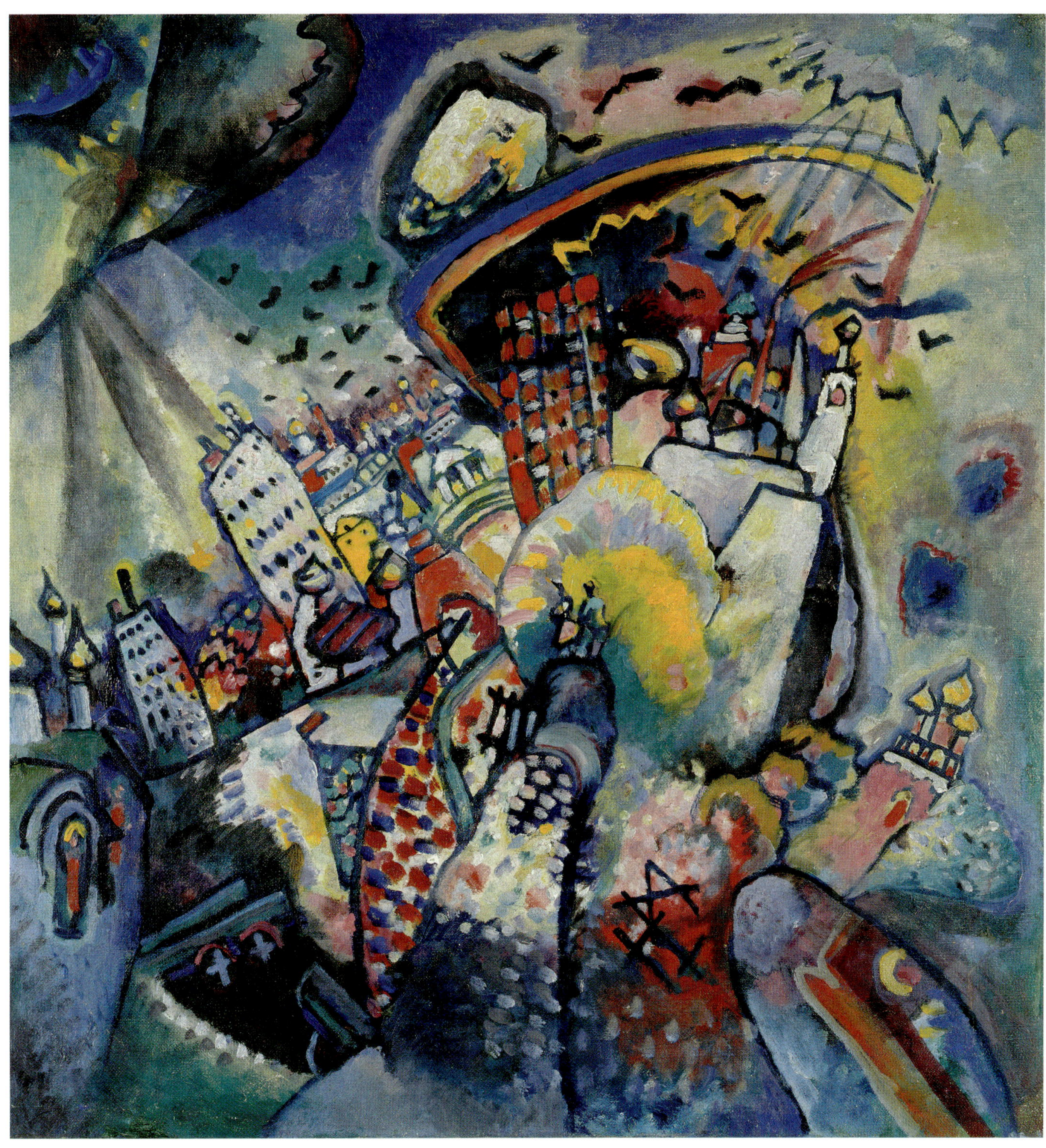

61 **Two Girls**
1917
Painting on glass 20 x 24.5
Private Collection, London

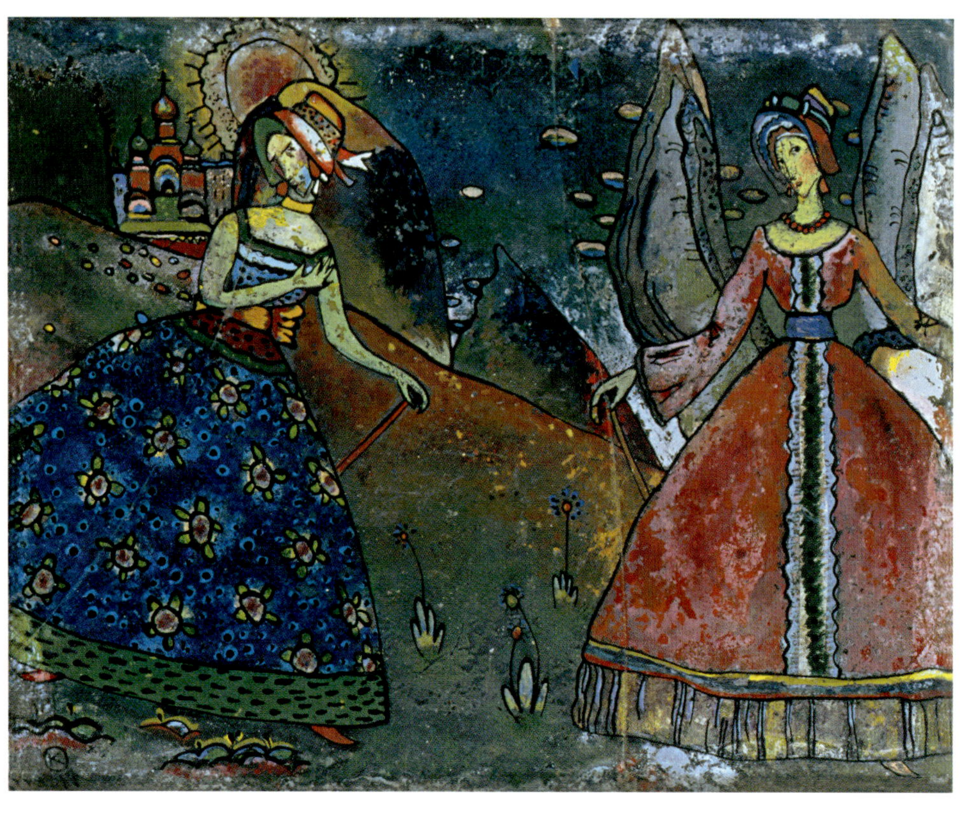

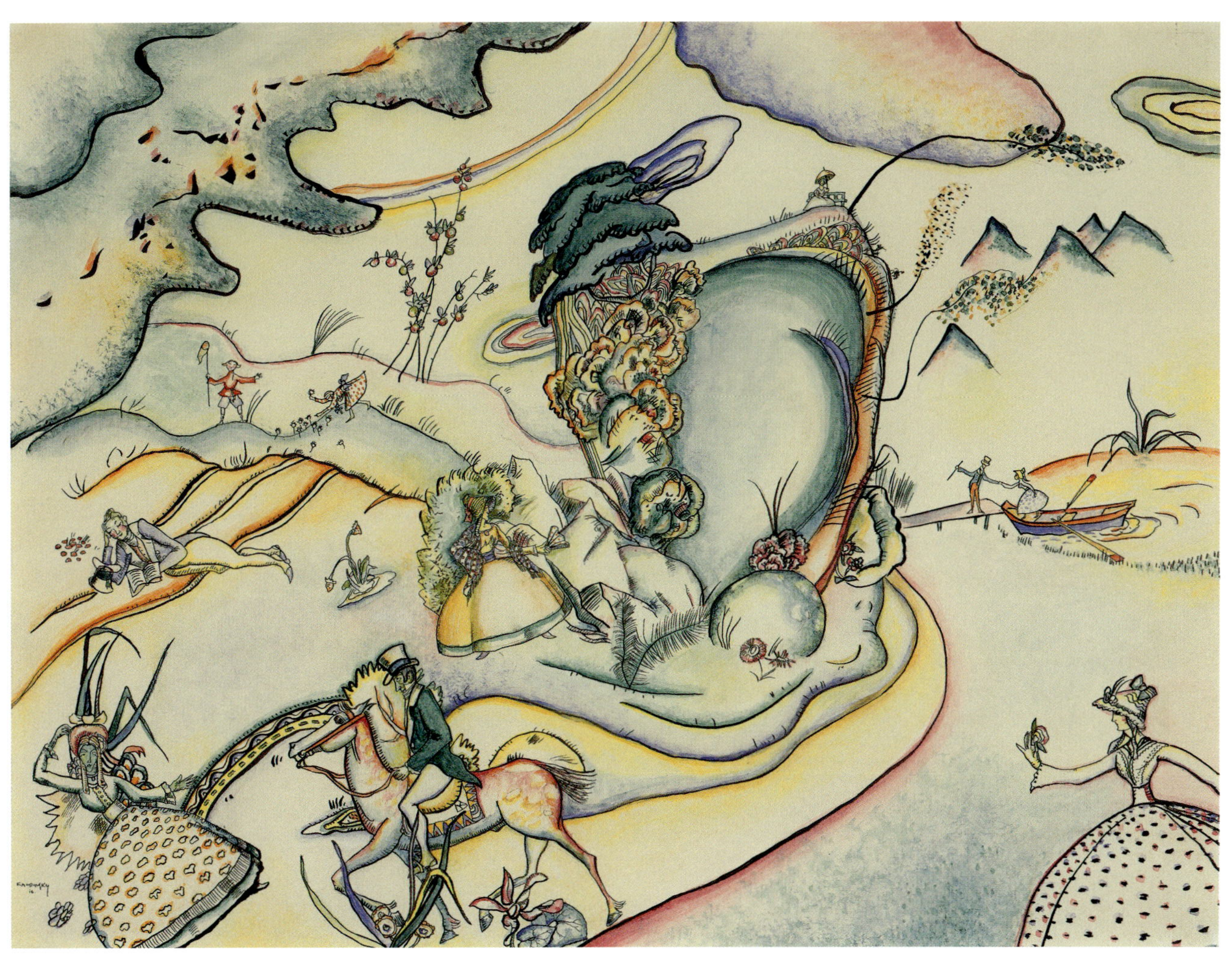

62 **Untitled**, also known as 'Bagatelle'
1916
Watercolour, Indian ink and pencil on paper 46 x 66.3
Private Collection, London

63 **Untitled**
1916
Ink on paper 15.5 x 23.5
Private Collection

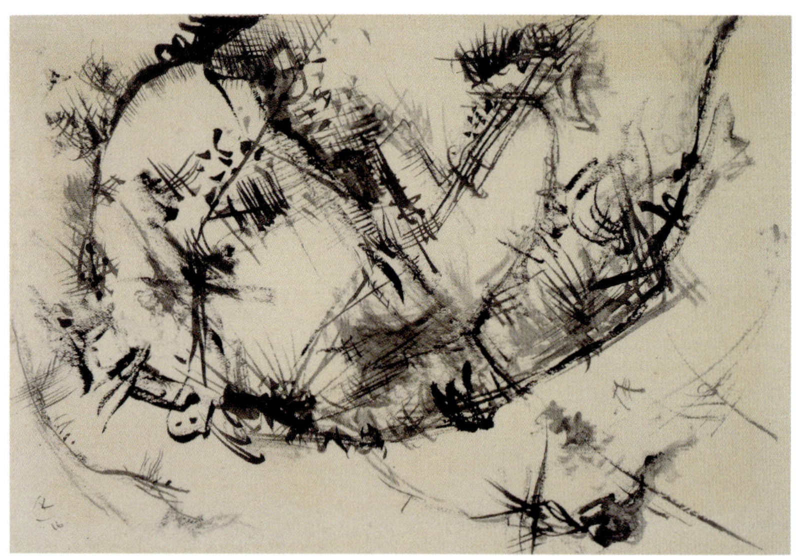

64 **Untitled**
1921
Watercolour, Indian ink and
pencil on paper 30.3 x 24.4
Kunstmuseum Basel,
Kupferstichkabinett.
Gift of Dr Richard Doetsch-Benziger,
Basel, 1939

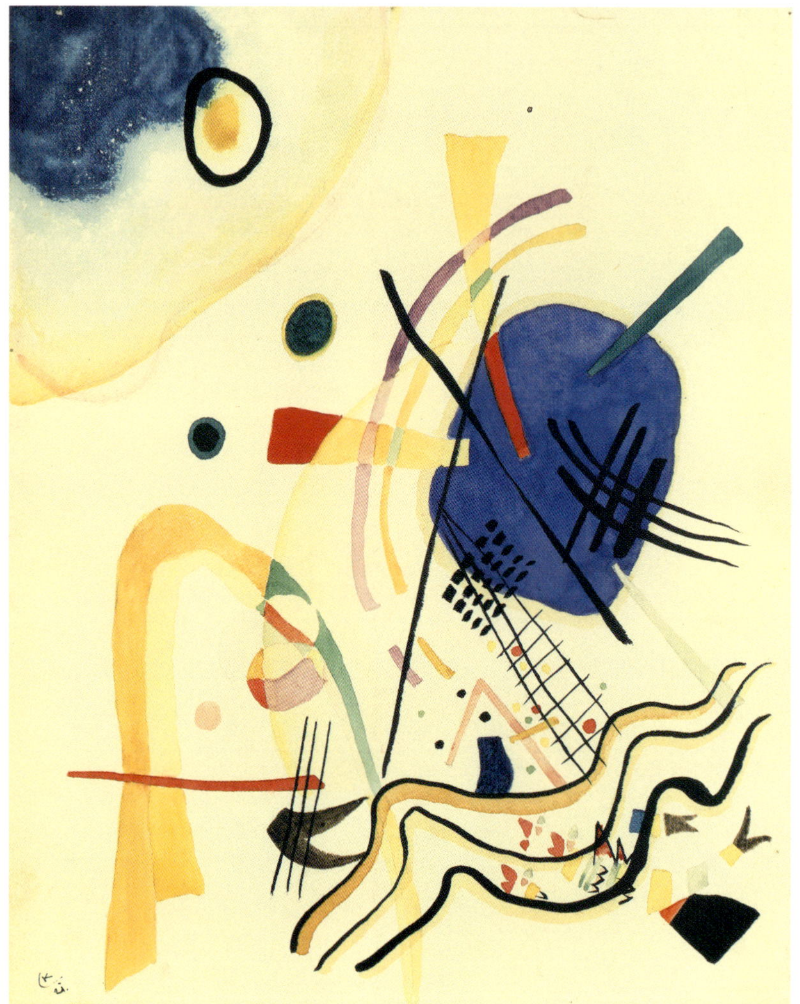

65 **Composition E**

1915

Watercolour on paper   22.6 x 37.1

The State Pushkin Museum, Moscow

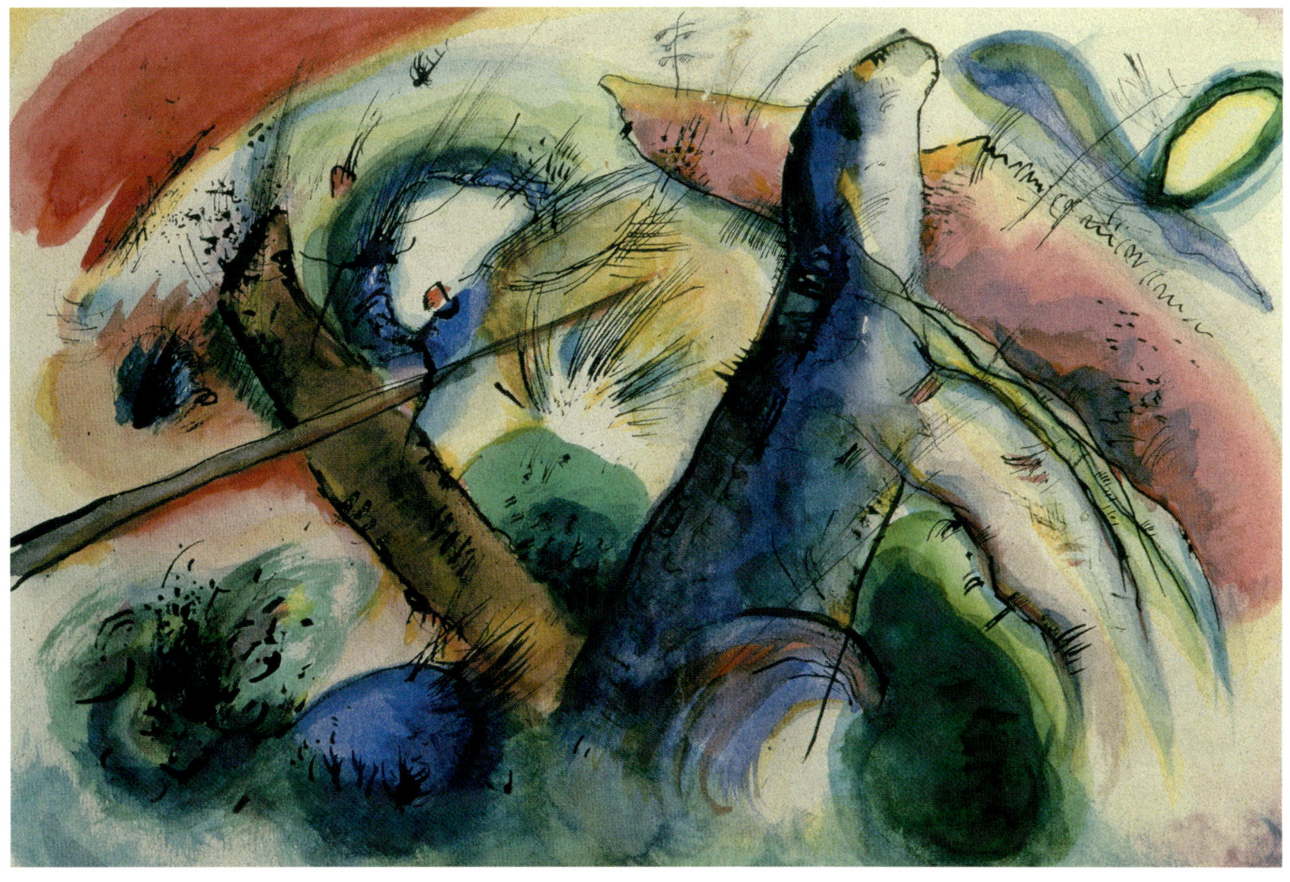

1917
Oil on canvas 91.5 x 69.5
The State Russian Museum, St Petersburg

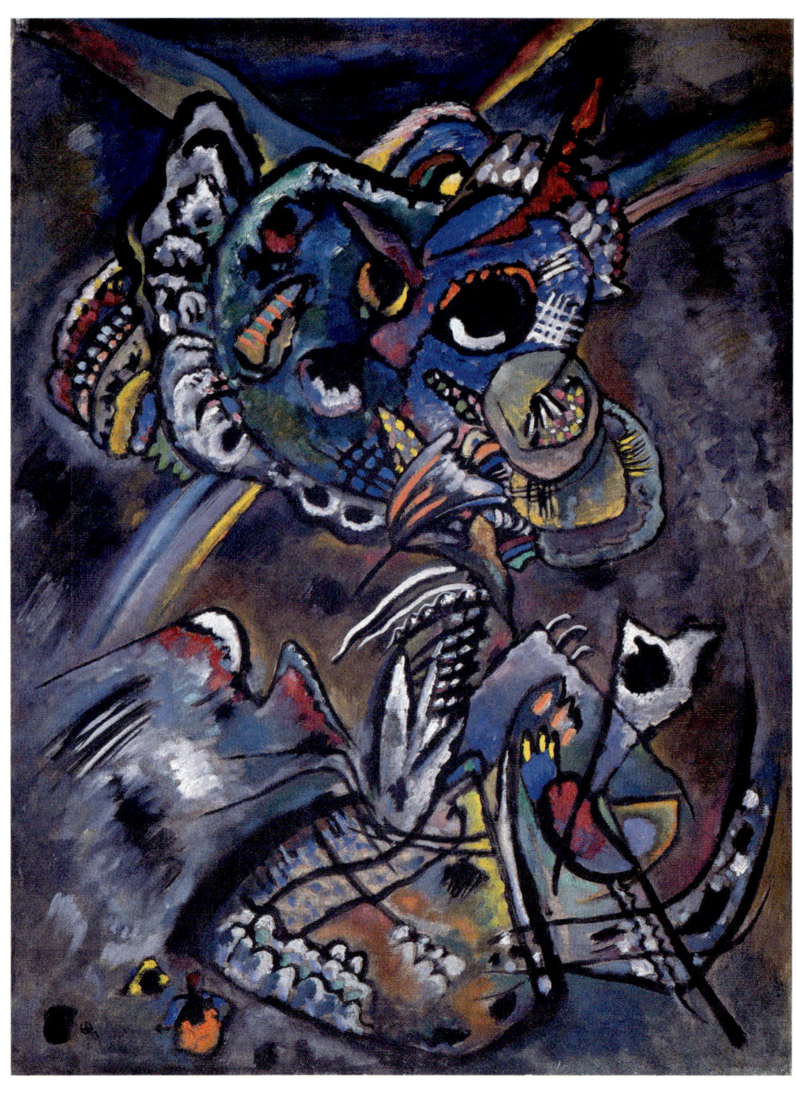

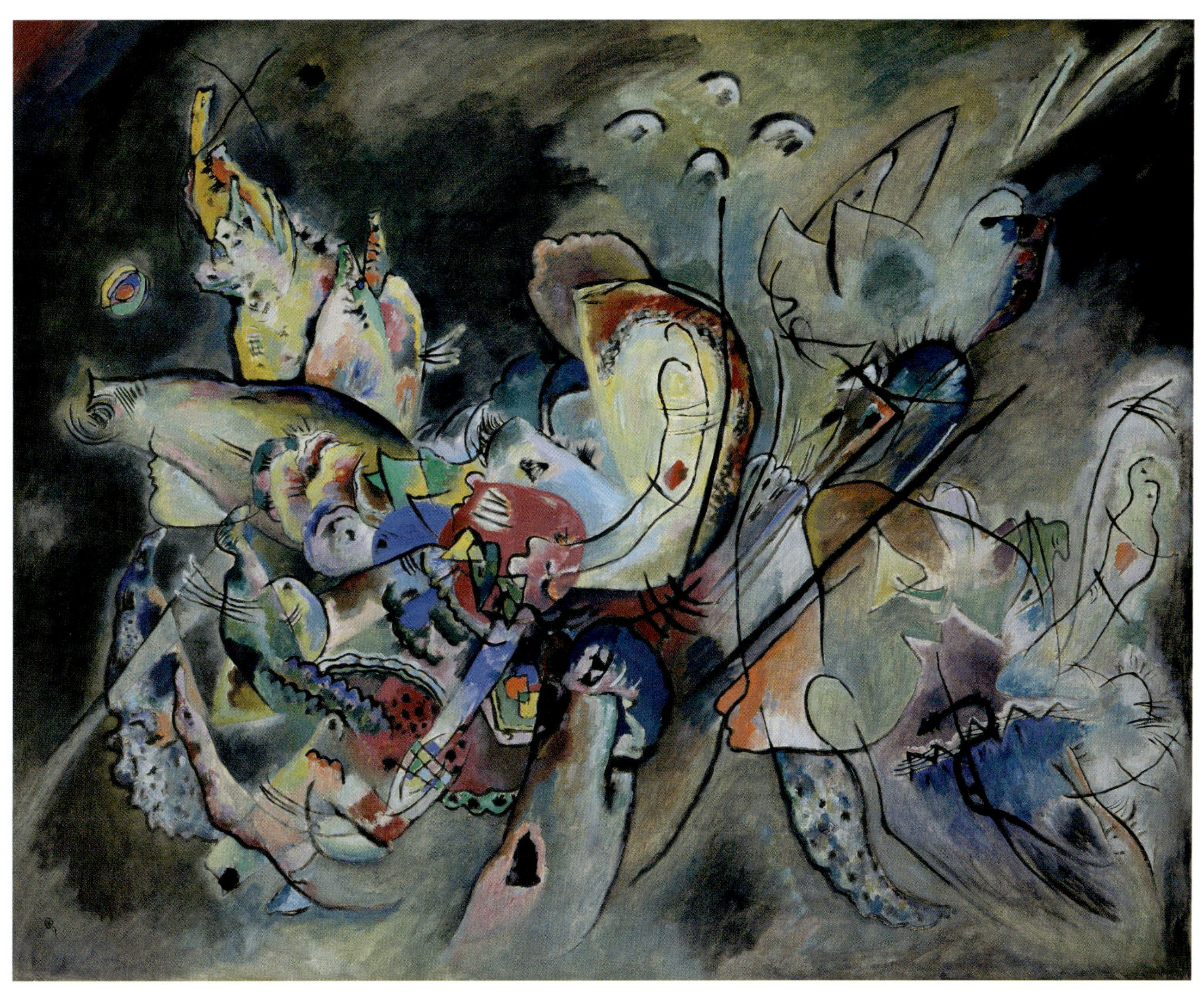

67 Overcast

1917
Oil on canvas   105 x 134
The State Tretyakov Gallery, Moscow

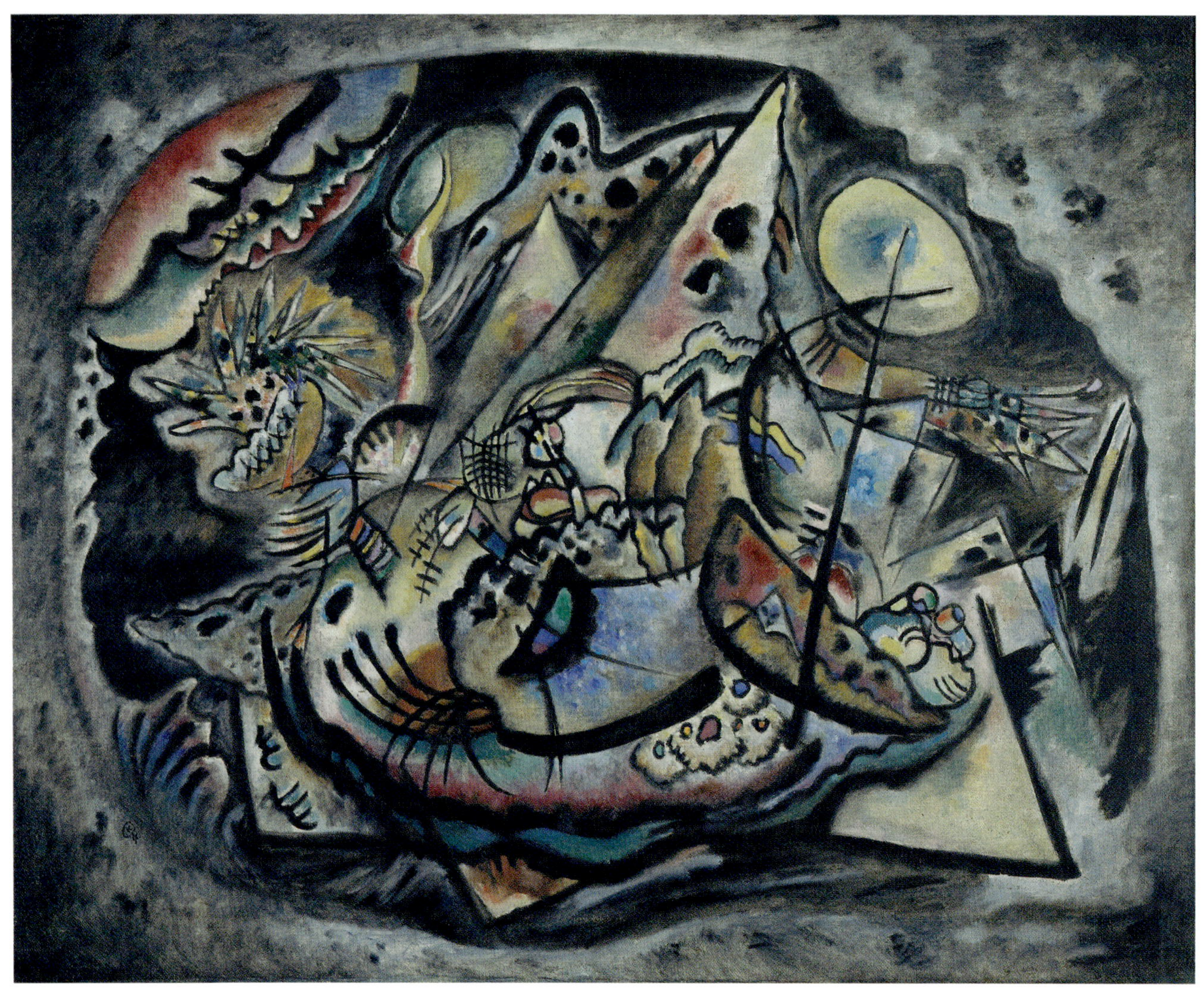

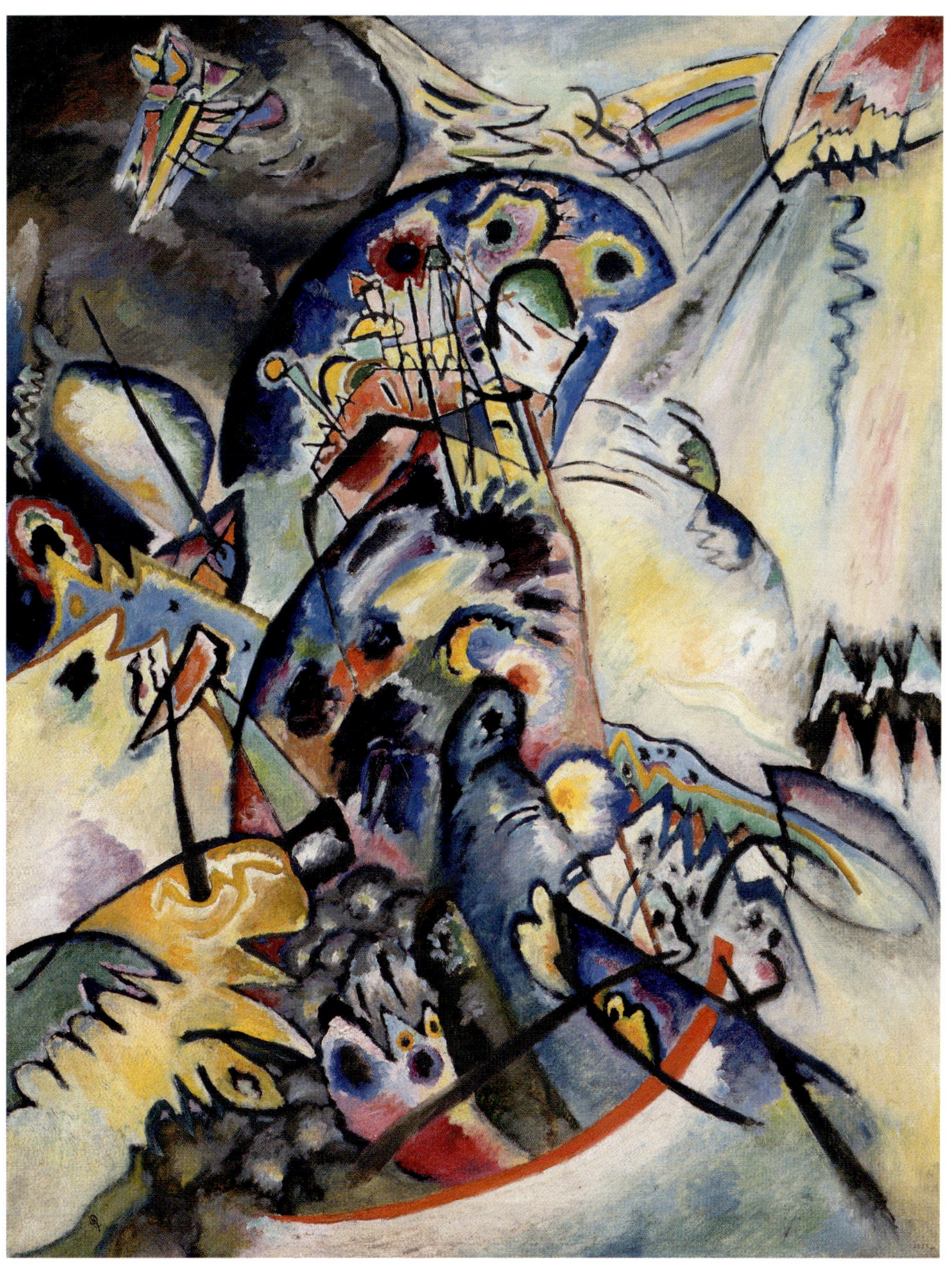

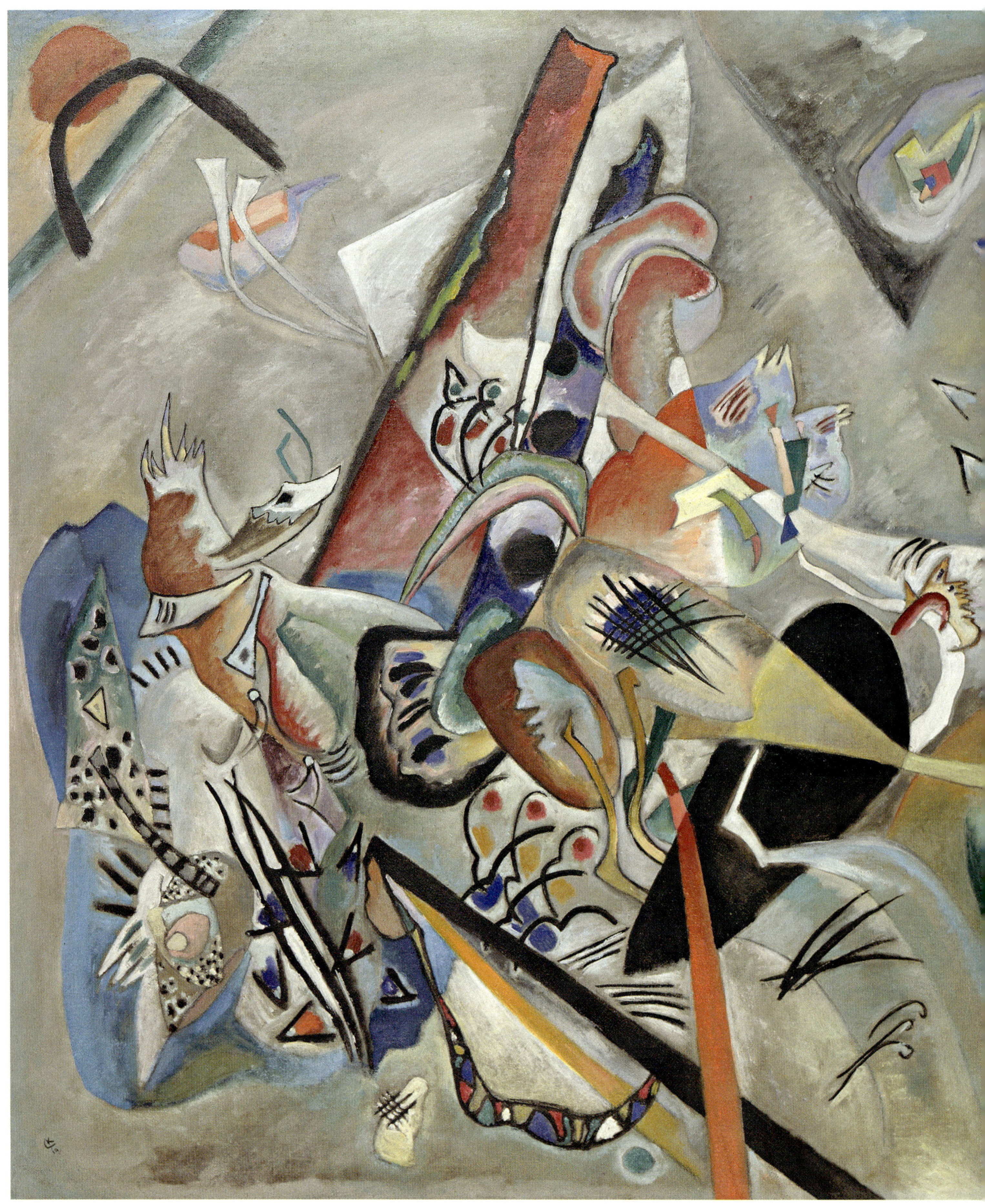

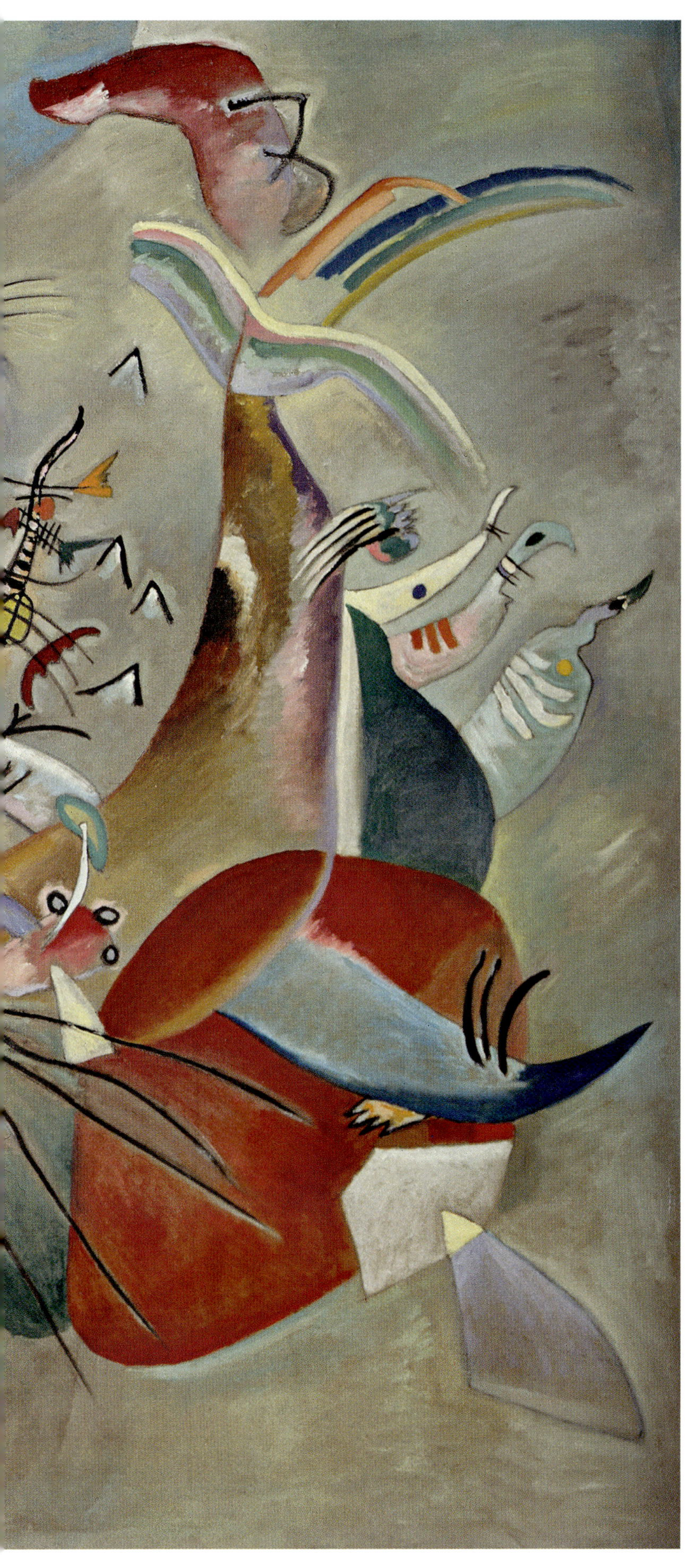

70 **In Grey**

1919
Oil on canvas 129 x 176

Musée National d'Art Moderne, Centre Georges Pompidou, Paris.
Centre de Création Industrielle. Bequest of Nina Kandinsky 1981

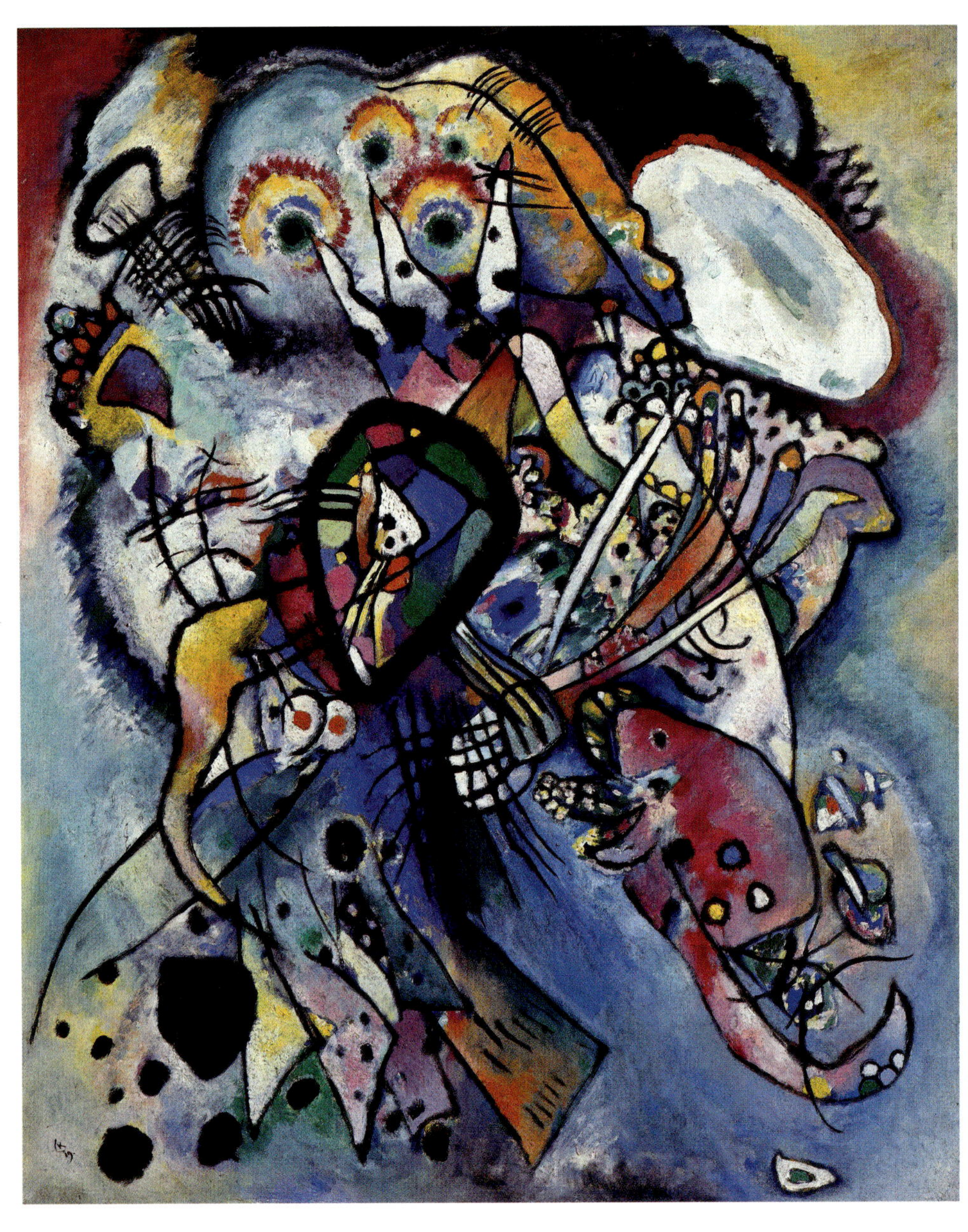

71 **Two Ovals**
1919
Oil on canvas 107 x 89.5
The State Russian Museum, St Petersburg

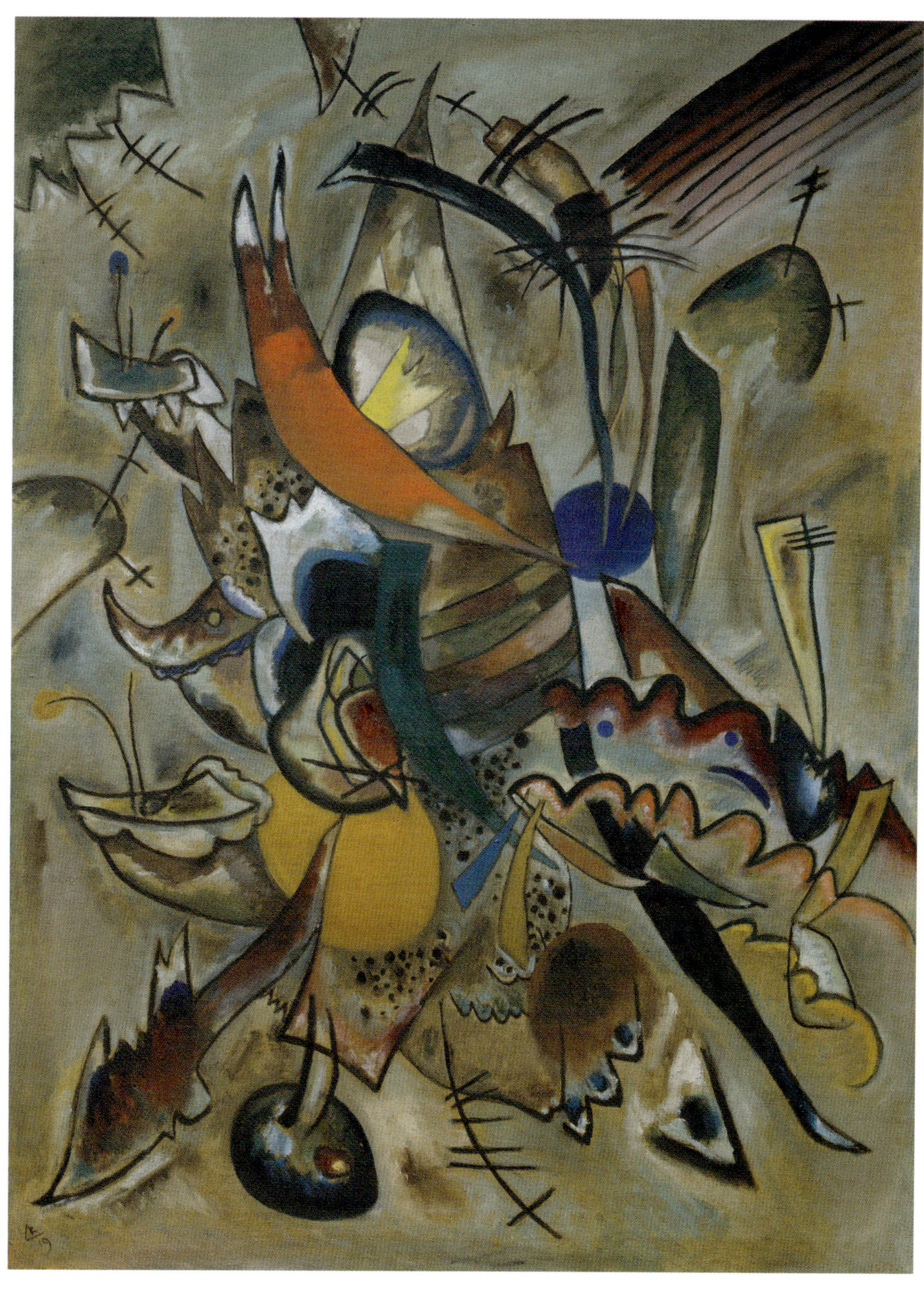

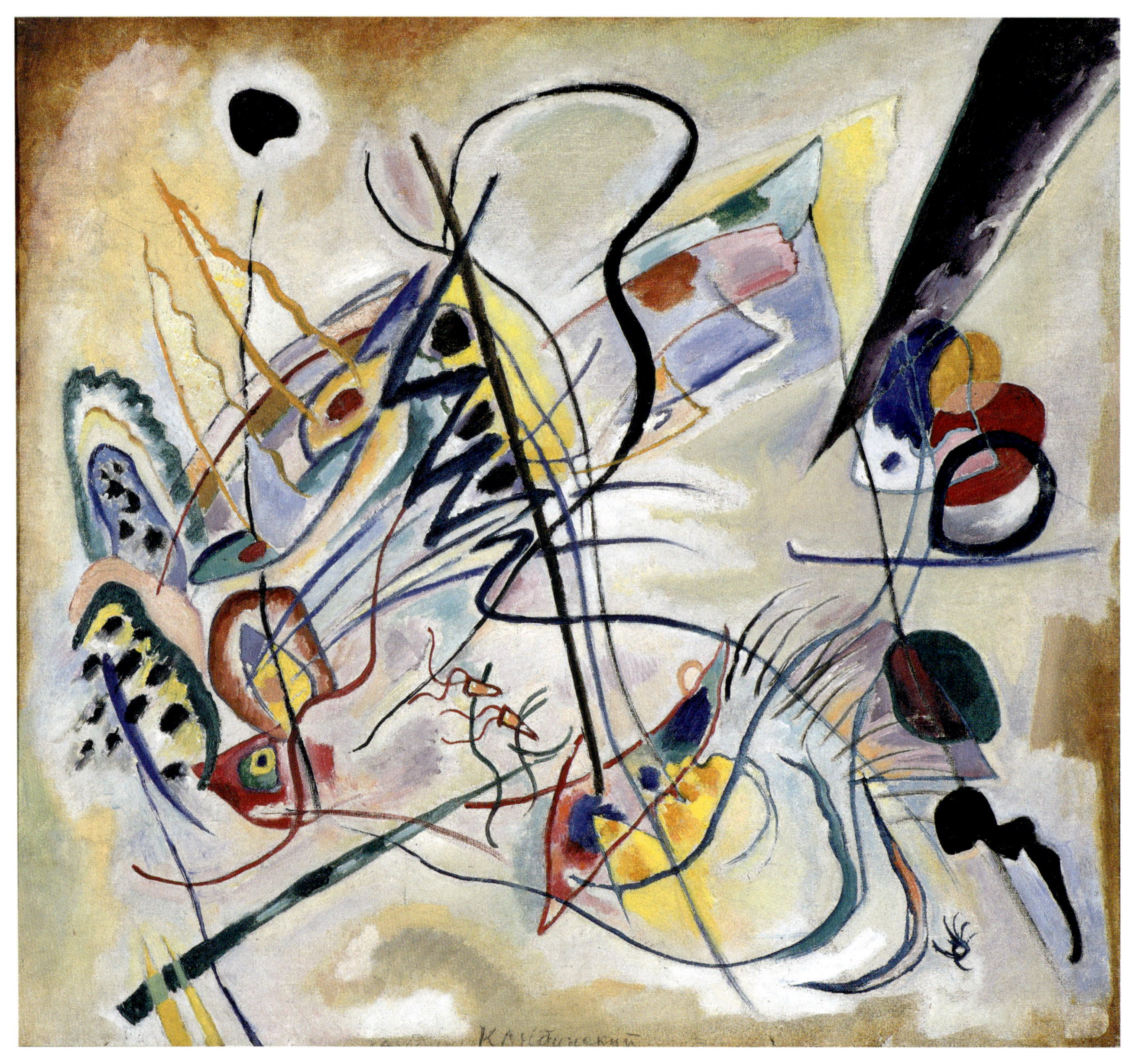

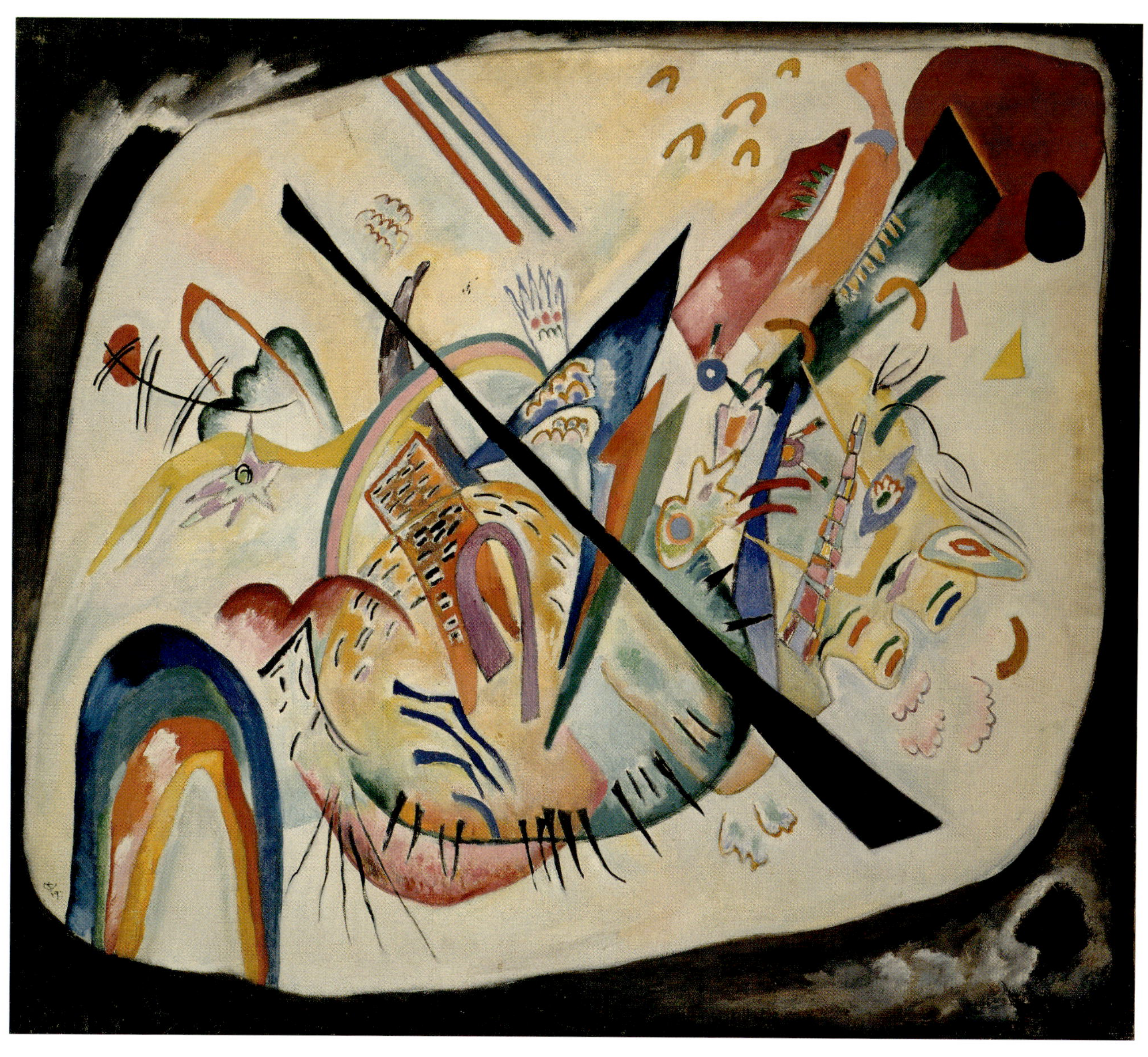

75 **Black Spot**
1921
Oil on canvas 138 x 120
Kunsthaus Zürich

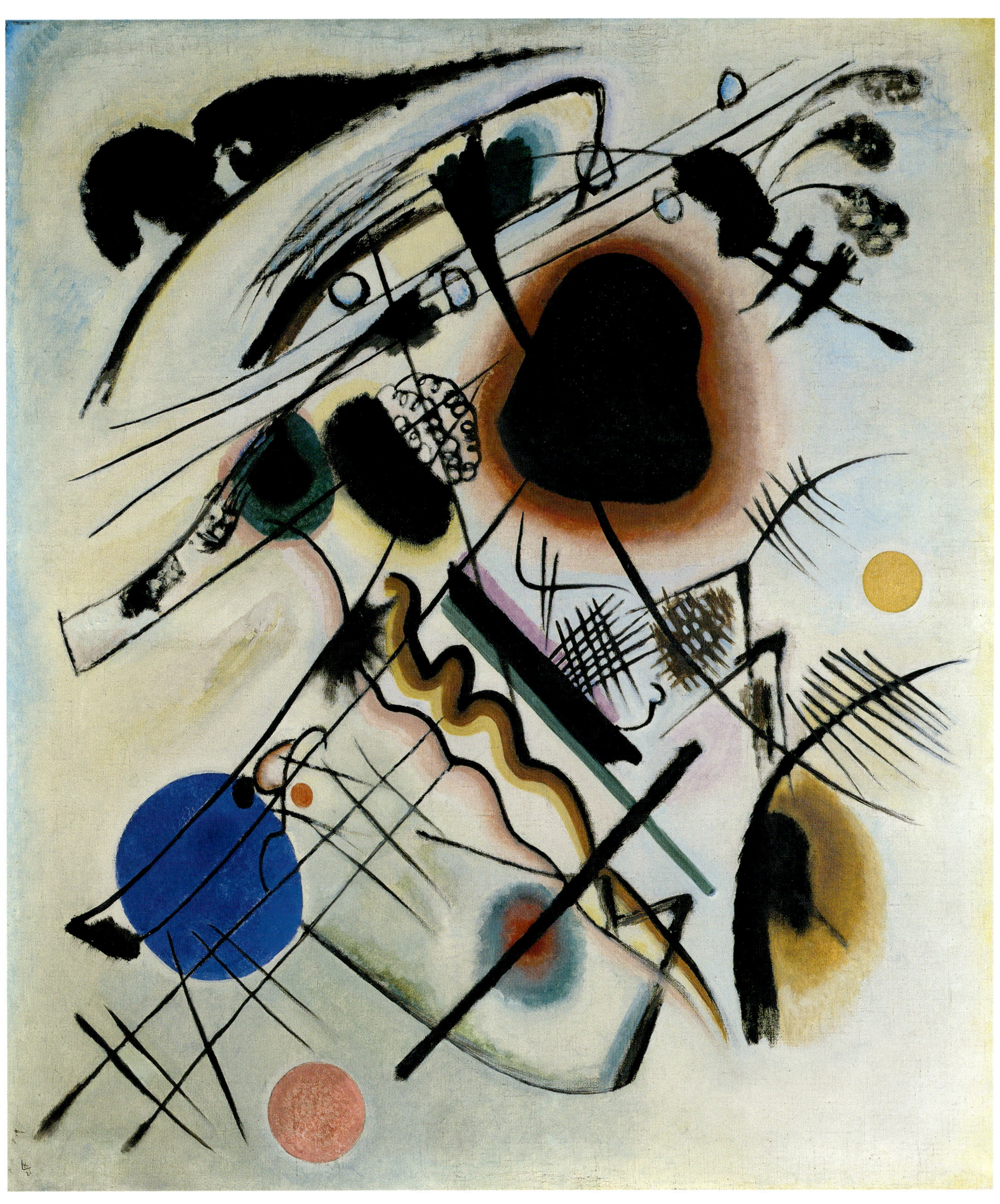

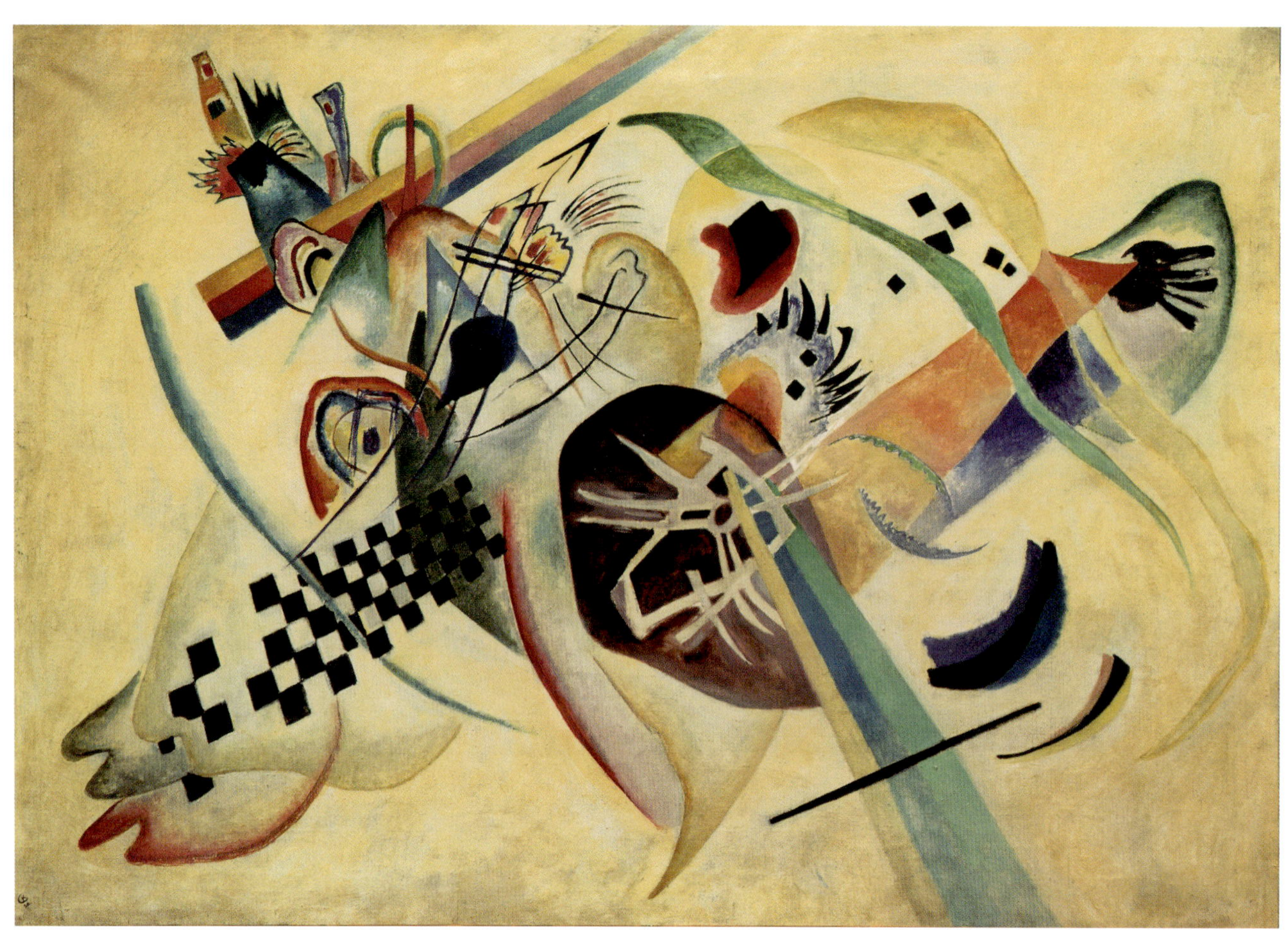

76 **On White I**
1920
Oil on canvas 95 x 138
The State Russian Museum, St Petersburg

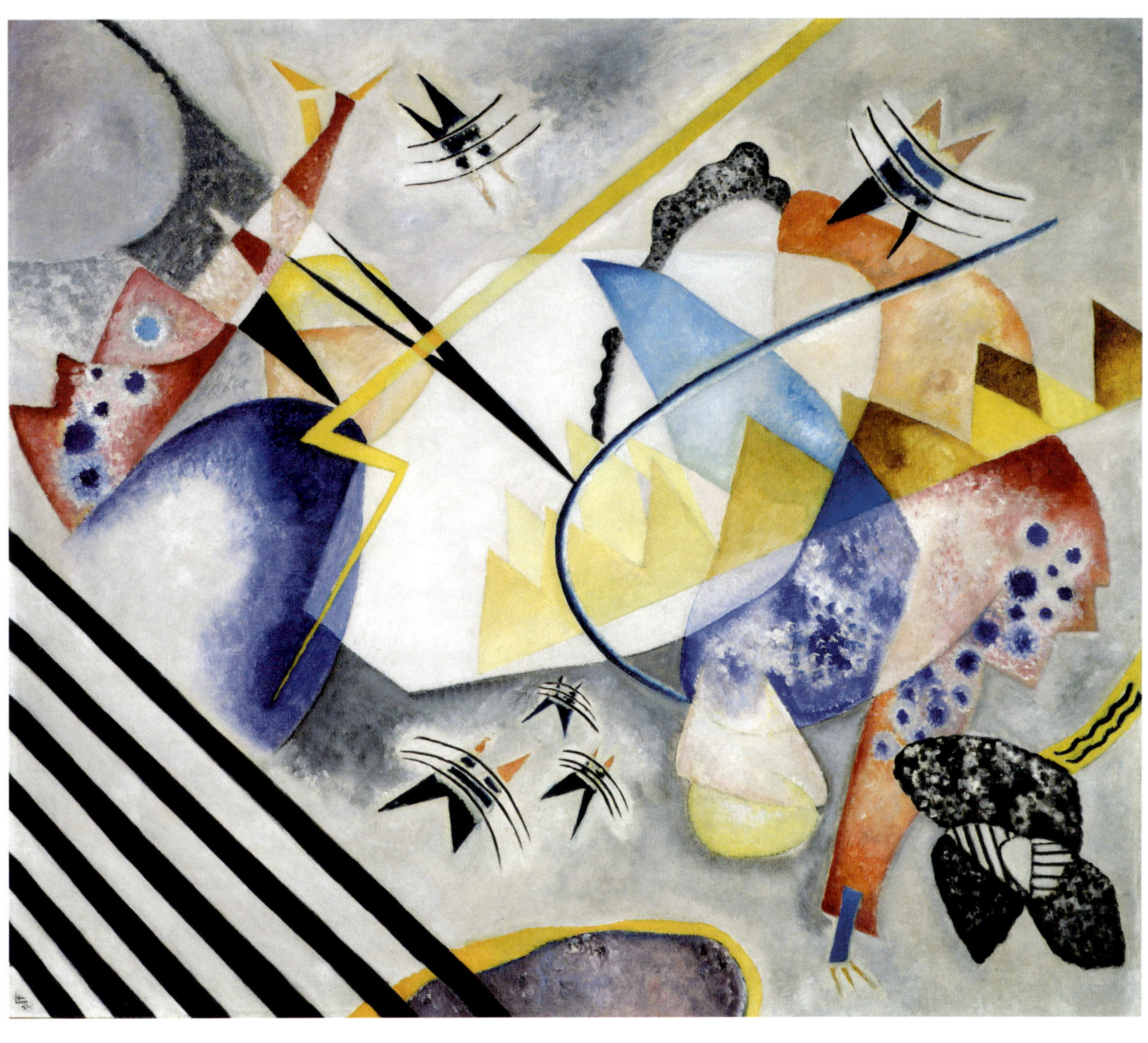

77 **White Centre**
1921
Oil on canvas   118.7 x 136.5
Solomon R. Guggenheim Museum, New York. Hilla Rebay Collection, 1971

78 **Blue Segment**
1921
Oil on canvas 120.6 x 140.1
Solomon R. Guggenheim Museum, New York

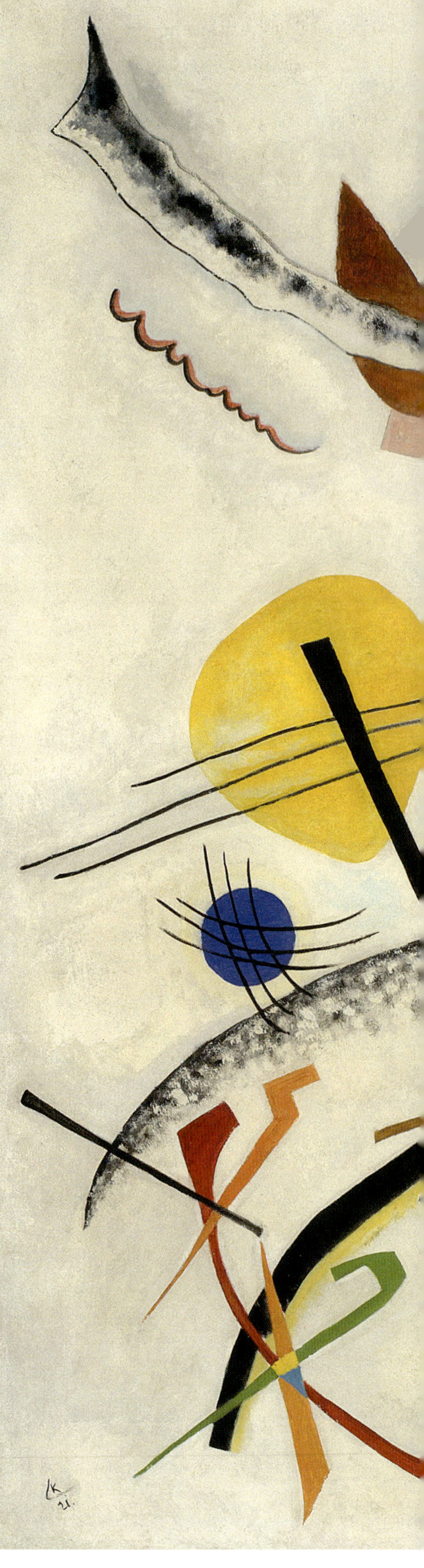

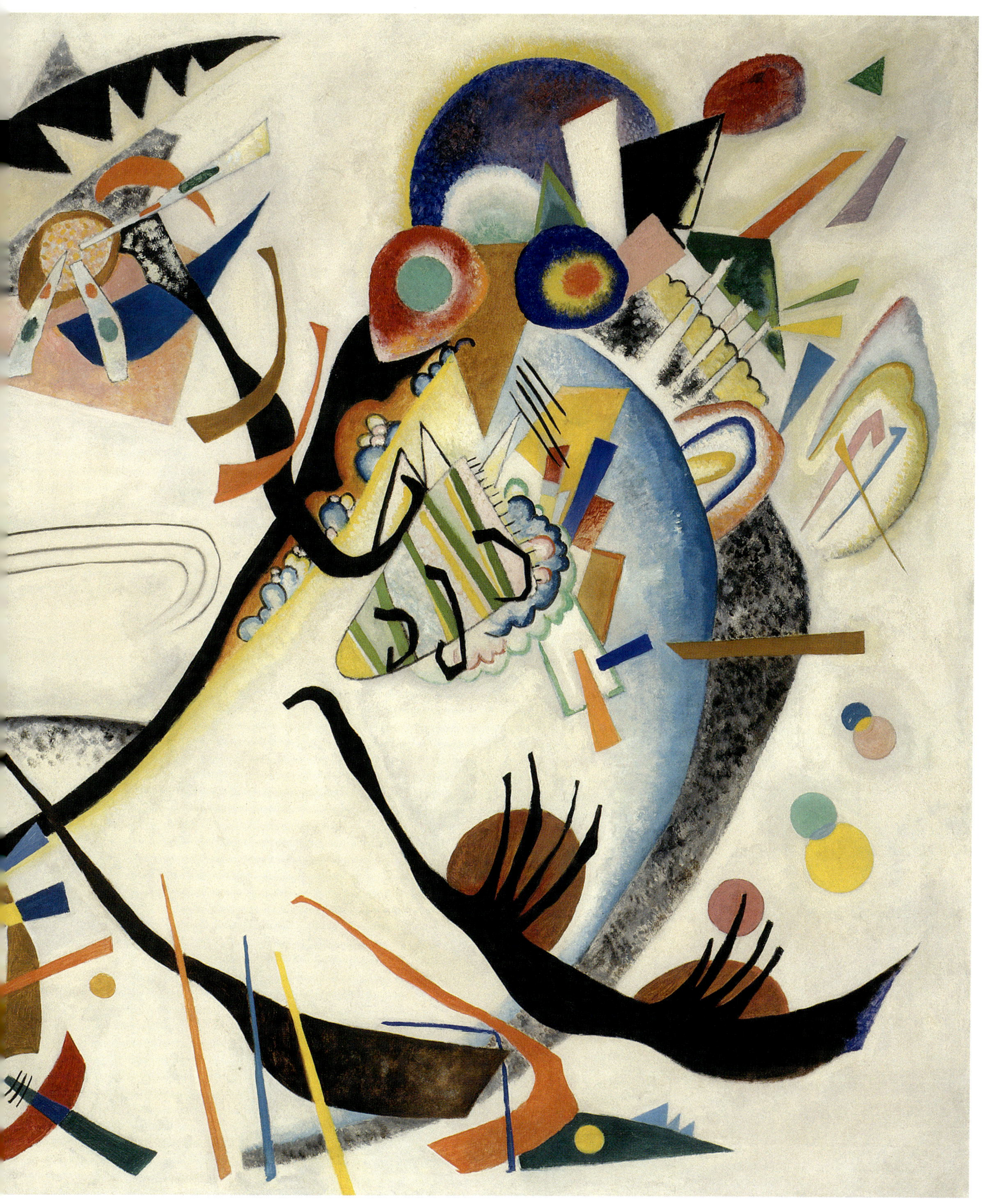

79 **Circles on Black**
1921
Oil on canvas   136.5 x 120
Solomon R. Guggenheim Museum, New York

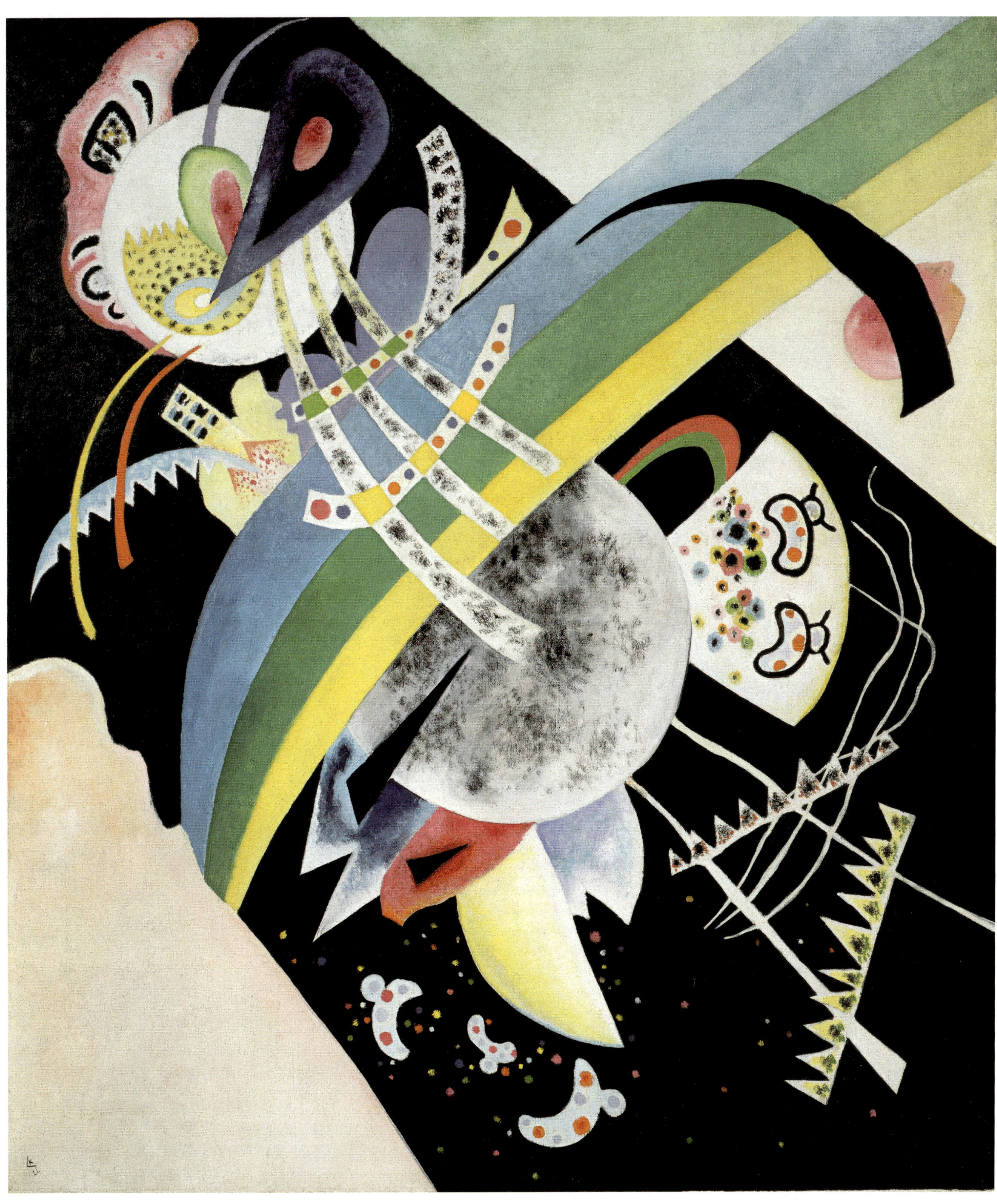

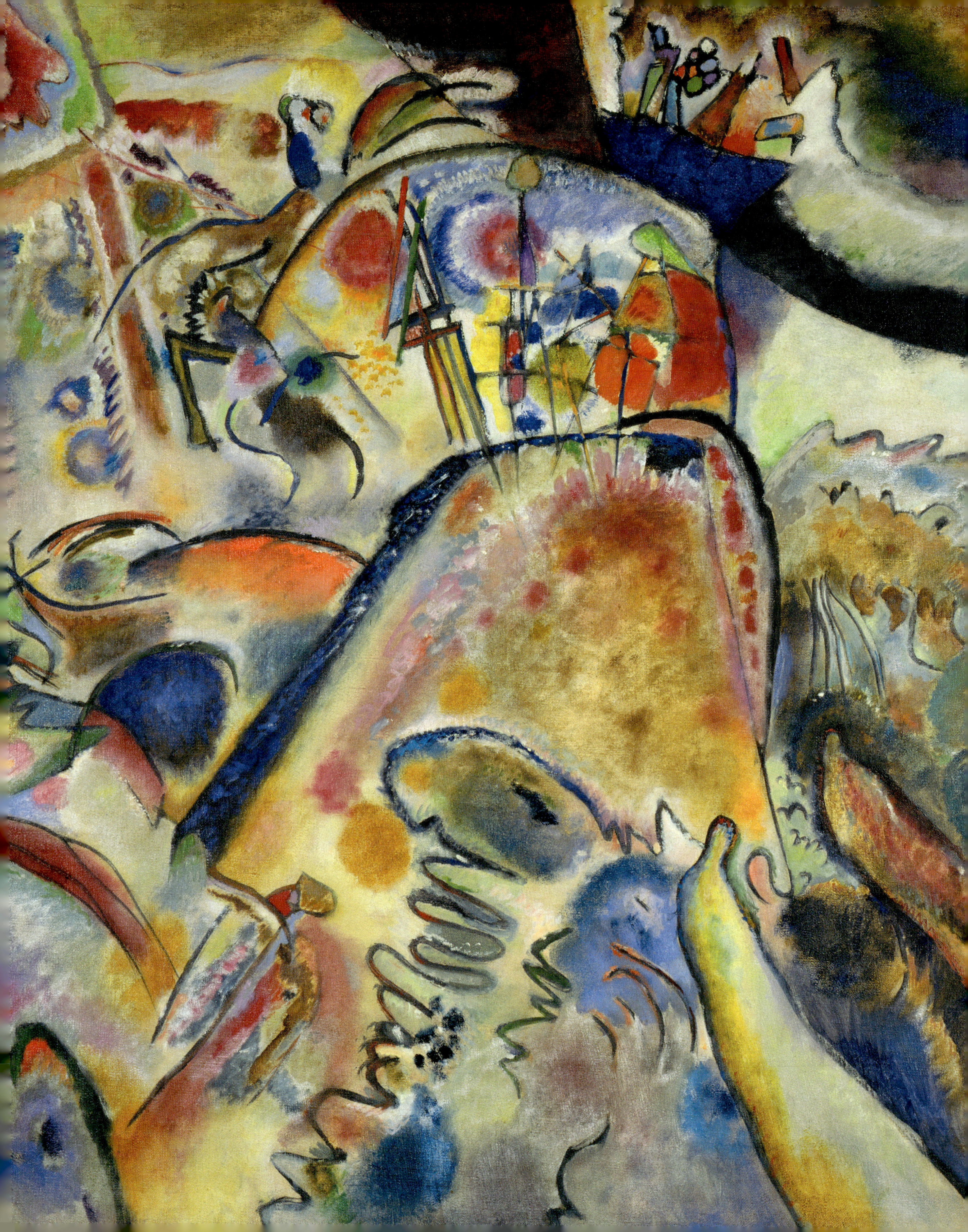

Syntax

BRUNO HAAS

'I painted only three or four such pictures, trying to infuse into every part an 'endless' series of initially concealed colour-tones. They had to lie in such a way that they were completely hidden at first (especially in the darker parts), revealing themselves only in the course of time to the engrossed, attentive viewer.'

Small Pleasures (DETAIL)
1913
Oil on canvas 109.8 x 119.7
Solomon R. Guggenheim Museum, New York

There is a passage in Kandinsky's 'Reminiscences' that mentions time as a compositional element.

I painted only three or four such pictures, trying to infuse into every part an 'endless' series of initially concealed colour-tones. They had to lie in such a way that they were completely hidden at first (especially in the darker parts), revealing themselves only in the course of time to the engrossed, attentive viewer. Indistinct and at the same time tentative, quizzical at first, and then sounding forth more and more, with increasing, 'uncanny' power. [1]

Though Kandinsky would later abandon these experiments, feeling that they leaned too strongly towards the Rembrandtesque, he would always remain interested in what he referred to as the 'question of time' – for example in his 1926 *Punkt und Linie zu Fläche* (*Point and Line to Plane*). It was not simply a matter of introducing the dimension of succession (that is, a sequence of events) into the picture. Rather, it was about certain colours revealing themselves *only in the course of time*, thereby resounding with *uncanny power*. Hence, time comes into play here as an interlude of patience that endures long enough to await the dawning of the uncanny.

Characters

In *Improvisation 35* 1914 (fig.33, no.56) we see a kind of middle field that is composed primarily of green, whitish and pale blue colours surrounded by a yellow–violet border at the edge of which, in turn, an intense vermilion radiates. It is difficult to describe the effects of colour accurately; let it suffice to say that the vermilion looks *strange* beside the yellow–violet border, for it is a colour of an entirely different nature and source. This is one reason why the red can be seen as emerging from behind the violet, shining out like a cold flame. If we let our gaze follow the yellow border that bounds the field to the upper left, we soon discover a pink glow that emerges between yellow and green, which again appears as a *strange* colour, albeit in a very different way from the vermilion. Compared to the vermilion, the effect of the pink is more localised, affecting only the relationship between the green–blue–white field and the yellow–violet border,

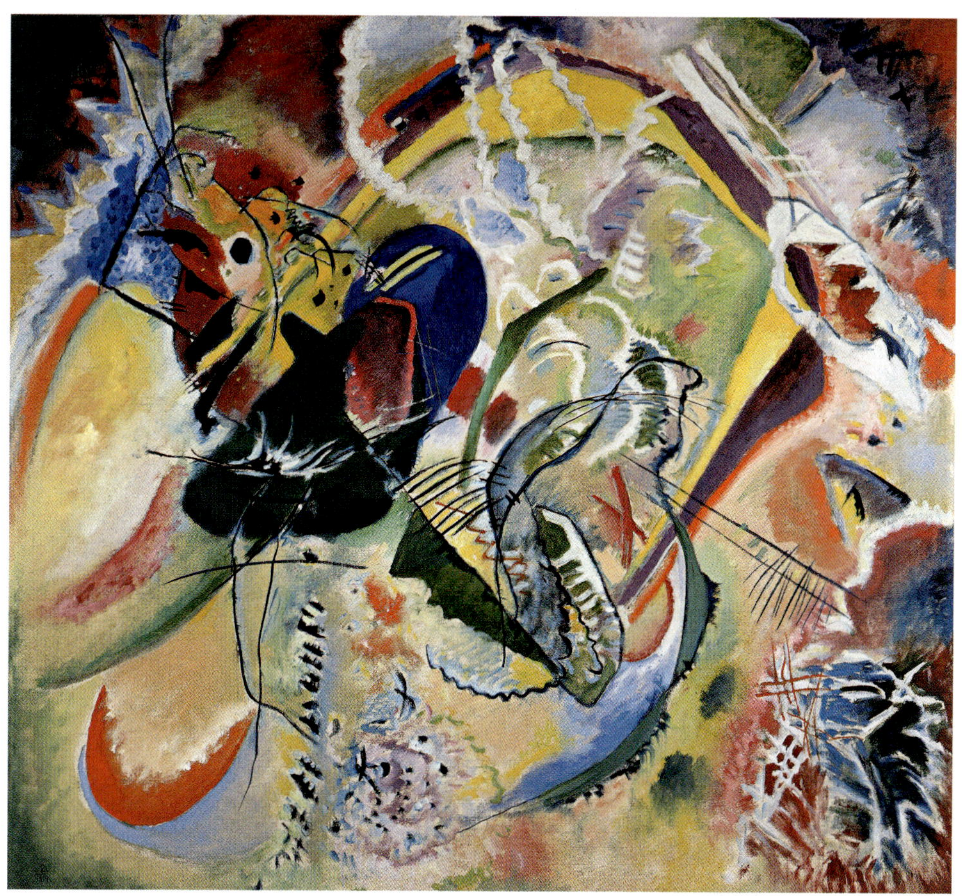

whereas the cold fire of the vermilion radiates throughout the entire picture. I say 'cold fire' because red, especially an orangey red, is generally considered to be warm (as Kandinsky also notes), and yet in this context it appears cold.[2]

Anyone who becomes accustomed to observing such chromatic effects will soon find Kandinsky's work teeming with them. In *Improvisation 35* alone there are countless further examples. Consider, for instance, the colours surrounding the little black patch in the upper left-hand corner that holds us in thrall from the start like an unseeing eye: there is an orange nearby that appears uncommonly intense, even hot – an effect that immediately fades as soon as we cover up, say, the pink or even the pale green in the immediate vicinity. At the lower left, a vermilion crescent is paired with pale blue, making both shine with a peculiar light. On the right-hand edge halfway up the picture, there is another pale blue patch that shines ever so gently and seems to come from another planet in comparison to the colours around it.

In his book *Concerning the Spiritual in Art*[3] Kandinsky famously developed a theory of colour in which, among other things, he characterised the individual colours. He tells us, for instance, that yellow is warm and blue is cold, that green balances them, and so on. What is less well known is the significance that these characteristics have in respect of the finished works. They should certainly not be regarded as a definitive reference list that might tell us how each colour is meant to be interpreted. If, for instance, the vermilion in *Improvisation 35* really does appear cold – even though, theoretically, it ought to have a warm tone – this does not contradict the theory. But we do have to ask ourselves what it actually says and what its rank and status is in terms of the painterly process. Kandinsky says in *Concerning the Spiritual in Art* that he sees 'no need to deal with the profound and refined complexities of colour', but that he will instead consider 'the direct use of simple colours'. And in his 1919 *Self-characterisation* he writes:

Every formal element has its absolute physical effect (= value); construction selects from among these resources, making an absolute into a relative value, so that, for example, a warm element can become cold and a sharp form blunt.[4]

In Kandinsky's later treatise *Point and Line to Plane* we find the following general reflections on the status of the elementary.[5]

It must, however, always be emphasised that elements completely pure in tone which radiate a single colour do not really exist; that even those elements designated as 'basic' or 'proto-elements' are not primitive but are, on the contrary, of a complex nature. All concepts having to do with the 'primitive' are likewise only relative concepts. Our 'scientific' language is, therefore, equally but relative. The absolute we do not know. Colour, then, might be understood only in context, and in this sense the whole would precede its parts or elements.[6]

Here, Kandinsky has formulated a fundamental tenet of Structuralism that we can apply in analysing the colours in his paintings. We shall view and describe the respective colours only in terms of their function and context, without entering into the fiction of supposedly simple elements. Complicated as that may sound, it delivers some very simple results. As we have seen, one of the characteristic features of Kandinsky's painting is that individual colours can appear *strange* when juxtaposed. In other words, Kandinsky's colours can have an appearance that is unfamiliar to us, with the painterly context giving them a 'face'[7] that they do not, by nature, possess the moment they are squeezed from the tube.[8] The question is, how does Kandinsky create these characters?

Colour Families

It would seem that these characters somehow arise through the painterly context and do so in such a manner that some of the colours appear to be related to one another while others appear unrelated. However, related is not the same as similar. Two colours are said to be similar if they are close to one another on the colour circle. Red madder lake (with a bluish tinge) is similar to vermilion, for both are red, but this does not mean they are related, as we can see in *Improvisation 35*. In the lower right-hand corner, some vermilion lines are juxtaposed with crimson so that the two clash. Further up in the picture, to the left, these two colours meet again: a broad vermilion stripe rises on the left-hand edge, running towards the right, where it meets with crimson fields surrounding the above-mentioned 'blind spot' or 'unseeing eye'. Once again, these two colours are fundamentally different. They belong to entirely discrete chromatic spheres, as though each came from a different world. Yet they do not clash like their counterparts on the lower right. In other words, the relationship between these two colours and their respective characters is subject to considerable variations within the same picture.

Just what is it that makes the distinction between the kinship and strangeness of colours? What is it that constitutes the chromatic context? The answer is *families*, or *chords* of colour.

What this means can be illustrated by way of a simpler example: the 1910 *Murnau – Mountain Landscape with Church* (fig.34, no.18). In this painting, too, individual colours are clearly separated, for instance at the horizon on the right, where the Neapolitan yellow[9] of the sky is set against the green, blue and ochre tones of the faraway mountains. The Neapolitan yellow seems *strange* and the context lends it a quite remarkable intensity. Stranger still, however, is the red of the cloud at the upper right-hand edge. While we might be able to imagine a more

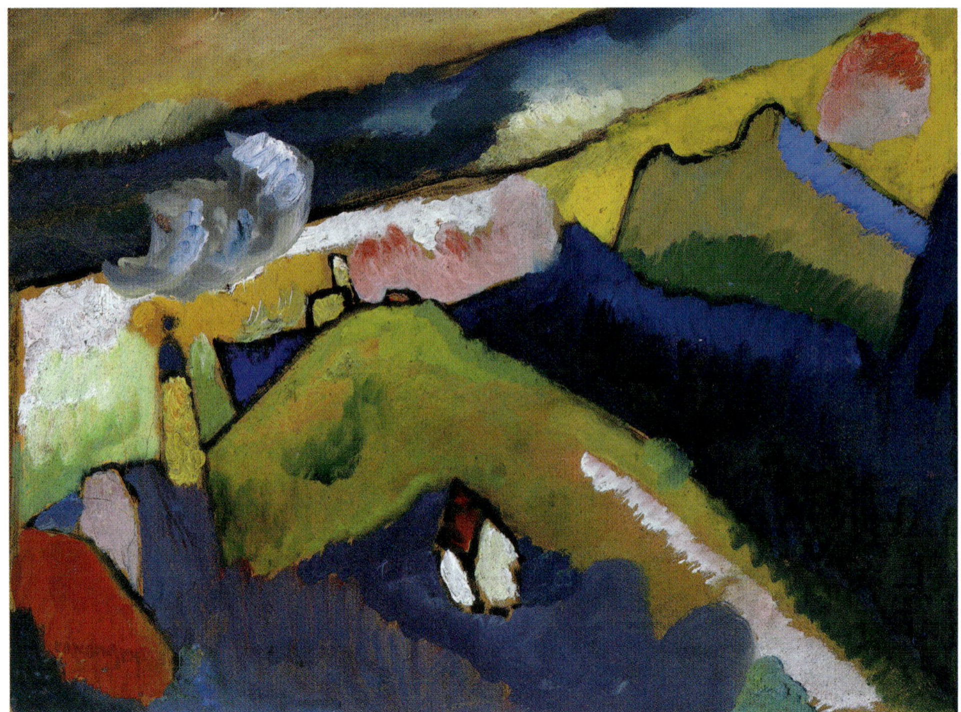

FIG 34
Murnau – Mountain Landscape with Church
1910
Oil on canvas 32.7 x 44.8
Städtische Galerie im Lenbachhaus, Munich

intense or radiant red if it were set, for instance, against a black ground, we can barely conceive of a red more rare or strange, let alone a red more intensely expressive. A passage in Kandinsky's 'Reminiscences' springs to mind:

In my studies, I let myself go. I had little thought for houses and trees, drawing coloured lines and blobs on the canvas with my palette knife, making them sing just as powerfully as I knew how. [10]

Though the Munich study is not painted with the palette knife, and while it is more mature than the studies of previous years to which Kandinsky was referring when he wrote that passage, the 'singing' of the colours is nevertheless the same. Indeed, it is elevated to another level here. Let us consider for a moment how this actually works.

Take a little Neapolitan yellow, ultramarine blue and emerald green on a palette. The result is nowhere near the profoundly charged, *strange* relationship we see in Kandinsky's picture. On the contrary, these colours can stand side by side quite indifferently. So there must be something within the painterly composition itself that creates this 'singing' effect. Below the white building with the red roof there is a touch of mauve bordering the violet shadow of the church. If we cover up this mauve with our hand, the Neapolitan yellow loses some of its depth and no longer appears to stand behind the mountains and push towards us. Instead, it seems to be on the same plane, as in a mosaic. The already mentioned *strangeness* of this yellow in relation to the blue, green and ochre is diminished. We conclude that the Neapolitan yellow is 'leaning' on the mauve. And in this context, we find that Neapolitan yellow and mauve – at least in the context of this particular painting – are anything but strangers to one another, but that they are indeed related. They support and sustain one another, without clashing. In this respect, we might say that they belong to the same *family of colours*. This family of colours (or *chord*) is rounded off by a third element: the otherwise unassuming grey of the little cloud above the church spire.[11] To prove that point, let us cover up this little cloud. Immediately, the relationship between the Neapolitan yellow and the mauve becomes two-dimensional; the two colours now appear like two sides of a coin and the spatial force of their relationship that drives the yellow forwards from behind the mountains is lost. But as soon as we uncover the grey again, the sky regains the compelling depth that comes from leaning on the mauve in the foreground. Hence, yellow, mauve and grey constitute a family of colours. Clearly, their ternary structure serves to organise not only the colours, but the space as well, and does so in a way that differs fundamentally from the familiar graphic handling of space (perspective, overlapping). The fact that a colour belongs to a chord automatically separates it from other colours so that an effect of *strangeness* between colours can occur.

Thus, the colour families form the basis of the painterly context while at the same time being based on it. After all, there is no reason why Neapolitan yellow, mauve and grey should constitute a chord at all times and in all places. Indeed, there are paintings in which the colours are not organised as families at all. This circular underlying structure that binds the whole and its parts (hermeneutic circle) indicates that it is not an optical phenomenon, but a semantic one in which, as in any semantic system, a certain arbitrariness and contingency hold sway. The relationship between colours in painting obeys historically mutable laws of meaning. This was the insight that led Kandinsky, in his *Point and Line to Plane*, to call for a new 'science of art' that would elucidate the rules of 'composition' from a historical point of view – a call that to all intents and purposes has remained a *desideratum* to this very day.[12]

Let us return to the Murnau landscape study. As part of a family of colours, the Neapolitan yellow counters the green and blue. But what about the green and blue? Here the ultramarine blue in particular possesses a wonderful depth and profound luminosity in spite of its darkness. This specific character of the blue that is so different from the raw colour squeezed fresh from the tube is once again the result of the painterly context. If, for instance, we cover up the white of the sky above the pink cloud, the sonority of the blue is less distinct. On the other hand, if we uncover the white again, we find that it seems to emerge out of the even deeper black on the lower edge of the blue chain of mountains. We can thus assume that the second family of colours is black–blue–white. Yet the green also seems closely related to the blue, even though it does not participate directly in the sonority of the blue within the black–blue–white chord. We must therefore conclude that the blue is also part of another family of colours and that two families overlap here: this second family of colours consists of ultramarine blue and emerald green plus a third colour that has been elided, or omitted, but which is nevertheless 'intended'. It is, in other words, an ellipse.

In order to describe this somewhat complex phenomenon we have to digress a little. The black–blue–white family of colours creates a generally chromatic character in which green plays a special role. The black–blue–white encompasses the entire colour sphere of this picture, bracketing it from darkest shadow to brightest white. Thus, the black–blue–white is an all-encompassing and universal chord of colour whose 'tone' or 'sound', as Kandinsky would have it, dominates the entire picture. The green, on the other hand, belongs more to the zone in which it actually occurs. It belongs to the forest and the meadow. The green–blue thus relates to a material entity that supports and sustains it, a material core that does not actually appear directly, but which is nevertheless present. We maintain that this underlying material core is formed by an elided and merely imagined brown, which we shall therefore mark with an asterisk (*). Accordingly, the *brown–blue–green[13] constitutes a third family of colours that intersects with the second one (black–blue–white). In graphic terms, this overlap might be envisaged as a cross, with the vertical beam formed by the black–blue–white and the horizontal by the brown–blue–green.

The red of the cloud, a stranger to the blue of the distant mountains and the Neapolitan yellow sky, clearly belongs to a different chord or family of colours. Of all the colours in the picture, this red probably achieves the highest degree of 'strangeness'. Not only is it set in the midst of utterly unrelated colour families; it is almost alienated from its own family as well. In fact, the same red crops up again right at the front in the lower left, but there it appears much less 'strange' and even seems quite 'normal' despite its luminosity. If we compare the relationship between these two patches of red with the relationship between the various areas that are, say, ultramarine blue, black or green, we notice that all these colours retain a uniform character, so that each ultramarine blue, for example, is part of the black–blue–white chord. At the same time, however, within the uniform character of this colour, the two patches of red achieve the greatest character contrast to be found in any single colour in this painting. The red in the foreground seems to be firmly rooted in the green of the meadow; it is a juicy, warm vermilion, against which the red of the cloud, in all its strangeness, glows with a certain coldness even though it clearly ought to be 'warm' according to conventional theory.

If we now place a hand over the light yellow in the picture (for instance, the church spire), we soon realise which family the red belongs to. This particular yellow has an affinity with the red that makes the red characteristically distinct from the Neapolitan yellow. Without the pale yellow, the red and the Neapolitan yellow move closer together so that they might almost belong to the same family of colours. If we cover up the pale yellow, the red cloud sinks back into the Neapolitan yellow sky and loses its incomparably strange expression. A third colour joins red and yellow as soon as we turn our attention to the area around the church spire. The light yellow and the red actually begin to flash as soon as we realise that they are carried by the same ultramarine blue that has already proved to belong to two other chords. This sparkling luminosity is most clearly evident in the place that is the source of tension in the picture: the church spire. The patches of red, yellow and blue act as reflexes or refractions of the light radiating from this hub. The red cloud on the far right is the 'strangest' place and the furthest removed from the centre of tension.

This shows us that the colours in the painting are more or less organised into the following groups: 1. Neapolitan yellow–mauve–grey; 2. black–blue–white; 3.*brown–blue–green; 4. red–yellow–blue.

Although these four chords do not constitute the entire arsenal of tools that Kandinsky uses in this picture in order to characterise colours through context, they do provide us with enough material to understand the following: first of all, how the juxtaposition of colours can create something akin to character in a colour, such as the way the extremely 'strange' effect of the red cloud in the upper right is achieved; and, secondly, how a pictorial space can be composed by colour alone. Let me dwell on this briefly. Earlier I mentioned that the Neapolitan yellow shines out from behind the mountains. While such luminosity is undoubtedly suggested by the figurative context, it would be rash to assume that this is the only factor at play here. As we have seen, we only have to disturb the interaction of the chords in order to diminish or even stifle such an effect. On the other hand, by focusing on the interaction of mauve and Neapolitan yellow, we begin to appreciate the singular spatial effect of the Neapolitan yellow in all its nuanced subtlety. The mauve is like a mist close up to us, in relation to which the Neapolitan yellow appears as a piercing distance pushing forwards, whereby the role played by the grey is not to be overlooked. But this entire chord of colour would completely miss its mark were it not contrasted with the black–blue–white – or rather, if it could not cross through it. It is in fact the black–blue–white that provides the (chromatic) framework for the Neapolitan yellow–mauve–grey to exercise its spatially formative power. But we now also notice that the chord that builds the 'framework' is itself dependent on being traversed by the *brown–blue–green, without which it would be left standing on only one leg, as it were. In order to stand firm, it needs two dimensions. We therefore maintain that chords 2 and 3 form a framework by dint of their contrast, in relation to which chord 1, by setting up its colours on either side of the framework and thus traversing it, opens up a space. However, what *occurs* within this space – the sudden, which has a *time* – is introduced by the fourth chord.

The fourth chord, as already mentioned, has a specifically luminous, sparkling character. It also constitutes the centre of tension from which movement radiates, of which the strange and elusive red of the cloud in the upper right is the most distant echo. Something *happens* in this picture. The sudden flash of temporality in the picture clearly has little to do with the rather banal notion that the various parts of the picture are successively grasped by the spectator. On the contrary, in this Murnau study of nature, time is emphatically

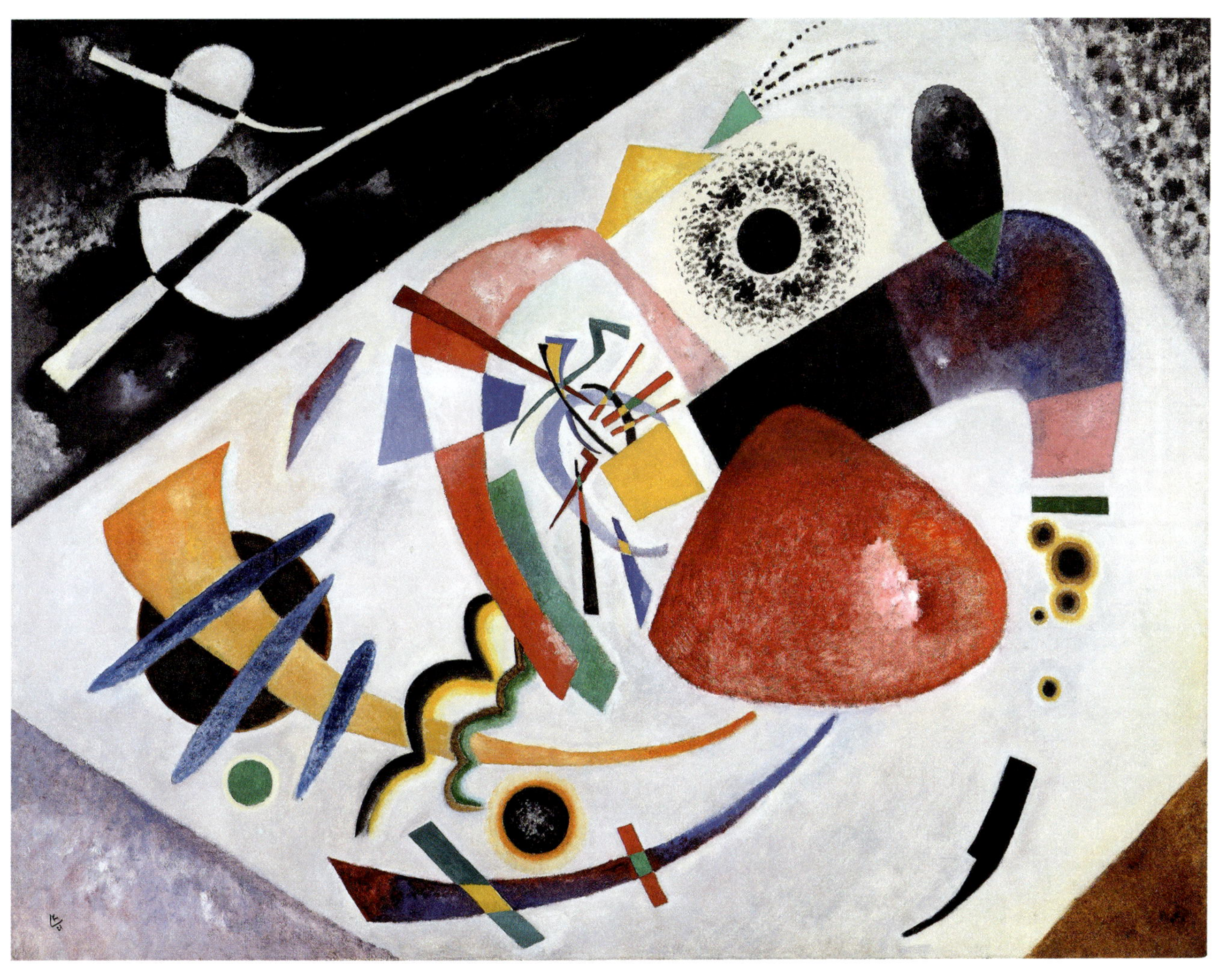

FIG 35
Red Spot II
1921
Oil on canvas 137 X 181.3
Städtische Galerie im Lenbachhaus, Munich

experienced suddenly, in the here and now. The moment, too, is time, and is perhaps more profoundly so than any simple sequence of movements in the eye of the beholder or the successive flow of motion of the spectator's attention. To summarise: pictorial space and pictorial time are opened up by four times three colours (that is, by four families each comprising three colours), so that in the context of these chords each colour takes on a dimension above and beyond its allegedly inherent natural character. I shall borrow an expression used by Albert Simon in calling this structure of four times three colours 'the construct'. [14] The construct is a basic structure of chromatic composition used in European painting since the nineteenth century and also adopted by Kandinsky. The very similar structures analysed here can be found throughout the artist's entire oeuvre, though it should be stressed that after leaving Russia, and especially since such works as *On White I* 1920 (no.76) and *Red Spot II* 1921 (fig.35), he radically revised his use of colours in ways that still throw up many unanswered questions.

On Orange and Gold

As we have already pointed out, the Murnau landscape study is an early and straightforward example of Kandinsky's use of colour. A more complex example can be found in *Improvisation 35* (fig.33, no.56). For this, let us first determine the four families of colours. In the upper left-hand corner of the picture there is a black patch that, to a certain degree, designates the dramatic centre of the painting. The black patch is itself inert, though it is at the hub of considerable 'tension'. Let us consider for a moment what is actually meant by the word 'tension', which Kandinsky himself often used. The black patch is bounded by orange and red (almost crimson) lake. [15] Beneath it, slightly to the right, is a rather large and dense form in green, which we shall refer to in the following as the 'stone', with an ultramarine bubble emerging from it on the right. In this picture, apart from the ultramarine blue, we can also find several areas of Paris blue – a fairly dark, slightly greenish hue as opposed to the ultramarine blue that tends somewhat towards red. The Paris blue, especially in most of the lines, appears as a dark, almost blackish colour, and is occasionally even mixed with black. Between the stone, the blue bubble and the 'blind spot' is where the primary event of the picture takes place (we shall see in a moment what that is). This event takes place at the edge of a 'field' of mainly pale green and pale yellow, bounded by yellow and violet, behind which the vermilion shines out. Having already discussed the way in which considerable strangeness can be evoked between certain colours, we shall now attempt to analyse the predominant colour families in order to grasp this effect more fully.

The orange surrounding the 'blind spot', for instance, is entirely separate from the crimson that in turn surrounds the orange. What sustains each of these colours? The following families of colour can be discerned and this can be checked by covering up each respective colour: 1. orange – violet – green earth,[16] and 2. crimson – emerald green (for example, the 'stone') – Paris blue (for example, the small shapes gravitating around the 'blind spot'). The first chord can be disrupted quite efficiently by covering up the violet that approaches the area around the blind spot from the right. This lessens the 'strangeness' of the orange in relation to its crimson surroundings, which alone suffices to collapse the 'tension' in this part of the picture. What is more, the orange no longer comes from 'elsewhere'; in other words, the spatial complexity is diminished. The orange becomes very 'strange' and intense when, sustained by its own family of colours, it is placed within the context of an entirely different family of colours.

Thus, whereas the second chord represents more of a material–physical state, the first chord appears as something that traverses it from behind. The second chord is held by a third: 3. ultramarine blue – yellow – white. This third chord appears to belong in a sense to the second, for both have blue in common, though it is not the same blue. It is the blue separating from blue that makes the rising blue bubble stand out so distinctly. Here, the ultramarine seems like a transmuted, transfigured blue, its specific character emanating from its proximity and difference in relation to the Paris blue. With this bubble, something akin to a separation, an elevation to other zones, takes place. These 'other zones' differ particularly from the highly charged zone at the 'blind spot' and from the solid darkness of the 'stone' and its surroundings.

The fourth chord in this construct is not formed by the participation of the vermilion, but by the participation of the ochre that occurs only once in the upper left and appears to play a subordinate role as an underlying background colour. This ochre relates to the white tone of the canvas, together with which it forms an elliptic chord of two colours. This chord, widely used in early twentieth-century painting, has a somewhat curious structure, which we shall not discuss in any great detail here. For our purposes, it is enough to note that the ochre, in its relation to the white of the canvas, carries the other colours like a quietly enduring background. If we cover up the ochre, the picture turns into a tapestry of motley colours.

But where does the vermilion that leaps out of the 'field' with such intensity, like a cold fire, belong? It belongs to what I should like to call the 'trumpet of light'. This is a structure that can, apparently, occur as part of a construct when it is slightly modified, as in the Murnau landscape study; or can just as easily occur independently, either without or alongside the construct, and which chromatically organises large areas of a picture or even entire paintings. As the name suggests, the 'trumpet of light' is invariably linked to some form of luminosity, the centre of which, in this particular case, is the 'blind spot'. Although the 'blind spot' itself is black, it has the character of an after-image of excessive brightness. There is a 'searing light' around this spot. The searing light falls into an imaginary space that is fundamentally dark. This darkness might even be described as the womb in which this image was originally conceived.[17] Without the darkness, how could the searing light seem so dazzling? Between the searing light and the conceiving black there emerges something like a refraction of light – or, in the words of Goethe, certain 'deeds and sufferings' of light,[18] a kind of flash of light that is formed here, as in the earlier Murnau landscape study, by the three primary colours: yellow–ultramarine–vermilion. However, in the earlier painting the red–yellow–blue occurs as part of the construct, while in this case the 'trumpet of light' is surplus to it – it is an independent element alongside the construct. This surplus, this exaltation, which can barely be kept within bounds, is typical of Kandinsky's use of colour from his 'wild' years right through to his Russian period when a profound transformation and radicalisation took place. At any rate, around 1914 Kandinsky achieved a chromatic diversity and richness that had been inaccessible to him four years earlier.

If we compare the two pictures under discussion here, we notice that the orange and Neapolitan yellow respectively play a similar role in both. In each painting these are the colours that designate the place and source of greatest 'tension'. We can trace this same function in many drawings by Kandinsky in which he specifies the colours. Let us take, by way of example, the untitled drawing at the Centre Pompidou (fig.36). The colours are designated 'w' for white, 'Neap' and 'N' for Neapolitan yellow and 'or' for orange. Needless to say, not all the colours that would be used in the painting are listed, but only the main colours. In order to understand this drawing and others like it, much depends on considering the designated colours as distinct and separate — as *members of different families of colour*. The shape labelled 'or' seems particularly luminous, even in this black and white sketch. A similar effect can be found in the preparatory sketch for *Improvisation 11* at the Centre Pompidou (fig.37), in which 'or' is reserved for the central sail. A cannon on the right seems to be aiming directly at this 'or'. In the painting *Improvisation 11* 1910 (no.39), the sail is yellow and the 'or', now Neapolitan yellow, has moved further to the left into the wave froth. Finally, let us consider one more untitled drawing (also at the Centre Pompidou, fig.38),[19] in which a formulaic group of riders at the upper edge rushes towards a sun designated 'or'.

The 'or' obviously refers to the colour orange, but in the second instance it also has a function that is independent of the absolute colour orange. In the finished paintings, at least, the colour orange can be replaced, as we have seen, by another colour. What they invariably have in common is that this is where the 'tension' reaches its height, or is at the centre. But what is tension? We may find some indication

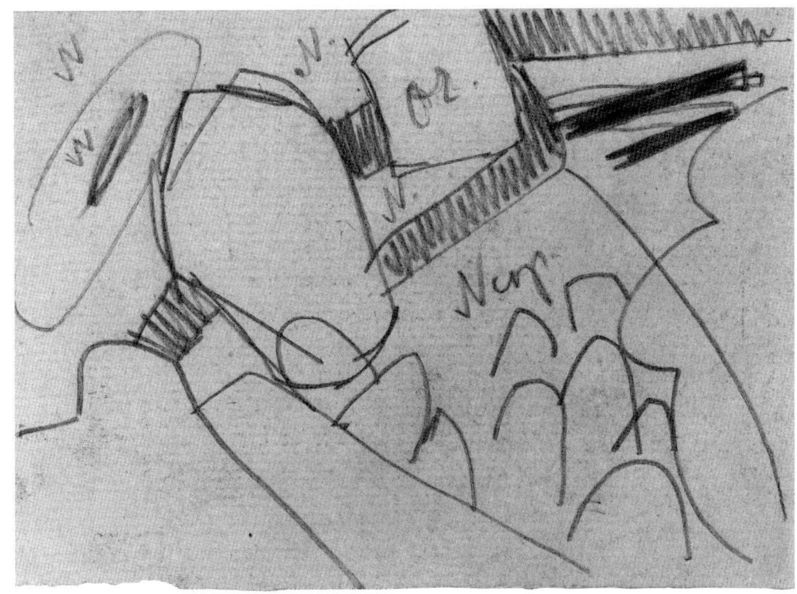

of this in the letters 'or' that designate such points in these and other drawings, primarily indicating orange, if we apply them to what Kandinsky described in his 'Reminiscences' as 'the most beautiful hour of the Moscow day' and of which he said, 'To paint this hour, I thought, must be for an artist the most impossible, the greatest joy.' [20]

This vision culminates in his description:

> [the] stiff, silent ring of the Kremlin walls, and above, towering over everything, like a shout of triumph, like a self-oblivious hallelujah, the long, white, graceful, serious line of the Bell Tower of Ivan the Great. And upon its tall, tense neck stretched up toward heaven in eternal yearning, the golden head of the cupola, which among the golden and coloured stars of the other cupolas, is Moscow's sun. [21]

The gold of the cupola, the 'or' of the drawings and the points of greatest 'tension' identified above, all seem to point to the same thing [22] – a profoundly orgiastic vision. In *Improvisation 35* the place of greatest tension at the 'blind spot' is also the place of greatest orgiastic release, to one side of which the blue bubble issues forth in all its purity. The abstract image thus becomes a figure of physical introspection, an expression of 'that invisible life that we ourselves are'. [23]

The Spectator Lost

The early Kandinsky has the reputation of being an expressive artist whose works are brimming with colours (such as *Composition VII* 1913, no.52), reaching an apex of complexity in the years 1913-14, while the later Kandinsky tends to be regarded as a more sober artist with a tendency towards the geometric, already foreshadowed in his Moscow period and emerging clearly in such works as *Red Spot II* and *Circles on Black* (no.79), both 1921. However, if we analyse the chromatic structure of these works, we find that they have become significantly more complex and, with that, more potent still – though only if we have the time and patience to commit ourselves to the study of these highly important works. Alexandre Kojève was aware of this and mentioned it in a (posthumously published) letter to Kandinsky, in which he writes that, following a period of transition, Kandinsky had overcome the uniformity and reference to unity in his early works. [24] Just what kind of unity Kojève meant may perhaps be clear from what has been pointed out above. Should not the 'blind spot' in *Improvisation 35* and its tension-charged surroundings be seen as the centre of an event which, though its effusive richness can barely be grasped in one glance, remains bound to that centre, thereby ensuring the picture's independence from its surroundings, that is, its autonomy? Our analysis of the construct and the 'trumpet of light' also shows the pictures as functioning units. It might be said that their unity is created by the functioning of one or another family of colours and their respective powers of spatial composition, provided that the families of colours are defined only within the unity of a picture and can thus, in turn, also define the unity of the picture. According to Kojève, the later Kandinsky had put this form of unity behind him.

In spite of its already geometric syntax, the painting *Red Spot II* is still a work of Kandinsky's transitional phase. As regards the colours, this painting indicates the direction of change. In the middle of the picture near the lower edge, there is a black spot surrounded by an orange ring. In some ways, the effect of this orange is similar to that

FIG 37
Untitled (Sketch for 'Improvisation 11')
1910
Pencil on envelope
18 x 11.7
Musée National d'Art Moderne, Centre Georges Pompidou, Paris

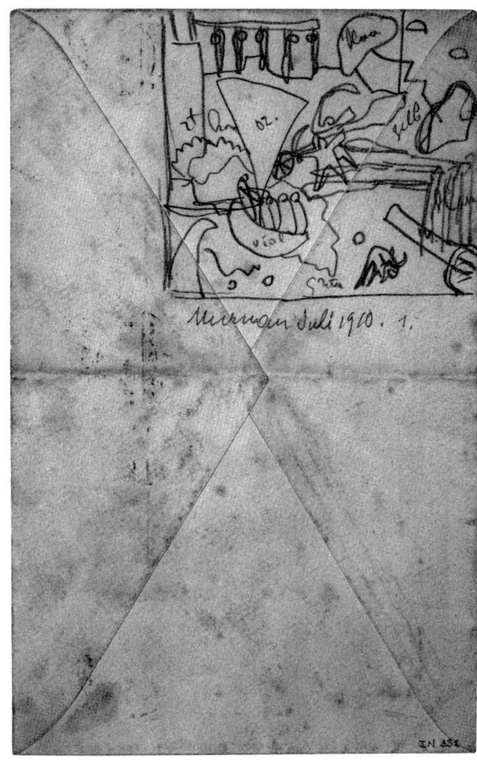

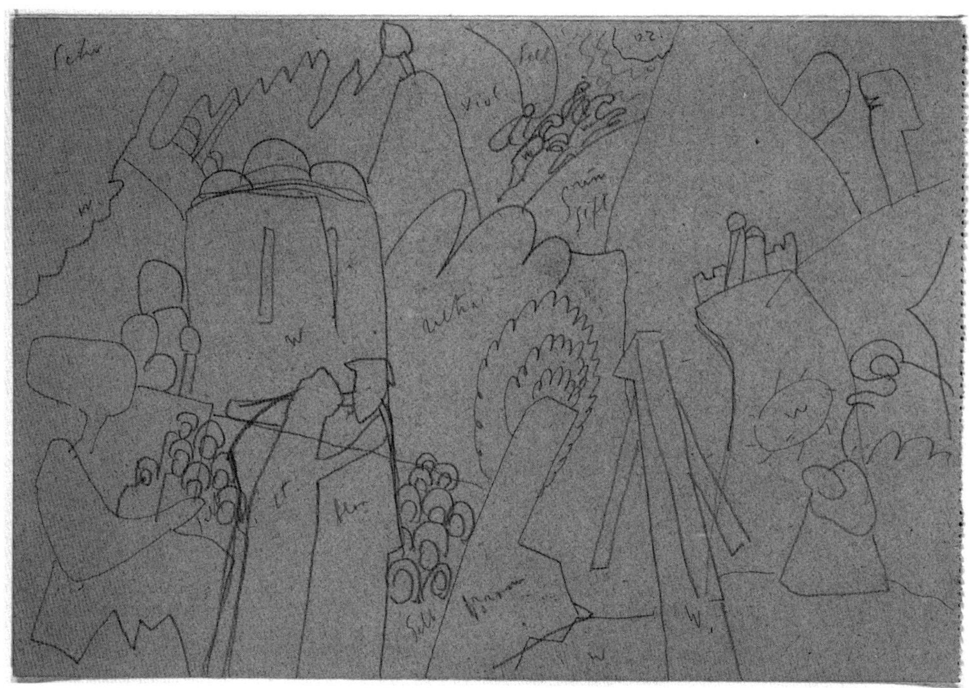

of the Neapolitan yellow in the Murnau landscape study and the orange next to the 'blind spot' in *Improvisation 35*. It is *detached* from the dominant tones, a *stranger* to the black of the large, bent shape with its point broken off, the brown of the sphere on the left towards which the point was aimed, the blue of the smaller broken point that aims directly at the place where the first pointed shape is broken, the double red of the red arc in the centre of the picture and the red 'spot' from which the painting takes its title. What is it that makes the orange ring out so clearly amid the concert of other colours?

The picture 'begins', in a way that will be described in more detail later, with the black point that aims towards the brown sphere. Black and brown are set against a white ground, with which they form a chord: white–brown–black. This chord exists as though buried beneath the rest; it emerges only gradually and can be perceived only in the course of time. Between the point and the sphere, we sense a droning tension. The ultramarine blue point that breaks into this tenseness lends the white of the background a different tone. The blue suddenly makes the white radiant, whereas the brown and black made it nebulous. What happens to the background here is remarkable: whereas the black and brown are merely set upon the white and in themselves bear no relationship to the four cut-off corners of the picture, the ultramarine blue suddenly turns the white area into a *sui generis* entity set against a background that is, in turn, brown – the brown of the lower right-hand corner. This gives us the blue–white–brown' chord.[25] The brown of this second chord is not the same as the brown of the first chord. It is a second brown, resulting from a transposition. Its character depends primarily on being the 'revenant' (*Wiedergänger*) of the first brown. If we focus on the picture and note the way the brown appears in the lower right-hand corner, we soon realise that the mauve in the lower left-hand corner is also brown, or, to be more precise, that this mauve is the result of a fading or discoloration of the brown – in other words, that the background of the white field is fundamentally and originally brown. We can imagine the entire picture being primed in brown, bearing the white field in the middle and finally turning to mauve in the lower left-hand corner. This change of colour responds to a painterly event in the main white field: the orange of the curved points below. The upper corners, too, are discolorations emanating from brown, but in such a way that the black/white at the upper left appears particularly rough and raw, especially in relation to the red arch in the centre of the picture. This corner harbours a terrible secret. Notwithstanding, it is the brown that is the underlying colour of all the corners, the colour that carries the white field. This discoloration from brown to mauve, brown to black, and so on, which we find in the four corners of the picture, is an effect that Kandinsky would later expand upon considerably (as in *Reciprocal Agreement* 1942, with its background painted in three colours; fig. 39).

Something happens where the blue and the black point meet. Not only do these points break and splinter. The actual point of collision is defined by the red arc into which the black point penetrates, while the 'red spot' of the title falls away to the right as though it had been severed. The chromatic structure of this complex is quite intricate, so we shall content ourselves with looking more closely at the difference between the two reds. The vermilion of the arc belongs in the context of a series of colours that possess a high degree of independence from one another: the yellow square in the centre, the blue, the black, the light green – all these colours are juxtaposed like blocks and it is inconceivable that they should ever mix. Similar characters can be found, for instance, in the works of Malevich from the same period and earlier. The carmine tone of the 'red spot', on the other hand, has a distinctly 'tonal' quality. It reverberates in the ultramarine of the black arc and these two colours also combine as chords with white and black. The impression we have here is almost as though these colours could be mixed together, as though interim tones might emerge.

A more detailed analysis than can be provided here would be needed in order to grasp these structures fully. For our purposes, however, it is enough to be able to see the three chromatic groups of white–brown–black (point and sphere), blue–white–brown (the other point and the background), the red of the arc and the carmine of the 'spot' as independent structures in dynamic interaction. Once we do so, it is no longer difficult to discern the chromatic orange group. The orange relates to the Paris blue of the three elongated ovals in the lower left and the violet–purple of the two smaller points near the point of collision between the black point and the red arc. Once again, we can check whether these colours belong together by covering the one or the other. The orange radiating around the black dot introduces a singular luminosity into the picture, an indescribable mellowness that betrays its affinity with the 'or' of earlier drawings and the corresponding areas in paintings.

But what is happening in the right-hand part of the picture, where the shaft of the large black pointed shape, perhaps influenced by the two bent points pushing towards it from below, hangs limply down? Could that also be the source of the rather odd black bump on the back of the same arc? In the actual curve itself, there is an ultramarine that belongs to the carmine red of the 'red spot'. But it is followed by a pink, a green and a group of dots with brown, black and yellow. These colours can no longer be linked to the four families of colour, or indeed to any family of colour. Although, in the construct, the individual colours generally crop up in different contexts, they remain identifiable ('pigmentary identity') throughout the entire picture as members of the same family of colours. In this way, a 'chromatic atmosphere' is defined that predominates in the entire picture. We also say that the colours of the construct form a 'palette', that is to say, a collection of colour tones grouped into chords, whose articulation itself creates a pictorial space. [26] Here, by contrast, we find individual colour tones that bear no relationship any more to this 'palette', each of them standing irrevocably alone.

This atomisation of the world of colour (as we shall put it for want of a better term), is, however, already inherent in the articulation

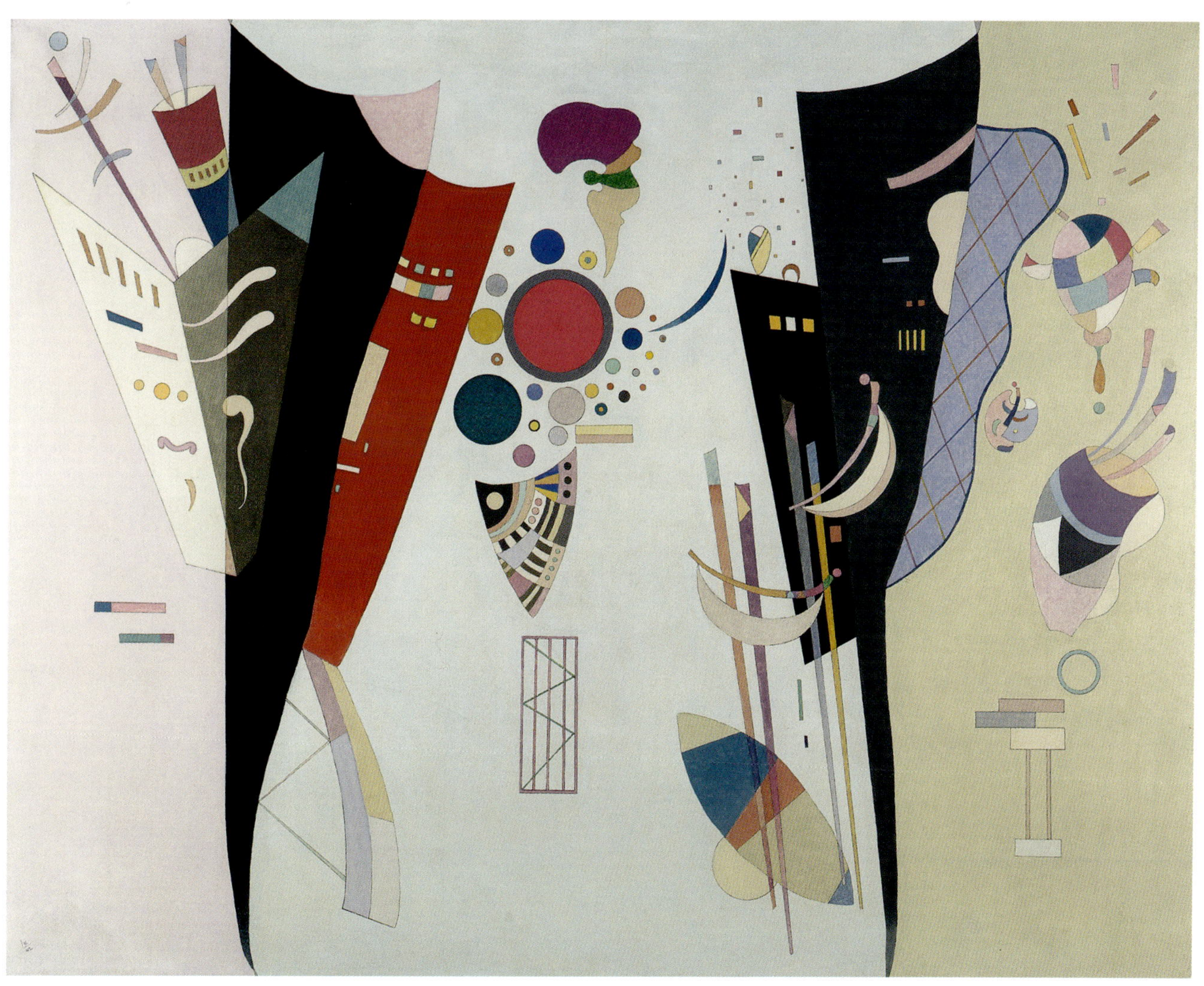

FIG 39
Reciprocal Agreement
1942
Mixed media on canvas
114 x 146
Musée National d'Art Moderne,
Centre Georges Pompidou, Paris

of the construct of *Red Spot II* itself. Indeed, the colour families here are already linked right from the start with certain complexes of forms, the white–brown–black of the point and sphere, the blue–white–brown of the other point and the brown background, and so on. These chromatically defined complexes of forms relate to one another dynamically. When looking at them, we have to move from event to event, thereby becoming involved in an occurrence that *destroys* the spectator as a homogeneous subject with a single viewpoint. The only trace that remains is the 'central point' which, admittedly, need not necessarily be at the geometric centre, but which is the last witness to what Kandinsky calls the 'prototype of pictorial expression', the 'point lying in the centre of a surface which is square in shape' (fig.40, *Point and Line to Plane*).[27] In *Red Spot II* this central point is constituted by the green circle in the lower left of the picture. This 'central point' is itself immutable, but each shape is ultimately accorded its place on the picture plane and its movement in relation to this point. It lends the picture plane a sense of tension and distinguishes between its zones. Thus its proximity lends the two curved points at the bottom of the picture their virulence and speed (just as a planet closer to the sun moves faster, as though fearing its heat). In the upper right, on the other hand, there is more of a sense of floating weightlessly. In this respect, the 'central spot' constitutes the picture plane as a unit of tension. Central spots of this kind can also be found in other works by Kandinsky and are especially in evidence in the works from his late Russian period and shortly afterwards. A particularly impressive example is the small green circle seen in *In Grey* 1919 (no.70), on the lower edge to the left of centre. This spot, too, serves as a point of reference for all positionings and as a trace of the defunct spectator.

Translated from the German by Ishbel Flett and Catherine Schelbert

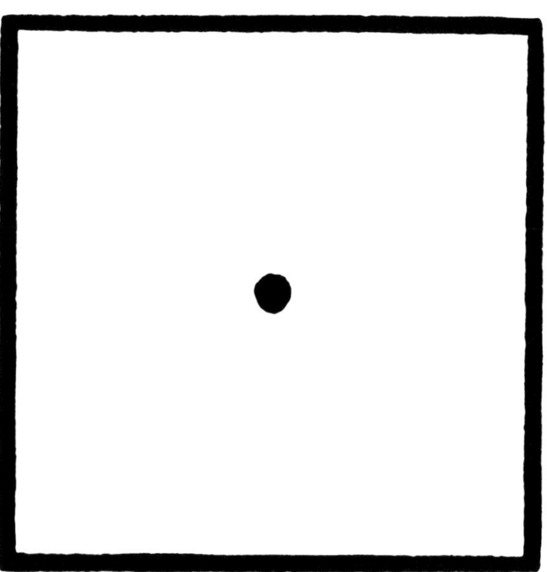

FIG 40
**Illustration in
'Punkt und Linie zu Fläche'**
1926

1866

Born in Moscow on 4 December, son of a wealthy Siberian tea merchant, Wassily, and a native of Moscow, Lydiya Ivanovna Tikheyeva. Moscow – 'the city with ten faces' – would shape his childhood imagination and continue to inspire him throughout his life.

1871

The Kandinskys move to Odessa where the climate is considered better for his father's health. Shortly afterwards, his parents divorce. Young Wassily stays with his mother and her elder sister Elizaveta. His aunt takes part in his upbringing and inspires his interest in music. Wassily takes piano and cello lessons. Many years later he will dedicate his book *Über das Geistige in der Kunst* (*Concerning the Spiritual in Art*, 1912) to Elizaveta.

1876

Attends a humanistic Gymnasium (secondary school) in Odessa (fig.41). From 1879 onwards spends the summers with his father in Moscow.

1885 – 1888

Moves back to Moscow. Enrols at the University of Moscow to study law and economics (fig.42). Becomes involved in the All-Russian student organisation and protests against a ruling by the Tsar which outlaws student unions. Paints in his spare time.

1889 – 1892

In the summer the Society of Natural Science and Anthropology sends him to Vologda province (north-eastern Russia).[1] Kandinsky discovers peasant folk art. Subsequently publishes two articles on peasant law and paganism among Siberian tribes. Sees Rembrandts at the Hermitage, St Petersburg and is impressed. Travels to Paris. Health problems interrupt his studies.

1892

Graduates after completing law studies. Marries cousin Anya Shemyakina with whom he lives until 1904. They divorce in 1911. Makes second trip to Paris.

1893

In November completes PhD dissertation *On the legality of Labourer's Wages*. Offered assistant position at Faculty of Law, University of Moscow.

1895

Becomes artistic manager of Kushnerev printing company in Moscow where he designs chocolate box covers.

1896

His interest in art is encouraged by seeing Claude Monet's *Haystacks* at *French Industrial and Art Exhibition* in Moscow, and attending Richard Wagner's *Lohengrin* at the Bolshoi Theatre in Moscow. A particular sensibility for synaesthetic experiences is already apparent. He later writes, 'I saw all my colours in spirit, before my eyes. Wild, almost mad lines drew themselves in front of me.'[2] Kandinsky is financially independent because of an inheritance from an uncle. Declines lectureship at University of Dorpat (now Tartu, Estonia). Moves in December to Munich where he enters private art school of Anton Ažbe.

1897

Moves to a flat in Giselastrasse and meets Alexei Jawlensky and Marianne Werefkin, who are also studying with Ažbe. Visits exhibitions at the Munich Secession with pictures by Max Liebermann, Lovis Corinth and Giovanni Segantini. Also Hermann Obrist, one of the earliest protagonists for reform of the arts and leading personality of the Munich Jugendstil movement, who founds, together with, among others, Peter Behrens, the Vereinigte Werkstätten für Kunst im Handwerk (United Workshops for Art in Applied Art).

1898

Rejected by Munich Art Academy. Works independently on drawing and anatomy. His work *Port of Odessa I* is shown at an exhibition of the South Russian Artists Association in Odessa. Exhibits with them until 1910.

1900

Becomes a student of Franz von Stuck at Academy in Munich, where Paul Klee also studies. Meets Hans Purrmann, Alexander von Salzmann, Ernst Stern and Albert Weisgerber. Stuck, one of the leading artists associated with Jugendstil, encourages Kandinsky to work with strong light/dark contrasts. Kandinsky makes first colour works on black paper and first woodcuts. The strictly organised curriculum does not meet Kandinsky's expectations. However, certain of Stuck's motifs have a lasting impact: the guardians of paradise, the snake as symbol of evil, the mysterious rider, the Greek warrior as symbol of the avant garde. Kandinsky keeps up contact with his homeland and sends work each February, until 1908, to the exhibition of the Moscow Artists' Union.

1901

Publishes his first art review on 17 April, 'Kritika kritikov' ('Critique of Critics'), in *Novosti Dnia*, Moscow.[3] Writes frequent articles from Munich for Sergei Diaghilev's progressive art journal *Mir Iskusstva* (St Petersburg) about exhibitions and art life there. Paints first gouaches, temperas and small oil studies, mainly landscapes, legends and scenes from medieval Russian life. Also designs furniture and ceramics. In May founds Phalanx group with Gustav Freytag, Waldemar Hecker, Wilhelm Hüsgen, Rolf Niczky and Ernst Stern. 14 July moves to Friedrichstrasse 1. First Phalanx exhibition in Munich, for which Kandinsky designs a poster. The show travels also to Wiesbaden, Krefeld and Barmen. Eleven more Phalanx exhibitions are held until 1904. Kandinsky's first exhibition in Germany. Finishes studies with Stuck. Kandinsky takes over the presidency of the Phalanx group. Travels to Hamburg, Stettin, St Petersburg and Rothenburg ob der Tauber. In September takes part in exhibition of South Russian Artists Association in Odessa. The Phalanx art school is established; Kandinsky becomes director and teaches drawing and painting. Unlike most art schools at this time, it is open to both sexes and most of the students are women.

1902

Meets Gabriele Münter, a 25 year old student at Phalanx art school. Friendship with Peter Behrens and Hermann Obrist. Produces his first woodcuts *Promenade*. Continues painting landscapes. Participates for the first time in the V Berlin Secession exhibition in the spring. Meets David Burlyuk. Second Phalanx exhibition (January to March) devoted to the Jugendstil. It features artists from Darmstädter Mathildenhöhe: Peter Behrens, Rudolf Bosselt, Hans Christiansen and Patriz Huber, also Erich Kleinhempel from Dresden, Natal'ya Davidova from Moscow. Works by members of Munich's United Workshops for Art in Applied Art are also shown; Kandinsky exhibits decorative designs, influenced by Jugendstil. Writes a survey of exhibitions in Munich titled 'Korrespondentsiia iz Miunkhena' for the Russian art journal *Mir Isskustva*. Third Phalanx exhibition (May-June) includes guest artists Lovis Corinth and Wilhelm Trübner. Travels with his pupils to Kochel during the summer. Fourth Phalanx exhibition (July–August) includes guest artists Akseli Gallen-Kallela and Albert Weisgerber.

1903

Kandinsky spends the summer with Phalanx students in Kallmünz, north of Regensburg. In August Behrens asks him to lead the class in decorative paintings at the Düsseldorf School for Arts and Crafts. Kandinsky declines and remains in Munich. In September he is impressed by St Marks during a trip to Venice; in Vienna on the way home, he admires paintings of the Italian Renaissance at the Kunsthistorisches Museum. In October he is in Moscow, where he writes to Gabriele Münter: 'I have a very strange sensation here in Moscow. Hundreds of memories, partly forgotten pictures, the whole character of the genuine Russian town which I feel and understand even today, these churches, carriages, flats, people who are so distant yet so familiar. I've been away from here for seven years and only now, for the first time, I am having these sensations.'[4] In Moscow he makes the album *Stikh bec slov* (*Poems without Words*) with twelve woodcuts inspired by the so-called 'Lubkis', or Russian folk picture books; it is published in Moscow. The Phalanx school closes at the end of the year, because of insufficient student numbers. Besides painting, Kandinsky works on embroidery, jewellery, clothes and furniture. He engages with contemporary French art and becomes a member of the Vereinigung für angewandte Kunst (Association for Applied Art) in Munich, founded in 1903; their exhibitions also include drawings.

1904

First notes towards a theory of colour. In May visits the exhibition *Linie und Form* (*Line and Form*) in Krefeld, with Gabriele Münter. Kandinsky's investigations into the question of form in art and the central notion of form created from inner necessity are adumbrated for the first time. Trip to Holland; visits museums. Kandinsky paints from nature, chiefly with the palette knife. In September Kandinsky separates from his wife Anya and moves alone to a flat in Aimmillerstrasse. Creates first, handwritten, chronological House catalogue, dated 20 September 1904. Kandinsky differentiates between 'paintings', 'small oil studies', 'coloured drawings' and 'decorative sketches'. Continues working on landscape motifs, imaginary Russian folk tales and pictures with medieval subjects. Writes to Gabriele Münter: 'I have a new path, which earlier masters might have intuited, but which will sooner or later be recognised.'[5] The effects of colour and how colour is perceived are of particular interest to him: 'I must consciously deepen my absorption in myself, to judge the effect of colour on my soul.'[6] In Paris, in November, he is awarded a medal at the newly founded, progressive Salon d'Automne. He shows there regularly until 1910.

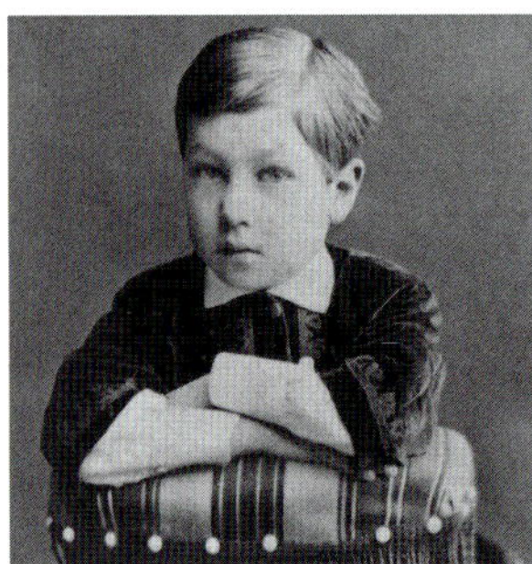

FIG.41
Kandinsky as a Student at the Secondary School in Odessa
Gabriele Münter-and Johannes Eichner-Stiftung, Munich

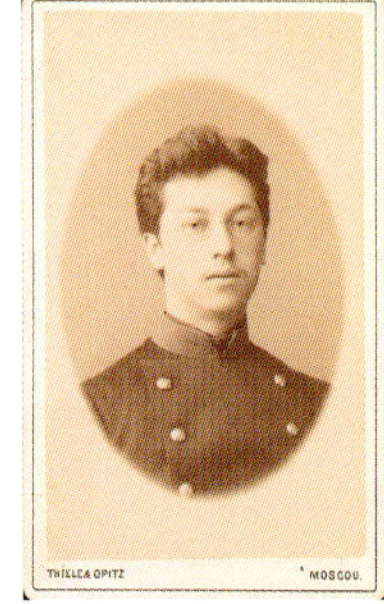

FIG.42
Kandinsky as a University Student in Moscow
c.1886
Gabriele Münter-and Johannes Eichner-Stiftung, Munich

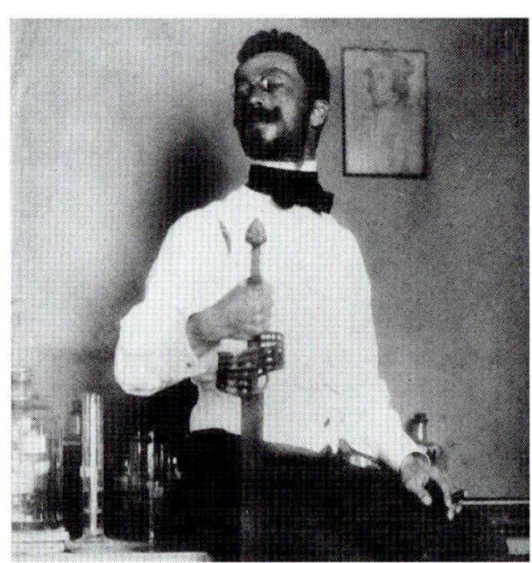

FIG.43
Kandinsky Posing with a Sword
1897
Gabriele Münter-and Johannes Eichner-Stiftung, Munich

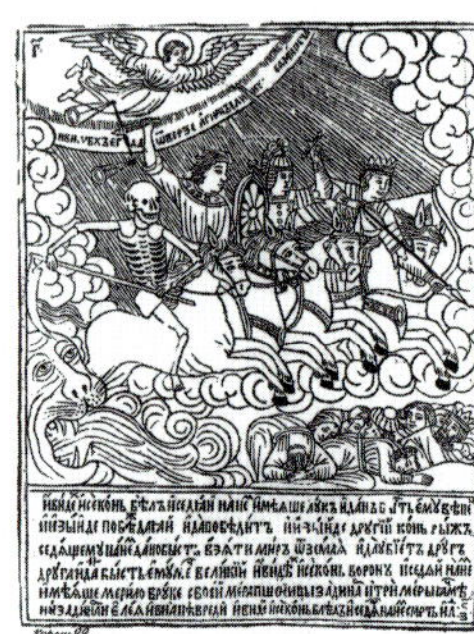

FIG.44
Russian Lubok (Folk Print): The Riders of the Apocalypse
D. Rovinskii 1881

At the end of the year he travels to Tunis and Italy, recording his impressions in 'coloured drawings': 'later I sometimes painted a landscape "from memory" better than from nature'. I painted 'The Old Town' like that and, later, many Dutch and Arab coloured drawings.'[7] The Phalanx Association is ended in December.

1905

Kandinsky and Gabriele Münter remain in Tunis until April, returning via Rome Florence, Bologna, Verona, Innsbruck, Igels, Starnberg and Dresden. Galerie Krause in Munich presents Kandinsky's first solo exhibition in mid-February. Kandinsky maintains his contracts in Russia and takes part in exhibitions in Moscow (Association of South Russian Artists) and St Petersburg (New Artist's Association). In October he exhibits for the first time in Paris at the Salon des Indépendants, where he continues to exhibit paintings until 1912. In the same month he travels to Odessa with his father and follows the political upheavals. Writes to Gabriele Münter, 'it has finally, finally happened. We have a proper constitution and are no longer subjects, but citizens, proper citizens with all the important rights. After anticipating this for 25 years I now experience the day […] Finally, finally, freedom.'[8] In December travels to Rapallo with Gabriele Münter, where they stay until April of the following year. Makes numerous landscape studies and small format oil sketches on cardboard or canvas board.

1906

On 1 May 1906 the couple moves to Sèvres (west of Paris). This sojourn lasts nearly 13 months and is plagued by personal and artistic difficulties. Kandinsky grieves at the death of his half brother Aleksandr Koyevnikov, has guilty feelings towards his wife, left behind in Munich. He watches with interest the art scene in Paris, shows interest in the Neo-Impressionists and encounters in exhibitions pictures by the Fauves (Henri Matisse at Berthe Weill, the Nabis and Neo-Impressionist at Bernheim, Pablo Picasso, Paul Cézanne, Vincent van Gogh, Paul Gauguin, Edvard Munch at Ambroise Vollard). Only limited contacts with other artists in Paris. Gets to know Gertrude Stein and sees her collection of works by Picasso and Matisse. Own work scarcely noticed when exhibited at the Salon d'Automne. Several visits to the exhibition of Russian art organised by Sergei Diaghilev, and to the Gauguin retrospective at the Grand Palais, in October and November. He is fascinated by the work of Georges Rouault and Henri Rousseau. In early December he begins designs for the picture *Riding Couple* (fig.7). End of December he shows drawings and woodcuts at the Berlin Secession, next to artists of the Brücke (Bridge).

1907

In January Kandinsky visits Chartres. The artist group Les Tendances Nouvelles, led by Alexis Mérodack-Jeaneau, Kandinsky's neighbour in Sèvres, offers him a professorship at their art school, which he declines. In May he shows a selection of 109 works in the Musée du Peuple in Angers. After his return to Paris, he goes to Bad Reichenhall, then on to Switzerland (Bex, Rapperswil, Immensee, Vierwaldstättersee, Lucerne, Brienz, Spiez and Brig). In September he moves to Berlin for eight months with Gabriele Münter and visits the great museums and theatres. He is introduced to the theosophy of Rudolf Steiner at a series of lectures in the Berlin Architects' House. He continues to be influenced by the theatrical concepts of Max Reinhardt and Edward Gordon Craig, and by his interest in of music and theosophy.

1908

Kandinsky and Gabriele Münter return from Berlin to Munich on 10 June. They go on cycling tours and reach Murnau (fig.47), which Kandinsky had already visited in August 1904, writing to Gabriele Münter in a postcard, 'it is very, very beautiful … The low-lying and slow-moving clouds, the dusky, dark-violet woods, the gleaming white buildlings, velvety-deep roofs of the churches, the saturated green of the foliage, remain with me; I even dreamt of these things.'[9] For the first time Kandinsky works again with artists with whom he conducts intensive discussions about art. Jawlensky also has close ties to artists of the school of Pont-Aven and to Matisse and is up to date on the latest artistic developments in France. The landscape in Murnau becomes a decisive motif in Kandinsky's artistic output (nos.3-11, 18, 19, 26). He also does paintings on glass, a skill found for over a century in Murnau and its surroundings; Kandinsky makes over 30 works, mainly with religious themes by 1914. For the pictures painted on cardboard, he elects a larger format. The colours become more vibrant and the motifs less naturalistic. Kandinsky gets to know the composer Thomas von Hartmann and works with him on theatrical projects in which music, dance, theatre and visual art combine to form a total work of art (*Daphnis and Chloe*, *The Garden of Eden*, *Yellow Sound*, *Black and White*).

1909

In January Kandinsky, Münter, Jawlensky and Werefkin, together with Alfred Kubin, Adolf Erbslöh and Alexander Kanoldt and the art historians Heinrich Schnabel and Oskar Wittenstein found the Munich New Artists' Association (NKVM, Neue Künstlervereinigung München). Kandinsky is the first chairman. The founding declaration reads, 'our assumption is that artists, apart from impressions observed in the outside world, progressively collects experiences of the inner world.'[10] Kandinsky ensures that each ordinary member has the right to submit two non jury-selected works for exhibition. In early 1909 he paints *Painting with Skiff* (fig.48). In his second House Catalogue II the work is described for the first time as 'Improvisation'. In the manuscript of *Concerning the Spiritual in Art*, dated 3 August 1909, Kandinsky explains 'Improvisations' as 'mainly sub-conscious, mostly suddenly created expressions of processes with an inner character, namely impressions of an "inner nature".'[11] In the summer Gabriele Münter buys a house in Murnau, the so-called Russian House (fig.49), where she and Kandinsky spend several months each year in the years to come. Kandinsky retains his flat in Ainmillerstrasse. A mystical and spiritual level can be perceived in Kandinsky's painting from this time. Kandinsky dispenses increasingly with narrative content and figuration. In early December the first exhibition of the NKVM is shown at the Moderne Galerie Thannhauser, before traveling on to other venues. Under Kandinsky's leadership the NKVM invites sculptors, poets and dancers, besides other painters, to its activities. From 1909 an exceptionally active and creative work phase begins for Kandinsky, which eventually leads him to abstraction. A second series of woodcuts, entitled *Xylographies,* published by Les Tendances Nouvelles.

1910

In his House catalogue list he notes the title 'C' for his large format figurative oil paintings, an abbreviation for 'Composition'. His ten Compositions, with seven completed by 1914, the last in 1939, are regarded as the artist's most important paintings (fig.12, nos.20, 21, 49, 50, 52). In January Kandinsky completes *Composition I*, in March *Composition II*, and in September he completes *Composition III*. Motifs such as horse and rider, boats with oarsmen, figures in long coats recur in his work up to 1919. In October Kandinsky travels to Paris and, after a long interval, to Moscow. His enthusiasm for the city can be sensed in his correspondence with Gabriele Münter. He comes into contact with the Russian avant garde (Nikolay Kul'bin, Natal'ya Goncharova, Mikhail Larionov, as well as David and Vladimir Burlyuk) and contributes

to exhibitions (International Salon Izdebsky in Odessa; Jack of Diamonds and Moscow Artist's Union in Moscow). For the catalogue of the International Salon Izdebsky he writes and essay called 'Content and Form' and translates Schoenberg's essay 'Octaves and Parallel Fifths'.[12] In the manuscript for *Concerning the Spiritual in Art* he further develops his theory of art. Of great importance is his meeting Franz Marc. Kandinsky feels himself understood by Marc at a time his own work is often heavily criticised in the press. A storm of protest is the response to his exhibition of *Composition II* and *Improvisation 10* (no.29) at the second exhibition of the NKVM. Marc writes a well-intentioned review about the spiritualisation of the material world and an immaterial inner sensation which expresses itself through pictures. Marc becomes a member of the NKVM.

1911

In response to a Schoenberg concert on 1 January Kandinsky paints *Impression III (Concert)* two days later (fig. 50). In the correspondence that arises from this experience he discusses pictorial and musical problems with the composer. They meet for the first time in September. By March Kandinsky completes five further *Impressions*. 'Impression' he defines in *Concerning the Spiritual in Art* as the direct impression of 'external nature', which is expressed in a drawn-pictorial form.[13] He defines 'Compositions' as planned and rationally structured 'Improvisations'.[14] On 10 January Kandinsky resigns as chairman of the NKVM because of increasing divergences of view with other members. During the hot summer he discovers the particular meaning of the colour white for his work. Kandinsky stresses that the inner character of a colour is defined by its specific functional interaction with other colours; 'he who can transform the visible into a chorus of colours is a master of vision. He who can make the visible impression with the simple means of this chorus of colours into the realisation of his thoughts, is master of himself. That is how one should judge an artist.'[15] When the majority of members of the NKVM refuse to include *Composition V* (fig.12) in the forthcoming Third Exhibition Kandinsky, together with Marc, leaves the Association, along with Gabriele Münter, Kubin, the composer von Hartmann and Henri Le Fauconnier (Jawlensky and Marianne Werefkin remain members). In only two weeks they organise an exhibition to coincide with the NKVM show, an exhibition with the title *First Exhibition of the Editors of Der Blaue Reiter* (fig.51). The exhibition takes place in the Moderne Galerie Thannhauser in Munich from 18 December 1911 until 12 January 1912, and travels thereafter to eleven

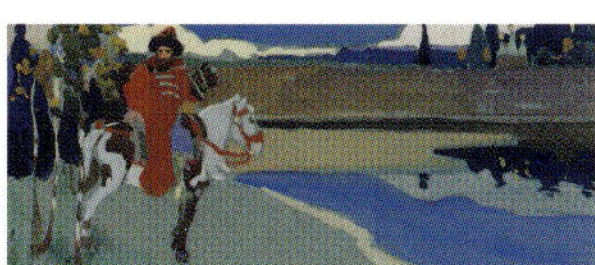

FIG.45
Russian Knight
1901-2
Gouache on cardboard 17.6 x 36.6
Städtische Galerie im
Lenbachhaus, Munich

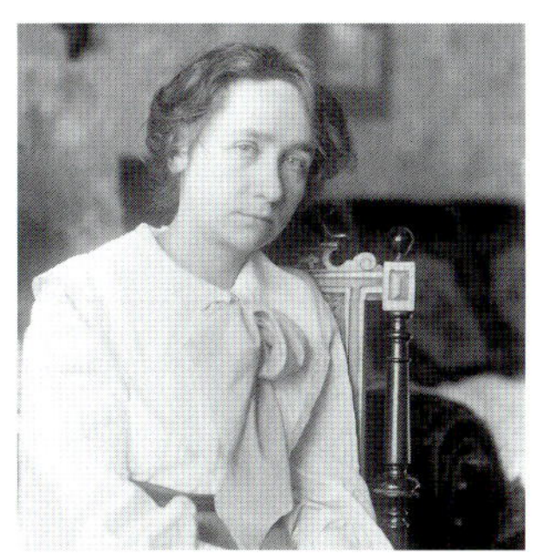

FIG.46
Gabriele Münter in Dresden
1905
Gabriele Münter-and Johannes
Eichner-Stiftung, Munich

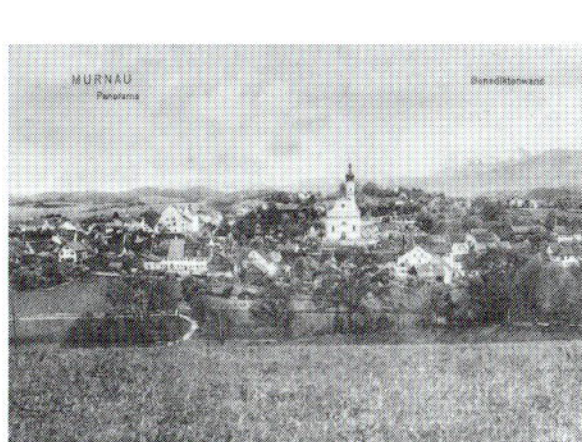

FIG.47
Murnau, View of the Church
1900
Schlossmuseum, Murnau

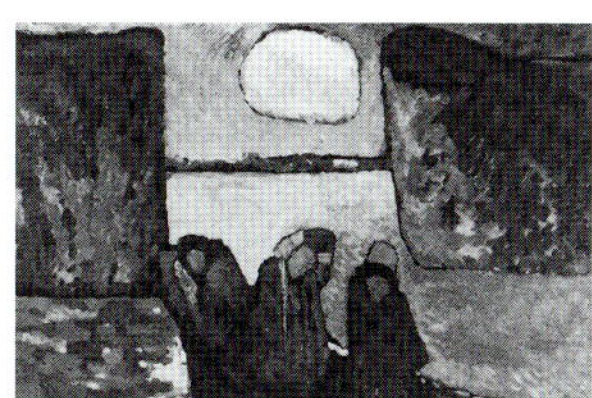

FIG.48
Painting with Skiff
1909
Oil on canvas 79 x 123
Private Collection, Sweden

European cities (Cologne, Berlin, Bremen, Hagen, Frankfurt, Hamburg, Budapest, Oslo, Helsinki, Trondheim and Göteborg). The *Second Exhibition of the Editors of Der Blaue Reiter. Black-White* opens a month later in the Galerie Goltz in Munich and presents the new tendencies in printmaking and drawings. Already on 19 June, five months before the row in the NKVM, Kandinsky had consulted Marc on his plan to produce 'a kind of almanac', which finally appears in May 1912, published by Reinhard Piper in Munich. Under the editorial leadership of Kandinsky, many artists contributed from different areas of visual and folk art, music and theatre; illustrations were chiefly reproductions of ethnographic and folk objects, childrens' and amateurs' pictures, as well as works by Robert Delaunay, Rousseau and van Gogh. Kandinsky contributed two articles, 'On the Question of Form' and 'On Stage Composition'. Religious themes, the Last Judgement (no.23), the Resurrection, Angels of the Apocalypse, *All Saints* (fig.25) and *Deluge* (no.44) appear frequently as subjects in Kandinsky's paintings of 1911 and 1912. Kandinsky has a particular affinity with the dragon-slaying St George (used, for example, on the cover of the *Almanac*). In the autumn makes the acquaintance of Paul Klee, who writes in his diary, 'he [Kandinsky] is someone and has an exceptionally beautiful, clear head'.[16]

1912

Kandinsky adds subtitles to his improvisations, such as *Orient* (no.47), *Funeral March* (no.17), *Cannons* (no.51) etc and he successively abstracts the motifs in his pictures. On 12 February he travels to Russia for three months. In June he shows several works at the Cologne Sonderbund Exhibition, one of the most significant exhibitions in Germany before 1914. It contains an overview of the development of the most important innovators from the late nineteenth century to the present day. In July he publishes extracts of *Concerning the Spiritual in Art* in Alfred Stieglitz's journal *Camera Work*. In July Kandinsky responds positively to Hans Arp's invitation to show with the Moderner Bund at the Kunsthaus Zürich. In the autumn he meets Hugo Ball. In October Herwarth Walden shows the first Kandinsky retrospective in his Berlin Galerie Der Sturm, with 73 works from the years 1902-12. Kandinsky travels on to Moscow for two months and visits in St Petersburg, among others, the Art and Theatre Society where he gives a lecture on value and judgement in painting. After his return he makes the first studies for *Composition VI* (no.49). Fifteen studies exist. He writes: 'I carried this picture within me for a year and a half and often thought I would not be able to complete it.

The point of departure was the Deluge. The point of departure was a painting on glass which I made more for my own pleasure.'[17] He completes *Composition VI* on 5 March of the following year.

1913

In February Kandinsky participates in the New York Amory Show with *Improvisation 27*, which is subsequently shown in Chicago and Boston. This exhibition gives him access to new collectors; Alfred Stieglitz acquires *Improvisation 27* and in the summer the American collector Arthur Jerome Eddy visits Kandinsky in Munich. Kandinsky and Marc prepare the second volume of the *Almanac Der Blaue Reiter* (*Blue Rider Almanac*), but never publish it. It would have contained an article by Wilhelm Worringer, who had published the influential book *Abstraction and Empathy* in 1909. Kandinsky, Erich Heckel, Klee, Oskar Kokoschka, Kubin and Marc work intensively on an illustrated bible, as a Blaue Reiter project, but this too never comes to fruition. The book *Klänge* (*Sounds*) appears, with poems and woodcuts, the high point and conclusion of Kandinsky's early graphic work. In July Kandinsky travels to Moscow. For the First German Autumn Salon in Herwarth Walden's Galerie Der Sturm he publishes a volume with an autobiographical text 'Rückblicke' ('Reminiscences'), as well as interpretations of *Composition IV* (no.32), *Composition VI* (no.49) and *Painting with White Border* (fig.9). After many months preparation, with stages in drawings, watercolours and oil sketches, he completes *Composition VII* (no.52) in only four days, between 25 and 28 November. Gabriele Münter takes photographs at four stages of the painting's execution (fig.22). Kandinsky shows the picture a little over a month later, on 1 January, in a solo show in Thannhauser's Moderne Galerie in Munich and at a second venue in the Kreis für Kunst in Cologne. In December he paints *Bright Picture* and *Black Lines* (fig.53), which Kandinsky later described as purely abstract pictures. In texts of this time he developed arguments about the problems of turning away from figuration.

1914

The first English translation of *Concerning the Spiritual in Art* appears with the title *The Art of Spiritual Harmony*.[17] Kandinsky paints *Improvisation Gorge* (no.54) after a walking trip to the Höllentalklamm, near Garmisch and, with *Improvisation 35* (no.56) he paints the final numbered improvisation. He travels with his mother to Meran and spends the rest of the summer in Murnau. Between June and August he paints four pictures for the New York flat

of Edwin A. Campbell. In June 1914, along with Martin Buber, Gustav Landauer, Walther Rathenau, Theodor Däubler and others, and invited by Erich Gutkind, Kandinsky joins an international group of intellectuals with the purpose of seeking understanding between different peoples, formed in 1910, but formally constituted only in 1914 in Potsdam as the Forte Circle. After the outbreak of war on 14 August Kandinsky leaves Munich and travels with Gabriele Münter to Switzerland, where they remain until 16 November. Aside from painting he is occupied by the play *Violet Curtain*. The war undermines plans by Hugo Ball to produce that play and *Yellow Sound* in Munich, as well as the publication of his works for theatre. Kandinsky begins writing another text, which he published in 1926 with the title *Punkt und Linie zu Fläche* (*Point and Line to Plane*). He writes to Marc on 8 November: 'Here I wrote the pictorial theory which I had been slowly preparing in the last few years. I have assembled the main, fundamental arguments.'[19] On 25 November he returns alone to Moscow via the Balkans and Odessa, and moves into a flat inherited from his uncle at 1 Dolgy Street. He lives there until he emigrates to Germany in December 1921. Gabriele Münter remains in Munich. Kandinsky takes Russian citizenship again.

1915

Kandinsky lives mainly in Moscow until 20 December. He paints no oils during this period, only drawings and watercolours. On 16 November he writes to Gabriele Münter, who had moved to Stockholm in the summer, 'it is filigree work and I learn something akin to goldsmithery. That will help me with the large pictures that are gradually forming within me. I would like to create a large painting of great depth and achieve this with discreet means that one first encounters when approaching the canvas, a thought I have already had about pictures, as you know. But I now understand this more comprehensively and more practically, the result of the many watercolours of recent times.'[20] Kandinsky participates in the Moscow exhibition *Picture Exhibition: The Year 1915* with *Composition VII* and *Painting with Circle*. life in Russia becomes more difficult as the war progresses, with supply problems in Moscow and St Petersburg due to the influx of refugees, leading to strikes and demonstrations. On 23 December Kandinsky travels to Sweden for three months at the invitation of the Stockholm Carl Gummeson Gallery. He meets up with Gabriele Münter and begins painting on canvas again. He paints figurative and abstract paintings, among them he starts a sequence of 14 watercolours with the title *Bagatelles* (no.62).

In his 21-page article 'Om konstnären' ('On the Artist'), which appears on the occasion of Gabriele Münter's exhibition in the Gummeson Gallery, he discusses the characteristics of the creative as against the merely virtuoso artist. Between 1915 and 1918 Kandinsky paints very few pictures, occupies himself instead with graphic work, paintings on glass, and preparatory works for future paintings.

1916

The only surviving painting from the Stockholm period is *Painting on a Bright Ground* (fig.54). In Stockholm Kandinsky has lively contact with the psychologist and author Paul Bjerre, a friend of Gutkind's, whose own research is into the origins of creativity. On 12 February Bjerre leads a discussion about Kandinsky's art, intended to give an insight into the biographical background of abstract art. In his exhibition *Kandinsky: Oljemalninger och Grafik* (Kandinsky: Painting and Graphic) at the Gummeson Gallery, Kandinsky shows *Composition IV* (no.32), *Improvisation 11* (no.39) and *Painting with White Border* (fig.9). Kandinsky separates permanently from Gabriele Münter and returns to Moscow on 16 March. The Dada exhibition of the Cabaret Voltaire in Zurich, which opens on 17 March, includes works by Kandinsky as well as those by Klee and Gabriele Münter. In June Hugo Ball performs poems from Kandinsky's *Sounds*. In September Kandinsky meets Nina Nikolayevna Andreyevskaya (1896-1980). He paints *Moscow. Red Square* (no.60) and he makes numerous pen drawings and watercolour which pick up on his abstract works of the years before 1915.

1917

On 11 February Kandinsky marries Nina Andreyevskaya; their honeymoon is spent in Finnland. In several of his figurative pictures Kandinsky refers to the social world of the Rococo and Biedermeier periods. He paints 29 non-figurative pictures, most with threatening, dark skies, or dark backgrounds and with suggestive titles, such as *Blue Arch*, *Twilight*, *Overcast* (nos.69, 66, 67). Nina Kandinsky gives birth to a son Vsevolod in September. In the October Revolution the Bolsheviks seize control of the interim government from by the social democratic Mensheviks following the February uprising. After the outbreak of the October Revolution Kandinsky produces no more paintings for three years. During this period he takes on important roles in the art institutions of the fledging Communist state, building new institutions in the areas of art education and the exhibition functions of museums.

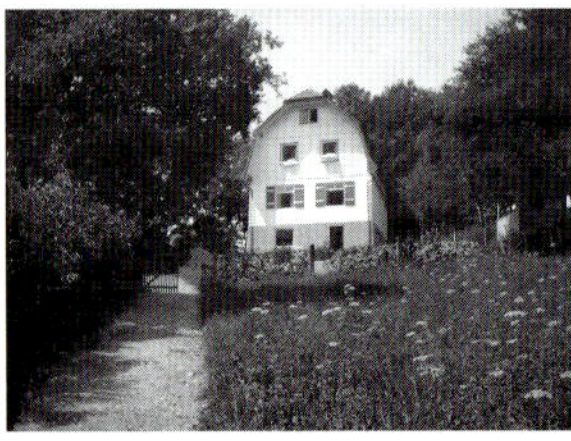

FIG.49
Gabriele Münter's House in Murnau
Gabriele Münter-and Johannes
Eichner-Stiftung, Munich

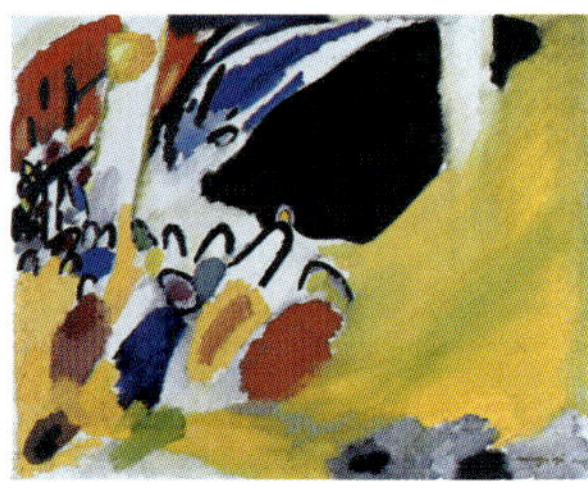

FIG.50
Impression III (Concert)
1911
Oil on canvas   77.5 x 100
Städtische Galerie im
Lenbachhaus, Munich

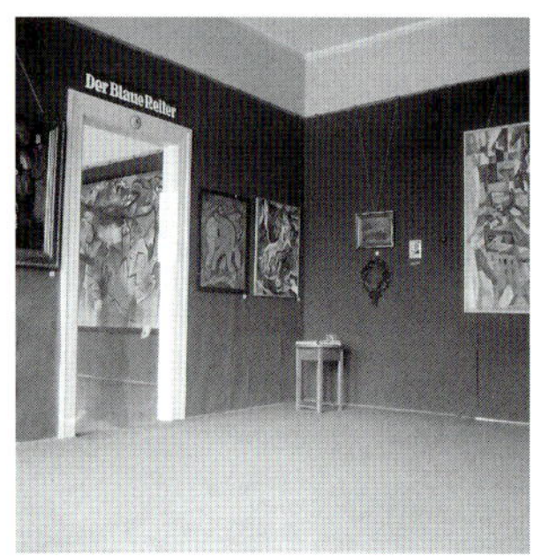

FIG.51
The First Exhibition of Der Blaue Reiter
1911
Gabriele Münter-and Johannes
Eichner-Stiftung, Munich

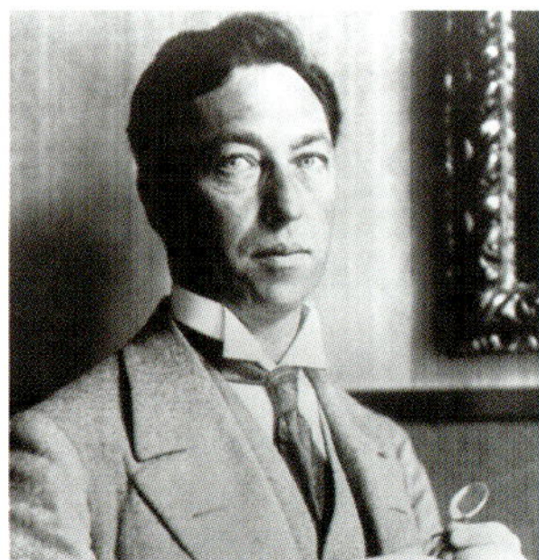

FIG.52
Kandinsky in Munich
1913
Gabriele Münter-and Johannes
Eichner-Stiftung, Munich

1918

In January Kandinsky sells his house in Moscow. As a result of the October Revolution he loses his entire fortune and his property. His economic circumstances rapidly worsen. The People's Commissariat for Enlightenment (NARKOMPROS) is founded on the initiative of the politician Anatoly Vassiliyevich Lunacharsky with the aim of establishing education and training following Communist principles. NARKOMPROS is divided into five sections; organisation, folk education, social training, science and art. The art section is divided into several subsections, among them the Department of Visual Arts (IZO). Vladimir Tatlin, Head of the IZO, requests Kandinsky's participation. IZO organises art exhibitions and administrates the newly formed art schools, the Free State Art Studios (SVOMAS), and the State Higher Artistic and Technical Workshops (VKHUTEMAS). In the art committee of the IZO Kandinsky comes into contract with younger artists of the Russian avant garde, such as Kasimir Malevich, Lyubov' Popova, Ol'ga Rozanova, Varvara Stepanova, Nadezhda Udal'tsova and Aleksandr Rodchenko. He maintains correspondence with German artists and architects, among them Walter Gropius. From October he runs one of the SVOMAS and develops a teaching curriculum based on his colour and form theory. He is also made director of the Film and Theatre section of the IZO and becomes a professor of the VKHUTEMAS. Kandinsky's 'Reminiscences' appear in Russian translation. He becomes a member of the Committee for the Foundation of The Museums of Painterly Culture in Moscow, St Petersburg and Other Cities, which open the following year. In the December issue of *Dada* several of Kandinsky's works are illustrated. His artistic production for the year is mainly watercolours and drawings.

1919

After a long interval Kandinsky begins to paint again. *Two Ovals* (no.71), *White Oval* (no.74), *Violet Wedge* (no.73) show a simplification of form and a more comprehensible structure. Kandinsky begins to integrate geometric elements into his works. He shows *Composition VI* in the First State Painting Exhibition in St Petersburg. On 1 April the State Bauhaus is founded in Weimar by Walter Gropius. The painters Johannes Itten and Lyonel Feininger and the sculptor Gerhard Marcks are employed as teachers. In June Kandinsky publishes his autobiographical 'Selbstcharakteristik' ('Self-Characterisation'). He repeats his fundamental position; the principle of inner necessity as the basis for art and the designation of a new era in world culture as the 'epoch of great spiritual people'.[21] In June Kandinsky becomes director of the Museum for Painting in Moscow, which

he heads until 1921. Together with Rodchenko and others, he founds 22 provincial museums and takes the trouble to acquire for them works of contemporary art, including his own.

1920

As a worker for the IZO Kandinsky is involved in the founding of the Institute of Artistic Culture (INKHUK) in Moscow, which has the task of systematising art theories in accordance with Communist principles. In May he takes over the section dealing with monumental art. His teaching programme is rejected at the first pan-Russian congress of the directors of the NARKOMPROS. He had formulated his view of the analysis and synthesis of the individual elements of the different artistic genres in the following manner: 'the aim of the activities of the institute for artistic culture is the science which researches analytically and synthetically the main elements of each genre, but also of art itself'.[22] According to Kandinsky art has three main problematic areas to address: the theory of the individual genres, the theory of the interaction between different genres and, finally, the theory of monumental art, or art in general. The Constructivists, led by Rodchenko, reject Kandinsky's concept as 'subjective' and 'intuitive' and boycott him. Kandinsky leaves the institute in May. In June he is given the title honorary professor by the University of Moscow. In September the SVOMAS are replaced by the VKHUTEMAS. The 19th exhibition of the Russian Central Exhibition Committee in Moscow shows 54 works by Kandinsky, among them *Composition VII* (fig.55).

1921

Kandinsky works with Peter Kogan and A. M. Rodionov to found the Russian Academy of Artistic Sciences (RAKHN), which opens in October. He takes over the direction of the physical-psychological department. Besides that he becomes chairman of the Commission for the Study of Historical and Theoretical Problems in Art and gives a series of lectures on the theme of the synthesis and coordination of all artistic genres. In July in an interview, Kandinsky criticises the main representatives of the Russian avant garde: 'instead of paintings, creating works, they experiment. They pursue experimental art in laboratories. I think these are two different things. People paint black on black, white on white. Colours are applied evenly and skillfully. Those who paint in this way say that they are experimenting, and that painting is the art of introducing a form to the canvas in such a way that it looks stuck on. Except it is impossible to stick black over yellow without the eye tearing it off the canvas …'[23] Kandinsky views artistic freedom

as increasingly threatened by the regime. His son Vsevolod dies. As Kandinsky is not a member of the Communist Party, he is overlooked for the presidency of the Academy. Peter Kogan becomes President. This disappointment, the rejection of his programme for the INKHUK, the intellectual isolation and the catastrophic state of supplies and economic situation following the civil war strengthen his resolve to leave Russia. In December he goes to Germany with official permission and remains in Berlin for six months. Many of his works are left behind because he is not granted permission to take them out of Russia.

1922

Kandinsky participates in several exhibitions during a six month stay in Berlin (Galerie Goldschmidt-Wallerstein, Galerie Guldendahl, Galerie Goltz). In March he receives the official invitation to join the Weimar Bauhaus during a visit to Berlin by Walter Gropius. Lyonel Feininger leads the graphic department, Johannes Itten the preparatory course, Klee the glass workshop, Oskar Schlemmer the sculptors' workshop and later stage design. A core part of the programme is the formulation of a theory that creates a common basis for the activities in art and design and the communal work towards a functional, humane design for all areas of human activity in the industrialised world. Kandinsky moves to Weimar in June. He never returns to Russia again. At the Bauhaus he teaches on the preparatory course and leads the workshop for mural painting. He creates large format murals with his students and exhibits them at the jury-free art exhibition in Berlin that autumn, in an octagonal room. Plans to site them permanently in the entrance hall of an art museum founder due to lack of funds. Kandinsky adapts quickly to the artistic life once more. His twelve-part graphic cycle *Kleine Welten* (*Small Worlds*) is published by the Propyläen Publishing House. The tendency towards greater geometry in his work, discernible over the past few years in Russia, continues in his paintings and works on paper.

1923

The circle becomes a prominent motif in Kandinsky's work. The Société Anonyme, founded by the collector Katherine S. Dreier, and the artists Marcel Duchamp and Man Ray, organises Kandinsky's first solo exhibition in New York. Kandinsky later becomes honorary vice-president of the Society. In July he completes *Composition VIII*.

1924

In Weimar Feininger, Jawlensky, Kandinsky and Klee found the artists' association the Blue Four (Blaue Vier). The German-American dealer and collector Galka Scheyer makes their work better known in the United States.

1925

In January *Composition VIII* is exhibited in a solo show at Neues Museum in Wiesbaden. Because of pressure from the National Socialists, the Bauhaus is forced to leave Weimar and, on 1 April, opens in Dessau. Kandinsky begins work in the new school in July. Eight collectors, led by Otto Ralfs, found the Kandinsky Society, to ensure his financial security.

1926

Kandinsky publishes his second major theoretical text *Punkt und Linie zu Fläche* (*Point and Line to Plane*). The Society of Friends of New Art (Gesellschaft der Freunde Junger Kunst) organise a retrospective in Brunswick Castle, on the occasion of Kandinsky's sixtieth birthday, which travels on to Dresden, Berlin, Dessau and other European cities. In June Kandinsky and his wife more to a house, shared with Klee and his family, designed by Gropius. At the end of the year the first issue of the journal *Bauhaus* appears, dedicated to Kandinsky, and includes his essay 'Der Wert des Theoretischen Unterrichts in der Malerei' ('The Value of Theoretical Training in Painting').

1927

Kandinsky teaches in the painting class at the Bauhaus. He becomes friends with the Parisian art critic and publisher Christian Zervos.

1928

In March Kandinsky and his wife become German citizens. He designs the stage set and costumes for Modest Mussorgsky's *Pictures at an Exhibition*, for the Friedrich–Theatre in Dessau. The journal *Bauhaus* publishes his article 'Analytisches Zeichnen. Kunstpädagogik' ('Analytical Drawing. Art Pedagogy'). Kandinsky paints mostly small scale or medium sized works with recurring forms and motifs (architectonic structures, geometric and organic figures).

1929

Gets to know Hilla Rebay and Solomon R. Guggenheim in the summer. Hilla Rebay enthuses Guggenheim for abstract art and acquires for his collection works by Kandinsky, Klee, Fernand Léger, László Moholy-Nagy, among others. They become Kandinsky's most important collectors. Galerie Zak in Paris mounts his first solo exhibition there, showing watercolours and drawings. Duchamp and Katherine S. Dreier visit Kandinsky in Dessau.

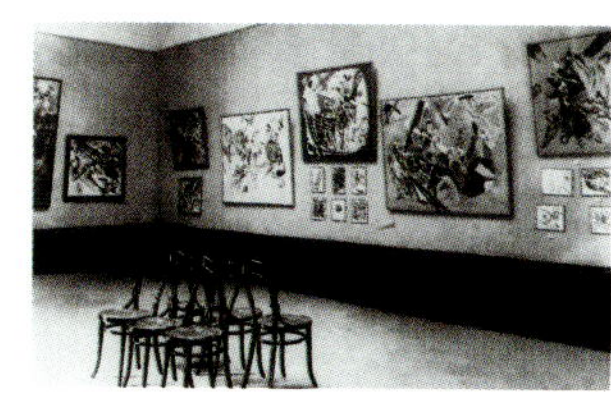

FIG.53
Black Lines
1913
Oil on canvas 129.4 X 131.1
Solomon R. Guggenheim Museum, New York.
Gift, Solomon R. Guggenheim

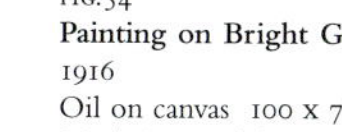

FIG.54
Painting on Bright Ground
1916
Oil on canvas 100 X 78
Musée National d'Art Moderne,
Centre Georges Pompidou, Paris

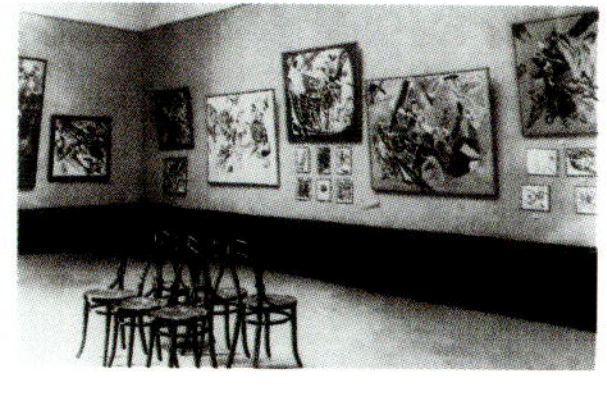

FIG.55
Room of Kandinsky Paintings in the 19th Exhibition of the Russian Central Exhibition Committee in Moscow
1920
Musée National d'Art Moderne,
Centre Georges Pompidou, Paris.
Société Kandinsky Archives

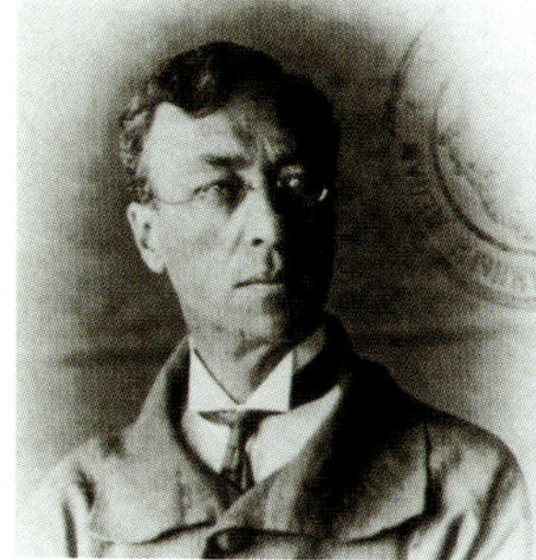

FIG.56
Kandinsky in Moscow
1921

1930

Kandinsky visits Paris again. He makes contact with the group Cercle et Carré, founded in 1929 by Michel Seuphor and Joaquín Torres García. In 1931 it is superseded by Abstraction-Création, which brings together representatives of non-figurative and abstract art. Paul Schultze-Naumburg, the National Socialist Director of Weimar University, removes works by Kandinsky, Klee and Schlemmer from the Weimar museum collections.

1931

Kandinsky designs a wall decoration for Mies van der Rohe's music room at the German Building Exhibition in Berlin. The Art Students League in New York offers him a teaching post, which he declines. In the autumn Zervos publishes Kandinsky's 'Reflexions sur l'art abstrait' ('Reflections on Abstract Art') in the journal *Cahiers d'Art*.

1932

After pressure from the National Socialist state government the Bauhaus moves from Dessau to Berlin on 22 August, and continues operations until July 1933 as a private institute. Kandinsky also moves to Berlin.

1933

Closure of the Bauhaus in July. In August Kandinsky paints his last picture in Germany, *Development in Brown* (fig.57). At the end of December he moves to France and settles in Neuilly-sur-Seine. He spends the last decade of his life there.

1934

Kandinsky continues working from February onwards. Illustrations of several of his works are included in the journal *Abstraction-Création*, published by Hans Arp and Sophie Taeuber-Arp. Between May and June Kandinsky shows his pictures in the editorial offices of the journal *Cahiers d'Art* in Paris. He meets up with Constantin Brancusi, Robert and Sonia Delaunay, Fernand Léger and Piet Mondrian.

1935

Between February and March participates in the exhibition *These, Antithese, Synthese* at the Kunstmuseum in Lucerne. Black Mountain College in the United States invites Kandinsky for a stay as artist in residence, which he declines.

1936

Kandinsky is included in many exhibitions; I. B. Neumann's New Art Circle in New York, Stendahl Art Galleries in Los Angeles, Lefevre Gallery in London and MoMA in New York. Neumann represents his interests on the east coast of America. Kandinsky publishes memoires of Franz Marc in *Cahiers d'Art*. Galerie Jeanne Bucher in Paris opens a Kandinsky exhibition in December.

1937

The National Socialists confiscate 57 works by Kandinsky from German museums and show 14 pictures in the travelling exhibition *Entartete Kunst* (*Degenerate Art*). Kandinsky visits Klee in Switzerland.

1938

Participates in the exhibition *Abstracte Kunst* (*Abstract Art*) exhibition at the Stedelijk Museum in Amsterdam. His essay 'L'Art Concret' is included in the first issue of San Lazzaro's journal *XXe Siècle*. The important avant garde journal *Transition* publishes four poems with woodcuts by Kandinsky.

1939

In January Kandinsky completes his final composition *Composition X* (fig.58). He and his wife become French citizens. The Second World War breaks out on 1 September. The French government purchases *Composition IX*.

1940

At the end of June Kandinsky flees to Cauterets in the Pyrenees, to escape from the German occupying troops. He returns to Neuilly-sur-Seine two months later.

1941

Kandinsky is offered an opportunity to emigrate to the United States, which he declines.

1942

Kandinsky writes the foreword for *10 Origin*, published by Max Bill. He paints his final major work, *Delicate Tensions*. Retrospective at the Nierendorf Gallery in New York.

1943

In March Kandinsky's works are included in the exhibition *15 Early – 15 Late* at Peggy Guggenheim's New York gallery Art of This Century.

1944

At the end of March Kandinsky completes his last painting, *Tempered Elan*. In spite of illness he continues to work until July. He dies on 13 December in Neuilly-sur-Seine.

Bettina Kaufmann with assistance from Jacob Dabrowski (quotations translated by Sean Rainbird)

Notes to the chronology

1. Translated into German as 'Beitrag zur Ethnographie der Sysol- und Vecegda-Syrjänen, Die nationalen Gottheiten' in Kandinsky, *Gesammelte Schriften*, pp.68–74; 'Über die Strafe in den Urteilen der Bauerngerichte im Bezirk Moskau' in Kandinsky, *Gesammelte Schriften*, pp.75–87.
2. *Autobiographische Schriften*, p.32.
3. Forthcoming in Helmut Friedel / Jessica Boissel, *Kandinsky: Farbensprache, Kompositionslehre und andere Texte, 1889–1916*, Munich 2006.
4. Vivian Endicott Barnett, *Das bunte Leben. Wassily Kandinsky im Lenbachhaus*, Cologne 1995, p.97.
5. Letter from Kandinsky to Gabriele Münter dated 25 April 1904, published in Gisela Kleine, *Gabriele Münter und Wassily Kandinsky. Biographie eines Paares*, Frankfurt 1990, p.259, letters to Kandinsky dated 8 December 1910.
6. Ibid. p.259.
7. *Autobiographische Schriften*, p.39.
8. Kleine, *Münter und Kandinsky*, p.230.
9. Postcard from Kandinsky to Gabriele Münter dated 25 August 1904, published in Kleine, *Münter und Kandinsky*, p.315.
10. Barnett, *Das bunte Leben*, p.192.
11. Ibid., p.219.
12. Published in: *Arnold Schönberg und Wassily Kandinsky, Briefe, Bilder und Dokumente einer aussergewöhnlichen Begegnung*, ed. Jelena Hahl-Koch, Salzburg and Vienna 1980, pp.173–5.
13. Wassily Kandinsky, *Über das Geistige in der Kunst*, Munich 1911, 2nd edn., Munich 1912, 4th edn, by Max Bill, Bern 1952, p.142.
14. Ibid., p.142.
15. Letter from Kandinsky to Marianne Werefkin, published in Marianne Werefkin, *Briefe an einen Unbekannten: 1901–1905*, p.42.
16. Paul Klee, *Tagebücher 1898–1918*, ed. Paul-Klee-Stiftung Kunstmuseum Bern, Stuttgart 1988, no.903, p.320.
17. *Über das Geistige in der Kunst*, p.172.
18. Wassily Kandinsky, *The art of spiritual harmony*, London 1914.
19. Wassily Kandinsky / Franz Marc, *Briefwechsel. Mit Briefen von und an Gabriele Münter und Maria Marc*, ed. Klaus Lankheit, Munich and Zurich 1983, p.265.
20. Letter from Kandinsky to Gabriele Münter dated 16 November 1915, published in Jelena Hahl-Koch, *Kandinsky*, Stuttgart 1993, p.236.
21. 'Self-Characterisation' (Potsdam, 1919), in *Complete Writings on Art*, ed. Kenneth C. Lindsay and Peter Vergo, 2 vols., Boston and London 1982; reprint, New York 1994, vol.1, pp.430–3.
22. Wassily Kandinsky, 'Schematitscheskaja programma instituta chudoschestwennoj kultury po planu W. W. Kandinskogo' in: N.B. Avtonomova (ed.) *Isbrannyje trudy po teoriji iskusstva (Gesammelte Werke über die Kunsttheorie)*, Moscow 2001, vol.2, p.46.
23. Interview by Charles-André Julien in 1921 with Kandinsky, in *Complete Writings on Art*, 1994 (see note 21), vol.1, p.476.

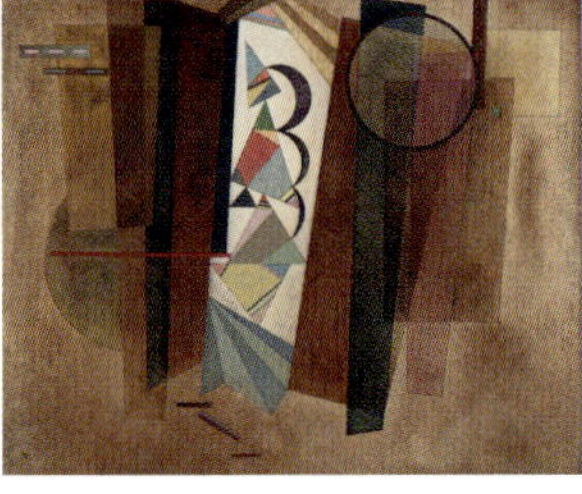

FIG.57
Development in Brown
1933
Oil on canvas 105 x 120
Musée National d'Art Moderne, Centre Georges Pompidou, Paris

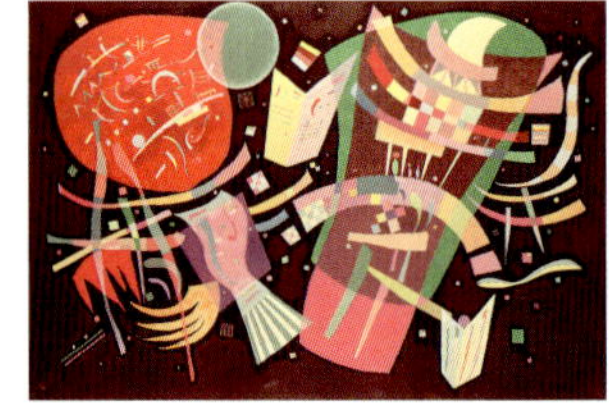

FIG.58
Composition X
1939
Oil on canvas 130 x 195
Kunstsammlung Nordrhein-Westfalen, Düsseldorf

Notes to the essays

Early Imprints and Influences

1. First published in *Kandinsky 1901–1913*, Berlin 1913, pp.iii–ixx; reprinted in Wassily Kandinsky, 'Autobiographische, ethnographische und juristische Schriften', in Hans K. Roethel and Jelena Hahl-Koch (ed.), *Kandinsky: Die Gesammelten Schriften*, Berne 1980, pp.27–50. Published in English in Kandinsky: *Complete Writings on Art*, 2 vols., ed. Kenneth C. Lindsay and Peter Vergo, London 1982, vol.1, pp.357–82.
2. Ibid. p.360.
3. Ibid. p.364.
4. Ibid. p.363.
5. Ibid. p.372.
6. The manuscript *Farbensprache* (written in German) probably dates to 1908; it is held in the Gabriele Münter and Johannes Eichner-Stiftung in Munich. On this see Reinhard Zimmermann, *Die Kunsttheorie von Wassily Kandinsky*, Berlin 2002, vol.2, p.19, no.(2).
7. In his hand-written inventories of his works, the so-called 'Hauskatalog', Kandinsky makes a distinction between 'paintings', 'small oil studies', 'coloured drawings' and 'decorative sketches'. The first category applies to oil paintings on canvases on stretchers; the second applies to smaller oil paintings on card or cardboard; the third and fourth include works in tempera in card or paper, with the fourth category a variant of the third.
8. Also known as *Die Postkutsche* (*The Mail Coach*; Private Collection; Barnett 18). This landscape, which measures 76 x 100, counts as a 'painting' (one of the larger ones) in Kandinsky's categorisation.
9. *Santa Margherita* 1906, oil on canvas, 23.7 x 32.7, Städtische Galerie im Lenbachhaus, Munich
10. *Nymphenburg – Large Fountain*, oil on cardboard, 13 x 18, Galerie Gunzenhauser, Munich.
11. Kandinsky 1980 (as note 1), pp.366f.
12. In a commentary on the painting *Heavenly and Earthly Sorrow* 1904, Kandinsky suggests that the effect of the black background takes one 'into the serious and sad', while white takes one 'into the joyous' (on this see Barbara Mackert-Riedel, *Wassily Kandinsky über eigene Bilder: Zum Problem der Interpretation moderner Malerei*, Weimar 2003, p.40). The serious and sad effect would be appropriate to the idea of bidding farewell.
13. *Picture with a Circle* 1911, oil on canvas, 139 x 111, The State Museum of Fine Arts of Georgia, Tbilisi.
14. Wassily Kandinsky, 'On the Spiritual in Art', 2nd ed., Munich 1912, in *Complete Writings on Art* (as note 1), p.218. *Über das Geistige in der Kunst* has also been translated in various editions as *Concerning the Spiritual in Art* and *The Art of Spiritual Harmony*
15. Vivian Endicott Barnett, *Vasily Kandinsky: A Colorful Life. The Collection of the Lenbachhaus, Munich*, Cologne 1995, no.279, illus. p.223.
16. This row of houses is derived from a votive painting in the Pfarrkirche in Murnau, which Kandinsky illustrated in *Der Blaue Reiter*. See Maurice Rummens, 'Kandinsky's "Painting with Houses" and a Votive Panel at Murnau', in *Burlington Magazine* 129 (1987), pp. 394–6.
17. *Improvisation 1* 1909, oil on canvas, 80.5 x 72, Roethel/Benjamin 271.
18. *Improvisation 5 – Variation 1* 1910, oil on canvas, 107 x 95, Roethel/Benjamin 330; *Improvisation 5 – Variation 2* 1910, oil on canvas, 130 x 110, Roethel/Benjamin 331.
19. Rose-Carol Washton Long, *Kandinsky: The Development of an Abstract Style*. Oxford 1980. For the critical response to this see, for instance, Felix Thürlemann, *Kandinsky über Kandinsky: Der Künstler als Interpret eigener Werke*, Berne 1986, pp.68f.; Günter Brucher, *Kandinsky: Wege zur Abstraktion*, Munich and elsewhere 1999, p.11.
20. Wassily Kandinsky, 'Picture with the White Edge', in *Kandinsky: Complete Writings on Art* (as note 1), pp.389–91; here: p.389).

21. *Murnau with Church II* 1910, oil on canvas, 96.5 x 105.5, Stedelijk van Abbe Museum, Eindhoven, Roethel/Benjamin 348. There is also a smaller, privately owned oil study for this painting (*Studie für Murnau mit Kirche II*, 1910, oil on card, 32 x 44, Roethel/Benjamin 347).
22. See the detailed discussion of this painting by Sixten Ringbom in idem, *The Sounding Cosmos. A Study in the Spiritualism of Kandinsky and the Genesis of Abstract Painting*, Acta Academia Åboensis, Ser. A. 28, 1970. As Ringbom points out (p.148), the composition of the painting is influenced by an illustration in the book *Gedankenformen* by Annie Besant and Charles W. Leadbeater (Leipzig 1908; first printed London/New York 1905), a 'visualisation' of the music of Richard Wagner.
23. The work, formerly entitled *Erstes abstraktes Aquarell* (*First Abstract Watercolour*) and retrospectively dated to 1910 on the basis of an erroneous inscription, is in fact a preparatory study – also made in 1913 – for *Composition 7*.
24. See Ringbom 1970 (as note 26).
25. On this see Zimmermann 2002 (as note 6), vol.1, pp.263–79.
26. As cited in ibid., vol.2, p.94. So far only excerpts from Kandinsky's letters to Gabriele Münter have been published.

Kandinsky, Münter and Creative Partnership

1. *Wassily Kandinsky and Gabriele Münter: Letters and Reminiscences 1902–1914*, Annegret Hoberg (ed.), Munich and New York 1994, p.70: Kandinsky to Münter, 20 October 1910. German edition: *Wassily Kandinsky und Gabriele Münter in Murnau und Kochel 1902–1914. Briefe und Erinnerungen*, Munich, London and New York 1994.
2. Ibid. p.66: Kandinsky to Münter, Moscow, 14 October 1910.
3. Edward Said succinctly observes this phenomenon in his essay, 'Reflections on Exile', in *Reflection on Exile and Other Literary and Cultural Essays*, London 2001, pp.173–87 (175).
4. Hoberg 1994 (see note 1), p.101: Kandinsky to Münter, Moscow, 16 December 1910.
5. The notion of 'artistic couples' as a phenomenon in the modern period has been considered in art historical literature and exhibitions on the theme. These have contributed insight in focusing on the impact of intimate partnerships on creativity. For the most recent publication, consult Renata Berger (ed.), *Liebe macht Kunst: Künstlerpaare im 20. Jahrhundert*, Cologne and Weimar 2000.
6. For a biographical interpretation of this painting consult Gisela Kleine, *Gabriele Münter und Wassily Kandinsky: Biographie eines Paares*, Frankfurt/Main 1990, pp.357–8. Kandinsky's knowledge of the muses and their representation can be ascertained from a photograph of the Phalanx school showing a model for his painting and drawing class posed as Clio, the muse of history. Indeed the entire costume detail and composition were modelled after Vermeer's painting *The Art of Painting* (*Die Malkunst*), c.1666, oil on canvas, Kunsthistorisches Museen, Vienna. For the photograph, consult the catalogue *Kandinsky: Oeuvres de Vassily Kandinsky (1866–1944)*, Christian Derouet and Jessica Boissel (ed.), Collections du Musée national d'art moderne, Paris, 1984, fig.4, p.19.
7. See Erwin Panofsky, *The Life and Art of Albrecht Dürer*, Princeton (NJ) 1945, pp.157–71. For a confirmation of Panofsky's reading of the *Melencolia* as an 'oblique' self-portrait consult Joseph L. Koerner, *The Moment of Self-Portraiture in German Renaissance Art*, Chicago and London 1993, pp.25–7.
8. Giulia Bartrum (ed.), *Albrecht Dürer and his Legacy: The Graphic Work of a Renaissance Artist*, London and Princeton 2002, no.128, p.188. The influential treatise *De occulta philosophia* (1509–10), of Cornelius Agrippa of Nettesheim, was almost certainly known to Dürer.
9. Sixten Ringbom's investigation of the theosophical referents of Kandinsky's mysticism was amplified by the significance Rose-Carol Washton Long attributed to the impact of Rudolf Steiner's eschatological writings and Symbolist aesthetic theory. Sixten Ringbom, *The Sounding Cosmos*, Acta Academia Åboensis 1970; Rose-Carol Washton Long, *Kandinsky: The Development of an Abstract Style*, Oxford 1980. Interestingly, Jelena Hahl-Koch cites the importance of 'Agrippa of Nettesheim [who] had predicted in the Middle Ages that there would be a historical upheaval in 1900 which would usher in a new era'. See her *Kandinsky*, London 1993, p.193.
10. Wassily Kandinsky, *Complete Writings on Art*, ed. Kenneth Lindsay and Peter Vergo, London 1982, vol.1, pp.143–5. Kleine 1990 (see note 6), p.356 states that, by 10 February 1910, the manuscript was lodged with the banker Gustav Meyrink for editorial comments. The publisher Reinhard Piper finally accepted the manuscript for publication in 1912.
11. *Kandinsky: Catalogue Raisonné of the Oil Paintings*, Hans K. Roethel and Jean K. Benjamin (ed.), vol.1, 1900–15, London 1982, no.344, *Gabriele Münter im freien vor der Stafellei*, 1910, oil on cardboard, 33 x 45, Private Collection.

12. Personified as a woman in Cesare Ripa's *Iconologia* (1593), Pittura is represented as a mute and beautiful muse, as nature, harbouring the seed for creative masculinity. For further discussion of this, consult Joanna Woodall, '"Every painter paints himself": Self-portraiture and Creativity', in *Self Portrait Renaissance to Contemporary*, exh. cat. National Portrait Gallery, London 2005, pp.26–8.
13. Hoberg 1994 (see note 1), pp.97–9: letters to Kandinsky dated 8 December 1910 and 12–13 December 1910.
14. In 1903, during one of the summer excursions of the Phalanx painting class to Kallmünz, Münter depicted a portrait of Kandinsky seated on a hill while painting. See Rosel Gollek, *Der Blaue Reiter im Lenbachhaus München: Katalog der Sammlung in der Städtischen Galerie*, exh. cat., Munich 1974, p.220: Gabriele Münter, *Kandinsky beim Landschaftsmalen*, 1903, oil on canvas board, 16.9 x 25. Interestingly, Gollek notes that Kandinsky is portrayed with the canvas board propped on his knees and using a palette knife.
15. Such questions are posed in Whitney Chadwick and Isabelle de Courtivron (ed.), *Significant Others: Creativity and Intimate Partnership*, London 1993.
16. Ibid. p.7. In their introduction, the editors refer to these concepts raised by the feminist and psychoanalyst Nancy Chodorow in her book, *The Reproduction of Mothering: Psychoanalysis and the Sociology of Gender*, Berkeley (CA) 1978.
17. Münter conveyed Kandinsky's observations on her talent to her second partner, the art historian Johannes Eichner, who wrote the book *Kandinsky und Gabriele Münter: Von Ursprüngen moderner Kunst*, Munich 1957, p.38.
18. Hoberg 1994 (see note 1), p.45–6.
19. See Wassily Kandinsky and Franz Marc, *Briefwechsel*, ed. Klaus Lankheit, Munich and Zurich 1983.
20. Further discussion of this term can be found in Jane Beckett, 'Book Review', *Women's Art Magazine*, no.54, September/October 1993, pp.29–30.
21. Brigitte Salmen, *Gabriele Münter malt Murnau: Gemälde 1908–1960 der Künstlerin des 'Blauen Reiter'*, exh. cat., Schlossmuseum Murnau 1996, p.122, note 15.
22. Only extracts of these have been published in Marianne Werefkin, *Briefe an einen Unbekannten 1901–1905*, ed. Clemens Weiler, Cologne 1960; 'Lettres á un inconnu, 1901–1905', in *Voicing our Visions: Writings by Women Artists*, Mara R. Witzling (ed.), London 1992, pp.132–46.
23. An outline of Werefkin's life and works can be found in Shulamith Behr, 'Marianne Werefkin', in *Dictionary of Women Artists*, vol.2, ed. Delia Gaze, London and Chicago 1997, pp.1441–4.
24. Further discussion of Munch's impact can be found in Bernd Fäthke, *Marianne Werefkin*, Munich 2001, pp.88–92; on Munch's exhibitions in Germany consult the catalogue, *Munch und Deutschland*, Kunsthalle der Hypo-Kulturstiftung, Munich 1994.
25. Hoberg 1994 (see note 1), pp.45–6. In 1911, in her diary, Münter referred chiefly to Jawlensky who 'talked about "synthesis"'. In his formulation of the programme for the catalogue of the first exhibition of the NKVM in 1909, Kandinsky also used the term as a veritable catchword. See Shulamith Behr, *Expressionism*, London 1999, p.41.
26. Further information can be found in the catalogue *Alexej Jawlensky 1864–1941*, Städtische Galerie im Lenbachhaus, Munich 1983.
27. Hoberg 1994 (see note 1), p.35: Kandinsky to Münter, Kochel, 9 September 1902.

28. For an incisive account of Kandinsky's technical methods consult Rudolf H. Wackernagel, 'Watercolour with "Oil" . . . , Oil with "Watercolour", and so on: On Kandinsky's Studio and his Painting Techniques', ed. Helmut Friedel, in *Vasily Kandinsky: A Colorful Life*, exh. cat., ed. Helmut Friedel, Städtische Galerie im Lenbachhaus. Munich 1995, pp.547-68 (561-2).

29. *Der Blaue Reiter und das neue Bild: von der 'Neuen Künstlervereinigung München' zum 'Blauen Reiter'*, exh. cat., Annegret Hoberg and Helmut Friedel (ed.), Städtische Galerie im Lenbachhaus, Munich 1999, pp.344-6. For a colour illustration see p.82, cat.133: Kandinsky, *Kahnfahrt* 1910, oil on canvas, 98 x 105, Tretjakov Gallery, Moscow.

30. Ibid. p.97, cat. 155: Münter, *Kahnfahrt 1910*, oil on board, 40.3 x 26, Ahlers Pro Arte Collection.

31. For an expanded gender-based discussion of 'painterly abstraction', consult Shulamith Behr, 'Veiling Venus: Gender and Painterly Abstraction in Early German Modernism', in Caroline Arscott and Katie Scott (ed.), *Manifestations of Venus: Art and Sexuality*, Manchester 2001, pp.126-41.

32. Griselda Pollock, 'Modernity and the Spaces of Femininity', in *Vision and Difference: Femininity, Feminism and the Histories of Art*, London and New York 1988, pp.70-177.

33. Wassily Kandinsky, *On the Spiritual in Art*, in *Complete Writings on Art*, 1982, p.183.

34. Hoberg 1994 (see note 1), pp.51-6: in a note dated 10 February 1933 for Johannes Eichner, Münter goes into detail about her discovery of traditional Bavarian painting.

35. Münter's portraiture and the interior genre are considered at greater length in Shulamith Behr, 'Beyond the Muse: Gabriele Münter as *Expressionistin*', in *Gabriele Münter: The Search for Expression 1906–1917*, exh. cat., Courtauld Institute of Art Gallery, London 2005, pp.43-71.

36. For an abridged text of Kandinsky's catalogue introduction, consult Kleine 1990 (see note 6), p.431: 'Die urwüchsige, innerliche, sagen wir gleich echt deutsche Begabung von Gabriele Münter . . . ist von vornherein und ausschliesslich als eine rein weibliche zu bezeichnen.' Reinhold Heller suitably comments that Kandinsky's linkage of a German identity with the feminine, with sensitivity and inward orientation is remarkable for the time. See his *Confronting Identities in German Art: Myths, Reactions, Reflections*, Chicago 2003, pp.66-7.

37. Kandinsky trained as an ethnographer in Moscow before deciding to pursue a career as an artist in 1896. See Peg Weiss, *Kandinsky and Old Russia: The Artist as Ethnographer and Shaman*, New Haven and London 1995.

38. Wassily Kandinsky, 'Reminiscences', in *Complete Writings on Art*, 1982, pp.368-9. 'Rückblicke' was published as part of a retrospective album of his essays in *Kandinsky 1901–1913*, Berlin 1913.

39. Ibid. p.369.

40. See Jörn Rüsen (ed.), 'Einleitung', *Geschichtsbewusstsein: Psychologische Grundlagen, Entwicklungskonzepte, empirische Befunde*, Cologne 2001, p.6. Rüsen emphasises that history as a temporal process and the content of historical consciousness is a relationship between present and future and appears with and in the remembered past: 'das eine [die Vergangenheit] ist ohne das andere [die Zukunft] nicht zu denken. "Wer die Vergangenheit vergisst, den bestraft die Zukunft"' (the one cannot be thought of without the other. 'Who forgets the past, punishes the future').

41. For the black and white photograph of *Composition II* 1910, oil on canvas, 200 x 275, consult *Kandinsky: Catalogue Raisonné of the Oil Paintings*, vol.I, p.314, no.334.

42. See Revelation of St John, 4: 'Throne in Heaven' and 6:1-8 'Opening of Seven Seals'.

43. Washton Long 1980 (see note 9), pp.110-12.

44. Peg Weiss 1995 (see note 37), pp.54-5.

45. In his essay 'Innenräume: Erlebnis, Erinnerung und Synthese in der Kunst Gabriele Münters', Reinhold Heller expands on Münter's abstract works. See *Gabriele Münter 1877–1962: Retrospektive*, exh. cat., Annegret Hoberg and Helmut Friedel (ed.), Munich 1993, pp.44-66.

46. Franz Marc, 'Zur Ausstellung der "Neuen Künstlervereinigung" bei Thannhauser', September 1910, in *Franz Marc: Schriften*, ed. Klaus Lankheit, Cologne 1978, p.127: 'Es ist schade, dass man Kandinskys grosse Komposition und manches andere nicht neben die muhamedanischen Teppiche im Ausstellungspark hängen kann. Ein Vergleich wäre unvermeidlich und wie lehrreich für uns alle! . . . Wir haben in Deutschland kaum ein dekoratives Werk, geschweige einen Teppich, den wir daneben hängen dürfen. Versuchen wir es mit Kandinskys Kompositionen – sie werden diese gefährliche Probe aushalten, und nicht als Teppiche, sondern als *"Bilder"*. . . . Die grosse Konsequenz seiner Farben hält seiner zeichnerischen [Willkür] Freiheit die Wage [sic.], – ist dies nicht zugleich eine Definition der Malerei?'

47. It is interesting that Marc's comparison of Kandinsky's painting with a Mohammedan carpet preceded G.J. Wolf's 'Ausstellungsrezension', *Die Kunst für Alle*, 1 November 1910, p.68, in which the critic stated that he would have fewer objections if Kandinsky's *Composition II* were labelled a '"Colour sketch for a modern carpet". But far from it! The people who are exhibiting here are too good to allow themselves to be put on a par with "designers."'

48. Wassily Kandinsky, 'Letters from Munich' ('Pis'mo iz Miunkhena'), *Apollon* (St Petersburg), 1909-10, in *Complete Writings in Art*, 1982, pp.73-6. Also consult the three-volume catalogue of this extensive exhibition (visited by Matisse in 1910), *Ausstellung von Meisterwerke muhammedanischer Kunst*, F. Sarre and F. R. Martin, Munich 1912.

49. Maurice Denis, 'Définition du néo-traditionalisme', *Art et Critique*, 23 August 1890, in *Théories, 1890-1910: du Symbolisme et de Gauguin vers un nouvel ordre classique*, Paris 1920, p.1: 'Se rappeler qu'un tableau – avant d'être un cheval de bataille, une femme nue ou une quelconque anecdote – est essentiellement une surface plane recouverte de couleurs en un certain ordre assemblées.'

50. For the theoretical sources in the Early Romantic period consult Klaus Lankheit, *Franz Marc: sein Leben und seine Kunst*, Cologne 1976, p.45.

51. In the catalogue *Kandinsky Compositions*, The Museum of Modern Art, New York 1995, p.18, Magdalena Dabrowski states that an annotated copy of Schopenhauer's *Ueber das Sehn und die Farben* (*On Vision and Colour*) was found among the books Kandinsky left with Münter in 1914. On Kandinsky's colour theory, consult John Gage, *Colour and Culture: Practice and Meaning from Antiquity to Abstraction*, London 1993, pp.188-9, 206-8, 212, 236-45.

52. August Macke and Franz Marc, *Briefwechsel*, Cologne 1964, pp.27-30: Marc to Macke, 12 December 1910.

53. Ibid. p.40: Marc to Macke, 14 January 1911. Also consult Shulamith Behr, 'The Relationship between the Works of Franz Marc and Wassily Kandinsky', unpublished MA thesis, University of Manchester 1983, pp.35ff.

54. Wassily Kandinsky and Franz Marc, *Briefwechsel*, ed. Klaus Lankheit, Munich and Zurich 1983, p.40: Kandinsky to Marc, 19 June 1911: 'In dem Buch muss sich das ganze Jahr spiegeln, und eine Kette zur Vergangenheit und ein Strahl in die Zukunft müssen diesem Spiegel das volle Leben geben . . . Da bringen wir einen Ägypter neben einem kleinen Zeh, einen Chinesen neben Rousseau, ein Volksblatt neben Picasso u. drgl. noch viel mehr!'

55. Wassily Kandinsky, *Klänge*, Munich 1912. Wassily Kandinsky, *Sounds*, Elizabeth R. Napier (trans.), New Haven and London 1981.

56. For consideration of his theatrical works consult Shulamith Behr, 'Wassily Kandinsky as Playwright: The Stage Compositions 1909-1914', unpublished PhD thesis, University of Essex 1991.

57. Wassily Kandinsky, 'Der blaue Reiter Rückblick', *Das Kunstblatt*, 1930.

58. The horse as emblematic of sexual passion dates from antique and medieval zoological literature. The rider/artist, thereby, channels or masters the irrational wildness through intellect and self-mastery. Consult Joseph Koerner 1993 (see note 7), pp.426-34.

59. Fäthke 2001 (see note 24), pp.184-6: Else Lasker-Schüler to Marianne Werefkin, 1913: 'Hochverehrte Prinzessin, vieladeliger, wilder Junge, Süsse Malerin, Wann darf ich kommen – ich trauma von der Süssigkeit Ihrer Bilder, (Der Prinz von Theben), Else Lasker-Schüler, (Des blauen Reiterreiterin Freundin)'.

60. See Annegret Hoberg, 'The Life and Work of Gabriele Münter', in *Gabriele Münter*, 2005 (see note 35), pp.35-6.

61. Behr 2005 (see note 35), pp.54-60.

62. *Kandinsky: Catalogue Raisonné of the Oil Paintings*, 1982, vol.I, p.352, no.373: *Impression II (Moscow)* was painted 1 January 1911.

63. Ibid. p.19.

64. Vivian Endicott Barnett, 'Evolution of Composition VII', in *Vasily Kandinsky*, 1995 (see note 28), pp.446-7.

65. Wassily Kandinsky, 'Cologne Lecture', 1914, *Complete Writings on Art*, 1982, vol.1, pp.393-400.

66. An in-depth account of the preliminary sketches in relation to the final painting and the iconography can be found in Magdalena Dabrowski, 'Composition VII', in *Kandinsky Compositions*, exh. cat., ed. Dabrowski, The Museum of Modern Art, New York 1995, pp.37-45.

67. For the diverse sources of this Dionysian concept, consult Rose-Carol Washton Long, 'Kandinsky's Vision of Utopia as a Garden of Love', *Art Journal*, vol.43, no.1, Spring 1983, pp.50-60.

68. Vivian Endicott Barnett, *Kandinsky and Sweden*, Malmö, Konsthall and Stockholm 1989, p.45, quoting Kandinsky's letter to Erich Gutkind, 11 July 1914.

69. The war interrupted this project. See Shulamith Behr, 'Wassily Kandinsky and Dimitrije Mitrinovic', 1992, *Oxford Art Journal*, vol.15, no.1, 1992, pp.81-8.

70. For detailed consideration of this consult Helmut Friedel and Marion Ackermann, 'A Colorful Life: History of the Collection of Vasily Kandinsky's Work in the Lenbachhaus', in *Vasily Kandinsky*, 1995 (see note 28), pp.15-31.

Kandinsky – Resurrection and Cultural Renewal

With thanks to Professor Dr Barbara Schellewald, University of Basel, for her generous input to the sections on icons in this essay.

1. As cited in 'A History of the Almanac' by Klaus Lankheit in *The Blaue Reiter Almanac*, ed. idem, trans. Henning Falkenstein with Manug Terzian and Gertrude Hinderlie, London 1974, p.17.

2. On the almanac and the exhibitions see *Der Blaue Reiter*, ed. Christine Hopfengart, exh. cat., Kunsthalle Bremen, Cologne 2000.

3. On this Leonid Sabaneyev, *Erinnerungen an Alexander Skrjabin (1925)*, ed. and trans. from Russian by Ernst Kuhn, Berlin 2005.

4. David Burlyuk, 'The "Savages" of Russia by D. Burliuk' in *The Blaue Reiter Almanac* (as note 1), pp.72-80.

5. For the purposes of this discussion the entire print run of *Mir Iskusstva* (1898–1904) was consulted in the Slavic Library of the Charles University in Prague. On Vrubel, Bilibin and Roerich, see *Michail Wrubel: der russische Symbolist*, exh. cat., Kunsthalle Düsseldorf and Haus der Kunst Munich, ed. Jürgen Harten and Christoph Vitali, Cologne 1997; Andreas Bode, *Ivan Jakovlevic Bilibin: der russische Märchenillustrator*, Wielenbach 1997; Jacqueline Decter, *Nicholas Roerich: Leben und Werk eines russischen Meisters*, Basle 1989.

6. Matters of guilt, criminality and retribution are central to Dostoevsky; witness works such as *Crime and Punishment* (1866), *The Demons* (1872) and *The Brothers Karamazov* (1880). See also the essay by Sigmund Freud, 'Dostoyevsky and Patricide' (1928), in *The Standard Edition of the Complete Psychological Works of Sigmund Freud*, London 1948, vol.14, pp.399-418. In the debate surrounding the retention of the peasants' legal system, Dostoevsky was supported by his younger friend, the philosopher Vladimir Solovyov.

7. Kasimir Malevich, *From Cubism and Futurism to Suprematism*, in Kasimir Malevich, *Essays on Art, 1915–1928*, Copenhagen 1968, vol.1, pp.19-41. Following the same line as Bulgakov, Malevich felt that Suprematism, far from being a continuation of Cubism, had ousted it.

8. Cf. note 7, passim.

9. Cf. note 1.

10. These included poets such as Andrey Bely and Aleksandr Blok. On Diaghilev see Richard Buckle, *Diaghilev*, Herford 1984; see also Janet Kennedy, *The 'Mir Iskusstva' Group and Russian Art 1898–1912*, New York 1977.

11. Malevich was later to engage in a lively correspondence with Gershenzon; see Kasimir Malevich, *Gott ist nicht gestürzt!*, ed. Aage A. Hansen-Loewe, Vienna 2004, pp.15-18.

12. Wassily Kandinsky, 'Rückblicke', in *Kandinsky 1901–1913*, Berlin 1913, pp.III–IXX, reprinted in Hans K. Roethel and Jelena Hahl-Koch (ed.), *Kandinsky, Die Gesammelten Schriften*, Berne, 1980, pp.27-50. Published in English as 'Reminiscences' in *Kandinsky: Complete Writings on Art*, 2 vols., ed. Kenneth C. Lindsay and Peter Vergo, London 1982, vol.1, pp.357-82, here note p.362. Hereafter referred to as Kandinsky, *Complete Writings on Art*.

13. Trans. into German as 'Beitrag zur Ethnographie der Sysol- und Vecegda-Syrjänen, Die nationalen Gottheiten' in Kandinsky, *Gesammelten Schriften* (as note 12) pp.68-74.

14. This article was published in a volume issued in 1889 by the Society of Friends of the Natural Sciences, Anthropology and Ethnography; translated into German as 'Über die Strafe in den Urteilen der Bauerngerichte im Bezirk Moskau' in Kandinsky, *Gesammelten Schriften*, pp.75-87.

15. 'Reminiscences' in Kandinsky, *Complete Writings on Art* (as note 12), vol.1, p.362.

16. Ibid.

17. Ibid. note (Kandinsky's own emphases).

Syntax

18. Wassily Kandinsky, 'Autobiographical Note' first published in exh. cat., *Kandinsky: Kollektive-Ausstellung, 1902–12*, Munich 1913, trans. in Kandinsky, *Complete Writings on Art* (as note 12), vol.1, p.343.
19. Wassily Kandinsky, *Text chudožnika*, Moscow 1918, p.50, trans. from Reinhard Zimmermann, *Die Kunsttheorie von Wassily Kandinsky*, vol.2, Berlin 2002, pp.31, 83–4.
20. See for instance *Apocalyptic Rider II* 1914, glass painting, 30 x 21.3, Munich, Städtische Galerie im Lenbachhaus, Roethel/Benjamin 507; *Rider* 1917–18, glass painting, 14 x 10, Baku, State Art Museum of Azerbaijan, Barnett 32; *Unknown Improvisation* 1914, oil on canvas, 111 x 111, Private Collection, Roethel/Benjamin 505.
21. *Large Resurrection* 1911, glass painting, 23.8 x 24, Munich, Städtische Galerie im Lenbachhaus, Roethel/Benjamin 420. *Sound of Trumpets (Large Resurrection)* 1910–11, watercolour, ink and pencil on paper, 21.7 x 21.8, Munich, Städtische Galerie im Lenbachhaus, Barnett 259.
22. See for instance, *Kandinsky: Compositions*, ed. Magdalena Dabrowski, exh. cat., New York, The Museum of Modern Art / Los Angeles, County Museum of Art, New York 1995, pp.34ff. and 40ff.
23. Wassily Kandinsky, 'Cologne Lecture', in Kandinsky, *Complete Writings on Art* (as note 12), vol.1, p.399.
24. *Sketch for 'Deluge I'* 1912, oil on card, 25.1 x 46.6, Pasadena, Norton Simon Museum, Roethel/Benjamin 433.
25. Trans. from talk given on 24 March 1905 in Moscow. Sergei Diaghilev, 'V čas itogov', in *Vesy*, 1905, no.4, p.46.
26. Georgi Ivanovi Chulkov, *Pokryvalo Izidy. Kriticeskie ocerki*, Moscow 1909, p.77.
27. Wassily Kandinsky, 'Concerning the Spiritual in Art' in Kandinsky, *Complete Writings on Art* (as note 12), vol.1, p.219.
28. Published with the title 'Steps' ('Stupeni') in Moscow in 1918. Additions by Kandinsky to Russian text translated in Kandinsky, *Complete Writings on Art* (as note 12), vol.2, pp.886-98, note 98, p.896.

1. Wassily Kandinsky, 'Reminiscences / Three Pictures' in *Complete Writings on Art*, ed. Kenneth C. Lindsay and Peter Vergo, Boston (MA) 1982, reprinted New York 1994, pp.362-3.
2. It is almost impossible to understand the issues outlined here when faced with colour reproductions. The reproduction is a translation of painting into another medium and format. Each medium, however, has its own functions and laws. This essay addresses the specific functions of Kandinsky's painting.
3. Wassily Kandinsky, *Concerning the Spiritual in Art*, trans. M.T.H. Sadler, 1914; revised F. Golffing, M. Harrison and F. Ostertag, New York 1947, p.54. [Originally published 1912 as Über das Geistige in der Kunst.]
4. Wassily Kandinsky, 'Self-characterisation', Potsdam 1919, in *Complete Writings on Art* (see note 1), p.428.
5. Wassily Kandinsky, *Point and Line to Plane*, trans. Howard Dearstyne and Hilla Rebay (ed.), New York 1947; reprint, New York 1979, p.31. [Originally published in 1926 as *Punkt und Linie zu Fläche*, the ninth in a series of fourteen Bauhaus books edited by Walter Gropius and L. Moholy-Nagy.]
6. Kandinsky repeatedly speaks of a 'science of art' to which he feels he can at best contribute only some initial remarks and suggestions (cf. *Point and Line to Plane* (see note 5), pp.19ff., clearly indicating how little he believed his own texts provided the concepts and insights necessary to respond to our question – even in relation to his own art, let alone in terms of the history of painting in a broader sense.
7. Felix Thürlemann mentions this in his seminal work *Kandinsky über Kandinsky: Der Künstler als Interpret eigener Werke*, Berne 1986, in which he addresses what Sedlmayr called the 'physiognomic semantics' of colours (pp.119 ff.). See also Matthias Haldemann, *Kandinskys Abstraktion: Die Entstehung und Transformation seines Bildkonzepts*, Munich 2001, pp.45-51.
8. The famous passage in 'Reminiscences', in which Kandinsky speaks of squeezing paint fresh from the tube and describes the wonders of the palette, does not disprove this. See: *Complete Writings on Art* (see note 1), p.127, pp.367-8. Sers observes that Kandinsky discovered the secret of a logic inherent in colours through his experience of pure pigments coming straight from the tube. See Philippe Sers, *Kandinsky. Philosophie de l'Abstraction: L'image métaphysique*, Geneva 1995, p.29 and pp.62-85, esp. pp.75ff.
9. Kandinsky calls a warm golden-yellow Neapolitan yellow. For example, an area of generous yellow is described as 'Neapolitan' in a preparatory drawing for *Improvisation 10* (Centre Pompidou). See *Oeuvres de Vassily Kandinsky (1866–1944), Collections du Musée national d'art moderne*, exh. cat., ed. Christian Derouet and Jessica Boissel, Paris 1984, p.94, fig.89.
10. Wassily Kandinsky, 'Reminiscences' in *Complete Writings on Art* (see note 1), p.363.
11. It is all but impossible to render this grey accurately in a colour reproduction.
12. *Point and Line to Plane* (see note 5), p.19.
13. Such elisions occur regularly, not only in Kandinsky's painting, and are used to achieve certain effects. For instance, in Kandinsky's picture, the ochre of the mountain on the upper right can be seen as a variation on the elided and merely imagined brown tone that lends the ochre its specific character, along with the red of the cloud and the pale blue reflex on the shoulder of the mountain. Its relationship to the merely imagined brown is due in part to the fact that it appears as a wan, pale and 'washed-out' colour.
14. Bernhard Haas, *Die neue Tonalität von Schubert bis Webern. Hören und Analysieren nach Albert Simon*, Wilhelmshaven 2004, pp.27-31.
15. Lake is a transparent pigment that becomes dark and intense when applied thickly.

16. I use 'green earth' to describe the colour that dominates the 'field' and is seen in especially pure form in an arabesque at the lowermost part of the field.
17. In the early years of the twentieth century Kandinsky even experimented with black and dark backgrounds.
18. In his *Die Kunsttheorie von Wassily Kandinsky*, Berlin 2002 (vol.1, pp.455-7), Reinhard Zimmermann recalls Ernest Harms' report on Kandinsky's intense study of Goethe's colour theory. See Ernest Harms, 'My Association with Kandinsky' in *American Artist*, 27, no.6, June–August 1963, pp.36-41 and 90-1.
19. This drawing makes a fairly clear reference to the theme of Ann and Joachim meeting by the Golden Gate. Christian Derouet relates it to *Improvisation 1* (Roethel/Benjamin 271) and *Paradise* of 1909 (Roethel/Benjamin 286); *Oeuvres de Vassily Kandinsky* (see note 9), p.86.
20. Wassily Kandinsky, 'Reminiscences' in *Complete Writings on Art* (see note 1), p.356.
21. Ibid. p.356.
22. 'Or' is the French word for gold. The word 'orange' is derived from the name of the fruit, formerly known as *pomme d'orenge* – golden apple or *aurantia*.
23. Michel Henry, *Voir l'invisible. Sur Kandinsky*, Paris 1988, p.25. What cannot be objectified because we cannot view it with detachment is what Henry means by the 'invisible' revealed in Kandinsky's abstract painting.
24. The letter is published in *Vassily Kandinsky. Correspondances avec Zervos et Kojève*, ed. Christian Derouet, trans. Nina Ivanoff, in an hors-série edition of *Cahiers du Musée National d'Art Moderne*, Paris 1992, pp.143-8.
25. The mark (') designates a colour that expressly reiterates another, while specifically not being identical to it in function.
26. This technique was already established among the Impressionists and was also employed in Cubism, Fauvism and Expressionism; cf. my *Historische Farbenlehre* (in prep.), which describes the historical context of this and other chromatic systems.
27. *Point and Line to Plane* (see note 5), pp.36-7. Matthias Haldemann (see note 7, pp.185ff., esp. p.187) has astutely associated the point at the heart of the central configuration of *Composition VII* with the 'point' in Kandinsky's theoretical treatise. It is evident, however, that much happened between 1913 and 1919 or 1921.

Select Bibliography

Kandinsky's writings and exhibition catalogues are arranged chronologically.

Catalogues raisonnés and secondary literature are arranged alphabetically

KANDINSKY'S WRITINGS

Über das Geistige in der Kunst, insbesondere in der Malerei, Munich 1911; 2nd revised ed., Munich 1912; 4th ed., ed. Max Bill, Berne 1952; reprint, ed. Jelena Hahl-Fontaine, Berne 2004. English trans. *The Art of Spiritual Harmony*, London 1914; *Concerning the Spiritual in Art and Painting in Particular*, 1912, New York 1947; *Concerning the Spiritual in Art*, New York 1977.

Almanac Der Blaue Reiter, ed. Wassily Kandinsky and Franz Marc. Munich 1912; 1st ed., with additional foreword, Munich 1912; documented new edition, ed. Klaus Lankheit, Munich 1965, reprint, Munich 1976, 1979, 1984, 1989, 2004.

Poems without Words, Church Enstone and Oxford 1978.

The Blaue Reiter Almanac, ed. Wassily Kandinsky and Franz Marc, ed. and intro. Klaus Lankheit; trans. from German Henning Falkenstein, Manug Terzain and Gertrude Hinderlie, London 1974.

'Über die Formfrage', in *Almanac Der Blaue Reiter*, pp.132–82.

'Über Bühnenkomposition', in *Almanac Der Blaue Reiter*, pp.189–208.

'Der Gelbe Klang', in *Almanac Der Blaue Reiter*, pp.210–29.

'Über Kunstverstehen', in *Der Sturm*, III, no.129, Berlin 1912, pp.157–58.

Klänge. Munich undated [1913]. English ed. *Sounds*, trans. and with intro. by Elizabeth R. Napier, New Haven and London 1981.

'Mein Werdegang', in *Kandinsky 1901–1913*, Berlin 1913, reprinted in *Kandinsky. Die gesammelten Schriften*, vol.1, ed. Hans K. Roethel and Jelena Hahl-Koch, Berne 1980, p.37, re-edited with the same pagination under the title *Autobiographische Schriften*, Berne 2004, pp.51–9.

'Rückblicke', in *Kandinsky 1901–1913* 1913, pp.III–IXX, reprinted in *Autobiographische Schriften*, pp.27–50.

'Komposition 4. Nachträgliches Definieren', in *Kandinsky 1901–1913*, 1913, pp.XXXIII–XXXIV, reprinted in Felix Thürlemann, *Kandinsky über Kandinsky: Der Künstler als Interpret eigener Werke*, Berne 1986, pp.219–20.

'Komposition 6', in *Kandinsky 1901–1913* 1913, pp.XXXV–XXXVIII, reprinted in Felix Thürlemann 1986, pp.221–24.

'Das Bild mit weissem Rand', in *Kandinsky 1901–1913*, 1913, pp.XXXIX–XXXXI, reprinted in Felix Thürlemann 1986, pp.225–7.

Om Konstnären [Über den Künstler], Stockholm 1916.

Punkt und Linie zu Fläche. Beitrag zur Analyse der malerischen Elemente, Munich 1926; 2nd ed., Munich 1928; 3rd and following eds., ed. Max Bill, Berne 1955 ff.; reprint, 2005. English ed., *Point and Line to Plane: Contribution to the Analysis of the Pictorial Elements*, trans. Howard Dearstyne and Hilla Rebay, eds. and prefaced Hilla Rebay, New York 1947.

Essays über Kunst und Künstler, ed. Max Bill, Stuttgart 1955; 2nd revised ed., Berne 1963; 3rd ed., Berne 1973.

Écrits complets, ed. Philippe Sers, Paris 1970–5 [vol.1, not published; vol.2, *La forme* (1970); vol.3, *La synthèse des arts* (1975)].

Kandinsky. Die gesammelten Schriften, ed. Hans K. Roethel and Jelena Hahl-Koch, 2 vols, Berne 1980.

Complete Writings on Art, ed. Kenneth C. Lindsay and Peter Vergo, 2 vols., Boston and London 1982; reprint, New York 1994.

Über das Theater. Du Théâtre. O teatre, ed. Jessica Boissel, Cologne 1998.

LETTERS TO KANDINSKY

Troels Andersen, 'Some Unpublished Letters by Kandinsky', in *Artes, Periodical of the Fine Arts*, 2 (October 1966), pp.90–110.

'Briefe von Wassily Kandinsky an Will Grohmann, 1924–1927', in Karl Gutbrod (ed.), *Künstler schreiben an Will Grohmann*, Cologne 1968, pp.45–71.

'Kandinsky – Briefe an Hermann Rupf 1931–1943', ed. Sandor Kuthy, in *Berner Kunstmitteilungen*, 150/1 (May/July 1974), pp.1–13; 152/3 (August 1974), pp.5–19.

'Briefe von Kandinsky an Paul Klee', in *Hommage à Wassily Kandinsky*, Wiesbaden 1976, pp.130–3.

'Zwölf Briefe von Wassily Kandinsky an Hans Thiemann 1933–1939', ed. Christian Beutler, in *Wallraf-Richartz-Jahrbuch*, 38 (1976), pp.155–66.

Wassily Kandinsky und Arnold Schönberg, Briefe, Bilder und Vienna 1980. English ed. *Arnold Schoenberg, Wassily Kandinsky: letters, pictures and documents*, trans. John C. Crawford, London 1984.

'Kandinsky – Briefe an Otto Nebel 1926–1940', ed. Therese Bhattacharya-Stettler, in *Berner Kunstmitteilungen*, 203 (January/February 1981), pp.1–19.

'Wassily Kandinsky and Franz Marc', *Briefwechsel. Mit Briefen von und an Gabriele Münter und Maria Marc*, ed. Klaus Lankheit, Munich and Zurich 1983.

Sandor Kuthy and Stefan Frey, 'Kandinsky und Klee, Aus dem Briefwechsel der beiden Künstler und ihrer Frauen – 1912–1940', in *Berner Kunstmitteilungen*, 234-6 (December 1984 – February 1985), pp.1–24.

'Die Briefe Wassily Kandinskys an Dmitrij Kardovskij', in Sibylle Ebert-Schifferer (ed.), *Wassily Kandinsky: Die erste sowjetische Retrospektive: Gemälde, Zeichnungen und Graphik aus sowjetischen und westlichen Museen*, exh. cat., Frankfurt, Schirn Kunsthalle, Frankfurt 1989, pp.47–54.

Vassily Kandinsky. Correspondances avec Zervos et Kojève, ed. Christian Derouet, Paris 1992.

Annegret Hoberg (ed.), *Wassily Kandinsky und Gabriele Münter in Murnau und Kochel 1902–1914. Briefe und Erinnerungen*, Munich 1994. English ed. *Wassily Kandinsky and Gabriele Münter: Letters and Reminiscences 1902–1914*, Munich 1994.

'Schriftwechsel. Korrespondenz zwischen Kandinsky, privaten Sammlern, Künstlerfreunden und Schweizer Museumsdirektoren, 1912–1943', in Manuela Kahn-Rossi (ed.), *Kandinsky nelle collezioni svizzere/in den Schweizer Sammlungen/dans les collections suisses*, exh. cat., Lugano, Museo cantonale d'arte, Milan 1995, pp.261–91.

Myriam Beck (ed.), 'Vasilii Kandinsky and Giovanni Antonio Colonna di Cesarò, Correspondence Regarding "On the Spiritual in Art" – Editorial Comment', in *Experiment. A Journal of Russian Culture*, 1 (1995), pp.82–139.

Kandinsky – Albers. Une correspondance des années trente. Ein Briefwechsel aus den dreissiger Jahren, ed. Jessica Boissel, Paris 1998.

Christian Derouet (ed.), 'Kandinsky – Delaunay. Un échange de lettres en avril 1912', in *Les Cahiers du Musée National d'Art Moderne*, 73 (2000), pp.74–85.

CATALOGUES RAISONNES

Vivian Endicott Barnett, *Kandinsky. Werkverzeichnis der Aquarelle*. 2 vols., Munich 1992-4. English ed. *Kandinsky: Watercolours: Catalogue Raisonné*, vol.I 1900–21 and vol.II, 1922–44, London 1992, 1994.

Hans K. Roethel, *Kandinsky. Das graphische Werk*, Cologne 1970.

Hans K. Roethel and Jean K. Benjamin, *Kandinsky. Werkverzeichnis der Ölgemälde*. 2 vols., Munich 1982, 1984. English ed. *Kandinsky: catalogue raisonné of the oil-paintings*, vol.I 1900–15 and vol.II 1916–44, London 1982,1984.

SECONDARY LITERATURE

Marion Ackermann, 'Eine Sprache, die besser wirkt als Esperanto. Überlegungen zum Einfluss des Spiritismus auf Kandinsky', in Moritz Bassler (ed.), *Mystique, mysticisme et modernité en Allemagne autour de 1900. Mystik, Mystizismus und Moderne in Deutschland um 1900*, Strasburg 1998, pp.187–201.

Natalja Avtonomova et al. (ed.), *Mnogogrannyj mir Kandinskogo* [International Congress Papers, Galerie Tretjakov, Moskau 1994], Moscow 1998.

Vivian Endicott Barnett, *Kandinsky at the Guggenheim*, New York 1983.

Vivian Endicott Barnett, 'Fairy Tales and Abstraction. Stylistic Conflicts in Kandinsky's Art 1915–1921', in Björn Springfeldt (ed.), *Nya perspektiv på Kandinsky/New perspectives on Kandinsky*, Malmö 1990.

Vivian Endicott Barnett, 'Kandinsky und die Naturwissenschaft', in Hubertus Gassner (ed.), *Elan vital oder Das Auge des Eros*, exh. cat., Munich, Haus der Kunst, Munich 1994, pp.39–55.

Shulamith Behr, 'Wassily Kandinsky and Dimitrije Mitrinovic. Pan-Christian Universalism and the Yearbook "Towards the Mankind of the Future through Aryan Europe"', in *Oxford Art Journal*, 1 (1992), pp.81–8.

Max Bill (ed.), *Wassily Kandinsky*, Paris 1951.

Konrad Boehmer (ed.), *Schönberg und Kandinsky. An Historic Encounter*, Amsterdam 1997.

John E. Bowlt and Rose-Carol Washton Long (ed.), *The Life of Vasilii Kandinsky in Russian Art. A Study of 'On the Spiritual in Art'*, 2nd ed., Newtonville (MA) 1984.

John E. Bowlt, 'Vasilii Kandinsky and Nikolai Kul'bin', in *Experiment. A Journal of Russian Culture*, 9, 2003, pp.69–81.

Ramon Tio Bellido, *Kandinsky*, trans. Jane Brenton, London 1988.

Marcel Brion, *Kandinsky*, trans. from French A.H.N. Molesworth, London 1961.

Günter Brucher, *Kandinsky. Wege zur Abstraktion*, Munich 1999.

Elisabeth Dämmer, *Kandinskys erste sieben Kompositionen. Betrachtung, Analyse, Versuch einer Deutung*, Dissertation, Munich 1986, 2 vols., Hillesheim and Buldorf 1991.

Johannes Eichner, *Kandinsky und Gabriele Münter. Von Ursprüngen moderner Kunst*, Munich 1957.

Ulrika Maria Eller-Rüter, *Kandinsky. Bühnenkomposition und Dichtung als Realisation seines Synthese-Konzepts*, Hildesheim 1990.

Claudia Emmert, *Bühnenkompositionen und Gedichte von Wassily Kandinsky. Im Kontext eschatologischer Lehren seiner Zeit 1896–1914*, Frankfurt 1998.

Jonathan David Fineberg, *Kandinsky in Paris 1906–1907*, Dissertation, Harvard University, Michigan, Ann Arbor (MI) 1984.

Helmut Friedel, *Wassily Kandinsky – Gesammelte Schriften*, Munich 2004.

Edna J. Garte, 'Kandinsky's Ideas on Changes in Modern Physics and their Implications for his Development', in *Gazette des Beaux-Arts*, 110 (1987), pp.137–44.

Adrian Glew, '"Blue spiritual sounds". Kandinsky and the Sadlers, 1911–16', in *Burlington Magazine*, 139 (1997), pp.600–15.

Will Grohmann, *Wassily Kandinsky*, Leipzig 1924.

Will Grohmann, *Kandinsky*, Paris 1930 [Les grands peintres d'aujourd'hui, 6].

Will Grohmann, *Wassily Kandinsky. Leben und Werk*, Cologne 1958; 2nd ed. 1961. English ed. *Wassily Kandinsky: Life and Work*, trans. from German by Norbert Guterman, London 2000.

Jelena Hahl-Koch, 'Kandinsky und der "Blaue Reiter"', in Karin von Maur (ed.), *Vom Klang der Bilder. Die Musik in der Kunst des 20. Jahrhunderts*, Munich 1985, pp.354–9.

Jelena Hahl-Koch, 'Kandinskys erstes abstraktes Ölbild 1989 wiedergefunden', in *Kunstchronik*, 43 (1990), pp.95–103.

Jelena Hahl-Koch, *Kandinsky*, Stuttgart 1993.

Jelena Hahl-Koch (ed.), 'Kandinsky, Schönberg and their Parallel Experiments', in Konrad Boehmer ed.), *Schönberg and Kandinsky*, pp.67–87.

Matthias Haldemann, *Kandinskys Abstraktion. Die Entstehung und Transformation seines Bildkonzepts*, Munich 2001.

Yule F. Heibel, '"They Danced on Volcanoes". Kandinsky's Breakthrough to Abstraction, the German Avant-Garde and the Eve of the First World War', in *Art History*, 12 (1989), pp.342–61.

Christoph Hölz (ed.), *Grenzgänger. Wassily Kandinsky – Maler zwischen Murnau, Moskau und Paris*, Munich 1997.

Johannes Huber, 'Wassily Kandinsky und Goldach', in *Rorschacher Neujahrsblatt*, 81 (1991), pp.37–48.

Georgia Illetschko, *Kandinsky und Paris. Die Geschichte einer Beziehung*, Munich 1997.

Nina Kandinsky, *Kandinsky und ich*, Munich 1976.

Gisela Kleine, *Gabriele Münter und Wassily Kandinsky. Biographie eines Paares*, Frankfurt 1990.

Verena Krieger, *Von der Ikone zur Utopie. Kunstkonzepte der russischen Avantgarde*, Cologne 1998.

Johannes Langner, '"Improvisation 13". Zur Funktion des Gegenstandes in Kandinskys Abstraktion', in *Jahrbuch der Staatlichen Kunstsammlungen in Baden-Württemberg*, 14 (1977), pp.115–46.

Johannes Langner, 'Impression V. Observations sur un thème chez Kandinsky', in *Revue de l'Art*, 45 (1979), pp.53–65.

Jacques Lassaigne, *Kandinsky. Biographisch-kritische Studie*, Geneva 1964. English ed. *Kandinsky: Biographical and Critical Study*, trans. from French H.S.B. Harrison, Geneva 1964.

Kenneth Lindsay, 'The Genesis and Meaning of the Cover Design for the First "Blaue Reiter" Exhibition Catalogue', in *Art Bulletin*, 35 (1953), pp.47–52.

Rose-Carol Washton Long, 'Kandinsky's Abstract Style. The Veiling of Apocalyptic Folk Imagery', in *Art Journal*, 34/3 (Spring 1975), pp.217–28.

Rose-Carol Washton Long, *Kandinsky. The Development of an Abstract Style*, Oxford 1980. Rose-Carol Washton Long, 'Kandinsky's Vision of Utopia as a Garden of Love', in *Art Journal*, 43 (1983), pp.50–60.

Rose-Carol Washton Long, 'Occultism, Anarchism, and Abstraction. Kandinsky's Art of the Future', in *Art Journal*, 46 (1987), pp.38–45. Rose-Carol Washton Long, 'Expressionismus, Abstraktion und die Suche nach Utopia in Deutschland', in Maurice Tuchman and Judi Freeman (eds.), *Das Geistige in der Kunst. Abstrakte Malerei 1890–1985*, Stuttgart 1988, pp.201–17.

Carol McCay, 'Kandinsky's Ethnography. Scientific Field Work and Aesthetic Reflection', in *Art History*, 17 (1994), pp.182–208.

Barbara Mackert-Riedel, *Wassily Kandinsky über eigene Bilder. Zum Problem der Interpretation moderner Malerei*, Weimar 2003.

Eva Mazur-Keblowski, *Apokalypse als Hoffnung. Die russischen Aspekte der Kunst und Kunsttheorie Vasilij Kandinskijs vor 1914*, Berlin 2000.

Paul Overy, *Kandinsky. Die Sprache des Auges*, Cologne 1970 [1st ed. London 1969].

Nadia Podzemskaia, *Colore, simbolo, immagine. Origine della teoria di Kandinsky*, Florence 2000.

Evelin Priebe, *Angst und Abstraktion. Die Funktion der Kunst in der Kunsttheorie Kandinskys*, Frankfurt 1986.

Hilla Rebay (ed.), *Kandinsky*, published upon the occasion of The Kandinsky Memorial Exhibition, New York 1945.

Peter Anselm Riedl, *Wassily Kandinsky in Selbstzeugnissen und Bilddokumenten*, Reinbek by Hamburg 1983.

Sixten Ringbom, 'Art in "The Epoch of the Great Spiritual". Occult Elements in the Early Theory of Abstract Painting', in *Journal of the Warburg and Courtauld Institutes*, 29 (1966), pp.386–418.

Sixten Ringbom, *The Sounding Cosmos. A Study in The Spiritualism of Kandinsky and the Genesis of Abstract Painting*, Acta Academia Åboensis, Ser. A. 38,2, Åbo 1970.

Sixten Ringbom, 'Kandinsky und das Okkulte', in *Kandinsky und München. Begegnungen und Wandlungen 1896–1914*, exh. cat., Munich, Städtischen Galerie Lenbachhaus, Munich 1982, pp.85–101.

Sixten Ringbom, 'Die Steiner Annotationen Kandinskys', in *Kandinsky und München: Begegnungen und Wandlungen, 1896–1914*, exh. cat., Munich, Städtische Galerie im Lenbachhaus, ed. Armin Zweite, Munich 1982, pp.102–5.

Sixten Ringbom, 'Überwindung des Sichtbaren. Die Generation der abstrakten Pioniere', in Maurice Tuchman and Judi Freeman (ed.), *Das Geistige in der Kunst. Abstrakte Malerei 1890–1985*, Stuttgart 1988, pp.131–53.

Sixten Ringbom, 'Kunst in der "Zeit des Grossen Geistigen". Okkulte Elemente in der frühen Theorie der Abstrakten Malerei', in *Jahresring. Jahrbuch für moderne Kunst (München)*, 40 (1993), pp.26–72.

Hans K. Roethel, 'Improvisation Klamm. Vorstufen einer Deutung', in *Eberhard Hanfstaengl zum 75. Geburtstag*, Munich 1961, pp.186–92.

Hans K. Roethel in collaboration with Jean K. Benjamin, *Kandinsky*, Oxford 1979.

Hans K. Roethel, *Kandinsky*, Munich and Zurich 1982.

Eva Rosenblum, 'Wassily Kandinsky und Franz Stadler – eine Freundschaft. Neue Funde aus der Blütezeit des Blauen Reiter', in *Pantheon*, 52 (1994), pp.142–7.

Mark Roskill, *Klee, Kandinsky, and the Thought of Their Time. A Critical Perspective*, Urbana and Chicago 1992.

Eberhard Roters, 'Wassily Kandinsky und die Gestalt des Blauen Reiters', in *Jahrbuch der Berliner Museen*, 5 (1963), pp.201–26.

Jorgen Schultz, 'Kandinsky's Kleine Welten. Theory and Practice', in *Hafnia, Copenhagen Papers in the History of Art*, 11 (1987), pp.39–75.

Philippe Sers, *Kandinsky. Philosophie de l'abstraction, l'image métaphysique*, Geneva 1995.

Philippe Sers, *Kandinsky. Philosophie de l'art abstrait, peinture, poésie, scénographie*, Milan 2003.

Richard Sheppard, 'Kandinsky's Early Aesthetic Theory. Some Examples of its Influence and some Implications for the Theory and Practice of Abstract Poetry', in *Journal of European Studies*, 5 (1975), pp.19–40.

Noemi Smolik, *Von der Ikone zum gegenstandslosen Bild. Der Maler Vasilij Kandinskij*, dissertation, Cologne 1987, Munich 1992.

Hai-Young Song, *Wassily Kandinsky. Von den frühen Landschaften zur Komposition (1901–1911)*, Regensburg 1995.

Björn Springfeldt (ed.), *Nya perspektiv på Kandinsky/New perspectives on Kandinsky*, Malmö 1990.

François Le Targat, *Kandinsky*, London 1988
Felix Thürlemann, *Kandinsky über Kandinsky. Der Künstler als Interpret eigener Werke*, Berne 1986.

Felix Thürlemann, 'Launelinien und schwarze Flecken. Kandinskys künstlerische Entwicklung im Spiegel der Bildtitel', in Manuela Kahn-Rossi (ed.), *Kandinsky nelle collezioni svizzere/in den Schweizer Sammlungen/dans les collections suisses*, exh. cat., Lugano, Museo cantonale d'arte, Milan 1995, pp.115–37.

Becke Sell Tower, *Klee and Kandinsky in Munich and at the Bauhaus*, Ann Arbor 1981.
Pierre Volboudt, *Die Zeichnungen Wassily Kandinskys*, Cologne 1974.

Rudolf H. Wackernagel, '" ... Ich werde die Leute ... in Öl und Tempera beschwindeln ...". Neues zur Maltechnik Wassily Kandinskys', in *Zeitschrift für Kunsttechnologie und Konservierung*, 11 (1997), pp.97–128.

Annika Waenerberg, 'Goethe und Kandinsky oder visuelle Motive und abstrakte Kunst zu Beginn des 20. Jahrhunderts', in Marja Terttu Knapas and Åsa Ringbom (ed.), *Icon to Cartoon. A Tribute to Sixten Ringbom*, Helsinki 1995, pp.339–53.

Peg Weiss, 'Kandinsky, Symbolist Poetics and Theater in Munich', in *Pantheon* 35 (1977), pp.209–18.

Peg Weiss, *Kandinsky in Munich. The Formative Jugendstil Years*, Princeton 1985.

Peg Weiss, 'Kandinsky and "Old Russia". An Ethnographic Exploration', in Gabriel P. Weisberg and Laurinda S. Dixon (ed.), *The Documented Image. Visions in Art History*, Syracuse and New York 1987, pp.187–222.

Peg Weiss, *Kandinsky and Old Russia. The Artist as Ethnographer and Shaman*, New Haven and London 1995.

Marit Werenskiold, 'Kandinsky's Moscow', in *Art in America*, 77 (1989), pp.96–111.

Stephan von Wiese, 'Landschaft und Abstraktion im Frühwerk von Kandinsky', in *Der frühe Kandinsky, 1900–1910*, ed. Magdalena M. Moeller, essays by Vivian Endicott Barnett et al., exh. cat., Berlin, Brücke-Museum and Tübingen, Kunsthalle Tübingen, Munich 1994, pp.91–8.

Reinhard Zimmermann, *Die Kunsttheorie von Wassily Kandinsky*, 2 vols., Berlin 2002.
Reinhard Zimmermann, 'Der Bauhaus-Künstler Kandinsky – ein Esoteriker?', in Christoph Wagner (ed.), *Johannes Itten, Wassily Kandinsky, Paul Klee. Das Bauhaus und die Esoterik*, exh. cat., Hamm, Städtisches Gustav-Lübcke-Museum, Bielefeld and Leipzig 2005, pp.46–55.

Armin Zweite, 'Kandinsky zwischen Tradition und Innovation', in Armin Zweite (ed.), *Kandinsky und München: Begegnungen und Wandlungen, 1896–1914*, exh. cat., Munich, Städtische Galerie im Lenbachhaus, ed. Armin Zweite, Munich 1982, pp.134–77.

EXHIBITION CATALOGUES

Hilla Rebay (ed.), *Wassily Kandinsky Memorial. In Memory of Wassily Kandinsky. The Solomon R. Guggenheim Foundation Presents a Survey of the Artist's Paintings and Writings*, exh. cat., Museum of Non-Objective Painting, New York 1945.

Wassily Kandinsky. Gemälde 1900–1944, exh. cat., Staatliche Kunsthalle, Baden-Baden 1970.

Kandinsky. Aquarelle und Zeichnungen, exh. cat., Kunstmuseum Basel, Basel 1972.

Vasily Kandinsky, 1866–1944, in the Collection of the Solomon R. Guggenheim Museum, exh. cat., Solomon R. Guggenheim Museum, intro. Thomas M. Messer, New York 1972.

Erika Hanfstaengl, *Wassily Kandinsky. Zeichnungen und Aquarelle. Katalog der Sammlung in der Städtischen Galerie im Lenbachhaus München*, Munich 1974; 2nd revised ed.,1981.

Christian Derouet et al., *Kandinsky. Trente peintures des musées soviétiques*, exh. cat., Musée national d'art moderne, Paris 1979.

Magdalena Droste, *Klee und Kandinsky. Erinnerung an eine Künstlerfreundschaft anläßlich Klees 100. Geburtstag*, exh. cat., Staatsgalerie, Stuttgart 1979.

Abstraction, Towards a New Art. Painting 1910–20, exh. cat., The Tate Gallery, London 1980.
Claudia Terenzi, *Wassily Kandinsky. 43 Opere dai Musei Sovietici*, exh. cat., Venice, Museum Correr and Rom, Comune di Roma, Milan 1980.

Rosel Gollek, *Der Blaue Reiter im Lenbachhaus München. Katalog der Sammlung in der Städtischen Galerie*, 2nd revised ed., Munich 1982.

Armin Zweite (ed.), *Kandinsky und München. Begegnungen und Wandlungen 1896–1914*, exh. cat., Städtische Galerie im Lenbachhaus, Munich 1982.

Christian Derouet and Jessica Boissel, *Kandinsky. Oeuvres de Vassily Kandinsky (1866–1944). Collections du Musée national d'art moderne*, Paris 1984.

Peter Hahn (ed.), *Kandinsky. Russische Zeit und Bauhausjahre 1915–1933*, exh. cat., Bauhaus-Archiv, Museum für Gestaltung, Berlin 1984.
Kandinsky in Paris 1934–1944, exh. cat., Solomon R. Guggenheim Museum, New York 1985.

Karin von Maur (ed.), *Vom Klang der Bilder. Die Musik in der Kunst des 20. Jahrhunderts*, exh. cat., Staatsgalerie Stuttgart, Munich 1985.

Hans Christoph von Tavel (ed.), *Der Blaue Reiter*, exh. cat., Kunstmuseum Berne, Berne 1986.

Vivian Endicott Barnett, *Kandinsky and Sweden*, exh. cat., Malmö, Konsthall and Stockholm, Moderna Museet, Malmö and others 1989.
Sibylle Ebert-Schifferer (ed.), *Wassily Kandinsky: Die erste sowjetische Retrospektive : Gemälde, Zeichnungen und Graphik aus sowjetischen und westlichen Museen*, exh. cat., Schirn Kunsthalle, Frankfurt 1989.

Susan B. Hirschfeld, *Kandinsky Aquarelle aus dem Guggenheim Museum. Eine Auswahl aus dem Guggenheim Museum und der Hilla von Rebay Foundation*, exh. cat., Historisches Museum der Stadt, Vienna, New York 1991.

Vivian Endicott Barnett and Armin Zweite (eds.), *Kandinsky. Kleine Freuden. Aquarelle und Zeichnungen*, exh. cat., Kunstsammlung Nordrhein-Westfalen and Stuttgart, Staatsgalerie Stuttgart, Munich 1992. English ed. *Kandinsky: watercolors and drawings*, Munich 1992.

Giorgio Cortenova, (ed.), *Vasilij Kandinskij*, exh. cat., Verona, Palazzo Forti, Milan 1993.
Nicoletta Misler (ed.), *Wassily Kandinsky tra Oriente e Occidente. Capolavori dei musei russi*, exh. cat., Palazzo Strozzi, Florence 1993.

Kandinsky, Mondrian. Dos caminos hacia la abstracción, exh. cat., Madrid and Barcelona, Fundación La Caixa, 1994.

Magdalena M. Moeller (ed.), *Der frühe Kandinsky 1900–1910*, exh. cat., Berlin and Tübingen, Munich 1994.

Vivian Endicott Barnett, *Das Bunte Leben. Wassily Kandinsky im Lenbachhaus*, Cologne 1995. English ed. *Vasily Kandinsky: A Colorful Life: The Collection of the Lenbachhaus*, Cologne 1995.

Magdalena Dabrowski (ed.), *Kandinsky Compositions*, ed. exh. cat., The Museum of Modern Art, New York, and Los Angeles County Museum of Art, New York 1995.

Manuela Kahn-Rossi (ed.), *Kandinsky nelle collezioni svizzere/in den Schweizer Sammlungen/dans les collections suisses*, exh. cat., Museo cantonale d'arte, Milan 1995.

Veit Loers (ed.), *Okkultismus und Avantgarde. Von Munch bis Mondrian 1900–1915*, exh. cat., Frankfurt, Schirn Kunsthalle, Ostfildern 1995.

Die Blaue Vier: Feininger, Jawlensky, Kandinsky, Klee in der Neuen Welt, eds. Vivian Endicott Barnett and Josef Helfenstein, exh. cat., Kunstmuseum Berne/Düsseldorf, Kunstsammlung Nordrhein-Westfalen, Cologne 1997. English ed. *The Blue Four: Feininger, Jawlensky, Kandinsky and Klee in the New World*, Cologne 1997.

Kandinsky: opere dal Centre Georges Pompidou, exh. cat., Milan, Fondazione Mazzotta, Milan 1997.

Vassily Kandinsky: la revolució del llenguatge pictòric: obres procedents del MNAM/CCI, exh. cat., Museu d'Art Contemporani, Barcelona 1997.

Farben-Klänge. Wassily Kandinsky, Bilder 1908 bis 1914. Arnold Schönberg, Konzerte und Dokumentation, exh. cat., Fondation Beyeler, Riehen / Basel 1998.

Magdalena M. Moeller (ed.), *Der Blaue Reiter und seine Künstler*, exh. cat., Brücke-Museum and Tübingen, Kunsthalle, Munich 1998.
Chagall, Kandinsky, Malewitsch und die russische Avantgarde, ed. Uwe M. Schneede, exh. cat., Hamburger Kunsthalle and Kunsthaus Zurich, 1998.

Annegret Hoberg and Helmut Friedel (ed.), *Der Blaue Reiter und das Neue Bild. Von der 'Neuen Künstlervereinigung München' zum Blauen Reiter'*, exh. cat., Städtische Galerie im Lenbachhaus, Munich 1999.

Kandinsky. Hauptwerke aus dem Centre Georges Pompidou Paris, exh. cat., Kunsthalle Tübingen, Cologne 1999.

Kandinsky, Chagall, Malevich e lo spiritualismo russo dalle collezioni del Museo Statale Russo di San Pietroburgo, exh. cat., Palazzo Forti, Milan 1999.

Kandinsky rond 1913. De wensdroom van een nieuwe kunst, exh. cat., Gemeentemuseum, Zwolle, The Hague 1999.

Kandinskys Aquarelle und andere Arbeiten auf Papier, exh. cat., London, Royal Academy of Arts, Munich 1999. English ed. *Kandinsky: Watercolours and Other Works on Paper*, exh. cat., Royal Academy of Arts, ed. Frank Whitford, London 1999.

Frank Whitford (ed.), *Kandinsky. Aquarelle und andere Arbeiten auf Papier*, London and Munich 1999.

Christine Hopfengart (ed.), *Der Blaue Reiter*, exh. cat., Kunsthalle Bremen, Cologne 2000.

Kandinsky et la Russie, exh. cat., Fondation Pierre Gianadda, Martigny 2000.

Wassily Kandinsky – tra Monaco e Mosca. 1896–1921, exh. cat., Complesso del Vittoriano, Milan 2000.

Wassily Kandinsky. Tradizione e astrazione in Russia 1896–1921, exh. cat., Fondazione Antonio Mazzotta, Milan 2000.

Fabrice Hergott u.a., *Kandinsky. Retour en Russie 1914–1921*, exh. cat., Musée d'art moderne et contemporaine, Strasburg 2001.

Jean-Louis Prat et al., *Vassily Kandinsky. Rétrospective*, exh. cat., Fondation Maeght, Paris 2001.

Richard W. Gassen (ed.), *Der Blaue Reiter. Die Befreiung der Farbe*, exh. cat., Ludwigshaven, Ostfildern-Ruit 2003.

Kandinsky – the Dissolution of Form, 1900–1920, exh. cat., Fundació Caixa Catalunya, Barcelona 2003.

Wassily Kandinsky: Der Klang der Farbe: 1900–1921, exh. cat., BA–CA Kunstforum Vienna and Wuppertal, Von der Heydt Museum, Bad Preisig 2004.

List of Exhibited Works

The numbers given under each entry refer
to plates. The references in brackets are to
entries in the following publications listed in
the Select Bibliography:

D: Derouet 1984
RB: Roethel and Benjamin 1982-4
VEB: Vivian Endicott Barnett 1994

Arab City
1905
Tempera on cardboard 67.3 x 99.5
*Musée National d'Art Moderne, Centre Georges
Pompidou, Paris. Centre de Création Industrielle.
Bequest of Nina Kandinsky, 1981*
LONDON ONLY
1 (VEB 184)

Song
1906
Gouache on cardboard 49 x 66
*Musée National d'Art Moderne, Centre Georges
Pompidou, Paris. Centre de Création Industrielle.
Bequest of Nina Kandinsky, 1981*
LONDON ONLY
2 (VEB 214)

Improvisation 2 (Funeral March)
1908
Oil on canvas 94 x 130
Moderna Museet, Stockholm
17 (RB 274)

Ludwigskirche in Munich
1908
Oil on cardboard 69.5 x 97
Museo Thyssen-Bornemisza, Madrid
NOT ILLUSTRATED (RB 254)

Murnau – Castle Courtyard I
1908
Oil on cardboard 33 x 44.3
The State Tretyakov Gallery, Moscow
8 (RB 216)

Murnau – Kohlgruberstrasse
1908
Oil on board 71 x 97.5
Private Collection, Switzerland
5 (RB 252)

Murnau – Staffelsee I
1908
Oil on paper laid on board 33 x 40.5
The Ashmolean Museum, Oxford
3 (RB 237)

Murnau – Village Street
1908
Oil on cardboard, mounted on wood
48 x 69.5
Private Collection, Switzerland
4 (RB 214)

St Peter's Chapel at Murnau
1908
Oil on cardboard 33 x 43
Private Collection, Hamburg
10 (RB 223)

Crinolines
1909
Oil on canvas 95 x 128.5
The State Tretyakov Gallery, Moscow
14 (RB 263)

Improvisation 4
1909
Oil on canvas 108 x 158.5
State Art Museum Nizhny Novgorod
12 (RB 282)

Kochel – Straight Road
1909
Oil on cardboard 33 x 44.8
Städtische Galerie im Lenbachhaus, Munich
9 (RB 306)

Murnau – Landscape with Green House
1909
Oil on cardboard 69 x 94
Private Collection, Israel
11 (RB 277)

Painting with Houses
1909
Oil on canvas 97 x 131
Stedelijk Museum, Amsterdam
13 (RB 269)

Study for Houses on a Hill
1909
Oil on cardboard 33 x 45
The State Russian Museum, St Petersburg
7 (RB 304)

Study for Improvisation 8
1909
Oil on cardboard 98 x 70
*Kunstmuseum Winterthur.
Permanent loan of the Volkart Foundation, 1960*
16 (RB 288)

**Study for Murnau – Landscape
with Church**
1909
Oil on cardboard 33 x 45
Collection Im Obersteg, Basel
6 (RB 278)

Boat Trip
1910
Oil on canvas 98 x 105
The State Tretyakov Gallery, Moscow
24 (RB 352)

Improvisation 9
1910
Oil on canvas 110 x 110
Staatsgalerie Stuttgart
LONDON ONLY
27 (RB 335)

Improvisation 10
1910
Oil on canvas 120 x 140
Fondation Beyeler, Riehen/Basel
BASEL ONLY
29 (RB 337)

Improvisation 11
1910
Oil on canvas 97.5 x 106.5
The State Russian Museum, St Petersburg
39 (RB 338)

Landscape with Factory Chimney
1910
Oil on canvas 66.2 x 82
*Solomon R. Guggenheim Museum, New York.
Gift, Solomon R. Guggenheim, 1941*
28 (RB 343)

**Murnau – Mountain Landscape
with Church**
1910
Oil on cardboard 32.7 x 44.8
Städtische Galerie im Lenbachhaus, Munich
18 (RB 345)

Murnau – The Garden II
1910
Oil on board 67 x 51
Private Collection, Switzerland
19 (RB 340)

Murnau with Church II
1910
Oil on canvas 96.5 x 105.5
Collection Van Abbe Museum, Eindhoven
BASEL ONLY
26 (RB 348)

Sketch for Composition II
1910
Oil on cardboard 57 x 47.5
Private Collection, Switzerland
20 (RB 325)

Sketch for Composition II
1910
Oil on canvas 97.5 x 131.2
Solomon R. Guggenheim Museum, New York
21 (RB 326)

The Last Judgement
1910
Oil on canvas 126.5 x 73
Private Collection. Courtesy Helly Nahmad
23 (RB 361)

Cossacks
1910-11
Oil on canvas 94.6 x 130.2
Tate. Presented by Mrs Hazel McKinley 1938
31 (RB 367)

Angel of the Last Judgement
1911
Oil on cardboard 64 x 50
Private Collection, Switzerland
22 (RB 407)

First sketch for Composition IV
1911
Pencil, charcoal and India ink on paper
10.2 x 20
*Musée National d'Art Moderne, Centre Georges
Pompidou, Paris. Centre de Création Industrielle.
Bequest of Nina Kandinsky 1981*
LONDON ONLY
34 (D 114)

Improvisation 19 A
1911
Oil and gouache on canvas 97.2 x 106.4
Städtische Galerie im Lenbachhaus, Munich
40 (RB 386)

Improvisation 20
1911
Oil on canvas 94.5 x 108
The State Pushkin Museum of Fine Arts, Moscow
41 (RB 394)

Lyrically
1911
Oil on canvas 94 x 130
Museum Boijmans Van Beuningen, Rotterdam
LONDON ONLY
30 (RB 377)

Nude
1911
Oil on canvas 147.3 x 99
Private Collection
38 (RB 389)

Study for Composition IV
1911
Pencil and ink 24.9 x 30.5
*Musée National d'Art Moderne, Centre Georges
Pompidou, Paris. Centre de Création Industrielle.
Bequest of Nina Kandinsky 1981*
LONDON ONLY
36 (D 113)

**Study for the Cover of
'The Blue Rider' Almanac**
1911
Watercolour, gouache and Indian ink on paper
29 x 21
*Musée National d'Art Moderne, Centre Georges
Pompidou, Paris. Centre de Création Industrielle.
Donated in 1994*
LONDON ONLY
37 (VEB 285)

Untitled, Sketch for Composition IV
1911
Charcoal on paper 10 x 14.9
*Musée National d'Art Moderne, Centre Georges
Pompidou, Paris. Centre de Création Industrielle.
Bequest of Nina Kandinsky 1981*
LONDON ONLY
35 (D 116)

Untitled, Study for Composition IV
1911
Charcoal on paper 10 x 14.9
*Musée National d'Art Moderne, Centre Georges
Pompidou, Paris. Centre de Création Industrielle.
Bequest of Nina Kandinsky 1981*
LONDON ONLY
33 (D 117)

Black Spot I
1912
Oil on canvas 100 x 130
The State Russian Museum, St Petersburg
42 (RB 435)

Deluge I
1912
Oil on canvas 100 x 105
Kaiser Wilhelm Museum, Krefeld
44 (RB 440)

Sketch for Deluge II
1912
Oil on canvas 95 x 107.5
Acquavella Galleries, Inc., New York
45 (RB 439)

Composition VI
1913
Oil on canvas 195 x 300
State Hermitage, St Petersburg
49 (RB 464)

Composition VII
1913
Oil on canvas 200 x 300
The State Tretyakov Gallery, Moscow
52 (RB 476)

Improvisation 30 (Cannons)
1913
Oil on canvas 110 x 110
Art Institute of Chicago
51 (RB 452)

Improvisation 34 (Orient II)
1913
Oil on canvas 120 x 140
*The State Museum of Fine Arts of
Tatarstan, Kazan*
47 (RB 469)

Landscape with Red Spots I
1913
Oil on canvas 78 x 100
Museum Folkwang, Essen
48 (RB 459)

Painting with White Form
1913
Oil on canvas 120.3 x 139.6
*Collection Gemeentemuseum,
Den Haag, The Hague*
BASEL ONLY
46 (RB 457)

Study for Composition VII
1913
Oil and tempera on canvas 78.5 x 100.5
Städtische Galerie im Lenbachhaus, Munich
50

Fugue
1914
Oil on canvas 129.5 x 129.5
Fondation Beyeler, Riehen/Basel
53 (RB 487)

Improvisation 35
1914
Oil on canvas 110.5 x 120
Kunstmuseum Basel
56 (RB 491)

Improvisation Gorge
1914
Oil and gouache on canvas 110 x 110.3
Städtische Galerie im Lenbachhaus, Munich
54 (RB 503)

Improvisation with Cold Forms
1914
Oil on canvas 120 x 140
The State Tretyakov Gallery, Moscow
58 (RB 485)

Painting with Red Spot
1914
Oil on canvas 130 x 130
*Musée National d'Art Moderne, Centre Georges
Pompidou, Paris. Centre de Création Industrielle.
Donated by Nina Kandinsky, 1976*
59 (RB 486)

Painting with Three Spots
1914
Oil on canvas 121 x 111
Museo Thyssen-Bornemisza, Madrid
LONDON ONLY
55 (RB 490)

Untitled Improvisation 2
1914
Oil on canvas 100.5 x 78
Museum Boijmans Van Beuningen, Rotterdam
LONDON ONLY
57 (RB 501)

Composition B
1916
Watercolour and ink on paper 20.8 x 30.6
The State Pushkin Museum of Fine Arts, Moscow
LONDON ONLY
NOT ILLUSTRATED (VEB 450)

Composition D
1916
Watercolour and ink on paper 31 x 20.8
The State Pushkin Museum of Fine Arts, Moscow
LONDON ONLY
NOT ILLUSTRATED (VEB 451)

Composition J
1916
Watercolour and ink on paper 31 x 20.8
The State Pushkin Museum of Fine Arts, Moscow
LONDON ONLY
NOT ILLUSTRATED (VEB 457)

Moscow, Red Square
1916
Oil on cardboard 51.5 x 49.5
The State Tretyakov Gallery, Moscow
60 (RB 605)

Untitled
1916
Watercolour and ink on cardboard 60.9 x 54.6
The State Pushkin Museum of Fine Arts, Moscow
LONDON ONLY
NOT ILLUSTRATED (VEB 465)

Untitled
1916
Ink on paper 15.5 x 23.5
Private Collection
LONDON ONLY
63

Untitled, also known as 'Bagatelle'
1916
Watercolour, Indian ink and pencil on paper
46 x 66.3
Private Collection, London
LONDON ONLY
62 (VEB 431)

Blue Arch (Ridge)
1917
Oil on canvas 133 x 104
The State Russian Museum, St Petersburg
69 (RB 614)

Grey Oval
1917
Oil on canvas 96 x 133
The Ekaterinburg Museum of Fine Arts
68 (RB 621)

Overcast
1917
Oil on canvas 105 x 134
The State Tretyakov Gallery, Moscow
67 (RB 615)

Twilight
1917
Oil on canvas 91.5 x 69.5
The State Russian Museum, St Petersburg
66 (RB 617)

Two Girls
1917
Painting on glass 20 x 24.5
Private Collection, London
LONDON ONLY
61 (RB 658)

In Grey
1919
Oil on canvas 129 x 176
*Musée National d'Art Moderne, Centre Georges
Pompidou, Paris. Centre de Création Industrielle.
Bequest of Nina Kandinsky 1981*
70 (RB 663)

Painting with Points
1919
Oil on canvas 126 x 95
The State Russian Museum, St Petersburg
72 (RB 664)

Two Ovals
1919
Oil on canvas 107 x 89.5
The State Russian Museum, St Petersburg
71 (RB 659)

Violet Wedge
1919
Oil on canvas 60 x 67
Tula Museum of Fine Arts
73 (RB 662)

White Oval
1919
Oil on canvas 80 x 93
The State Tretyakov Gallery, Moscow
74 (RB 661)

On White I
1920
Oil on canvas 95 x 138
The State Russian Museum, St Petersburg
76 (RB 665)

Black Spot
1921
Oil on canvas 138 x 120
Kunsthaus Zürich
75 (RB 681)

Blue Segment
1921
Oil on canvas 120.6 x 140.1
Solomon R. Guggenheim Museum, New York
78 (RB 676)

Circles on Black
1921
Oil on canvas 136.5 x 120
Solomon R. Guggenheim Museum, New York
79 (RB 682)

Untitled
1921
Watercolour, Indian ink and pencil on paper
30.3 x 24.4
*Kunstmuseum Basel, Kupferstichkabinett.
Gift of Dr Richard Doetsch-Benziger, Basel, 1939*
64 (VEB 546)

White Centre
1921
Oil on canvas 118.7 x 136.5
*Solomon R. Guggenheim Museum, New York.
Hilla Rebay Collection, 1971*
77 (RB 677)

Lenders and Credits

Index

A

All Saints II 147-8, 150, 154-5; fig.25
Andreyevskaya, Nina (second wife) 99
Angel of the Last Judgement no.22
angels 36, 151-2, 154
Apollon journal 145
Arab City no.1
Arrival of the Merchants 29; fig.8
auras 40, 42
Autumn I
   study for 198-9; fig.36
Autumn Landscape no.25

B

Bagatelle watercolours 13; no.62
Ballets Russes 140
Basileios the Great 148
Bauhaus 13
Bely, Andrey
   Na perevale 157
Berdyaev, Alexandrovich 142-4
Bilibin, Ivan 26, 140, 145-6
Black Spot no.75
Black Spot I no.42
Der Blaue Reiter (Blue Rider) 86, 91-5
   exhibitions 95-6; fig.20
Der Blaue Reiter almanac (1912) 82, 92-3,
   94-5, 140
   cover 95, 150, 154; figs.19, 31; no.37
   original name 92
Blue Arch (Ridge) no.69
Blue Segment no.78
Boat Trip 86; no.24
Boris and Gleb, Saints 146-7; fig.24
Braque, Georges 82
Bulgakov, Sergei 140, 141-5
   From Marxism to Idealism 141-2
   New Paths 142-3
Burlyuk, Vladimir 140

C

Cézanne, Paul 140
Christological symbolism 89-90, 97-8, 155
Christopher, Saint 148, 155; fig.26
Chulkov, Georgy Ivanovich 157
Circles on Black 200; no.79
cloisonnisme 84
'Cologne Lecture' 97, 155
colour and colour theory 12-13, 19-21, 32,
   42, 92, 186-206
   blue 94, 188
   colour families (colour chords) 27, 31,
   189-99, 202-3
   colour patches 21-2, 23, 29-32
   colour revealed in the course of time 186
   colour and sound 92
   Concerning the Spiritual in Art 87, 188
   Point and Line to Plane 188, 191-2
   tonal contrast 24-5, 29
   unvarnished surfaces 84, 86
   yellow 87, 188
coloured drawings 21, 26-7, 29; figs.6-8
Colourful Life 146-7; fig.23
Compositions 14, 30, 89-90, 95
Composition E no.65
Composition II 90, 91, 155
   sketches for 33, 90; nos.20, 21
Composition IV 35, 39; no.32
   studies for nos.33-6
Composition V 39, 95, 97, 155; fig.12
Composition VI 97, 155; no.49
Composition VII 36, 39-40, 96-8, 150,
   155, 200; no.52
   photographs by Münter 96-8; fig.22
   sketch 3 fig.21
   study for no.50
compositional elements
   ambivalent spaciality 14, 15, 23-4, 26,
   31, 40, 42
   colour *see* colour in Kandinsky's work
   contrasts, interplay 25-6, 32
   diagonals 23-4, 25-6, 31
   dynamic composition 12, 14, 40
   linear elements 12
   perspective 23-4, 31
   planarity 23-4, 31
   Point and Line to Plane 191-2
   raised horizon line 23, 25

time as compositional element 24, 186,
   194, 196
   tonal contrast 24-5, 31, 32
Concerning the Spiritual in Art 158
   colour theory 87, 188
   cover 150, 154
   on the Improvisations 33
   original title 20
   on Theosophy 81
Constructivism 15
'Contribution to the Ethnography of the
   Sysola and Vychegda Zyrians. Their
   National Deities' 144
Corinth, Lovis 78
Cossacks no.31
Crinolines no.14
Cubism 15
Cupolas no.15

D

Deluge I 155; no.44
Deluge II
   sketch for 155; no.45
Denis, Maurice
   'Définition de néo-traditionalisme' 91
Diaghilev, Sergei 140, 143-4, 155, 157
   Mir Iskusstva 140, 145, 146
distortion of natural forms 32
Doppelbegabung 94
Dorpat University 145
Dostoevsky, Fyodor 141, 142, 145, 155, 157
Dürer, Albrecht
   Melencolia I 79, 81; fig.14
dynamic composition 12, 14, 40

F

Fauvism 30, 36
First World War 15, 98
folk art, influence 33, 82, 83, 86, 87-9, 92-3,
   140, 145-7
France 15, 18
Franck, Maria 91, 94
Fugue no.53

G

*Gabriele Münter Painting Outdoors in
   Front of an Easel* 81
Gauguin, Paul 91
George, Saint 36, 95, 150-1, 154; fig.28
German Idealism 92
Germany 14, 15, 18, 89
Gershenzon, Mikhail O. *Vechi* 144
glass paintings 87-8, 140, 148, 155; fig.27
Goethe, Johann Wolfgang von 198
Goltz, Hans 90
Gregory Nazianzus 148
Grey Oval 42; no.68
grounds
   coloured 26
   unprimed boards 84

H

Hartmann, Thomas von 140
Hinterglasbild *see* glass paintings
Hoberg, Annegret 82
Holland – Beach Chairs 22-3; fig.3
Houses on a Hill
   study for no.7

I

icons 148, 150-2, 154, 155
   The Archangel Michael 152; fig.30
   *The Ascension of the Prophet Elijah in a
   Chariot of Fire* 155; fig.32
   Boris and Gleb with Scenes from their Lives
   146-7; fig.24
   St George on Horseback Slaying the Dragon
   150-1; fig.28
   Stephanos and Christophoros 148; fig.26
Impression II (Moscow) 95-6; fig.20
Impressionism 12, 18-19, 21, 29, 30
Impressions 89, 95
Improvisations 14, 30, 32-3, 35-6, 89, 95
Improvisation 1 33
Improvisation 2 (Funeral March) no.17

Improvisation 4 no.12
Improvisation 5 33, 35
Improvisation 8
   study for no.16
Improvisation 9 no.27
Improvisation 10 33, 36; no.29
Improvisation 12 96, 138, 151-2; fig.29
Improvisation 19 39; fig.11
Improvisation 19A no.40
Improvisation 20 no.41
Improvisation 28 (Second Version) no.43
Improvisation 30 (Cannons) no.51
Improvisation 34 (Orient II) no.47
Improvisation 35 186-9, 196-8, 200, 201; fig.33;
   no.56
Improvisation with Cold Forms no.58
Improvisation Gorge no.54
Improvisation II 199; no.39
   sketch for 199; fig.37
In Grey 42, 206; no.70
Interior (with Two Ladies) 87, 88; fig.16

J

Jawlensky, Alexei 78, 83-4, 86, 87
Jawlensky, Andreas 86
John Chrysostomos 148
John the Forerunner 148, 155
Jugendstil 15, 20, 82

K

Kallmünz – Stormy Weather 22; fig.2
Klee, Paul 19, 140
Kochel – Straight Road no.9
Koehler, Bernhard 96
Kojève, Alexandre 200-1
Krötz, Johann 87
Kubin, Alfred 95

L

Lady (Gabriele Münter) 79, 81; fig.13
Landscape with Factory Chimney no.28
Landscape with Red Spots I 36, 39; no.48
landscapes 29-32, 81, 83-4
Large Resurrection 155
Lasker-Schüler, Else 95
The Last Judgement no.23
legal training 89, 141, 144, 145
'Letters from Munich' 91
Lissitzky, El 15
Lyrically no.30

M

Macke, Auguste 91, 92, 140
Macke, Elisabeth 91
Makovsky 145
Malevich, Kasimir 15, 140, 144, 203
   Black Square 15, 142
   From Cubism and Futurism to Suprematism
   142, 157
Marc, Franz 82, 83, 91, 94-5; fig.19
   creative partnership with Kandinsky 91-5,
   100
   Kandinsky's correspondence with 82,
   140-1
Marxism 141-2
materialist positivism 142, 144
Matisse, Henri 30, 86, 91
Michael, Saint 151-2, 154; fig.30
Mir Iskusstva journal 140, 145, 146
Mitrinovic, Dimitrije 100
modernism 86, 155-7
Mondrian, Piet 42
Monet, Claude
   Haystack 18-19
Moscow 14, 18, 35-6, 78, 98, 200
Moscow, Red Square 13; no.60
Moscow University 82, 141, 142, 145
Munch, Edvard 84
Munich 14, 18, 24, 84
   Neue Künstlervereinigung München
   (NKVM) 78, 86, 91, 95
   Phalanx School 78
Munich – Planegg I 22; fig.1
Münter, Gabriele 40
   abstraction 90
   Abstraktion 25.4.1912 90

After Tea I 90
After Tea II 90
archiving of Kandinsky's work 82, 96-8,
   99
Boat Trip 86
creative partnership with Kandinsky
   83-91, 99-100
glass painting 87-8
interiors 90
Kandinsky at the Tea-table 76, 86; fig.15
Kandinsky's correspondence with 42, 78,
   82, 98
Murnau house 36, 78, 84; fig.17
photographs 83, 95-8, 99
   First Blaue Reiter Exhibition 95-6; fig.20
   four photographs documenting
   Kandinsky's *Composition VII* 96-8; fig.22
   Interior of Sitting Room in Murnau 87; fig.17
   *Kandinsky in his Home in Ainmillerstasse 36,
   Munich* 92-3; fig.18
portraits by Kandinsky 78-9, 81; figs.13, 16
relationship with Kandinsky 78-9, 81-3,
   95-100
retrospective exhibition (1913) 88-9
Murnau 13, 78, 81, 83-9, 90
Murnau landscapes 13, 15, 29-32, 81, 83-4
Murnau – Castle Courtyard I no.8
Murnau – The Garden II 32; no.19
Murnau – Kohlgruberstrasse 31-2; no.5
Murnau – Landscape with Church
   study for no.6
Murnau – Landscape with Green House no.11
Murnau – Mountain Landscape with Church
   189-90, 192-4, 196, 198, 201; fig.34; no.18
Murnau – Staffelsee I no.3
Murnau – Village Street 31; no.4
Murnau with Church II 36; no.26
music
   abstraction 18
   'colour chords' 27, 31
   influence in Kandinsky's work 13-14,
   20-1, 92
   'inner sound' 20-1
   time as compositional element 24, 186
   Wagner's influence on Kandinsky 18, 19

N

Neo-Impressionism 30
Neue Künstlervereinigung München (NKVM)
   78, 86, 91, 95
New Paths journal 142-3
Nude no.38
Nymphenburg – Large Fountain 24

O

occult, Kandinsky's interest in 40, 42, 81
oil sketches 21, 22-6; figs.1-5
Old Town II 25-6; fig.5
'On the Legality of Workers' Wages' 145
'On Punishment as Meted Out in Peasant
   Courts in the Moscow District' 144-5
On White I 196; no.76
Overcast 42; no.67

P

Painting with Houses 33; no.13
Painting with Points no.72
Painting with Red Spot no.59
painting technique 190
   coloured drawings 26-7
   Murnau landscapes 30-2, 84
Painting with Three Spots no.55
Painting with White Border 35-6; fig.9
Painting with White Form no.46
Painting with White Lines 36; fig.10
Paris 15, 18
Park of St Cloud – Clearing 24-5; fig.4
Peredvischniki 140
Picasso, Pablo 82, 92
Picture with a Circle 32, 39
poetry 93-4
Point and Line to Plane 186, 188, 191-2, 206;
   fig.40
Pont Aven School 84, 91
Post-Impressionism 21
primitives, Kandinsky's interest in 33, 90,
   92-3, 145-7
'pure painting' 12

R
Rambold, Heinrich 88
Realism 140
Reciprocal Agreement 203; fig.39
Recollections of Venice 1-4 27
Recollections of Venice 4 (Ponte Rialto) 27, 29;
    fig.6
Red Spot II 196, 200, 201-4, 206; fig.35
Rembrandt van Rijn 24, 186
'Reminiscences' 18, 89, 190, 200
    on his use of tonal contrast 24
    on Russia 158
    on time as a compositional element 186
Repin, Ilya 19, 84
representational motifs in Kandinsky's work
    35-6
    angels 36, 151-2, 154
    Christological symbolism 89-90, 97-8,
    155
    dual iconography 36
    mountains 154, 155
    riders 90, 94-5, 150-1, 154
    Russian fairy-tales and songs 145-6
    Russian saints 147-8, 150-1, 154-5
Resurrection 148; fig.27
riders, depictions of 90, 94-5, 150-1, 154
Riding Couple 16, 29; fig.7
Roerich, Nicholas Konstantinovich 140, 145-6
Rousseau, Henri 92, 140
Russia 14-15, 18, 26, 78, 89, 95, 98, 100,
    145, 158
    legal system 141-5
    October Revolution 14, 15
Russian Renaissance (Russian Resurrection)
    143-4, 155, 157

S
Sabaneyev, Leonid 140
St George 150-1
St Peter's Chapel at Murnau no.10
Santa Margherita 23
Schoenberg, Arnold 92, 140
Schopenhauer, Arthur
    On Vision and Colour 92
    The World as Will and Representation 92
Seidl, Emanuel von 83
'Self-characterisation' 188
Sèvres 78
Shemyakina, Anya (first wife) 78, 82-3
Simon, Albert 196
Skriabin, Alexander 140
Small Pleasures 184
Solovyov, Vladimir Sergeyevich 142, 145,
    155, 157
Song no.2
Sound of Trumpets (Large Resurrection) 155
Sounds (poetry and graphic works) 93
spaciality in Kandinsky's work 14, 15, 23-4,
    26, 31, 40, 42
Spasovich, Vladimir Danilovich 141
Staffelsee 83, 86; no.3
Steiner, Rudolf 90
Stephanos and Christophoros 148
Stravinsky, Igor
    The Firebird 146
Structuralism 188
Stuck, Franz von 19
Surrealism 18
Sweden 83, 98
Switzerland 98
Symbolists 84
Synthesism 84

T
tempera 26-7, 29
Theosophy 40, 42, 81
time as compositional element 24, 186, 194,
    196
tonal contrast 24-5, 31, 32
Twilight 42; no.66
Two Girls no.61
Two Ovals no.71

U
Untitled (1916) no.63
Untitled (1921) no.64
Untitled (Bagatelle) 13; no.62
Untitled Improvisation 2 no.57
Untitled (Sketch for Improvisation 11) 199; fig.37
Untitled (Study for Autumn 1) 198-9; fig.36
Untitled (Study for Improvisation 1 and Paradise)
    fig.38

V
Varangians 146
Vechi almanac 144
Venice 27
Vesy journal 157
Violet Wedge no.73
Vologda, ethnographic expedition to 89, 90,
    144-5
Vrubel, Mikhail 140, 145-6

W
Wagner, Richard 19
    Lohengrin 18
Washton Long, Rose-Carol 35, 90
Weiss, Peg 90
Werefkin, Marianne 78, 83-4, 86, 87, 95; fig.16
    Letters to an Unknown 84
White Centre no.77
White Oval no.74

Z
Zyrians 90, 144

Supporting Tate

Tate relies on a large number of supporters – individuals, foundations, companies and public sector sources – to enable it to deliver its programmes of activities, both on and off its gallery sites. This support is essential in order to acquire works of art for the Collection, run education, outreach and exhibition programmes, care for the Collection in storage and enable art to be displayed, both digitally and physically, inside and outside Tate. Your donation will make a real difference and enable others to enjoy Tate and its Collection both now and in the future. There are a variety of ways in which you can help support Tate and also benefit as a UK or US taxpayer. Please contact us at:

The Development Office
Tate
Millbank
London SW1P 4RG

Tel: 020 7887 8945
Fax: 020 7887 8098

American Patrons of Tate
1285 6th Avenue (35th fl)
New York, NY 10019
USA

Tel: 001 212 713 8497
Fax: 001 212 713 8655

Donations
Donations, of whatever size, from individuals, companies and trusts are welcome, either to support particular areas of interest, or to contribute to general running costs.

Gifts of Shares
Since April 2000, we can accept gifts of quoted shares and securities. These are not subject to capital gains tax. For higher rate taxpayers, a gift of shares saves income tax as well as capital gains tax. For further information please contact the Development Office.

Gift Aid
Through Gift Aid, you can provide significant additional revenue to Tate. Gift Aid applies to gifts of any size, whether regular or one-off, since we can claim back the tax on your charitable donation. Higher rate taxpayers are also able to claim additional personal tax relief. Contact us for further information and a Gift-Aid Declaration.

Legacies
A legacy to Tate may take the form of a residual share of an estate, a specific cash sum or item of property such as a work of art. Legacies to Tate are free of Inheritance Tax, and help to secure a strong future for the Collection and galleries.

Offers in lieu of tax
Inheritance Tax can be satisfied by transferring to the Government a work of art of outstanding importance. In this case the amount of tax is reduced, and it can be made a condition of the offer that the work of art is allocated to Tate. Please contact us for details.

Tate Annual Fund
A donation to the Annual Fund at Tate benefits a variety of projects throughout the organisation, from the development of new conservation techniques to education programmes for people of all ages and abilities.

American Patrons of Tate
American Patrons of Tate is an independent charity based in New York that supports the work of Tate in the United Kingdom. It receives full tax exempt status from the IRS under section 501(c)(3) allowing United States taxpayers to receive tax deductions on gifts towards annual membership programmes, exhibitions, scholarship and capital projects. For more information contact the American Patrons of Tate office.

Membership Programmes
Tate Members enjoy unlimited free admission throughout the year to all exhibitions at Tate Britain, Tate Liverpool, Tate Modern and Tate St Ives, as well as a number of other benefits such as exclusive use of our Members' Rooms and a free annual subscription to *Tate Etc.*

Whilst enjoying the exclusive privileges of membership, you are also helping secure Tate's position at the very heart of British and modern art. Your support actively contributes to new purchases of important art, ensuring that the Tate's Collection continues to be relevant and comprehensive, as well as funding projects in London, Liverpool and St Ives that increase access and understanding for everyone.

Tate Patrons
Tate Patrons are people who share a strong enthusiasm for art and are committed to giving significant financial support to Tate on an annual basis. The Patrons support the Tate Collection, helping Tate acquire works from across its broad collecting remit: historic British art, modern international art and contemporary art. The scheme provides a forum for Patrons to share their interest in art and to exchange knowledge and information in an enjoyable environment. United States tax payers who wish to receive full tax exempt status from the IRS under Section 501(c)(3) may want to pay through our American office. For more information on the scheme please contact the Patrons office.

Corporate Membership
Corporate Membership at Tate Modern, Tate Liverpool and Tate Britain offers companies opportunities for corporate entertaining and the chance for a wide variety of employee benefits. These include special private views, special access to paying exhibitions, out-of-hours visits and tours, invitations to VIP events and talks at members' offices.

Corporate Investment
Tate has developed a range of imaginative partnerships with the corporate sector, ranging from international interpretation and exhibition programmes to local outreach and staff development programmes. We are particularly known for high-profile business to business marketing initiatives and employee benefit packages. Please contact the Corporate Fundraising team for further details.

Charity Details
The Tate Gallery is an exempt charity; the Museums & Galleries Act 1992 added the Tate Gallery to the list of exempt charities defined in the 1960 Charities Act. Tate Members is a registered charity (number 313021). Tate Foundation is a registered charity (number 1085314).

Tate Modern Donors to the Capital Campaign

FOUNDERS
The Arts Council of England
English Partnerships
The Millennium Commission

FOUNDING BENEFACTORS
Mr and Mrs James Brice
The Clore Duffield Foundation
Gilbert de Botton
Richard B. and Jeanne Donovan Fisher
Noam and Geraldine Gottesman
Anthony and Evelyn Jacobs
The Kresge Foundation
The Frank Lloyd Family Trusts
Ronald and Rita McAulay
The Monument Trust
Mori Building Co.Ltd
Peter and Eileen Norton,
    The Peter Norton Family Foundation
Maja Oeri and Hans Bodenmann
The Dr Mortimer and Theresa Sackler
    Foundation
Ruth and Stephan Schmidheiny
Mr and Mrs Charles Schwab
Peter Simon
London Borough of Southwark
The Starr Foundation
John Studzinski
The Weston Family
Poju and Anita Zabludowicz

BENEFACTORS
Frances and John Bowes
Donald L Bryant Jr Family
Sir Harry and Lady Djanogly
Donald and Doris Fisher
Lydia and Manfred Gorvy
The Government Office for London
Mimi and Peter Haas
The Headley Trust
Mr and Mrs André Hoffmann
Pamela and C. Richard Kramlich

MAJOR DONORS
The Annenburg Foundation
The Baring Foundation
Ron Beller and Jennifer Moses
Alex and Angela Bernstein
Mr and Mrs Pontus Bonnier
Lauren and Mark Booth
Ivor Braka
Melva Bucksbaum
Edwin C. Cohen
Michel and Hélène David-Weill
English Heritage
Esmée Fairbairn Charitable Trust
Tate Friends
Bob and Kate Gavron
Giancarlo Giammetti
Horace W.Goldsmith Foundation
The Government of Switzerland
Mr and Mrs Karpidas
Peter and Maria Kellner
Mr and Mrs Henry R Kravis
Irene and Hyman Kreitman
Catherine and Pierre Lagrange
Edward and Agnes Lee
Ruth and Stuart Lipton
James Mayor
The Mercers' Company
The Meyer Foundation
Guy and Marion Naggar
The Nyda and Oliver Prenn Foundation
The Rayne Foundation
John and Jill Ritblat
Barrie and Emmanuel Roman
Lord and Lady Rothschild
Belle Shenkman Estate
Hugh and Catherine Stevenson
David and Linda Supino
David and Emma Verey
Clodagh and Leslie Waddington
Robert and Felicity Waley-Cohen

DONORS
The Asprey Family Charitable Foundation
Lord and Lady Attenborough
David and Janice Blackburn
Mr and Mrs Anthony Bloom
Mr and Mrs John Botts
The British Land Company PLC
Cazenove & Co.
The John S. Cohen Foundation
Sir Ronald and Sharon Cohen
Sadie Coles
Carole and Neville Conrad
Giles and Sonia Coode-Adams
Alan Cristea
Thomas Dane
Julia W. Dayton
Paul Smith and Pauline Denyer-Smith
The Fishmongers' Company
The Foundation for Sports and the Arts
Alan Gibbs
Mr and Mrs Edward Gilhuly
Helyn and Ralph Goldenberg
The Worshipful Company of Goldsmiths
Pehr and Christina Gyllenhammar
Richard and Odile Grogan
The Worshipful Company of Haberdashers
Hanover Acceptances Limited
Jay Jopling
Howard and Lynda Karshan
Madeleine, Lady Kleinwort
Brian and Lesley Knox
The Lauder Foundation –
    Leonard and Evelyn Lauder Fund
Ronald and Jo Carole Lauder
Leathersellers' Company Charitable Fund
Lex Service Plc
Mr and Mrs Ulf G. Linden
Anders and Ulla Ljungh
Mr and Mrs George Loudon
Nick and Annette Mason
Viviane and James Mayor
Solita and Steven Mishaan
Anthony and Deidre Montague
Sir Peter and Lady Osborne
Maureen Paley
William A. Palmer
Mr Frederik Paulsen
The Pet Shop Boys
David and Sophie Shalit
William Sieghart
Mr and Mrs Sven Skarendahl
Mr and Mrs Nicholas Stanley
The Jack Steinberg Charitable Trust
Carter and Mary Thacher
Insinger Townsley
The 29th May 1961 Charitable Trust
Dinah Verey
The Vintners' Company
Gordon D.Watson
Mr and Mrs Stephen Wilberding
Michael S. Wilson

and those donors who wish to remain anonymous.